The Constitution and Criminal Procedure

The Constitution and Criminal Procedure

First Principles

Akhil Reed Amar

Yale University Press   New Haven and London

Designed by James J. Johnson set in Meridien Roman type by Ink, Inc., New York, New York
Printed in the United States of America by BookCrafters, Inc., Chelsea, Michigan

Library of Congress Cataloging-in-Publication Data

Amar, Akhil Reed.
The constitution and criminal procedure: first principles/Akhil Reed Amar.
p. cm.
Includes bibliographical references and index.
ISBN 0-300-06678-3 (alk. paper)

1. Criminal procedure—United States. 2. United States—Constitutional law. I. Title
KF9619.A72196   1997
345.73'05—dc20
[347.3055]   96-21079 C

A catalogue record for this book is available from the British Library.

The paper in this book meets the guidelines for permanence and durability of the Committee on Production Guidelines for Book Longevity of the Council on Library Resources.

10 9 8 7 6 5 4 3 2 1

To all my teachers—especially my parents and my wife

Contents

Preface

This book is a collection of essays, but it is, I hope, much more than that. Taken as a whole, these interlocking essays aim to fundamentally reorient the field now known as constitutional criminal procedure.

Constitutional criminal procedure—the very label tugs in different directions. Not all of our Constitution is about criminal procedure, and not all criminal procedure should be constitutionalized. This logical gap between the Constitution and criminal procedure is matched by a sociological gap in today's law schools: constitutional law and criminal procedure are typically taught as separate courses, by separate groups of scholars. Very few of our most prominent constitutional law scholars have devoted extensive analysis to the Fourth, Fifth, and Sixth Amendments, individually or as a group. Conversely, very few of America's leading academic voices in criminal procedure are broad-gauged students of the Constitution.

One obvious explanation, of course, is that prior to the Warren Court, remarkably little criminal procedure had been constitutionalized. Most criminal cases are rooted in state law and tried in state courts; and before the 1960s, the Fourth Amendment exclusionary rule, the Fifth Amendment self-incrimination clause and double jeopardy clause, and all the protections of the Sixth Amendment applied only to federal cases. And so, for the generation of legal scholars coming of age before 1960, criminal procedure and (federal) constitutional law were rather distinct fields.

Today, however, constitutional law pervades criminal procedure casebooks, courses, and scholarship. Yet the kind of constitutional law discourse and scholarship that now dominates criminal procedure is generally, in a word, *bad* constitutional law—constitutional law insouciant about constitutional text, ignorant of constitutional history, and inattentive to constitutional structure. Or, at least, so I shall argue in the pages that follow.

Good constitutional criminal procedure must be, first and foremost, good constitutional law—developed with respect for things like text, history, and structure. In this book I attempt to analyze the Fourth, Fifth, and Sixth Amendments from these perspectives, to lay bare their first principles.

Good constitutional law must of course also pay heed to precedent, but Supreme Court case law in this field is remarkably complex, sometimes perverse, and often contradictory. Part of the problem is that the Burger and Rehnquist Courts have not always shared the Warren Court's vision but have regularly chosen to distinguish away disfavored cases without overruling them. After twenty-five years of this strategy, *U.S. Reports* bristles with language poking out in opposite directions at every level of abstraction. But this intergenerational tension is only part of the problem. The deeper problem is that at no time has the Supreme Court had a coherent and clearly developed vision of constitutional criminal procedure. The Warren Court contradicted itself, and so has the post-Burger Court. Cases come to the Court one by one, under different clauses and amendments; and the Justices have failed to see how these clauses fit together into a coherent whole.

And that is the aim of this book—to show how the Fourth, Fifth, and Sixth Amendments fit together. To ease exposition, I have organized each of the first three chapters around a particular amendment or clause. Each chapter can thus stand alone and be read profitably by a lawyer or judge who needs to understand a particular clause or amendment to deal with the case at hand. But each chapter is also designed to interlock with the others; and in a brief concluding chapter, I try to pull the camera back and identify broader themes connecting the different parts of my project. In this concluding chapter, as in the ones that precede it, I stress the need to construe the Constitution in ways that protect the innocent without needlessly advantaging the guilty. Taken as a whole, this book seeks to provide both scholars and general readers with a coherent, integrated vision of the entire field now known as constitutional criminal procedure.

Each of the following chapters has been previously published in a slightly different form, and each is used by permission of the original publisher. Chapter 1 appeared in the February 1994 *Harvard Law Review* and is based on the Samuel Rubin Lecture delivered on October 27, 1993, at Columbia Law School. Chapter 2 derives from an article, cowritten with Renée B. Lettow, in the March 1995 *Michigan Law Review*. Chapter 3 was published as the Foreword to the *Georgetown Law Journal*'s Twenty-Fifth Annual Review of Criminal Procedure in April 1996. Chapter 4 appeared in the summer 1996 *American Criminal Law Review*. The Appendix was published in the summer 1995 *U.C. Davis Law Review* and derives from the seventh Edward L. Barrett, Jr., Lecture, delivered on October 25, 1994, at the University of California at Davis School of Law.

The Constitution and Criminal Procedure

1 Fourth Amendment First Principles

> The right of the people to be secure in their persons, houses, papers, and effects, against unreasonable searches and seizures, shall not be violated, and no Warrants shall issue, but upon probable cause, supported by Oath or affirmation, and particularly describing the place to be searched, and the persons or things to be seized.

The Fourth Amendment today is an embarrassment. Much of what the Supreme Court has said in the last half-century—that the amendment generally calls for warrants and probable cause for all searches and seizures, and exclusion of illegally obtained evidence—is initially plausible but ultimately misguided. As a matter of text, history, and plain old common sense, these three pillars of modern Fourth Amendment case law[1] are hard to support; in fact, today's Supreme Court does not really support them. Except when it does. Warrants are not required—unless they are. All searches and seizures must be grounded in probable cause—but not on Tuesdays. And unlawfully seized evidence must be excluded whenever five votes say so. Meanwhile, sensible rules that the amendment clearly does lay down or presuppose—that all searches and seizures must be reasonable, that warrants (and only warrants) always require probable cause, and that the officialdom should be held liable for unreasonable searches and seizures—are ignored by the Justices. Sometimes. The result is a vast jumble of judicial pronouncements that is not merely complex and contradictory, but often perverse. Criminals go free while honest citizens are intruded upon in outrageous ways with little or no real remedy. If there are good reasons for these and countless other odd results, the Court has not provided them.

Nor has the academy. Indeed, law professors have often been part of the problem, rather than the solution. Begin in the classroom. The Fourth Amendment is part of the Constitution yet is rarely taught as part of constitutional law. Rather, it unfolds as a course unto itself, or is crammed into criminal procedure. The criminal procedure placement is especially pernicious. For unlike the Fifth, Sixth, and Eighth Amendments, which specially apply in criminal contexts,[2] the Fourth Amendment applies equally to civil and criminal law enforcement. Its text speaks to all government searches and seizures, for whatever reason. Its history is not uniquely bound up with criminal law. And the amendment presupposes a civil damage remedy, not exclusion of evidence in criminal trials; its global command that all government searches and seizures be reasonable sounds not in criminal law, but in constitutional tort law.[3]

Placing the Fourth Amendment in criminal procedure thus distorts, causing us to see things that are not there. It also obscures, leading us to miss things that are there—as does teaching the amendment in a stand-alone course. What we miss is how the Fourth Amendment connects up with the rest of the Constitution, procedurally and substantively. From a legal-process perspective, we fail to focus clearly on basic constitutional questions like: Who should decide whether a search or seizure is reasonable? Legislatures? Administrators? Judges? Juries? Some combination? Who should be allowed to issue warrants, and how should their decisions be reviewed? From a substantive perspective, we give short shrift to questions like: How should searches and seizures outside the criminal context be constitutionally regulated? What makes a search or seizure substantively unreasonable? How should other constitutional principles—protecting speech, privacy, property, due process, equality, democratic participation, and the like—inform the reasonableness determination?

When we move from law school classrooms to law reviews and legal treatises, things do not improve. Leading scholars ponder every nuance of the latest Supreme Court case but seem unconcerned about the amendment's text, unaware of its history, and at times oblivious or hostile to the common sense of common people. Like the Justices, leading scholars seem to think the amendment requires warrants, probable cause, and exclusion but then often abandon all this to avoid absurdity. Fourth Amendment case law is a sinking ocean liner—rudderless and badly off course—yet most scholarship contents itself with rearranging the deck chairs.

There is a better way to think about the Fourth Amendment—by returning to its first principles. We need to read the amendment's words and take them seriously: they do not require warrants, probable cause, or exclusion of evidence, but they do require that all searches and seizures be reasonable. While keeping our eyes fixed on reasonableness, we must remember the historic role played by civil juries and civil damage actions in which government officials were held liable for unreasonable intrusions against person, property, and privacy. We need to recover the lost linkages between the Fourth and Seventh Amendments—linkages obscured by teaching the Fourth in criminal procedure and the Seventh in civil procedure. We must self-consciously consult principles embodied in other parts of the Constitution to flesh out the concrete meaning of *constitutional* reasonableness. Finally, we must use twentieth-century legal weaponry like *Bivens* actions, class actions, structural injunctions, entity liability, attorney's fees, administrative regulation, and administrative remedies, to combat twentieth-century legal threats—technology and bureaucracy—to the venerable values protected by the Fourth Amendment.

In what follows, I shall first critique the current doctrinal mess and then attempt to sketch out a better way—a package that, taken as a whole, strikes me as far superior to the status quo along any number of dimensions. It is more faithful to constitutional text and history. It is more coherent and sensible. It is less destructive of the basic trial value of truth seeking—sorting the innocent from the guilty. It is more conducive to the basic appellate value of truth speaking; it will help courts to think straight and write true, openly identifying criteria of reasonableness rather than mouthing unreasonable principles that are blindly followed, and then blandly betrayed.[4] Finally, my package, taken as a whole,[5] can be understood by, and draws on the participation and wisdom of, ordinary citizens—We the People, who in the end must truly comprehend and respect the constitutional rights enforced in Our name.

Make no mistake: I come to praise the Fourth Amendment, not to gut it. It is a priceless constitutional inheritance, but we have not maintained it well. Refurbished, it is a beauty to behold, for it was once—and can once again be—one of our truly great amendments.

The Mess: A Critique

The words of the Fourth Amendment really do mean what they say. They do not require warrants, even presumptively, for searches and seizures. They do not require probable cause for all searches and seizures without warrants. They do not require—or even invite—exclusions of evidence, contraband, or stolen goods. All this is relatively obvious if only we read the amendment's words carefully and take them seriously.

Warrant Requirement?

The modern Supreme Court has claimed on countless occasions that there is a warrant requirement in the Fourth Amendment.[6] There are two variants of the warrant requirement argument—a strict (per se)

4 • **Fourth Amendment First Principles**

variant that insists that searches and seizures always require warrants, and a looser (modified) variant that concedes the need to craft various common-sense exceptions to a strict warrant rule. Both variants fail.

The Per Se Approach.   The first (per se) variant interpolates but nevertheless purports to stay true to the text. The amendment contains two discrete commands—first, all searches and seizures must be reasonable; second, warrants authorizing various searches and seizures must be limited (by probable cause, particular description, and so on). What is the relation between these two commands? The per se approach reasons as follows: Obviously, the first and second commands are yoked by an implicit third that no search or seizure may take place except pursuant to a warrant.[7] Although not expressing the point in so many words, the amendment plainly presumes that warrantless searches and seizures are per se unreasonable. Surely executive officials should not be allowed to intrude on citizens in a judicially unauthorized manner. And the mode of proper judicial authorization is the warrant. Why else would the warrant clause exist?

Standing alone, this line of argument is initially plausible. But when all the evidence is in, we shall see that it is plainly wrong. Begin by noting that the per se interpolation is only one of several possible ways of understanding the relationship between the amendment's two commands. Perhaps, for example, there is no logical relation between the two: the first speaks globally to all searches and seizures, whereas the second addresses the narrower issue of warrants. Or, if this reading seems insufficiently holistic, the same result obtains under a more aesthetic reformulation: warrants are not required, but any warrant that does issue is per se unreasonable if not supported by probable cause, particular description, and the rest. As we shall see, this reading ultimately squares more snugly with the amendment's specific words, harmonizes better with its historic context, and makes considerably more common sense.[8]

If a warrant requirement was intended but not spelled out—if it simply went without saying—we might expect to find at least some early state constitutions making clear what the federal Fourth Amendment left to inference. Yet although many states featured language akin to the Fourth Amendment, none had a textual warrant requirement.[9] Of course, it could be argued that here, too, a warrant requirement was generally presumed—it went without saying. But in leading antebellum cases, the state supreme courts of Pennsylvania, New Hampshire, and Massachusetts briskly dismissed claims of implied warrant requirements under state constitutional provisions that were predecessors of, and textually quite similar to, the federal Fourth Amendment.[10] And these cases harmonize with nineteenth-century opinions from many other states.[11] Supporters of the warrant requirement have yet to locate any antebellum cases contra.

Nor have proponents of a warrant requirement uncovered even a handful of clear statements of the "requirement" in common law treatises, in the debates over the Constitution from 1787 to 1789, or in the First Congress, which proposed the Fourth Amendment. On the contrary, when we consult these and other sources, we see a number of clear examples that disprove any implicit warrant requirement.

Arrests without warrants. At common law, arrests—seizures of persons—could take place without warrants in a variety of circumstances. So said the major founding-era commentators.[12] In 1792—one year after ratification of the Fourth Amendment—the Second Congress explicitly conferred this common law arrest power on federal marshals.[13] Relying on this and other broad historical evidence, the modern Supreme Court in *United States v. Watson* carved out an "arrest exception" to its so-called "warrant requirement."[14] But all this raises an obvious logical problem with the "requirement" itself. If an arrest—one of the most intrusive kinds of seizures imaginable—does not require a warrant, why do less intrusive searches and seizures?[15]

Searches pursuant to arrests. In his brilliant study of the Fourth Amendment, Professor Telford Taylor reminds us that, since at least the seventeenth century, the common law has recognized broad authority to search an arrestee and his immediate surroundings without a search warrant, and even when the arrest itself was warrantless:

> Whether the chase was in hot pursuit, by hue and cry, or by a constable armed with an arrest warrant, the object was the person of the felon, and the weapon he had used or the goods he had stolen. A seventeenth-century work on the function of constables gives a broad description of the power of search incident to arrest. . . .
>
> Neither in the reported cases nor the legal literature is there any indication that search of the person of an arrestee, or the premises in which he was taken, was ever challenged in England until the end of the nineteenth century. When the power was belatedly contested, . . . the English courts gave the point short shrift. That the practice had the full approval of bench and bar, in the time of George III when Camden and Mansfield wrote, and when our Constitution was adopted, seems entirely clear.[16]

Indeed, Taylor goes on to remark that, even at a time when other searches for "mere evidence" were disallowed by American courts, officers without warrants could search an arrestee for "mere evidence."[17]

On the basis of this and other data, the modern Supreme Court has carved out an "incident to arrest exception" to its so-called "warrant requirement" for all searches.[18] But once again, this exception seems to *dis*prove the rule: why should various less intrusive, nonarrest searches be subject to requirements that arrest searches are not?

Not only were warrants unnecessary for "mere evidence" arrest searches; but also warrants could not, historically speaking, support a search for certain types of "mere evidence." The common law search warrants referred to in the warrant clause were solely for stolen goods;[19] various early American statutes extended warrants to searches for smuggled or dangerous goods (gunpowder, diseased and infected items, and the like), contraband, and criminal instrumentalities.[20] If there was probable cause to believe that a place contained these items, an ex parte warrant could issue, without notice to the owner of the place, lest he be tipped off and spirit away the goods, or lest the items cause imminent harm. Even if ultimately innocent, mere possession of these items was suspicious or dangerous enough to justify summary process, and the standard for this process was probable cause. But once searches for mere evidence are allowed, wholly innocent and unthreatening citizens are much more likely to be implicated.[21] With modern forensic techniques, virtually any place could yield "evidence" of some offense, civil or criminal—fingerprints of a next-door neighbor suspected of a traffic offense, carpet fibers relevant to products liability issues, and so on. Under these circumstances, the summary and ex parte procedures underlying warrants become quite problematic on due process grounds. Strictly read, the warrant clause applies only to search warrants akin to traditional search warrants—warrants for contraband, stolen goods, and the like.[22] Once uprooted from this soil, the amendment's "probable cause" formulation becomes awkward and oppressive. (There is always probable cause to believe the government will find *something* in a house—walls, for example—yet surely *that* kind of probable cause cannot always suffice to support an ex parte warrant.) The upshot is not that government may never conduct reasonable searches for "mere evidence" like a murderer's bloodstained shirt, believed to be stashed in the car of an unsuspecting neighbor—that would be silly[23]—but that the *warrant clause* cannot always be stretched to reach these searches.[24] And this straightforward result is yet another signal that many of the most important searches and seizures can and must take place without warrants.

Searches of ships and storehouses. In a statute passed during the same session at which it adopted the Fourth Amendment, the First Congress pointedly authorized federal naval inspectors to enter ships without warrants and, again without warrants, to search for and to seize any goods that they suspected violated customs laws.[25] Similar provisions were contained in congressional acts passed in 1790, 1793, and 1799.[26] Other provisions of the 1789 act authorized, but did not require, warrants to search houses, stores, and buildings; the statute did not say that no search or seizure could occur without a warrant, but only that, under certain conditions, naval officers and customs collectors would "be entitled to a warrant."[27] In yet another early statute, the First Congress authorized warrantless entry into and inspection of all "houses, store-houses, ware-houses, buildings and places" that had been registered (as required by law) as liquor storerooms or distilleries.[28]

If any members of the early Congresses objected to or even questioned these warrantless searches and seizures on Fourth Amendment grounds, supporters of the so-called warrant requirement have yet to identify them.

Successful searches and seizures. At common law, it seems that nothing succeeded like success. Even if a constable had no warrant and only weak or subjective grounds for believing someone to be a felon or some item to be contraband or stolen goods, the constable could seize the suspected person or thing. The constable acted at his peril. If wrong, he could be held liable in a damage action. But if he merely played a hunch and proved right—if the suspect *was* a felon, or the goods *were* stolen or contraband—this ex post success apparently was a complete defense.[29] Variants of the ex post success defense appeared prominently in several landmark English cases that inspired the Fourth Amendment[30] and in the 1818 Supreme Court case of *Gelston v. Hoyt,* authored by Justice Story.[31] We shall return to this point later, but for now it is yet another historical example casting doubt on the so-called warrant requirement.

Other historical examples exist,[32] but the four we have already considered suffice to make clear that, if a warrant requirement truly did go without saying, leading eighteenth- and nineteenth-century authorities did not think so.

Of course, this hardly ends the matter. Perhaps early judges and lawmakers simply misunderstood the true spirit of the principles the Constitution embodied. For example, less than a dozen years after the adoption of the Constitution and the ratification of the Bill of Rights, Congress passed and federal judges upheld the now-infamous Sedition

Act. Surely this act was unconstitutional in any number of ways. And surely the self-serving actions of early Congresses and judges do not end the matter. Is it possible that in the Fourth Amendment, too, the early implementation betrayed the underlying principle?

No. The problem with the so-called warrant requirement is not simply that it is not in the text and that it is contradicted by history. The problem is also that, if taken seriously, a warrant requirement makes no sense. Consider just a few common-sense counterexamples to the notion that all searches and seizures must be made pursuant to warrants.

Exigent circumstances. In a wide range of fast-breaking situations—hot pursuits, crimes in progress, and the like—a warrant requirement would be foolish. Recognizing this, the modern Supreme Court has carved out an "exigent circumstances exception" to its so-called warrant requirement.[33]

Consent searches. If government officials obtain the uncoerced authorization of the owner or apparent owner, surely they should be allowed to search a place, even without a warrant. And the modern Supreme Court has so held. It is tempting to claim that this is no exception to a warrant requirement but merely a "waiver" of Fourth Amendment rights by the target of a search. However, the waiver argument surely cannot justify *A*'s "waiving" *B*'s Fourth Amendment rights, and yet the Court has allowed searches when a wife consented to a search of her husband's property.[34] It has also upheld searches when the consenting party did not really have authority to permit the police to search—because, say, someone else was the true owner—but the police reasonably thought the consenter was the owner.[35] The explicit logic here has been that, even though the police had neither a true warrant nor a true waiver, they acted *reasonably*.[36] But this is a recognition that reasonableness—not a warrant—is the ultimate touchstone for all searches and seizures.

Plain view searches. When a Secret Service agent at a presidential event stands next to her boss, wearing sunglasses and scanning the crowd in search of any small sign that something might be amiss, she is searching without a warrant. Yet surely this must be constitutional, and the Supreme Court has so suggested. At times, however, the Court has played word games, insisting that sunglass or naked-eye searches are not really searches.[37] But if high-tech binoculars or X-ray glasses are used, then maybe . . .[38]

These word games are unconvincing and unworthy. A search is a search, whether with Raybans or X rays.[39] The difference between these two searches is that one may be much more reasonable than another. In our initial hypothetical, the search is public—the agent is out in the open for all to see; nondiscriminatory—everyone is scanned, not just, say, blacks; unintrusive—no X-ray glasses or binoculars here; consented to—when one ventures out in public, one does assume a certain risk of being seen; and justified—the President's life is on the line. But change these facts, and the outcome changes—not because a nonsearch suddenly becomes a search, but because a search at some point becomes *unreasonable*. (Imagine, for example, a government policy allowing government officials, as a perk of power, to stand unobservably under bleachers and take snapshots of women's panties.)[40]

Because it creates an unreasonable mandate for all searches, the warrant requirement leads judges to artificially constrain the scope of the amendment itself by narrowly defining *search* and *seizure*. If a "search" or a "seizure" requires only reasonableness rather than a warrant, however, judges will be more likely to define these terms generously.[41] (Interestingly, in the landmark *Katz* case, the Court, perhaps unconsciously, smuggled reasonableness into the very definition of the amendment's trigger: the amendment comes into play whenever government action implicates a "reasonable expectation of privacy.")[42]

Real life. Finally, consider the vast number of real-life, unintrusive, nondiscriminatory searches and seizures to which modern-day Americans are routinely subjected: metal detectors at airports, annual auto emissions tests, inspections of closely regulated industries, public school regimens, border searches, and on and on. All of these occur without warrants. Are they all unconstitutional? Surely not, the Supreme Court has told us, in a variety of cases.[43] What the Court has not clearly explained, however, is how all these warrantless searches are consistent with its so-called warrant requirement.

It is no answer to point out that most of these searches are designed to enforce not "criminal" but "civil" laws—safety codes, pollution laws, and the like. The text of the amendment applies equally to both civil and criminal law.[44] The unsupported idea that the "core" of the amendment is somehow uniquely or specially concerned with criminal law is simply an unfortunate artifact of the equally unsupported exclusionary rule. If two searches are equally unintrusive to the target, why should the criminal search be more severely restricted than the civil search?[45] In any event, aren't metal detectors there to detect and deter crimes like attempted hijacking? And what about warrantless weapons frisks conducted by police officials as a routine part of their criminal enforcement policy?[46]

We have now seen at least eight historical and commonsensical exceptions to the so-called warrant requirement. There are many others[47]—but I am a lover of mercy. And by now I hope the point is clear: it makes no sense to say that all warrantless searches and seizures are per se unreasonable.

The Modified Per Se Approach. At this point, a supporter of the so-called warrant requirement is probably tempted to concede some exceptions and modify the per se claim: warrantless searches and seizures are per se unreasonable, save for a limited number of well-defined historical and commonsensical exceptions.

This modification is clever, but the concessions give up the game. The per se argument is no longer the textual argument it claimed to be; it no longer merely specifies an implicit logical relation between the reasonableness command and the warrant clause. To read in a warrant requirement that is not in the text—and then to read in various non-textual exceptions to that so-called requirement—is not to read the Fourth Amendment at all. It is to rewrite it. What's more, in conceding that, above and beyond historical exceptions, common sense dictates various additional exceptions to the so-called warrant requirement, the modification seems to concede that the ultimate touchstone of the amendment is not the warrant but reasonableness.[48]

According to the modified approach, the Framers did not say what they meant, and what they meant—warrants, always—cannot quite be taken seriously, so today we must make reasonable exceptions. On my reading, the Framers did say what they meant, and what they said makes eminent good sense: all searches and seizures must be reasonable. Precisely because these searches and seizures can occur in all shapes and sizes under a wide variety of circumstances, the Framers chose a suitably general command.

The Per Se Unreasonableness of Broad Warrants. If all this is so, why has the Court continued to pay lip service to the so-called warrant requirement? What *is* the purpose of the warrant clause, and how does it relate to the more general command of reasonableness? And what is wrong with the logic that drives the warrant requirement—namely, that executive officials should be prohibited from searching and seizing without judicial approval, and that the warrant clause specifies the proper mode of this approval?

To anticipate my answers to these related questions: Perhaps the Justices have been slow to see the light because they do not understand that juries, as well as judges, are the heroes of the Founders' Fourth Amendment story. Indeed, at times, the Founders viewed judges and certain judicial proceedings with suspicion; this unflattering truth may not immediately suggest itself to modern-day judges.[49] The amendment's warrant clause does not require, presuppose, or even prefer warrants—it *limits* them. Unless warrants meet certain strict standards, they are per se unreasonable. The Framers did not exalt warrants, for a warrant was issued ex parte by a government official on the imperial payroll and had the purpose and effect of precluding any common law trespass suit the aggrieved target might try to bring before a local jury after the search or seizure occurred. The logic driving the warrant requirement is doubly flawed: it sees warrants as judicial, when they lack certain judicial attributes, and it ignores the after-the-fact judicial review that the common law furnished against warrantless intrusions, in which the jury loomed large.

Begin with the doubly flawed logic driving the warrant requirement. Consider the person who issues the warrant. In England, certain Crown *executive* officials regularly exercised this warrant power.[50] We need only recall the facts of the 1763 English case, *Wilkes v. Wood*, whose plot and cast of characters were familiar to every schoolboy in America, and whose lessons the Fourth Amendment was undeniably designed to embody.[51] *Wilkes*—and not the 1761 Boston writs of assistance controversy, which went almost unnoticed in debates over the federal Constitution and Bill of Rights[52]—was *the* paradigm search and seizure case for Americans. Indeed, it was probably the most famous case in late eighteenth-century America, period.[53] In *Wilkes*, a sweeping warrant had been issued by a Crown officer, Secretary of State Lord Halifax. In colonial America, Crown executive officials, including royal governors, also claimed authority to issue warrants.[54] Well into the twentieth century, states vested warrant-issuing authority in justices of the peace—even when such justices also served as prosecutors—and today states confer warrant authority on clerks and "magistrates" who are neither lawyers nor judges and who at times look rather like police chiefs.[55]

Even when a judge issued a warrant, revolutionary Americans greeted the event with foreboding. Before the American Revolution, colonial judges lacked the independence from the Crown that their British brothers had won after the Glorious Revolution.[56] Sitting at the pleasure of the monarch, the King's judicial magistrates in America were at times hard to distinguish from his executive magistrates—especially when a single Crown lackey wore several hats, as often occurred.[57] Nor did the foreboding disappear after the American Revolution, when judges won a measure of institutional independence from the executive branch. Even an Article III judge, after all, had been appointed by the President, looked to the President for possible promotion to a higher court, and drew his salary from the government payroll. What's more, such a judge was an official of the central government—perhaps not so imperial as his Crown-directed colonial predecessors, but suspicious nonetheless. Would the handful of elite federal judges truly be able to empathize with the concerns of ordinary folk? And a single bad apple could spoil the bunch; if even one federal judge was a lord or a lackey, executive officials shopping for easy warrants would know where to go. Far more trustworthy were twelve men, good and true, on a local jury, independent of the government, sympathetic to the legitimate concerns of fellow citizens, too numerous to be corrupted, and whose vigilance could not easily be evaded by governmental judge-shopping.

Consider next the process by which warrants issued in eighteenth-century America. This, too, was hardly likely to inspire enthusiasm for a blanket warrant requirement. The typical search warrant for stolen goods or contraband was issued at the request of an accuser or the government, ex parte, with no notice or opportunity to be heard afforded the target.[58] Lacking the adverse presentation characteristic of Anglo-American judicial proceedings, the summary warrant procedure was justified only because of a unique combination of highly suspicious or dangerous circumstances: there was very good reason—probable cause—to think that an owner, however ultimately innocent of personal wrongdoing, was harboring something he had no right to have in the first place. Outside this narrow situation—particular description, probable cause, and items akin to contraband or stolen goods—the ex parte search warrant had the potential to become an engine of great oppression.

What would happen if no warrant issued? Here we come to the second big error in the doubly flawed logic driving the warrant requirement. Warrantless intrusions were hardly immune from judicial review in the early years of the Republic. Rather, any official who searched or seized could be sued by the citizen target in an ordinary trespass suit—with both parties represented at trial and a jury helping to decide between the government and the citizen. If the jury deemed the search or seizure unreasonable—and reasonableness was a classic jury question[59]—the citizen plaintiff would win and the official would be obliged to pay (often heavy) damages. Any federal defense that the official might try to claim would collapse, trumped by the finding that the federal action was unreasonable, and thus unconstitutional under the Fourth Amendment, and thus no defense at all.

Fearing this, federal officials would try to get ex parte warrants whenever they could, for a lawful warrant would provide—indeed, was designed to provide—an absolute defense in any subsequent trespass suit.[60] Warrants, then, were friends of the searcher, not the searched. They had to be limited; otherwise, central officers on the government payroll in ex parte proceedings would usurp the role of the good old jury in striking the proper balance between government and citizen after hearing lawyers on both sides.

Now we can see why the Fourth Amendment text most emphatically did not require warrants—why, indeed, its reference to warrants is so plainly negative: "*no* Warrants shall issue, but . . ."[61] The warrant clause says only when warrants may not issue, not when they may, or must. Even if all the minimum prerequisites spelled out in the warrant clause are met, a warrant is still unlawful, and may not issue, if the underlying search or seizure it would authorize would be unreasonable.

The history of the federal Bill of Rights powerfully supports this textual analysis. In every state constitution prior to the federal Bill, "the warrant is treated as an enemy, not a friend."[62] No state convention proposes a warrant requirement for the federal Bill of Rights.[63] And in early drafts of the federal Fourth, it is the loose warrant, not the warrantless intrusion, that is explicitly labeled "unreasonable."[64]

History also reveals strong linkages between the Fourth and Seventh Amendments that previous clause-bound scholarship about each amendment in isolation has overlooked. All the major English cases that inspired the Fourth Amendment were civil jury actions, in which defendant officials unsuccessfully tried to use broad warrants as shields against liability.[65] Indeed, in *Wilkes v. Wood* itself, plaintiff's attorneys went out of their way to stress the jury's role:

> That the constitution of our country had been so fatally wounded, that it called aloud for the redress of a jury of Englishmen. . . . He then congratulated the jury, that they now had in their power, the present cause. . . . [T]he jury would effectually prevent the question from being ever revived again. He therefore recommends it to them to embrace this opportunity . . . of instructing those great officers in their duty, and that they (the jury) would now erect a great sea mark, by which our state pilots might avoid, for the future, those rocks upon which they now lay shipwrecked.[66]

A companion case featured the following noteworthy passage: "'Whether there was a probable cause or ground of suspicion' was a matter for the jury to determine: that is not now before the Court. So [too with the issue] 'whether the defendants detained the plaintiff an *unreasonable* time.'"[67] Here we have clear evidence of a role for the civil jury in deciding the reasonableness of government searches and seizures—and from none other than Lord Mansfield, a judge with notoriously statist sympathies.[68]

On this side of the Atlantic, Americans enthusiastically embraced the role of the civil jury in government search and seizure cases. Consider, for example, the words of a Pennsylvania Anti-Federalist in a 1787 essay: "[If a federal constable searching] for stolen goods, pulled down the clothes of a bed in which there was a woman and searched under her shift . . . a trial by jury would be our safest resource, heavy damage would at once punish the offender and deter others from committing the same; but what satisfaction can we expect from a lordly [judge] always ready to protect the officers of government against the weak and helpless citizens. . . ."[69] In the Pennsylvania ratifying convention, Robert Whitehill made a similar point, though less colorfully, by invoking "the Case of Mr. Wilkes"—a trespass action that had been tried to a jury—and reminding his audience that "the Doctrine of general Warrants show[s] that Judges may be corrupted."[70] To similar effect was the Anti-Federalist essayist Hampden: "Without [a jury] in civil actions, no relief can be had against the High Officers of State, for abuse of private citizens. . . ."[71] Government officials shared Hampden's sense of the importance of the civil jury in proto–Fourth Amendment cases, as shown by a mournful 1761 comment of Massachusetts royal Governor Bernard in response to a citizen trespass suit: "A Custom house officer has no chance with a jury."[72]

The Fourth-Seventh Amendment linkage was especially visible in the Maryland ratification debates. The prominent Anti-Federalist essayist "Maryland Farmer" set the tone:

> [S]uppose for instance, that an officer of the United States should force the house, the asylum of a citizen, by virtue of a general warrant, I would ask, are general warrants illegal by the [C]onstitution of the United States? . . . [N]o remedy has yet been found equal to the task of deterring and curbing the insolence of office, but a jury—[i]t has become an invariable maxim of English juries, to give ruinous damages whenever an officer had deviated from the rigid letter of the law, or been guilty of any unnecessary act of insolence or oppression. [By contrast,] an American judge, who will be judge and jury too [would probably] spare the public purse, if not favour a brother officer.[73]

The fire-breathing Luther Martin also clearly had in mind what we now call "Fourth Amendment cases" in emphasizing the importance of juries "[in] every case, whether civil or criminal, between government and its officers on the one part and the subject or citizen on the other. [Without civil juries] every arbitrary act of the general government, and every oppression of [its officers] for the collection of taxes, duties, imports, excise, and other purposes must be submitted to by the individual. . . ."[74] Notes from a speech delivered by Marylander Samuel Chase suggest that the future Justice likewise saw juries and warrants as linked and stressed the need for civil juries in trespass suits against government "officers."[75] In response, a Maryland ratifying convention committee recommended a federal constitutional amendment requiring civil jury trial in "all cases of trespasses"—plainly contemplating *government officer* trespasses—and prohibiting appellate relitigation of the jury's factual findings.[76] Committee members went on to warn that loose warrants should be "forbidden to those magistrates who are to administer the general government."[77]

The First Congress heeded all this in its proposed Bill of Rights, but also in its statutes. In a law authorizing federal agents to inspect distilleries, Congress explicitly provided that in citizen suits against abusive agents "the trial shall be by jury."[78]

Whereas the modern Court has described how a warrant reassures a search target,[79] earlier judges understood how it barred a target from suing after the fact. Indeed, the immunity it conferred was part of its very purpose, its definition; as Lord Mansfield put it in 1785, it would be a "solecism" if "the regular execution of a legal warrant shall be a trespass."[80] Speaking not merely of general warrants but of all warrants, the Supreme Court of Kentucky in 1829 described search warrant process as uniquely "distressing to the citizen" because of its "humiliating and degrading effects."[81] In 1859, the Massachusetts Supreme Judicial Court, with Lemuel Shaw presiding, proclaimed that the purpose of the state counterpart to (and prototype of) the federal Fourth was not to prefer or require warrants, but "strictly and carefully to limit, restrain and regulate" them.[82] And both the nineteenth- and twentieth-century editions of Judge Thomas Cooley's monumental treatise on constitutional law describe *all* search warrants as "a species of process exceedingly arbitrary in character, and which ought not to be resorted to except for very urgent and satisfactory reasons[;] the rules of law which pertain to them are of more than ordinary strictness."[83]

Indeed, even some modern Justices have at times understood that at least arrest warrants were friends of the government, not the citizen:

"Far from restricting the constable's arrest power, the institution of the warrant was used to expand that authority by giving the constable delegated powers of a superior officer such as a justice of the peace. Hence at the time of the Bill of Rights, the warrant functioned as a powerful tool of law enforcement rather than as a protection for the rights of criminal suspects."[84] What was true of warrants to arrest persons was likewise true of warrants to search and seize property. As Blackstone put it, "a lawful warrant will at all events indemnify the officer, who executes the same ministerially."[85]

But what, precisely, *is* a lawful warrant under the Fourth Amendment? Beneath this seemingly simple question lurks considerable complexity, especially at the remedial level. These issues are not free from all doubt, and some interpolation between the points pricked out thus far may be necessary.

At a minimum, of course, a lawful warrant can issue only from one duly authorized, and only if it meets the explicit textual requirements of probable cause, oath, particular description, and so forth. By analogy to the traditional eighteenth-century search warrant, and in order to avoid serious due process concerns, an ex parte search warrant arguably should be allowed only for items akin to contraband and stolen goods, for the probable cause test and the ex parte process both presuppose this limited context; if extended to warrants for "mere evidence," the warrant clause at a minimum should require "probable cause" to believe that the custodian would defy a subpoena or—stricter still—would destroy the evidence.[86] It also seems clear that no warrant should issue if the underlying search or seizure would be unreasonable, even if the minimal elements of the warrant clause are met. (Consider, for example, a strip search of high school girls to be conducted by an individual policeman with a 55 percent probability of finding tobacco cigarettes.)[87]

But who should decide what is unreasonable, or whether probable cause is truly met? In the first instance, the issuing magistrate. But what if the citizen target disagrees, and tries to (re)litigate the matter by bringing it before a trial judge and jury for full adversarial adjudication?

If an executive (or only quasi-judicial) magistrate issued the warrant, the verdict of *Wilkes v. Wood* and of Blackstone seems clear. Just as in England, where a general warrant issued by Lord Halifax was, in Blackstone's phrase, "no warrant at all,"[88] so too, in America, an unreasonable executive warrant or one without probable cause (from the perspective of the civil jury) is no warrant at all and should therefore support a cause of action against the executive issuer himself. (In England, Wilkes recovered the princely sum of 4,000 pounds from Lord Halifax.)[89] Because the defect of "unreasonableness" or "improbable cause" typically does not appear on the face of the warrant—unlike the defect in the *Wilkes* warrant—inferior officers who merely execute the warrant ministerially might escape liability altogether; if held liable, they should probably be able to implead the executive issuer for indemnification.[90]

When an unreasonable or improbable warrant (from the jury's perspective) issues from a judge—a member of a court of general jurisdiction—things take on a different hue. For unlike an executive official, the judge can claim that, in issuing the warrant, he made the requisite findings of reasonableness and probability and that these findings are res judicata and thus cannot be questioned by a jury but can be overturned only by a higher court. Surely the officials who executed this judicial warrant must be held immune—this immunity is of course why they sought the judicial warrant in the first place—for even if the search was *substantively* incorrect (from the jury's perspective), it was *jurisdictionally* authorized.[91] The usual remedy for an incorrect judicial act is an appeal to a higher court, but this remedy rings hollow in certain contexts, like search warrants and ex parte temporary restraining orders; much of the damage is done before the target has had any real day in court.

This last result should trouble us. From the perspective of the later civil jury, an unreasonable search *has* occurred, or a warrant *has* issued without probable cause. Arguably, the Fourth Amendment was designed to privilege the perspective of the civil jury. If so, perhaps the fairest solution—though one not provided by the common law—would be for the government itself to make amends. After all, its officials sought and executed the warrant, and its judges approved it. An analogy to modern-day inverse condemnation law under the just-compensation clause suggests itself—an analogy perhaps strengthened by the textual parallels between the Fourth Amendment's ban on "seizures" of "papers, houses, and effects" and the Fifth Amendment's rules regarding "tak[ings]" of "private property."

Probable Cause Requirement?

In recognizing various exceptions to its so-called warrant requirement, the modern Court has routinely said that even warrantless searches and seizures ordinarily must be backed by "probable cause."[92] But like its kindred warrant requirement, the probable cause requirement stands the Fourth Amendment on its head.

Begin with the text. The "probable cause" standard applies only to "warrants," not to all "searches" and "seizures." None of the other warrant rules—oath or affirmation, particular description, and so forth—

sensibly applies to all searches and seizures; and the Court, bowing to the text and common sense, has never so applied them.[93]

Why, then, has the Court tried to wrench the words "probable cause" from one clause and force them into another? Because of the "fundamental and obvious" notion that "less stringent standards for reviewing the officer's discretion in effecting a warrantless arrest and search would discourage resort to the procedures for obtaining a warrant."[94] In the words of a leading commentator, "the concept of probable cause lies at the heart of the fourth amendment," and it would be "incongruous" if police officers have "greater power to make seizures than magistrates have to authorize them."[95]

But this is simply our old friend, the doubly flawed logic driving the warrant requirement, now dragging along its yoked mate, the probable cause requirement. Contrary to this flawed logic, the Framers did not mind "discourag[ing] resort to . . . a warrant." They wanted to *limit* this imperial and ex parte device, so they insisted on a substantial standard of proof—and even that standard, understood in context, justified searches only for items akin to contraband or stolen goods, not "mere evidence." Precisely because officers carrying out warrantless searches and seizures would be accountable to judges and juries in civil damage actions after the fact, no fixed constitutional requirement of probable cause was imposed on all these searches and seizures; they simply had to be reasonable.

Of course, certain intrusive subcategories of warrantless action— arrests, for example—might generally require probable cause at common law, but this is a far cry from the idea that *all* searches and seizures must meet this standard to be reasonable. Supporters of a global probable cause requirement have yet to identify even a single early case, treatise, or state constitution that explicitly proclaims probable cause as the prerequisite for all searches and seizures. On the other side of the ledger, the First Congress clearly authorized various suspicionless searches of ships and liquor storehouses.[96] And let us recall once again the apparent common law rule that a warrantless intrusion could be justified after the fact, even in the absence of objective probable cause ex ante, if it succeeded in turning up an actual felon.

So much for text and history. Now consult common sense. If "probable cause" is taken seriously—a good probability of finding items akin to contraband or stolen goods—surely it cannot provide the standard for all searches and seizures. What happens when the government wants to search or seize other items? Here the probable cause test is unilluminating and we need to revert instead to the real "heart of the fourth amendment": reasonableness. In other situations, a probable cause test is not merely unilluminating but downright silly. Must a search that has been consented to by the apparent owner be backed by probable cause? How about a search of items in plain, public view, as when our Secret Service agent scans the crowd, searching for anything unusual? What about metal detector and X-ray searches at airports? Or building code inspections? Or weapons pat-downs by police officers who legitimately fear for their personal safety? Or prison searches? What if a grand jury subpoenas a person precisely to determine whether there may be probable cause to believe a crime has occurred?

Justices and other supporters of the so-called probable cause requirement have only two responses. The first is to claim that all these things are not really "searches" or "seizures." But a search is a search even if consented to, or of an item in plain view, or if conducted via modern magnetic or X-ray technology, or if part of noncriminal law enforcement, or if no more intrusive than a frisk, or if done in prison. And if successfully commanding someone, upon pain of contempt and imprisonment, to appear downtown before the grand jury on Monday at nine o'clock A.M. does not "seize" that person, I do not know what does. Beneath the Justices' unconvincing and unworthy word game, we see again how unjustified expansions of constitutional rights often lead to dangerous and unjustified contractions elsewhere. To avoid some of the absurdities created by the so-called warrant and probable cause requirements, the Justices have watered down the plain meaning of "search" and "seizure."[97]

The second response also involves a possible watering down of the text—here, the *probable cause* idea itself. At first blush, the phrase seems to connote a standard akin to more than 50 percent, or at least something higher than, say, 1 percent: a warrant should issue only if it is probable—more likely than not, or at least not highly *un*likely—that the search will turn up the goods. And if limited to the context that gave it birth—the common law search warrant—these words could probably (!) be taken at face value.[98] The words would, no doubt, strictly limit the number of ex parte warrants that could issue; but of course, that was just the point of the warrant clause. However, once wrenched from the warrant clause and (wrongly) proclaimed the heart of the Fourth Amendment, these words must be defined differently.

To begin with, probable cause cannot be a *fixed* standard. It would make little sense to insist on the same amount of probability regardless of the imminence of the harm, the intrusiveness of the search, the reason for the search, and so on. Also, probable cause cannot be a *high* standard. It would make no sense to say that I may not be searched via metal detectors and X-ray machines at JFK unless there is a high likelihood—more than 50 percent, or at least more than 1 percent—that I am toting a gun.[99]

In effect, this approach reads "probable cause" as "reasonable cause."[100] Is it not easier to read the words as written, and say that warrantless searches must simply be reasonable? For unlike the seemingly fixed and high standard of probable cause, reasonableness obviously does require different levels of cause in different contexts, and not always a high probability of success—if, say, we are searching for bombs on planes.

More than intellectual honesty and interpretive aesthetics are at stake, for once "probable cause" is watered down for warrantless searches, how can it be strictly preserved in the warrant clause itself? If 0.1 percent is good enough for airports, why not for warrants? The watering down of "probable cause" necessarily authorizes ex parte warrants on loose terms that would have shocked the Founders. Indeed, the modern Court has explicitly upheld "newfangled warrants" on less than probable cause in explicit violation of the core textual command of the warrant clause.[101] History has been turned on its head, and loose, ex parte warrants—general warrants, really—now issue from central officialdom. Once again, apparent textual expansion leads to contraction elsewhere in an inversion of the original amendment's first principles.

Exclusionary Rule?

The modern Court not only has misunderstood the nature of Fourth Amendment rights but also has distorted Fourth Amendment remedies. This distortion has pushed in many directions at once. The Court has failed to nurture and at times has affirmatively undermined the tort remedies underlying the amendment, has concocted the awkward and embarrassing remedy of excluding reliable evidence of criminal guilt, and has then tried to water down this awkward and embarrassing remedy in ad hoc ways.[102]

Let us return once again to the text of the Fourth Amendment. Its global command that all searches and seizures be reasonable applies equally to civil and criminal searches. And its reference to Americans' right to be "secure in their persons, houses, papers, and effects" should remind us of background common law principles protecting these interests of personhood, property, and privacy—in a word, the law of tort.[103]

Typically, if one's person or house or papers or effects are unreasonably trespassed upon, one can bring a civil action against the trespasser. And this is exactly what happened in pre-Revolutionary England and America. In a series of landmark English cases—most famously, *Wilkes v. Wood*—oppressive general warrants were struck down in civil jury trespass actions brought against the officials who committed or authorized the unreasonable searches and seizures.[104] In America, both before and after the Revolution, the civil trespass action tried to a jury flourished as the obvious remedy against haughty customs officers, tax collectors, constables, marshals, and the like.[105]

Tort law remedies were thus clearly the ones presupposed by the Framers of the Fourth Amendment and counterpart state constitutional provisions. Supporters of the exclusionary rule cannot point to a single major statement from the Founding—or even the antebellum or Reconstruction eras—supporting Fourth Amendment exclusion of evidence in a criminal trial. Indeed, the idea of exclusion was so implausible that it seems almost never to have been urged by criminal defendants, despite the large incentive that they had to do so, in the vast number of criminal cases litigated in the century after Independence. And in the rare case in which the argument for exclusion was made, it received the back of the judicial hand. Consider carefully the words of Justice Joseph Story in a famous circuit court opinion in 1822:

> In the ordinary administration of municipal law the right of using evidence does not depend, nor, as far as I have any recollection, has ever been supposed to depend upon the lawfulness or unlawfulness of the mode, by which it is obtained. . . . [T]he evidence is admissible on charges for the highest crimes, even though it may have been obtained by a trespass upon the person, or by any other forcible and illegal means. . . . In many instances, and especially on trials for crimes, evidence is often obtained from the possession of the offender by force or by contrivances, which one could not easily reconcile to a delicate sense of propriety, or support upon the foundations of municipal law. Yet I am not aware, that such evidence has upon that account ever been dismissed for incompetency.[106]

When the bookish Story tells us that he has never heard of a case excluding evidence because it was "obtained by a trespass [or] illegal means," surely we should sit up and take notice. A generation after Story's remarks, the Supreme Judicial Court of Massachusetts reached a similarly brisk result under its state constitutional predecessor of the federal Fourth: "If the search warrant were illegal, or if the officer serving the warrant exceeded his authority, the party on whose complaint the warrant issued, or the officer, would be responsible for the wrong done; but this is no good reason for excluding the papers seized as evidence. . . ."[107] As late as 1883, the leading evidence treatise clearly proclaimed illegally procured evidence admissible,[108] a result that universally obtained in America before 1886, according to Dean Wigmore's definitive scholarship.[109]

Lochner's Legacy. How then, did exclusion creep into American law? By a series of missteps and mishaps. Because the detailed story has been well told by others,[110] I shall only summarize.

The confusion began with the Supreme Court's landmark 1886 case, *Boyd v. United States*.[111] Collapsing the Fourth Amendment rule against unreasonable seizures into the Fifth Amendment ban on compelled self-incrimination, the *Boyd* Court excluded various papers that the government had in effect subpoenaed and sought to use in a quasi-criminal case against the target of the subpoena. The Fourth Amendment's reasonableness clause and the Fifth Amendment's incrimination clause, said the Court, "run almost into each other" and "throw great light on each other."[112] Continuing this conflation of clauses, later cases expanded exclusion to searches and seizures in which the compelled self-incrimination of subpoenas was wholly absent.[113]

Boyd and its immediate progeny involved corporate and regulatory offenses rather than violent crime. These cases took root in a judicial era that we now know by the name *Lochner,*[114] and the spirit inspiring *Boyd* and its progeny was indeed akin to *Lochner*'s spirit: a person has a right to his property, and it is unreasonable to use his property against him in a criminal proceeding.

Several things can be said about this intriguing claim. For starters, it surely cannot explain excluding contraband or stolen goods, which were never one's property to begin with—and the Court's eventual expansion of exclusion, four decades after *Boyd*, to cover these categories occurred without cogent explanation.[115] Next, this claim has a certain initial plausibility in the context in which it arose, involving personal papers. To introduce a man's diary as evidence against him is perhaps perilously close to forcing him to take the stand himself.[116] In both cases he is being done in against his will by his own words, words that he has never chosen to share with anyone else. Through a diary, a defendant arguably becomes an involuntary "witness"—one whose words testify against himself at trial. But whatever one thinks of a diary or personal papers, where Fourth and Fifth Amendment concerns may overlap and reinforce, a bloodstained shirt is something else entirely.

Diaries and personal papers arguably testify—in the defendant's words, as might the defendant himself as an actual "witness" at trial—but a bloody shirt does not. Only the most peculiar property fetishist could say that everything one owns, bloody shirts and all, is simply an extension of the "person" protected by the Fifth Amendment, in the same way that a diary or a personal paper arguably is.

Property worship was of course once in vogue, but this aspect of the *Lochner* era was supposedly laid to rest in the 1930s. If a person's very blood can be forcibly taken and used against him because it is not "testimonial"—as Justice Brennan held for the Warren Court in *Schmerber*[117]—it is hard to understand why his bloody shirt is entitled to greater protection. Indeed, much of *Boyd* has been explicitly repudiated by modern Supreme Court decisions.[118]

Once we reject *Lochner*-era property worship, none of the arguments in *Boyd* or its exclusionary offspring holds up. *Boyd* claimed roots in a landmark English case that followed *Wilkes v. Wood*, but Professor Taylor has shown that the murky dictum on which *Boyd* relied was most probably off point.[119] In any event, and no matter how we parse this single ambiguous passage, exclusion is not and never has been the British rule.[120]

Despite *Boyd*'s expansive vision of the right against compelled self-incrimination, leading nineteenth-century cases in America and England viewed the right as exceedingly narrow outside the context of political crime and thought crime, as the right (if broadly construed) was in derogation of truth. Indeed, before *Boyd*, the dominant American view took the wording of the right seriously and allowed into evidence fruits of the defendant's compelled pretrial disclosures. Under the logic of a landmark New York opinion decided in 1861, which construed a state constitution whose language tracked the federal Fifth Amendment almost verbatim, the suspect could be obliged to tell the grand jury where the body was buried, and at trial the body itself (but not the suspect's words) could be introduced.[121] A defendant did indeed enjoy a right not to "be compelled in any criminal case to be a witness against himself," but this right applied only when the government introduced a defendant's own words—testimony—against him at trial.[122]

Boyd's effort to fuse the Fourth and Fifth Amendments has not stood the test of time and has been plainly rejected by the modern Court. *Boyd*'s mistake was not in its focus on the concept of Fourth Amendment reasonableness, nor in its laudable effort to read the Fourth Amendment reasonableness clause in light of other constitutional provisions. (Indeed, I shall later call for just such an approach.)

Rather, *Boyd*'s mistake was to misread both the reasonableness clause and the incrimination clause by trying to fuse them together. At heart, the two provisions are motivated by very different ideas; they do not "run almost into each other" as a general matter. The Fourth, unlike the Fifth, applies equally to civil searches, and the Fifth, unlike the Fourth, is strictly limited to compelled testimony. Even with compelled testimony, it is hard for some to see what transcendent constitutional norm is served by the incrimination clause outside the context in which it arose—political and religious thought crime and speech crime.[123] When it comes to murders and rapes, the intuitive appeal of an expansive reading of the incrimination clause drops dramatically. In ordinary morality, people are encouraged and often obliged to admit their misdeeds, and the law requires a person to testify truthfully even against her dearest childhood friend (when her reluctance to testify is supported by more worthy motives than the urge of thugs to save their skins).[124] To expand the Fifth beyond compelled testimony by fusing it with the Fourth does not serve any overarching constitutional value, apart from now-discredited property fetishism. As we shall see later, it is far more sensible to try to read the Fourth in light of other norms that do embody our overall constitutional structure today—free speech, free press, privacy, equal protection, due process, and just compensation.[125]

Even if ultimately wrong, *Boyd*'s Fourth-Fifth fusion at least had an internal logic that could explain the source, scope, and limits of the so-called exclusionary rule. For example, even if ultimately incorrect, the fusion was an intelligible and principled response to the claim that, by excluding highly relevant evidence of criminal guilt, judges were simply conjuring up out of thin air a wholly unprecedented and nontraditional Fourth Amendment remedy. Under the Fifth Amendment, excluding evidence is not a *remedy* for an earlier constitutional violation, but a *prevention* of the violation itself. A Fifth Amendment wrong occurs only at trial, when testimony is introduced *"in a[] criminal case."*[126] (It was no Fifth Amendment violation to force Oliver North to testify before Congress; but it would have been to introduce that compelled testimony, over North's objection, in his criminal trial.) Likewise, the Fifth Amendment's explicit reference to "criminal" cases can explain why evidence must be excluded from criminal trials, but not from civil trials.[127] Standing alone, the Fourth Amendment cannot justify this difference, for its global command of reasonableness nowhere distinguishes between criminal searches and seizures and civil ones. The Fifth Amendment further explains why unlawful arrests do not require releasing the suspect, whereas unlawful searches of property require exclusion of evidence:[128] compelling the defendant himself to appear at trial has never been seen as raising a Fifth Amendment problem.[129] So too, the Fourth Amendment, standing alone, cannot explain why an unconstitutional search of *A*'s home that uncovers criminal evidence against both *A* and *B* calls for exclusion in *A*'s criminal trial, but not *B*'s.[130] The Fifth helps explain this, for *A* may be compelled to testify against *B* but not against himself. The Fourth-Fifth fusion—our old friend, *Lochner*-era property fetishism, dressed up as a textual argument—treats *A*'s property like *A* himself.

Modern Moves. Once we reject the Fourth-Fifth fusion, we are left with a variety of slogans wholly inadequate to the task at hand. These slogans—"judicial integrity and fairness," "preventing government from profiting from its own wrong," and "deterrence"—cannot explain basic elements of exclusionary doctrine.[131] They cannot explain where this nontextual and unprecedented remedy comes from. They cannot explain why it applies only in criminal and not civil cases. They cannot explain why unlawful arrests are different from unlawful searches. They cannot explain Fourth Amendment standing doctrine. In short, they prove too much—and also too little, for each slogan sits atop a pile of dubious assumptions and inferences.

Consider first "judicial integrity and fairness." Do courts in England—and many other countries, for that matter—lack integrity and fairness because they generally allow material and relevant evidence of criminal guilt?[132] Surely the practices of other civilized and respected judicial systems should give pause to those who claim exclusion is mandated by basic notions of fair play. Do all American courts lack integrity and fairness in civil cases brought by the government as plaintiff? Given that civil exclusion is not the rule, never has been the rule,[133] and shows little sign of becoming the rule, it seems that the near-unanimous verdict of the American bench is that integrity does not invariably require exclusion. If the primary justification for exclusion is that federal judges have inherent power over what happens inside their own courtrooms, whence their authority to impose the exclusionary rule on the states? It is hard to attribute any exclusionary purpose to the Fourteenth Amendment Framers, given the universal law against exclusion in the 1860s and the utter absence of any challenge to this universal practice by the Reconstruction Republicans.[134] More generally, we must remember that integrity and fairness are also threatened by excluding evidence that will help the justice system to reach a true verdict. Thus the courts best affirm their integrity and fairness not by closing their eyes to truthful evidence, but by opening their doors to any civil suit brought against wayward government officials, even one brought by a convict.

Consider next the nice-sounding idea that government should not profit from its own wrongdoing. Our society, however, also cherishes the notion that cheaters—or murderers, or rapists, for that matter— should not prosper. When the murderer's bloody knife is introduced, it is not only the government that profits; the people also profit when those who truly do commit crimes against person and property are duly convicted on the basis of reliable evidence. When rapists, burglars, and murderers are convicted, are not the people often *more* "secure in their persons, houses, papers, and effects?"[135]

The classic response is that setting criminals free is a cost of the Fourth Amendment itself, and not of the much-maligned exclusionary rule.[136] If the government had simply obeyed the Fourth Amendment, it would never have found the bloody knife. Thus, excluding the knife simply restores the status quo ante and confers no benefit on the murderer. The classic response is too quick.

In many situations, it is far from clear that the illegality of a search is indeed a but-for cause of the later introduction into evidence of an item found in the search. Suppose the police could easily get a warrant, but fail to do so because they think the case at hand falls into a judicially recognized exception to the so-called warrant requirement. A court later disagrees—and so, under current doctrine, the search was unconstitutional. But if the court goes on to exclude the bloody knife, it does indeed confer a huge benefit on the murderer. The police could easily have obtained a warrant before the search, so the illegality is not a but-for cause of the introduction of the knife into evidence.

This causation gap would remain even if the Court sensibly abandoned its so-called warrant and probable cause requirements. Suppose the police search without enough justification to be "reasonable," and five minutes later, independent information comes to the police station that would have nudged the probability needle enough to make the search reasonable. Here, too, the illegality of the search when conducted is not a but-for cause of the later introduction of the bloody knife, and exclusion makes the murderer better off than he would have been had no Fourth Amendment violation ever occurred. Once tipped off that the cops are onto him, the suspect may well destroy other evidence that the police might have found, had the illegal search not occurred. Here, too, exclusion makes the criminal better off.

The point is generalizable and raises big questions concerning burdens of proof. Given the almost metaphysical difficulties in knowing whether the bloody knife or some evidentiary substitute would have come to light anyway, should not the law strongly presume that somehow, some way, sometime, the truth would come out? Criminals get careless or cocky; conspirators rat; neighbors come forward; cops get lucky; the truth outs; and justice reigns—or so our courts should presume, and any party seeking to suppress truth and thwart justice should bear a heavy burden of proof.[137]

But even if a defendant could conclusively establish but-for causation, the bloody knife should still come in as evidence. Not all but-for consequences of an illegal search are legally cognizable. If the police buy fancy surveillance equipment from HiTek, Inc., to conduct illegal searches, and competitor Low-Tech Corp. is thereby driven into bankruptcy, Low-Tech's *factual* harm—though (by stipulation) a but-for consequence of the illegal searches—does not constitute *legally* cognizable injury. Now for a far more vivid example: if an illegal search turns up a ton of marijuana, the government need not return the contraband even if the government's possession of the marijuana is clearly a but-for consequence of its illegal search.[138] Indeed, the government may sell the marijuana (say, for legitimate medical uses) and use the proceeds to finance the continued war on drugs. In a very real way, the government *has* "profited from its own wrong." Put differently, just as the illegality in the HiTek example was in unreasonably searching—and not in bankrupting Low-Tech—so here the illegality was in unreasonably searching prior to finding the marijuana, and not in seizing the marijuana itself, once found. And what is true of seizing should also be true of using the marijuana—or some noncontraband item like the suspect's bloodstained shirt—as evidence.

This last point is not merely wishful thinking or a personal view. It is the residue of a two-century tradition of civil damage actions in America. Consider the following situation. Police suspect identical twins, who live in identical, adjoining houses. Police search both equally with equal but insufficient justification. In twin Adam's house, they find nothing; in twin Bob's, the bloodstained shirt. The shirt is introduced as evidence in Bob's murder trial, and he gets twenty years. Both Adam and Bob then bring independent civil actions for damages. The result: under traditional principles, Adam and Bob recover equal amounts.[139] Bob does not recover more for his twenty years. The factual harms of seizure, evidentiary use, conviction, and sentence are not legally cognizable; only the prior unconstitutional search is.[140]

This brings us, finally, to deterrence. Government must be deterred from violating the people's Fourth Amendment rights. But the exclusionary rule is a bad way to go about this.

For starters, note that, unlike "integrity and fairness" or the "non-profit" principle, deterrence does not posit some inherent right in the criminal defendant. Deterrence is concerned with the government; it is concerned with systematic impact. It treats the criminal defendant merely as a surrogate for the larger public interest in restraining the government. The criminal defendant is a kind of private attorney general.

But the worst kind. He is self-selected and self-serving. He is often unrepresentative of the larger class of law-abiding citizens, and his interests regularly conflict with theirs. Indeed, he is often despised by the public, the class he implicitly is supposed to represent. He will litigate on the worst set of facts, heedless that the result will be a bad precedent for the Fourth Amendment generally. He cares only about the case at hand—his case—and has no long view. He is not a sophisticated repeat player. He rarely hires the best lawyer. He cares only about exclusion—and can get only exclusion—even if other remedies (damages or injunctions) would better prevent future violations. He is, in many ways, the exact opposite of the litigants the NAACP sought out in its carefully orchestrated campaign to revive the equal protection clause in the 1930s through the 1960s. He is, in short, an awkward champion of the Fourth Amendment.

He is also overcompensated. In an antitrust or securities class action, we must give the private attorney general enough to induce her to bring the suit, but a small percentage of the total take will suffice. In a criminal case, if we insist on using criminal defendants as private attorneys general, why not give a defendant who successfully establishes a Fourth Amendment violation only a 10 percent sentence discount—surely a tangible incentive—and substitute for the remaining 90 percent some other structural remedy, injunctive or damages, that will flow to the direct benefit of law-abiding citizens?[141] (Floating class actions and fluid recovery in antitrust and consumer-fraud cases are the model here.)[142]

Put differently, if deterrence is the key, the idea is to make the government pay, in some way, for its past misdeeds, in order to discourage future ones. But why should that payment flow to the guilty? Under the exclusionary rule, the more guilty you are, the more you benefit. And when we think about this upside-down effect clearly, our minds balk—just as they did when we focused clearly on the notion that Bob should somehow recover higher damages than Adam simply because Bob was a murderer. Instead of excluding the bloodstained shirt, why not assess damages against the police department set at a level to achieve the same quantum of total deterrence, and use the money as a fund to educate the police and the citizenry about the Fourth Amendment, or to comfort victims of violent crime, or to build up neighborhoods that have borne the brunt of police brutality?[143] (All of these would be more apt to make the people "secure in their persons, houses, papers, and effects" than would freeing murderers and rapists.)[144] In sum, when it comes to private attorneys general, the exclusionary rule's deterrence rationale looks in the wrong place—to paradigmatically guilty criminal defendants rather than to prototypically law-abiding civil plaintiffs.[145]

The Framers understood the deterrence and private attorney general concepts perfectly. As civil plaintiffs, John Wilkes and company, after all, had recovered a King's ransom from civil juries to teach arrogant officialdom a lesson and to deter future abuse.[146] In *Wilkes v. Wood* itself, Lord Chief Justice Camden proclaimed in a famous passage that "a jury have it in their power to give damages for more than the injury received. Damages are designed not only as a satisfaction to the injured person, but likewise as a punishment to the guilty, *to deter from any such proceeding for the future*, and as a proof of the detestation of the jury to the action itself."[147] And we have already encountered clear Founding references in America to the "invariable maxim" of "ruinous damages" to "*deter*[] and curb[]" government "insolence or oppression"[148] and "heavy damages . . . [to] punish the offender *and deter others* from committing the same."[149] The point is not simply that these civil forms of deterrence and private attorney generalship are deeply rooted in our Fourth Amendment tradition whereas criminal exclusion is wholly unprecedented (once we abandon Fourth-Fifth fusion). The point is also that these traditional forms make much more sense, *as deterrence*.

On distributional grounds, the traditional civil model is not skewed to reward the guilty. Murderer Bob does not get more than innocent Adam. On efficiency grounds, money damages are often far superior to exclusion. Money is infinitely divisible; exclusion is clunky. If less deterrence is desired, the punitive damages multiplier can be ratcheted down; but under an exclusion scheme, a Tuesday exception tends to look unprincipled. Money is more visible and quantifiable, and therefore democratic; the public can more easily see the costs of bad police conduct. And many of the advantages of money also apply to standard injunctive relief.

Of course, the traditional eighteenth-century civil model must be brought into the twenty-first century. Time-honored rules of trespass need to be supplemented to deal with new technology like wiretapping, as the Court held in *Katz*.[150] State common law suits must be joined by the more modern *Bivens* action.[151] The increased bureaucratic density of government officialdom calls for government-entity rather than individual-officer liability. Widespread, low-grade Fourth Amendment violations provide a textbook example of the need for modern class action aggregation techniques. Civil injunctions have become a more routine regulatory mechanism elsewhere; why not here, too? And here, as elsewhere, a civil jury model must make its peace with the modern administrative state. I shall have more to say about all of this later. But for now, the basic point is that faithful interpretation upgrades the civil model rather than inventing out of whole cloth a criminal one. The modern-day equivalent of a horse and buggy is a car, not an Andy Warhol poster.[152]

"But," someone unconcerned about text and history might ask, "why not keep both the poster and the car (and the buggy as well)? The more the merrier! To be sure," the argument might run, "if forced to choose between civil and criminal deterrence, clearly we must choose civil, not merely on grounds of text and tradition, but on grounds of common sense. Much government searching and seizing is not motivated by an effort to secure criminal convictions, and even traditional criminal law enforcement officers may often seek to harass or brutalize rather than convict. Civil deterrence is the only game in town, much of the time. But why abandon or even trim the exclusionary rule rather than supplement it?"

Perhaps there is no logical or causal connection between the attention lavished on the exclusionary rule in the twentieth century and the woeful failure to nurture the civil model, not to mention the affirmative efforts to weaken this model with newfangled immunities. Perhaps the judges' positioning of themselves as exclusionary guardians of the amendment is unrelated to the diminished role of the civil jury. Perhaps the rise of exclusion as a Fourth Amendment remedy has nothing to do with the coincidental mess that has been made in defining the meaning of Fourth Amendment rights.

I am doubtful. The exclusionary rule renders the Fourth Amendment contemptible in the eyes of judges and citizens. Judges do not like excluding bloody knives, so they distort doctrine, claiming that the Fourth Amendment was not really violated. In the popular mind, the amendment has lost its luster and become associated with grinning criminals getting off on crummy technicalities. When rapists are freed, the people are *less* secure in their houses and persons[153]—and they lose respect for the Fourth Amendment. If exclusion is the remedy, all too often ordinary people will want to say that the right was not really violated. At first they will say it with a wink; later, with a frown; and one day, they will come to believe it. Here, too, unjustified expansion predictably leads to unjustified contraction elsewhere.

Thus, even if exclusion achieves short-term deterrence, it creates long-term instability, driving a wedge between We the People and Our Constitution. We have never enshrined Fourth Amendment exclusion in Our Constitution, nor endorsed its upside-down logic that the guilty should benefit more than the innocent. In the long run, popular sentiment will (quite literally) have its day in court, for the people elect Presidents, who in turn appoint federal judges. Judges who value long-run stability and sustainability should prefer institutions that connect the People to Our Constitution, rather than ones that alienate Us from it.

The Better Way: A Proposal

As announced at the outset, my aim here is to provide a way out of the mess that is the current Fourth Amendment. Implicit in my critique are the basic elements of an attractive alternative approach. In developing this approach, we need not abandon all that the modern Court has said and done. To be sure, we should reject the extravagant textual and historical claims that the Court has at times made—that the amendment's words implicitly require warrants; that all warrantless searches require probable cause, lest warrants be discouraged; that the incrimination and reasonableness clauses "run almost into each other" as a general matter; and that Founding history supports all this. But beneath this sloppy textual and historical analysis lay genuine concerns to which the Justices were probably responding. As government power became increasingly bureaucratic, and as highly organized paramilitary police departments emerged, perhaps the Justices sensed a need to go beyond the common law jury system of policing the police—and so they latched onto the warrant, and modified the notion of probable cause. And beneath *Boyd*, we find a praiseworthy effort to look to other clauses of the Constitution to inform the idea of Fourth Amendment reasonableness,[154] and to press the Fourth Amendment into the service of the organizing constitutional idea of the era: property.[155]

As it turns out, however, there is a better way to adapt to changes in the structure of government, and to bring the Fourth Amendment into the center of constitutional discourse today. And this better way does not require us to twist the text or to manhandle the historical evidence. Let us now assemble the elements of this better model, by considering in turn Fourth Amendment rights, remedies, and regimes of enforcement.

Rights

Rights first. The core of the Fourth Amendment, as we have seen, is neither a warrant nor probable cause, but reasonableness. Because of the Court's preoccupation with warrants and probable cause—ordaining these with one hand while chiseling out exception after exception with the other—the Justices have spent surprisingly little time self-consciously reflecting on what, exactly, makes for a substantively unreasonable search or seizure.[156]

Common-Sense (Tort) Reasonableness. Consider ordinary common-sense reasonableness. Probability—"probable cause" or something more or less—is obviously only one variable in a complex equation. To focus on probability alone as the sine qua non of reasonableness would be a mistake. Sometimes 0.1 percent is more than enough—consider bombs on planes—and other times 100 percent may still be unreasonable. (Even if the government knows with certainty that honest Abe's business log is in his bedroom and contains a notation relevant to a civil suit between Betty and Carol, a surprise nighttime search—as opposed to a subpoena—would typically be unreasonable.) Common sense tells us to look beyond probability to the importance of finding what the government is looking for, the intrusiveness of the search, the identity of the search target, the availability of other means of achieving the purpose of the search, and so on.

As obvious as all this seems, the Court's obsession with warrants, probable cause, and criminal exclusion has often made it difficult for the Justices to admit what common sense requires. At times, the Court has suggested that, because the core of the amendment involves criminal investigation, exceptions to strict probable cause should be specially disfavored here.[157] If taken seriously, this upside-down idea would mean that, as between two equally unintrusive but low-probability searches, the search justified by a *more* compelling purpose—criminal enforcement to protect person and property—is *less* constitutionally proper.[158]

On the other hand, on those occasions when common sense breaks through into the *United States Reports,* it often comes wrapped in a sheepish, apologetic tone. Here, for example, are two of the most noted judicial statements—both from the pen of Justice Robert Jackson—that argue that more serious crimes may justify more expansive searches:

> I should be human enough to apply the letter of the law with some indulgence to officers acting to deal with threats or crimes of violence which endanger life or security.[159]
>
> But if we are to make judicial exceptions to the Fourth Amendment, . . . it seems to me they should depend somewhat upon the gravity of the offense. If we assume, for example, that a child is

kidnaped and the officers throw a roadblock about the neighbor-hood and search every outgoing car, it would be a drastic and undiscriminating use of the search. The officers might be unable to show probable cause for searching any particular car. However, I should candidly strive hard to sustain such an action, executed fairly and in good faith, because it might be reasonable to subject travelers to that indignity if it was the only way to save a threat-ened life and detect a vicious crime. But I should not strain to sus-tain such a roadblock and universal search to salvage a few bottles of bourbon and catch a bootlegger.[160]

In remarkable imagery, Justice Jackson "candidly" confesses that as a "human" (rather than as a judge) he would "strive" to stretch and "strain" the law—"to apply the letter of law with some indulgence," to "make judicial exceptions to the Fourth Amendment"—in cases of seri-ous crime. Lost in these commonsensical but confused confessions is the idea that, in upholding a "reasonable" roadblock to find kidnappers and save kids, judges would be sticking strictly to "the letter of the law" rather than "mak[ing] judicial exceptions to the Fourth Amendment."

If Justice Jackson's language is too embarrassed, at least it is not embarrassing. It clearly states a global truth that makes intuitive sense to police officials and citizens alike: serious crimes and serious needs can justify more serious searches and seizures. Consider, by contrast, the way that the modern Court recently articulated this insight when it recognized yet another epicycle in its Ptolemaic system of Fourth Amendment rules. Because the seriousness of a crime matters, the Court in *Welsh v. Wisconsin* in effect proclaimed that there should be a "minor offense" *(Welsh)* exception to the "exigent circumstances" *(War-den)* exception to the "home arrest" *(Payton)* exception to the usual "arrest" *(Watson)* exception to the so-called "warrant requirement" *(Johnson)*.[161] Got that?

For another example of how common-sense reasonableness could straighten out Fourth Amendment thinking and writing, consider elec-tronic surveillance. In love with the warrant, the Court has blessed hid-den audio and video bugs—even ones that must be installed by secret physical trespass—so long as these bugs are approved in advance by judicial warrant.[162] The problem here is not in considering audio bugs Fourth Amendment "searches"—by ears rather than eyes—of the tar-get's home, and "seizures" of some of her most valuable "effects," namely, her private conversations. The problem is trying to stretch the warrant clause to cover these things. It is not simply that, as Justice

Black pointed out in *Katz*, the words of the warrant clause don't seem to fit, contemplating as they do physical things already in existence that can be "particularly described," rather than intangible conversations that don't yet exist.[163] Rather, the problem is that these words, as we have seen, presuppose a search for items akin to contraband or stolen goods, not "mere evidence," such as where the target was and when she was there, which video surveillance could establish.

Moreover, even though the warrant contemplated by the Fourth Amendment would be issued ex parte, it would be served on the owner or occupant of the searched premises, or left there, giving the target clear notice of what had been searched or seized, and when. This notification was contemporaneous with the intrusion itself. By contrast, targets of audio and video warrants may never learn that they have been searched and that their words have been seized—or they may find out years after the fact.[164] (As Telford Taylor has noted, such "warrants" severely strain the paradigmatically adversarial nature of Anglo-American judicial proceedings and traditional Article III notions of "case" or "controversy.")[165]

Now secrecy does not necessarily equal unconstitutionality. But it does raise a problem. And if the answer to our problem does not lie in a secret newfangled warrant, neither does it lie in probable cause. It lies in reasonableness. Simply put, are secret searches and seizures reasonable? Regardless of one's answer, at least one will be asking the right question—talking sense rather than nonsense.[166]

Once we see that secrecy is a key issue raised by electronic surveillance, we also see that the issue arises in many other contexts, too. Consider the undercover cop who poses as someone she is not. From one perspective, whether she carries a bug or not, she is acting openly, not secretly. The target who speaks with our agent and lets her into his confidence knows that his eyes are being "searched" and his words "seized" by his conversation partner. What he does not know, however, is that she is a government official. So here, too, we have an element of secrecy and deception.

When is such deception permissible? Is winning a suspected hit man's confidence by posing as a mobster different from winning entrance into someone's home or car by posing as a stranded motorist? If so, what are the factors that distinguish among deceptions?[167] Once again, the issues here must be organized not around warrants or probable cause but around reasonableness.

Just as a more secret search may be more unreasonable, so too with a more intrusive search. Today's Court recognizes that intrusiveness can make a difference, but the language of warrants and probable cause does not easily accommodate this insight. As we have seen, intrusiveness at times sneaks sub rosa into the judicial definition of what counts as a "search" or "seizure." But once we focus on reasonableness, we can more easily admit the truth: metal detection is often more acceptable than a strip search, not because the former is not a search but because it is less intrusive and thus more reasonable. All other things being equal, a compulsory urine test is more problematic if government officials insist on monitoring the production of the specimen. Greater intrusiveness requires greater justification. Only by keeping our eyes fixed on reasonableness as the polestar of the Fourth Amendment can we steer our way to a world where serious, sustained, and sensible Fourth Amendment discourse can occur.

Constitutional Reasonableness. Fourth Amendment reasonableness is not simply a matter of common sense: it is also an issue of constitutional law. For the Fourth Amendment is not merely tort law (in which issues of common-sense reasonableness loom large); it is also emphatically constitutional law.[168] Of course, many obvious intuitions may resonate in both common sense and constitutional law. For example, the common-sense intuition about the special intrusiveness of monitored urine tests can easily be packaged in the language of constitutional privacy.

With this caveat in mind, let us recall a standard technique of constitutional interpretation: parsing one provision—especially if somewhat open-ended—in light of other constitutional provisions.[169] In thinking about the broad command of the Fourth Amendment, we must examine other parts of the Bill of Rights to identify constitutional values that are elements of *constitutional* reasonableness.[170] These other clauses at all times stand as independent hurdles, above and beyond composite reasonableness, that every search or seizure must clear, but the clauses can also serve other functions. They can furnish benchmarks against which to measure reasonableness and components of reasonableness itself. A government policy that comes close to the limit set by one of these independent clauses can, if conjoined with a search or seizure, cross over into constitutional unreasonableness.[171]

For example, a search or seizure of newspaper files should cause special alarm and require special safeguards. The *Wilkes v. Wood* case should have taught us all about the special dangers posed by the government's searching and seizing documents from the press, but the lesson was lost on the Court in *Zurcher v. Stanford Daily,* a 1978 case involving Stanford University's student newspaper.[172] Law enforcement officials wanted evidence against violent student protesters and thought they would find some in the files of the *Stanford Daily*. There was no claim that the *Daily* had been part of the protests, but the paper had covered the events and was believed to have photographs and other material in its files that might help to identify the culprits. Armed with an ex parte warrant, police officers searched the *Daily*'s offices. The *Daily* then brought a civil suit for declaratory and injunctive relief, and the Supreme Court sided with the government, thereby blessing the search and inviting others like it.[173]

The facts in *Zurcher* cried out for comparison with *Wilkes*—a civil suit brought to challenge a search carried out under an oppressive warrant for inflammatory newspaper articles—yet the greatest search and seizure case in Anglo-American history went unmentioned and unanalyzed. Warrants were good—required—said the Court, and this search had a warrant. Bowing to this Fourth Amendment worship of the warrant, Justice Stewart, joined by Justice Marshall, dissented solely on First Amendment grounds.[174]

What was missing was a way of integrating First Amendment concerns explicitly into the Fourth Amendment analysis. And the vehicle for this integration is of course not the warrant, not probable cause, but constitutional reasonableness. Indeed, the *Zurcher* majority mouthed the right words but then proceeded to ignore them: "Where the materials sought to be seized may be protected by the First Amendment, the requirements of the Fourth Amendment must be applied with 'scrupulous exactitude.' *Stanford* v. *Texas*, [379 U.S. 476, 485 (1965)]. 'A seizure reasonable as to one type of material in one setting may be unreasonable in a different setting or with respect to another kind of material.' *Roaden* v. *Kentucky*, 413 U.S. 496, 501 (1973)."[175] Under this approach, First Amendment concerns could well trigger special Fourth Amendment safeguards—heightened standards of justification prior to searching, immediate (presearch) appealability of any proposed search (with the premises sealed to prevent interim destruction of evidence), specially trained nonpartisan marshals or magistrates or masters to carry out the search, and so on.[176]

The First Amendment lesson can be generalized. For example, searches of attorneys' offices implicate special concerns of attorney-client privilege protected by the Sixth Amendment. Unless these searches are conducted with special precautions—say, an on-the-scene special master to screen out privileged material before any document is probed by police eyes—they, too, should be deemed constitutionally unreasonable.[177]

As we have already seen, the Fifth Amendment's incrimination clause arguably counsels special sensitivity when the government is trying to seize a personal diary to testify against its author in a criminal case.[178] Any search for such a diary will often be especially intrusive, involving governmental perusal of various personal papers in ways that also implicate the First Amendment and more general privacy principles.[179] Note that the reasonableness clause singles out "papers" for explicit protection above and beyond all other "effects"[180] and seems especially concerned with the private domain—"houses" as opposed to other "buildings," following the Third Amendment's explicit reference to "house[s]."

So, too, the Fifth Amendment's takings clause reminds us that governmental compensation can sometimes render an otherwise illegitimate seizure constitutionally acceptable. Although textually limited to property, perhaps the clause's underlying principle—that an innocent individual not be singled out to bear a special burden for the benefit of the entire community—radiates further. Imagine, for example, an apathetic grand jury under the thumb of a malicious prosecutor. The grand jury subpoenas a witness of modest means to appear before it, at her own expense, for weeks upon end. Surely, this is a Fourth Amendment seizure, and even if the takings clause does not strictly apply—the grand jury is seizing and using a person, not property[181]—could the clause not inform a ruling that, at some point, minimum compensation would be required to render the Fourth Amendment seizure reasonable?[182]

Consider next equal protection. Even if racially disparate impact alone does not violate the Constitution, surely equal protection principles call for concern when blacks bear the brunt of a government search or seizure policy. Thus, in a variety of search and seizure contexts, we must honestly address racially imbalanced effects and ask ourselves whether they are truly reasonable. As long as courts organize Fourth Amendment discourse around warrants, probable cause, and exclusion, rather than reasonableness, this open engagement of race will likely not occur in Fourth Amendment case law. Indeed, it is probably no coincidence that one of the most open Fourth Amendment discussions of race to date occurred in *Terry v. Ohio,* in which Chief Justice Warren carved out exceptions to both the probable cause and the warrant requirements, and self-consciously focused instead on the amendment's "general proscription against unreasonable searches and seizures."[183]

To justify a search or seizure that lands with disproportionate impact on poor persons or persons of color, the government may at times claim that the poor or the nonwhite are also disproportionate *beneficiaries* of the scheme, because the government search is designed to reduce the risk that they will be victimized by violent crime, or drugs, or what have you. The interests of victims are hard to squeeze into the language of probable cause and warrants but comfortably fit under the canopy of reasonableness. Make no mistake, the issues of race and class—of the police officer, the target of the search or seizure, and the victim of the crime—will not be easy to sort out, but once again we will be asking the right questions, honestly and openly.[184]

As with race and class, so too with sex. Searches and seizures that create opportunities for sexual oppression, harassment, or embarrassment are unreasonable both as a matter of common sense and constitutional morality, whether one uses the language of privacy or equality or both. Throughout my exposition, I have intentionally traded on these intuitions, purposely using gendered hypotheticals to illustrate quintessentially unreasonable searches.[185] These intuitions are neither merely personal nor of recent vintage. Recall, for example, the striking language used by a Pennsylvania Anti-Federalist to conjure up a nightmarish search: an obviously male federal constable might invade the bedroom and the bed of a "woman," "pull[] down the clothes of [her] bed" and "search[] under her shift."[186] These remarks appeared in 1787.

As the equal protection clause should remind us, constitutional reasonableness encompasses procedural regularity as well as substantive fairness, and the two are often tightly intertwined. Rule-of-law values affirmed in various constitutional ways—the due process, equal protection, and attainder clauses, and the more general separation of powers—teach us to be especially wary of searches and seizures that allow too much arbitrariness and ad hoc-ery, unbounded by public, visible rules promulgated in advance by legislatures and executive agencies. Recall here Justice Jackson's confession, in which he described searches of "every outgoing car," if "executed fairly and in good faith," as possibly "reasonable" even if "undiscriminating."[187] I would say that such a search might well be constitutionally reasonable *precisely because* it is undiscriminating. A broader search is sometimes better—fairer, more regular, more constitutionally reasonable—if it reduces the opportunities for official arbitrariness, discretion, and discrimination. If we focus only on probabilities and probable cause, we will get it backwards. The broader, more evenhanded search is sometimes more constitutionally reasonable even if the probabilities are lower for each citizen searched.[188]

Due process values may even call for judicial preclearance of certain types of government searches and seizures, if there are good reasons for suspecting strong and systematic overzealousness on the part of certain segments of executive officialdom. In some situations, a search or seizure could be deemed constitutionally unreasonable because no prior approval was sought from a more neutral and detached decision maker. Preclearance might also help firm up the record of what facts the government had before the intrusion, thereby preventing officials from dreaming up post hoc rationalizations.[189] But this selective judicial preclearance is a far cry from the warrant requirement I have been attacking so insistently. Judicial preclearance would not be a per se requirement of all searches and seizures, nor even a presumptive mandate, subject to well-defined categorical exceptions. Rather it would apply only when it was reasonable—and only *because* it was reasonable. This determination of reasonableness would be pragmatic, contingent, and subject to easy revision. It would not apply specially to criminal law enforcement under the unsupportable claim that the Fourth Amendment was somehow at its core about criminal rather than civil searches and seizures. (It could, however, apply specially to police departments on the pragmatic and empirical claim that these paramilitary organizations do pose a qualitatively different threat than do other government officials.)[190] Most importantly, judicial preclearance would be in addition to, rather than instead of, after-the-fact review in civil actions brought by the citizen target. Unlike a warrant, judicial preclearance would offer absolutely no immunity for a search later deemed unreasonable. (This immunity is, of course, precisely the point—the definition, really—of a judicial warrant.)[191] Judicial preclearance, even if sometimes necessary, would never be sufficient.[192] Of course, a later civil jury would remain free to take the fact of preclearance into account, and in an otherwise close case, preclearance could, in the jury's mind, tip the balance in favor of reasonableness.

The above examples show just how broad and powerful constitutional reasonableness could become as a way of talking and thinking about the Fourth Amendment. Indeed the potential breadth and power of this new tool will no doubt trouble some. But it should surprise no one. For the Fourth Amendment, literally and in every other way, belongs at the center of the Bill of Rights and discussion about the Bill—in civil cases as well as criminal, on matters of both constitutional procedure and constitutional substance. By focusing on constitutional reasonableness, we restore the Fourth to its rightful place. To be sure, the amendment is triggered only by a search or seizure, and to ignore these triggers is to rewrite the amendment into a global command of reasonableness. Yet a great many government actions can be properly understood as searches or seizures, especially when we remember that a person's "effects" may be intangible—as the landmark *Katz* case teaches us.[193] Unlike the due process clause, in whose name so much has been done, the Fourth Amendment clearly speaks to substantive as well as procedural unfairness and openly proclaims a need to distinguish between reasonable and unreasonable government policy. For those who believe in a "substantive due process" approach to the Constitution, the Fourth Amendment thus seems a far more plausible textual base than the due process clause itself.[194] For those who believe in general rationality review, the Fourth, here too, is more explicit than its current doctrinal alternative, the equal protection clause.[195]

Remedies

Fixated on the exclusionary rule, the twentieth-century Supreme Court has, through acts of omission and commission, betrayed the traditional civil-enforcement model. What follows are illustrative but not exhaustive suggestions for refurbishing the traditional civil-enforcement model.

Entity Liability and Abolition of Immunity. Eighteenth-century common law allowed suit against the officers personally, but everyone understood that the real party in interest was the government itself, which would typically be forced to indemnify officials who were merely carrying out government policy. (Without indemnification, who would agree to work for the government?) Thus, we have already seen the Maryland Farmer speaking of damage awards deriving from "the public purse"[196]—no doubt a reference to the notorious fact that the English government had indemnified all the government officials in the Wilkes affair, to the tune, it appears, of £100,000.[197] In modern parlance the Framers, well before Coase, understood the Coase Theorem.[198] Precisely because officials would be indemnified, it was not unfair to hold them strictly liable for constitutional torts, even if they acted in the good faith (but incorrect) belief that their behavior was fully constitutional.[199] Recall, for example, the Maryland Farmer's insistence on "ruinous damages whenever an officer had deviated from the rigid letter of the law"[200]—and recall further that heavy damages were assessed in the Wilkes affair, even though the officials there had followed an executive practice stretching back seventy years.[201]

In our century, however, judges for the first time have created wide zones of individual officer immunity for constitutional torts. Within these zones, the innocent citizen victim is in effect held liable and left to pay for the government's constitutional wrong. The Framers would have found the current remedial regime, in which a victim of constitutional tort can in many cases recover from neither the officer nor the government, a shocking violation of first principles, trumpeted in *Marbury v. Madison*, that for every right there must be a remedy.[202]

The best way to close this shocking remedial gap today would be to recognize direct liability of the government entity.[203] (Of course, in keeping with Coase, the government could seek indemnification from, dock the pay of, or otherwise discipline, any officers who triggered the government's liability; this would most likely occur if officials were violating the entity's own internal policies.)[204] If the search or seizure is ultimately deemed unreasonable, the government entity should pay. And the damages assessed will be a visible sign to legislators and the general public of the true costs of unreasonable government conduct.

Strict entity liability in the twentieth century makes perfect sense as the substitute for—indeed, the exact equivalent of—strict officer liability in the eighteenth century. The intervening years have brought us vastly increased bureaucratic density. The Framers' constables have become our police *departments;* their watchmen, our environmental protection *agencies;* and so on. The true locus of decision-making authority has shifted from the individual to the organization. The deterrence concept implicit in both the text and history of the amendment[205] calls for placing (initial) liability at the level best suited to restructure government conduct to avoid future violations. For the Framers, that level was the constable; for us, the police department.

This system of liability could be fashioned by legislatures, and in fact bears a striking resemblance to Congress's Privacy Protection Act of 1980,[206] passed to undo the damage done by *Zurcher*.[207] But courts need not await legislative action. They need only interpret section 1983 to mean what it says—strict government-entity liability[208]—and exercise their traditional remedial powers against federal officialdom in keeping with the promise of *Marbury* and its modern descendant, *Bivens*.[209] The deeply rooted power of judges to infer damage remedies for violations of constitutional norms was of course a strong theme of Justice Harlan's careful and traditional concurring opinion in *Bivens;*[210] and properly understood, sovereign immunity principles do not bar damage actions for constitutional violations. Such actions enforce, rather than offend, the sovereignty of the People over officialdom.[211]

Punitive Damages.   Because only a fraction of unconstitutional searches and seizures will ever come to light for judicial resolution, merely compensatory damages in the litigated cases would generate systematic underdeterrence. The problem is hardly unique to the Fourth Amendment, and a widespread technique today is to use multipliers and punitive damages. As we have seen, the Framers were well aware of these techniques of "heavy" and "ruinous" damages. By 1789, punitive damages in search and seizure cases were "an invariable maxim."[212] In fact, Lord Camden's explicit approval of punitive damages in *Wilkes v. Wood* and two companion search and seizure cases in the 1760s[213] appears to mark the first clear acknowledgment in English case law of the very concept of punitive damages.[214] *Wilkes*'s lesson for us here is that modest and thoughtful remedial creativity *within the civil model* is in the truest spirit of the cases that gave birth to our Fourth Amendment.[215] And in keeping with that spirit of modest remedial creativity, we should note an insight of modern tort theory: deterrence requires that the defendant must pay more than the plaintiff suffered, but not all this amount need go directly to the plaintiff. (This insight is actually implicit in Lord Camden's initial formulation, if read with care.) Perhaps some portion of punitive damages could flow to a "Fourth Amendment Fund" to educate Americans about the amendment and comfort victims of crime and police brutality, and thereby promote long term deterrence, compensation, and "security."

Class Actions, Presumed Damages, and Attorney's Fees. Large categories of unreasonable searches and seizures—street harassment, for example—will affect many persons, but each only a little. The offenses may be largely dignitary, and the citizen's out-of-pocket losses may be small or nonexistent. Here too, the problem is hardly unique to the Fourth Amendment, and modern law has developed general tools to address it. Class action aggregation techniques and minimum presumed damages are often the answer. Presumed damages are especially appropriate in Fourth Amendment cases, given Lord Camden's explicit embrace of an award of 300 pounds to a journeyman printer—a small fry of low "station and rank" caught up in the Wilkes affair—who had suffered in "mere personal injury only, perhaps 20 [pounds'] damages," but whose case raised a "great point of law touching the liberty" of "all the King's subjects."[216]

In an isolated Fourth Amendment wrong involving a small dollar amount but large dignitary concerns, any plaintiff who proves a violation should receive reasonable attorney's fees, even if the fees bulk larger than the plaintiff's out-of-pocket damages, unless the government was willing to concede that a Fourth Amendment violation had indeed occurred.[217]

Injunctive Relief. Early prevention is often better than after-the-fact remedy. The Fourth Amendment says its right "shall not be violated." When judges can prevent violations before they occur, they should do so—especially if after-the-fact damages could never truly make amends. Damages cannot bring back African-American males killed as a result of the unreasonable choke hold policy of the Los Angeles police department in the 1970s and 1980s.[218] And yet in 1983 the Supreme Court in *Los Angeles v. Lyons* prevented federal courts from enjoining various forms of racially discriminatory police brutality.[219] Like *Zurcher, Lyons* was a sad entry in the annals of the Fourth Amendment. One can only wonder how much of the racial tragedy visited upon Los Angeles in recent years might have been avoided had the Supreme Court done the right thing in *Lyons* and sent a different signal to the LAPD.[220]

Administrative Relief. The traditional judicial system is slow and cumbersome. Executive departments are typically the source of unconstitutional searches and seizures; is it too much to expect them to establish internal mechanisms to process citizen complaints quickly? Citizen review panels could serve a function akin to a traditional jury, and in many cases, victims of government unreasonableness might willingly forgo a judicial lawsuit in favor of a cheaper, less adversarial, quicker administrative solution that would vindicate their dignitary claims.[221]

Regimes

At least four overlapping, reinforcing, and non–mutually exclusive enforcement regimes should exist to enforce the reasonableness norm.

Consider first a regime of *legislative* reasonableness. Legislatures are, and should be, obliged to fashion rules delineating the search and seizure authority of government officials. General rule of law, structural due process, and separation of powers principles frown on broad legislative abdications. In cases of borderline reasonableness, the less specifically the legislature has considered and authorized the practice in question, the less willing judges and juries should be to uphold the practice.

Now consider *executive/administrative* reasonableness. Professors John Kaplan, Anthony Amsterdam, and Kenneth Culp Davis and Judge Carl McGowan have generated thoughtful blueprints for this regime, and they deserve our most serious attention.[222] Even if a search or seizure is broadly authorized by statute, administrators and agencies—including police departments—should promulgate implementing guidelines that publicly spell out more concrete search and seizure policies for recurring fact patterns. Advisory input from citizen panels may be particularly helpful here,[223] but even if citizens do not participate in initial policy formation, public promulgation of agency guidelines will enable the citizenry to better assess things done in their name. Agencies should not only lay down substantive rules and standards but also implement these policies through good faith training programs and disciplinary mechanisms. Once again, judges and juries should be less willing to defer to official intrusions in borderline cases in which the agency fails to live up to this regime of reasonableness.

Next consider a regime of *judicial* reasonableness. Judges should continue to build up doctrine specifying certain actions that, as a matter of law, violate the Fourth Amendment.[224] But unlike the current doctrinal mess, this new edifice would be built on the foundation of reason, not probability or warrant. Although no clear line divides common-sense reasonableness from constitutional reasonableness, judges should concentrate their doctrinal energies on the latter, especially in cases in which searches or seizures implicate constitutional principles beyond the Fourth Amendment, or in which judges have strong reasons to suspect unjustified jury insensitivity to certain claims or claimants. Although judicial preclearance may at times be appropriate, courts must strictly limit warrants. Civil litigation after the fact, with both citizen and government represented in the courtroom, would be far more deliberative and reviewable than the current system of practically unreviewable rubber-stamp magistrates acting ex parte.

Last, but not least, imagine a regime of *jury* reasonableness. Even when legislature, administrator, and judge have all accepted a search or seizure as reasonable, the government often should also be obliged to convince a civil jury of this. In the criminal context, the government may not prevail if the citizen can win over a jury under the Sixth Amendment. In the civil context, the parties' positions are reversed—the citizen is plaintiff, the government, the defendant[225]—but a basic principle that governs the Sixth should inform the Seventh: the government should generally not prevail—at least on the issue of reasonableness—if the citizen can persuade a jury of her peers.[226] Reasonableness is largely a matter of common sense, and the jury represents the common sense of common people.[227] Threats to the "security" of Americans come from both government and thugs; the jury is perfectly placed to decide, in any given situation, whom it fears more, the cops or the robbers. This judgment, of course, will vary from place to place and over time. "Reasonableness" is not some set of specific rules, frozen in 1791 or 1868 amber, but an honest and sensible textual formula to organize candid jury deliberations and fair jury decisions.[228] And in the course of deliberating and deciding, citizen jurors will become educated—will educate each other—about the meaning of the Constitution, about government policy, about competing conceptions of reasonableness, and about citizenship in a self-governing republic.[229] The jurors will become participants in the ongoing enterprise of constitutionalism and will come over time to better appreciate how the Fourth Amendment, rightly understood, protects *them*. To discharge this weighty representative, educative, and policy-making function, the civil jury must be made truly inclusive along race, gender, and class lines. Recent developments in the Supreme Court give ground for hope here.[230]

And this seems a good note on which to end. For I hope it is not too late to remember that the Fourth Amendment boldly proclaims a right of "the people." What better body than a jury of "the people"—a jury that truly looks like America—to cherish and protect this precious right?[231]

2 Fifth Amendment First Principles: The Self-Incrimination Clause

No person . . . shall be compelled in any criminal case to be a witness against himself . . .

The self-incrimination clause of the Fifth Amendment is an unsolved riddle of vast proportions, a Gordian knot in the middle of our Bill of Rights. From the beginning it lacked an easily identifiable rationale; in 1789, the words of the clause were more a slogan than a clearly defined legal rule, and in the preceding four centuries the slogan had stood for at least four different ideas.[1] Today, things are no better: the clause continues to confound and confuse. Because courts and commentators have been unable to deduce what the privilege is for, they have failed to define its scope in the most logical and sensible way. This chapter tries to solve the riddle and untie the Gordian knot. It proposes both a rationale for, and a definition of the proper scope of, the self-incrimination clause.

The Supreme Court's interpretation of the Fifth Amendment is currently in a jumbled transitional phase. The key question, though rarely recognized as such, is what sort of immunity the clause requires before a person may be made to tell all outside his own "criminal case," beyond the earshot of the petit jury. Over the years the answers have varied considerably. In its 1892 chestnut *Counselman v. Hitchcock*, the Supreme Court required total ("transactional") immunity from prosecution whenever a person is compelled to testify against himself outside the courtroom.[2] But in 1972, *Kastigar v. United States* in effect overruled *Counselman* and established a new, narrower rule of "use plus use-fruits immunity": a person forced to speak pretrial may be prosecuted, but neither the compelled statement nor any evidence it led to ("fruits") can be introduced in the criminal trial.[3] *Kastigar* provided no persuasive basis for stopping where it did in fashioning its new rule, and the Court is slowly—if not always consciously—chipping away at the foundations of the new rule, emphasizing the difference between testimony and physical evidence. The time is ripe to take a decisive step in the direction the Court has been leaning: the Court should move beyond the way station of *Kastigar* and declare that a person's (perhaps unreliable) compelled pretrial statements can never be introduced against him in a criminal case but that reliable fruits of such statements virtually always can be. Thus the government should be allowed to require a suspect to answer relevant questions in a civilized pretrial hearing presided over by a judge or magistrate. Under penalty of contempt, a suspect must answer truthfully, but he will be entitled to "testimonial immunity": that is, the compelled words will never be introduced over the defendant's objection in a criminal trial—the defendant will never be an involuntary *witness* against himself *in* a criminal *case*—but the fruits of these compelled pretrial words will generally be admissible.

This clean rule of testimonial immunity would openly vindicate the Court's recent emphasis on reliability as a preeminent criminal procedure value, but it has many other virtues as well. For starters, it has some important history on its side. Testimonial immunity, supported by English precedent, was the majority rule in America before *Counselman* and was explicitly endorsed by Congress at the time it adopted the Fourteenth Amendment, which reglossed the Bill of Rights and made its privileges and immunities applicable against the states. More importantly—as the long history of compelled self-incrimination is admittedly tangled—testimonial immunity makes the best sense of the words of the Fifth Amendment and kindred constitutional provisions, like those of the Sixth Amendment. Read my way, the words of the clause fit neatly together and tightly cohere with the rest of the Constitution. In short, this reading works, textually and functionally—no small thing in so muddy a field. Indeed, the proposal creates a rare win-win solution in criminal procedure: more guilty persons will be brought to book, while the plight of the truly innocent defendant will be improved.

Once we see the clear meaning of the rule against compelled self-incrimination—that self-incriminating *words* compelled from a defendant must be excluded from his criminal case—and the best reason underlying that rule—reliability—we can also see the independent roles that other rules must play, radiating from other clauses of the Constitution and motivated by other rationales. As we shall see, in both civil and criminal contexts, needlessly intrusive questioning, fishing expeditions, and offensive impositions upon a person's body raise obvious Fourth Amendment concerns; attempts to probe a citizen's mind for heresy or political incorrect-ness or a map of his inner life or conscience implicate the First Amendment; unregulated and lawless police behavior must be stamped out in the name of due process and the rule of law; and so on. By misreading—and often overreading—the scope and rationale of the self-incrimination clause, courts and commentators have often obscured the proper role of other clauses, and so another happy side effect of my reading is that it yields a sensible division of labor among constitutional provisions.

The very breadth of the self-incrimination clause, as currently construed, creates huge challenges, substantively and doctrinally. Substantively, we must note that an enormous amount of modern criminal law enforcement has been shaped by the self-incrimination clause, as (mis)construed over the years. By narrowing government's ability to tap suspects as testimonial resources in civilized pretrial proceedings, the clause has driven some interrogation underground into less-than-civilized police station rooms and squad cars; has spurred on surprise searches, wiretaps, and other intrusions that fall outside the Fifth Amendment; has increased pressure to use sting operations and government informants, who often must be bribed in unappealing ways; and has ramified in countless other directions. A different reading of the self-incrimination clause would likewise ripple out far and wide, and a single chapter cannot trace all these likely ripples with precision. On the other hand, the vast substantive significance of the self-incrimination clause only deepens the puzzle of current doctrine and scholarship, which cannot persuasively explain what the clause means and why.

Doctrinally, the vastness of the self-incrimination clause, sprawling across the *U.S. Reports* into a great many doctrinal corners and crevices, makes exposition difficult. It is hard to get one's hands on the beast, and there is no self-evidently superior way of taming the multiheaded case law for exposition and analysis. In what follows I use the technique—call it a gimmick, if you like—of organizing the argument around key words of the clause itself.[4] Each word offers a window onto a different cluster of doctrinal difficulties. Although these clusters might at first seem unconnected, by the end of our journey we shall see how each cluster of current problems can be solved by the same elegant rereading of the self-incrimination clause.

The Puzzle

Under current interpretations, courts cripple innocent defendants while the guilty wrap themselves in the self-incrimination clause and walk free. Modern understandings of the clause deviate far from its early American implementation, from plain meaning, and from common sense. The catalogue of interpretive difficulties is long: the privilege protects the wrong "person"—the guilty witness rather than the innocent defendant; courts struggle with impractical definitions of "compulsion"; what is excluded from "any criminal case" by grants of immunity has fluctuated widely over the years; and reliable physical fruit, such as a bloody knife or a dead body, is now excluded because it is "witnessing" against oneself, while other reliable physical evidence (the defendant's own blood, for example) is allowed because it is not testimonial. In short, virtually every word and phrase—*person, compelled, in any criminal case,* and *witness*—sits atop considerable confusion or perversion because courts do not yet understand how the words fit together, or what big idea(s) might underlie the clause.

"Person"?

Perhaps the most striking flaw in current application of the privilege is that in some important cases defendants are not helped but harmed. And worse: the privilege seems perversely designed to aid the guilty defendant while punishing the innocent one. Indeed, an overbroad reading of the privilege ends up undercutting the most basic of all criminal procedure rights—the right of an innocent defendant to mount a truthful defense.

Begin with the following question: Does the self-incrimination clause prevent a *person* in a criminal case from being compelled to testify against himself even when that person is not on trial but only a witness? Today the answer is yes. As a result, the Fifth Amendment prevents an innocent defendant from compelling self-incriminating testimony from a guilty witness. But this invocation of the Fifth Amendment by the witness denies the accused her explicit Sixth Amendment right "to have *compulsory* process for obtaining *witnesses* in [her] favor." The Fifth and Sixth Amendments seem to be at war with one another, and the Fifth Amendment rights of a witness apparently trump the Sixth Amendment rights of the defendant, even though the defendant is, of course, the *person* whose criminal case it is.[5]

Let's consider a simple situation—a single defendant truthfully claiming that she is innocent and that another specific person committed the crime—and trace the sequence of events that would most likely follow in a criminal trial.[6] Defendant subpoenas the guilty party to testify at her trial, in accordance with her explicit Sixth Amendment right to "comp[el]" the production of "witnesses in [her] favor." The guilty witness notifies defense counsel before trial that he will refuse to testify, invoking his Fifth Amendment privilege not to be "compelled" to be a "witness" against himself. After defense counsel informs the judge of the witness's intent, the judge conducts a hearing to determine whether the witness may assert the privilege. At the hearing, the witness refuses to answer questions. This refusal, combined with other evidence the defense has discovered suggesting the witness's guilt, convinces the judge that the witness might incriminate himself were he to testify truthfully. The court therefore holds that the witness may assert the privilege.

Faced with the witness's silence, the defendant begs the prosecution to grant the witness immunity to compel him to testify.[7] Note the imbalance of power here. While the prosecution can freely grant immunity and compel witnesses to testify, the defense has no such power. At a minimum, one might have thought the defendant's explicit Sixth Amendment right of compulsory process should put her on a level playing field with the prosecution; if the prosecutor is empowered to subpoena a reliable witness, the defendant should be so empowered.[8] Prima facie, it might seem that the same should hold true for the immunity-granting power. But instead, the defendant is forced to rely on the good graces of the prosecutor.[9] The prosecution, however, has little incentive to grant immunity in this situation. Although our defendant is (by hypothesis) innocent, the prosecutor may not know or believe this. And so the prosecutor reasons as follows: If the witness confesses falsely and the defendant is acquitted, a guilty party gets off;[10] and if the witness confesses truthfully, the immunity itself will make it hard to ever prosecute and convict him—and so, here too, a guilty party gets off.[11] The prosecutor therefore refuses the defendant's request that the government grant the witness immunity. Frustrated, the defendant asks that the court require the prosecution to grant immunity. The vast majority of courts would reject such a request,[12] and the reasons here are obvious. Immunity can create a major stumbling block to prosecuting the witness on anything related to his testimony. (The government will have to prove that nothing in its case is in any way derived from the testimony, and as we shall see in more detail, this can be a very hard thing to prove.) Indeed, in organized crime settings the first defendant will be tempted to give all his partners an immunity bath.

To add insult to injury, the jury would not even hear, from the witness or anyone else, that the witness claimed the privilege. At trial, the defendant could introduce evidence against the witness but could not force him to invoke the privilege in front of the jury.[13] At most the defendant could request an instruction that the jury must not draw any inference against either side from the witness's failure to appear.[14] On the other hand, merely forcing the witness to assert the privilege before the jury might make collusion between defendant and witness easier.[15] In general, the jury would be left with considerable uncertainty about why the witness is asserting the privilege; jurors could learn far more from actual testimony than from a mere assertion of the privilege.

Of course, even if immunity were conferred, the guilty witness might take the stand and lie, denying all involvement. But the witness need not break down and deliver a full-blown Perry Mason–style confession to make all the difference for an innocent defendant. A lying witness may well sound unconvincing or trip himself up with inconsistent testimony; he will also be subject to impeachment via cross-examination and defense introduction of other evidence and witnesses. The jury would then be perfectly poised to assess witness credibility and to resolve factual disputes. This, of course, is what we pay jurors to do.[16]

So in the end we are left with the following puzzle. Precisely because Fifth Amendment immunity is so strong, innocent defendants are crippled in their effort to mount a Sixth Amendment defense. Might the solution be to rethink Fifth Amendment immunity?[17]

"Compelled"?

The Fifth Amendment does not prohibit all self-incrimination but only *compelled* self-incrimination. How should we go about construing the word *compelled?* Some leading Framers thought of the self-incrimination clause as a protection against torture, which might often lead to unreliable confessions.[18] Our main concerns today should still be protecting against third-degree tactics and assuring reliability in evidence. Instead, at times the Justices of the Supreme Court have become engrossed by relatively trivial forms of compulsion; at other times they have zigged and zagged erratically; and at still other times they have turned a blind eye to dangerous compulsion threatening our core concerns.

In-Court Compulsion. At times, *compulsion* seems to be defined as making someone who "takes the Fifth" worse off in any way than one who sings without reservation. Under this definition, the government may not draw any adverse inference if a person insists on standing mute in the face of an accusation of criminal wrongdoing. In its controversial 1965 opinion in *Griffin v. California,* the Supreme Court established this as the test of in-court compulsion.[19] A defendant had an absolute right not to take the stand, and no adverse inference of guilt could be drawn from the exercise of this trial right. Any inference, said the Court, was tantamount to criminal punishment of trial silence itself, a core violation of the clause's command.[20]

But this begs the question: if the adverse inference was indeed probabilistically sound, was it truly punishing *silence,* or the (more probable) guilt signaled by the silence? On its facts, however, the in-court rule may well make sense. As we shall see in more detail later, many innocent defendants may decline to take the stand for reasons that have little to do with their guilt in the case at hand, and so an adverse inference might be statistically *un*sound and *un*reliable and therefore may punish silence itself, rather than underlying guilt on the predicate offense.[21] Under the reliability theory we shall explore below, *Griffin* can stand.

The Supreme Court, however, has failed to make clear how *Griffin* should apply when a criminal court acts in the sentencing phase rather than the guilt-determination stage of a criminal case and seeks to draw inferences from a defendant's earlier (preverdict) silence. Even if adverse inferences are unreliable to *prove* guilt, perhaps they may be reliably used in the sentencing process, *after* guilt has already been reliably established. The Federal Sentencing Guidelines, for example, authorize a lower sentence for a defendant who "accept[s] . . . responsibility for his offense" as evidenced by, among other things, "truthfully admitting the conduct comprising the offense(s) of conviction" or "assist[ing] authorities in the investigation or prosecution of his own misconduct by taking one or both of the steps set forth in subsection (b)."[22] One of the steps in subsection (b) involves the "timely provision of complete information to the government concerning his own involvement in the offense."[23] The common-sense logic and morality of these guidelines are easy to see: those who repent and admit their misdeeds in open court before conviction may need less rehabilitation and deserve less punishment in the sentencing process.

But can this everyday morality be squared with the logic of the self-incrimination clause and *Griffin?* Are courts in effect punishing silence—and in a criminal case, no less? On the other hand, if the Sentencing Guidelines can be upheld, and *Griffin* limited, on the basis of a distinction between guilt determination and sentencing, what would such a distinction imply about the meaning and purpose of the self-incrimination clause? (Wouldn't it, for example, suggest that the key to the clause is reliability?) Finally, if a defendant appeals, wins, and is retried, can he exclude, in the guilt-determination stage of his second trial, any earlier statements on the grounds that they were compelled by the "silence penalty" imposed by the Sentencing Guidelines? Lower courts need to know which silence penalties are valid under the self-incrimination clause, and the Supreme Court has not yet announced a theory of the clause that can inform them.[24]

Out-of-Court Compulsion: Government Employment. In a series of cases involving public employees, the Supreme Court tried to stretch the in-court *Griffin* rule to govern conduct well outside the courtroom—indeed, outside the criminal justice system.[25] The cases held that the threat of removal from government employment was compulsion for the purposes of the Fifth Amendment, incorporated through the Fourteenth; they concerned such individuals as allegedly corrupt police officers and dishonest state contractors who successfully claimed a right to keep their government jobs while refusing to respond to allegations of wrongdoing.[26]

But outside the courtroom, the "no worse off" test seems extravagant and unworkable: the logical consequences are absurd. Couldn't President Reagan have refused to appoint Oliver North to be Secretary of State—or fired him from his subcabinet White House office, for that matter—on the simple ground that North's invocation of the Fifth Amendment raised sufficient doubt about his worthiness to serve in a position of high honor and power? Merely focusing preliminary investigation on someone who takes the Fifth also makes that person worse off, and yet—so far—the courts have allowed the government to do just that.[27] Even if *within* a courtroom a jury should be barred from drawing adverse inferences from trial silence, the real world outside the courtroom cannot be regulated by so nice a test of compulsion; people in everyday life must draw reasonable inferences.[28] A responsible private employer may draw sensible inferences from silence and fire the bank clerk who refuses to respond to accusations of pilfering.[29] Yet the "no worse off" test forces the government to act as an irresponsible employer—ignoring common sense—or else confer immunity and possibly lose valuable evidence in its capacity as sovereign enforcer of criminal law. (Once again, it loses this evidence unless it can conclusively prove at trial that the evidence was in no way connected to the earlier "compelled" words.)[30] Is it possible that, here too, this immunity rule is too broad?

So it seems that the "no worse off/no adverse inference" test simply will not work as a global rule of impermissible compulsion outside the courtroom. Indeed, in the 1976 case of *Baxter v. Palmigiano*, the Court seemed to reject the "no worse off" test even for prison disciplinary hearings.[31] The Court allowed adverse inferences to be drawn in a *disciplinary* hearing against a prisoner who refused to respond to questions unless he was immunized.[32] Once we reject the "no worse off" test, however, we flounder in a sea of murky rules. How much pressure to talk is *too* much? And how can we even begin to answer this question without a theory of why pressure is bad?

Out-of-Court Compulsion: Required Records.   A prime example of the confusion that results when the Court strays from the "no worse off" test is the required records doctrine. The Court has been unable to develop a consistent rule for the use in criminal proceedings of records that the government requires citizens to keep for administrative purposes.[33] The cases essentially set up an open-ended test that allows the Court to swing from admitting the records to excluding both the records and their fruits without any principled basis.

The 1948 case that spawned the doctrine, *Shapiro v. United States,* arose out of emergency wartime regulations and seemed to place few limits on the required records exception to the Fifth Amendment.[34] Shapiro, a produce wholesaler during World War II, was required to keep price, sale, and delivery records and to make them available for inspection under the Emergency Price Control Act.[35] Shapiro complied with a subpoena to produce his records but claimed his constitutional privilege. The government, however, proceeded to prosecute him for illegal tie-in sales, using the records and their fruits. A closely divided Supreme Court held that the self-incrimination clause did not apply to the subpoenaed documents; because Shapiro was required by law to keep the records, they were unprotected public documents rather than protected private papers.[36] In his dissent, Justice Frankfurter pointed out some of the deep flaws in the Court's reasoning: "Subtle question-begging is nevertheless question-begging. Thus: records required to be kept by law are public records; public records are non-privileged; required records are non-privileged. If records merely because required to be kept by law *ipso facto* become public records [and therefore fall outside the scope of the privilege], we are indeed living in glass houses."[37]

We must keep in mind that the rule of immunity at that time was laid down by *Counselman*—complete immunity from prosecution for the crime.[38] This no doubt encouraged the *Shapiro* Court's failure to define any limits to the "public" records Congress might require, except those limits imposed by its enumerated powers. Government had legitimate regulatory need of the information, and the Court was unwilling to force the government to vindicate its legitimate regulatory needs only by abdicating—via sweeping immunity—its role as criminal law enforcer. As in the employment context, is it possible that the real problem here is that immunity has been defined too broadly?

In later cases, the Court has struggled to establish limits to the required records exception, but the limits have remained fuzzy. In 1968, the Court decided three required documents cases on the same day, all authored by Justice Harlan and all reversing convictions because of violations of the Fifth Amendment. The first, *Marchetti v. United States,* controlled the rest.[39] Marchetti had been convicted of willful failure to pay the occupational tax associated with gambling and of willful failure to register as a wagerer. Justice Harlan cobbled together bits from earlier cases into a three-pronged pseudo-test to distinguish *Shapiro,* but the test failed to undo the confusion produced by earlier cases. Under the test, courts were to inquire, first, whether the defendant was obliged to keep records "of the same kind as he has customarily kept;" second, whether there were "public aspects" involved in the records required; and third, whether a records requirement was "imposed in 'an essentially non-criminal and regulatory area of inquiry'" or was instead "directed to a 'selective group inherently suspect of criminal activities.'"[40] The prongs were intriguing but not well defined or well justified.

Although the Court found Fifth Amendment violations in the 1968 *Marchetti* trilogy, in 1971 the Court lurched the other way and upheld the constitutionality of California's hit-and-run statute in *California v. Byers.*[41] Byers had been convicted of failing to stop at the scene of an accident and failing to leave his name and address. The California Supreme Court required a use restriction on the information,[42] but the U.S. Supreme Court held that because the statute did not violate the Fifth Amendment, no use restriction was required.[43] Chief Justice Burger, writing for a plurality, struggled to find a rationale for holding that the privilege did not apply. He invoked some elements of the *Marchetti* test, but the opinion elsewhere veered away from the test. At one point, the Chief Justice seemed to announce a new principle in self-incrimination cases, and one completely lacking in textual support: questions about whether the privilege should apply "must be resolved in terms of *balancing* the public need on the one hand, and the individual claim to constitutional protections on the other."[44]

The Court further stretched the required records doctrine in the 1990 *Bouknight* case, in which Justice O'Connor relied heavily on the exception to prevent the privilege from applying in a disturbing case of child abuse.[45] In *Bouknight,* a mother suspected of child abuse was given custody of her injured child with extensive conditions imposed by a protective order. The mother violated those conditions, and a court ordered her to produce the child in order to verify that the child was alive and well. When she refused, the court held her in contempt and rejected her contention that the Fifth Amendment protected her from having to produce him. The Supreme Court invoked *Shapiro, Marchetti,* and *Byers,* explaining that the requirement to produce the child involved a "broadly directed, noncriminal regulatory regime"—that the state was attempting to help "a child in need of assistance" and was not solely concerned with criminal law enforcement.[46]

The inconsistency of these cases is striking and revealing. The Court hems and haws and then often holds that the privilege does not apply at all: the government often needs information for nonpenal purposes and should not be forced to let criminals go free to get it, the Court intuits. The Court is understandably reluctant to apply the privilege in a heinous crime such as child abuse; granting use plus use-fruits immunity would make it difficult, and in some cases (including the hit-and-run) almost impossible, to prosecute. But that is what *Kastigar* currently demands.[47] Unable to live with that result, the Court zigs, zags, and balances, ad hoc. But the language of the self-incrimination clause does not balance: it states a bright-line rule. Is it possible that if immunity were narrower than *Kastigar* indicates, judges could indeed live with the logic of the bright-line rule?

Out-of-Court Compulsion: Police Interrogation. When it comes to genuine out-of-court coercion, courts at times turn a blind eye. While *Miranda* purported to establish propriety in police-station interrogation, our system in fact can still be quite ugly.[48] Despite *Miranda*'s promise to open up the black box of the police station, it did not require that lawyers, magistrates, or even tape or video recorders be present in interrogation rooms. In the absence of these monitors, detectives and police have often engaged in ingenious, but troubling, forms of interrogation.

In some instances, courts actually succeed in chilling clever tactics, with a resulting loss of information for the prosecution, but in other cases the judicial decisions have created a divergence between theory and practice. A good recent description of this divergence—and of suspect interrogation in general—is found in David Simon's 1991 book based on unlimited access to the Baltimore homicide detective unit over the course of a year.[49] Some of the techniques used by detectives could aptly be described as physically intimidating, teetering on the brink of violence. Simon describes detectives doing everything from slamming doors and kicking chairs, swearing, and interrogating late at night to lying about the evidence against the suspect and about the detective's ability and willingness to get the suspect a lower sentence.[50] Several of the techniques are ingenious, most notably "polygraph by photocopier."[51] But most people would find them uncivilized, at best. We do not tolerate such behavior in civil litigation.[52] Rather, we use depositions—with court reporters, lawyers, and judicial oversight.

Here, too, we are left with a puzzle. Perhaps the police are tempted to subvert formal rules because the rules make no sense. A suspect, even if ultimately innocent, is often someone close to the action, someone who can tell the government what really happened so that the case can be solved.[53] But formal doctrine prevents the government from using the suspect as an involuntary testimonial resource unless the government confers a sweeping immunity that will often preclude prosecution. By effectively preventing formal, civilized depositions—by creating an overly strong Fifth Amendment immunity—perhaps we are driving interrogation underground, in ways that make some citizens more vulnerable and the weakest most vulnerable of all.[54] So could it be that here, again, the most sensible solution would be to rethink immunity?

"In Any Criminal Case"?

The government compels persons to be witnesses to their own criminal conduct all the time—in strict conformity with the Constitution, we are told. All that is required is immunity of a certain sort, enforced by rules of exclusion "in any criminal case" against the witness.[55] But immunity of what sort? This is the hidden key to the Fifth Amendment.[56] Exactly what must be excluded from "a criminal case"? Over the years, courts have been all over the map.

As we shall see in more detail later, the earliest American courts addressing the immunity issue required only a narrow form of immunity.[57] But the U.S. Supreme Court brushed these cases off in its 1892 decision in *Counselman v. Hitchcock*.[58] *Counselman* established an extraordinarily sweeping form of immunity that came to be known as "transactional" because it absolutely prohibited prosecution for any criminal transaction to which a question might relate.[59] In effect, *Counselman* prevented a suspect who had been made to sing pretrial from being a witness against himself "in any criminal case" by preventing him from being a defendant—by preventing the case against him from ever going forward. Put another way, *Counselman* excluded the prosecution itself "in" a "criminal case." But where, textually, does *that* rule come from? And would its logic require that if a person is made to sing *after* he has been convicted of a crime, the conviction must be vacated? Does that make sense?[60]

Formally, *Counselman* reigned until 1972, but for much of its rule, the so-called dual sovereignty doctrine created an important chink in its armor: before 1964, testimony compelled from a person by federal officials could be used against him in a state prosecution and vice versa.[61] The Court so held because the self-incrimination clause, and therefore exclusion, applied not to the states but only to the federal government.[62] With its 1964 decision in *Malloy v. Hogan*, however, the Court incorporated the clause against the states, rejecting the notion that the Fourteenth Amendment contained "only a 'watered-down, subjective version of the individual guarantees of the Bill of Rights.'"[63] The same day it decided *Malloy*, the Court reconsidered its rule of self-incrimination dual sovereignty. In light of *Malloy*, it made little sense that two governments acting in tandem could do what neither could do alone: extort testimony out of court and then introduce it in a criminal case against the testifier. Thus, in *Malloy*'s companion case, *Murphy v. Waterfront Commission*, the Court declared that "there is no continuing legal vitality to, or historical justification for, the rule that one jurisdiction . . . may compel a witness to give testimony which could be used to convict him of a crime in another jurisdiction."[64] According to *Murphy*, a state witness could not be compelled to give testimony that might be incriminating under federal law unless the *compelled testimony and its fruits* could not be used in any way by federal officials in a criminal prosecution against him.[65]

Although the *Murphy* Court cited *Counselman*, it actually introduced a narrower standard of immunity that was elaborated in a separate opinion by Justices White and Stewart.[66] *Counselman* transactional immunity would create huge intersovereign friction: government *A* could confer immunity and thereby in effect veto government *B*'s law enforcement efforts. To reduce this friction, immunity must be rethought, argued White and Stewart. If only a narrower immunity were required, government *B* could prosecute even after *A*'s grant of immunity so long as *B* could prove that all its evidence came from truly independent sources.[67] (Note, of course, that the difficulty of proving this meant that intersovereign friction would be reduced but not eliminated.)[68]

Eight years after *Murphy*, its newfangled immunity rule was formally approved outside the dual sovereignty context in *Kastigar v. United States*.[69] Unlike *Counselman*, *Kastigar* held that the government at times could indeed prosecute a person who had earlier been obliged to testify against himself under a grant of immunity.[70] *Kastigar* held that in order to compel incriminating testimony from a witness, the government merely had to grant the witness immunity from the use of his testimony and of its fruits in a criminal trial against him.[71] This became known as "use plus use-fruits immunity" and is, theoretically, the standard still in operation today.[72] The Court aimed to find "a rational accommodation between the imperatives of the privilege and the legitimate demands of government to compel citizens to testify" and stated that the new standard "leaves the witness and the prosecutorial authorities in substantially the same position as if the witness had claimed the Fifth Amendment privilege. The immunity is therefore co-extensive with the privilege and suffices to supplant it."[73]

In effect, this new rule prevents a suspect from being a witness against himself "in any criminal case" by excluding his words and all things they lead to from the "criminal case." But the *Kastigar* Court failed to explain persuasively where its new rule came from. *Counselman* was out, but what, precisely, was the source of *Kastigar's* "rational accommodation"? How would introducing a physical fact (fruit), but not anything a defendant ever said, make a defendant a *witness* against himself *in* a criminal trial? *Kastigar* provided few satisfying answers— perhaps because the Court failed to see the huge stakes involved: the entire Fifth Amendment pivots on the precise rule of immunity required.[74] Beyond its mushy rational accommodation balancing, *Kastigar's* main argument seems to be that a suspect must be placed in "substantially the same position" whether or not he sings out of court. But this is precisely the "no worse off" test that, as we have seen, is wholly unworkable as a global principle.

Recently, however, even *Kastigar* has come under attack. Pressure is growing for efficient law enforcement. When an immunized witness is later prosecuted, *Kastigar* places the burden on the government "to prove that the evidence it proposes to use is derived from a legitimate source wholly independent of the compelled testimony."[75] At times, this burden can be staggering.[76] The government may try to build a Chinese wall between prosecutors exposed to the testimony and prosecutors working on the case against the witness.[77] But sometimes a Chinese wall cannot be built, and sometimes the wall leaks. Another common technique is "canning" the results of an investigation before a potential defendant testifies,[78] but this involves even greater administrative burdens. To make matters worse, courts have adopted varying interpretations of the independent source standard.

At one extreme is the D.C. Circuit's holding in *United States v. North*.[79] Oliver North, as many will recall, received a grant of immunity to testify in a congressional hearing involving the Iran-Contra affair. The prosecutor had not seen the testimony, nor did he seek to use it in the prosecution. Several prosecution witnesses, however, had seen the testimony on their own. The court announced that the Fifth Amendment is violated "whenever the prosecution puts on a witness whose testimony is shaped, directly or indirectly, by compelled testimony, regardless of *how or by whom* he was exposed to that compelled testimony."[80] The court imposed additional administrative burdens on prosecutors in its suggestion that the government's burden could be met by "canning the testimony beforehand, just as wise prosecutors meet their burden of showing independent investigation by canning the results of the investigation before the defendant gives immunized testimony."[81] The D.C. Circuit's superstrict approach leaves little difference between use plus use-fruits and transactional immunity.

On the other hand, several circuits have diverged from a superstrict approach, and with good reason.[82] Besides its sometimes-crushing burdens on prosecutors, the D.C. Circuit approach at times can embroil courts in a futile attempt to resolve never-neverland counterfactuals: What would the world look like if Oliver North had never testified? God knows![83] In light of these metaphysical imponderables, why should the law not simply *presume*—irrebuttably—that somehow, some way, the truth and the fruit might have come to light anyway? (This presumption would in effect simply expand the scope of current inevitable discovery doctrine and would track the approaches followed in England and Canada.)[84] But under this theory, what would be left of use-fruits immunity? Only the testimony itself would be excluded.

In the same way that the Supreme Court in *Murphy* chipped away at *Counselman*'s transactional immunity before overruling it in *Kastigar,* the Court is now chipping away at use plus use-fruits immunity in the context of *Miranda* warnings. When the police interrogate a suspect without giving complete warnings, *Miranda* bars the prosecution from using any resulting confession in its case in chief. However, the Supreme Court has repeatedly chosen to admit the fruits of such confessions. In *Michigan v. Tucker,* the defendant, arrested for rape, was informed of his right to remain silent and right to counsel, but not of the fact that he would be given counsel if he were indigent.[85] The defendant told the police he was with his friend Henderson at the time of the crime, and the police then questioned Henderson. Henderson's information suggested that Tucker was guilty. His testimony was admitted at trial, over the defendant's objection, and the defendant was convicted. Emphasizing reliability, the Court held that while the failure to give the full *Miranda* warning required the exclusion of defendant Tucker's statement, it did not require exclusion of his friend Henderson's testimony: "There is plainly no reason to believe that Henderson's testimony is untrustworthy simply because *respondent* was not advised of *his* right to appointed counsel. Henderson was both available at trial and subject to cross-examination by respondent's counsel, and counsel fully used this opportunity, suggesting in the course of his cross-examination that Henderson's character was less than exemplary and that he had been offered incentives by the police to testify against respondent. Thus the reliability of his testimony was subject to the normal testing process of an adversary trial."[86]

In *Tucker,* the Court did not categorically declare that a mere violation of *Miranda* would always allow use of a confession's fruits, but other decisions seem to be heading that way. In a concurring opinion in *New York v. Quarles,*[87] Justice O'Connor advocated a bright-line rule that physical evidence obtained as a result of a confession after a *Miranda* violation should be admissible.[88] In *Quarles,* a woman told police officers that she had just been raped, described her assailant, and said that he had just entered a nearby supermarket and was carrying a gun. One of the officers chased the defendant, who matched the description given by the woman, through the supermarket. The officer caught him and found a holster but no gun; the officer asked him where the gun was, the defendant told him, and the gun was recovered there. The officer then read the defendant his *Miranda* rights, and the defendant admitted that he owned the gun. In the ensuing prosecution for criminal possession of a weapon, the trial judge excluded both the defendant's initial statement of where the gun was and the gun itself. Justice O'Connor thought the gun itself should come in: "Admission of non-testimonial evidence of this type is based on the very sensible view that procedural errors should not cause entire investigations and prosecutions to be lost."[89] O'Connor relied on the *Schmerber* line of cases, which emphasized the difference between physical and testimonial evidence, as support for her approach.[90] Writing one year later in *Oregon v. Elstad,* this time for the majority, Justice O'Connor again invoked *Schmerber*—"[t]he Fifth Amendment, of course, is not concerned with nontestimonial evidence"—and declined to suppress the fruits of a "mere" *Miranda* violation.[91] Once again, the Court stressed "the Fifth Amendment goal of assuring trustworthy evidence."[92] This approach has led most circuits to embrace the view that all fruits of a (merely) *Miranda*-defective confession are admissible—even though the confession itself is inadmissible.[93]

But if *Miranda* is ultimately rooted in the self-incrimination clause, we need to ask what the courts have not (yet) asked: Why not enforce the clause itself by excluding confessions and allowing fruits?[94]

"Witness"?

What does it mean to be a "witness" against oneself? Here, too, the courts have been all over the map.

In the 1886 case of *Boyd v. United States,* the Supreme Court held that seizing or compelling production of a defendant's private papers to be used in evidence against him was equivalent to compelling him to be a witness against himself.[95] *Boyd*'s basic rule—that a person's property could not be used against him in a criminal proceeding—is plausible in the context of personal papers such as diaries.[96] A defendant's diary *testifies:* it speaks in the defendant's own words, much as would the defendant himself as a witness on the stand.[97] Diaries often express secret thoughts that implicate First Amendment concerns and sometimes pose reliability problems because of the use of personal shorthand, fantasy, and so forth.

But not all papers pose these difficulties. In particular, papers kept in connection with such legal matters as taxes or customs duties are quite different. *Boyd* involved a subpoena requiring the defendant to produce not a diary but books, invoices, and papers for enforcement of customs laws. *Boyd*'s exclusion of such records was inspired by a spirit akin to the spirit of *Lochner:*[98] that a person's right to his property includes the right not to have it introduced against him in a criminal case.[99] (Significantly, *Boyd* and its immediate progeny involved corporate crime and breaches of regulatory requirements, not violent crime like rape or murder.)[100]

In a less extreme version of *Boyd,* many courts in the late nineteenth and early twentieth centuries held that using the defendant's body as physical evidence was in effect compelling the defendant to be a witness against himself.[101] The question, however, was hotly contested; some jurisdictions admitted such evidence. Courts divided on whether a defendant could be compelled to undergo a physical examination,[102] to make a footprint or fingerprints,[103] or to display himself to the jury or perform physical acts.[104] Courts adopted various rationales for excluding or allowing the evidence.[105] The reason for this uncertainty is obvious: using a defendant's body is different in some ways from forcing him to take the stand and testify as a witness, and yet in other ways it does treat him like a witness to be observed by the jury. Is a witness someone who testifies—or merely someone who is observed at trial? To answer this question, we need an overall theory of the self-incrimination clause—and that is precisely what the legal community seems to lack.

As the twentieth century wore on, the spirit of the *Lochner* era declined, and so did *Boyd* and its progeny. Beginning with the landmark case of *Schmerber v. California,*[106] a series of cases in the 1960s and 1970s rejected *Boyd*'s approach. *Schmerber,* announced a week after the Court's decision in *Miranda,* gave rise to a sweeping assertion of the need to let in reliable physical evidence, via a definition of *witness* that drew a sharp distinction between words and physical evidence. The defendant was arrested at a hospital while being treated for injuries from a car accident. A police officer directed a doctor at the hospital to take a blood sample, and an analysis of the alcohol percentage showed that the defendant was intoxicated. The analysis report was introduced at trial, and the defendant was convicted of driving under the influence of alcohol. Justice Brennan wrote for the Court: "We hold that the privilege protects an accused only from being compelled to testify against himself, or otherwise provide the State with evidence of a testimonial or communicative nature, and that the withdrawal of blood and use of the analysis in question in this case did not involve compulsion to these ends."[107] In support of the Court's position, Justice Brennan cited *Holt v. United States*,[108] a case where a defendant had been compelled before the trial to try on a blouse related to the crime; the fact that the blouse fit him served as incriminating evidence. The *Holt* Court, per Justice Holmes, rejected the defendant's objection as "an extravagant extension of the Fifth Amendment;" Holmes declared that "the prohibition of compelling a man in a criminal court to be a witness against himself is a prohibition of the use of physical or moral compulsion to extort communications from him, not an exclusion of his body as evidence when it may be material."[109] Justice Brennan summed up the distinction thus: "[T]he privilege is a bar against compelling 'communications' or 'testimony,' but . . . compulsion which makes a suspect or accused the source of 'real or physical evidence' does not violate it."[110]

Although *Schmerber* did not explicitly overrule *Boyd*, its logic is hard to square with *Boyd*'s.[111] *Boyd* fused the Fourth and Fifth Amendments, holding that the two provisions "run almost into each other."[112] *Schmerber* analyzed each amendment separately.[113] In dissent, Justice Black argued that it was a "strange hierarchy of values" that allowed the state to convict someone with his own blood but not with his "lifeless papers."[114] If Black is wrong and *Schmerber* is right, perhaps the Fifth Amendment is *not* about bodily privacy, as is the Fourth. And if the two amendments reflect separate ideas, rather than the same one, then perhaps we should exclude not *things*—the Fourth Amendment's concern in its "effects" language[115]—but only *words*, as in testimonial witnessing, from a criminal case.

But if so, *Kastigar* unravels. Justice O'Connor in *Quarles* noted the broad implications of *Schmerber* and quoted Judge Friendly's view that "[u]se of a suspect's answers 'merely to find other evidence establishing his connection with the crime . . . differs only by a shade from the permitted use for that purpose of his body or his blood.'"[116] O'Connor's own words went one step further: "Certainly interrogation which provides leads to other evidence does not offend the values underlying the Fifth Amendment privilege any more than the compulsory taking of blood samples. . . ."[117]

Schmerber's progeny continued the division between testimonial or communicative evidence and physical evidence. A series of cases allowed a defendant to be compelled to stand in a lineup,[118] to give handwriting exemplars,[119] to give voiceprints,[120] and to take sobriety tests measuring mental acuity and physical coordination.[121] Property, too, was no longer sacrosanct. *Warden v. Hayden,* which involved the seizure of an armed robber's clothing found in a washing machine in his house, simultaneously rejected the Fourth Amendment mere evidence rule established under *Boyd's* regime and reaffirmed *Schmerber* in holding that because the clothing was not "testimonial" or "communicative," it could be introduced.[122] Perhaps property protections were not so enticing to the Court when violent crime was involved.

In the 1970s, the Court began to turn away from *Boyd* even in the context of nonviolent crime and to lessen protection for papers. In a series of cases that all but overruled *Boyd,* the Court held that even a defendant's subpoenaed papers—except, perhaps, personal papers like diaries—could be introduced at a criminal trial. The Court's theory was that although they were *testimonial,* and although their production was *compelled,* these papers were not *compelled testimony* within the meaning of the Fifth Amendment because the defendant was not compelled to create the papers in the first place but only to hand them over.[123] (In this last respect, such papers differed from the "required records" whose creation the government had mandated.) If this is the Court's logic, however, it applies to diaries, too; so why did the Court pointedly leave this question open?[124] And in order to decide whether subpoenaed papers are indeed compelled testimony within the meaning of the Fifth Amendment, we need an overall theory of the clause—which, again, is precisely what we now lack. Until we have such a theory, it is impossible to decide whether it was the *Boyd* Court or the modern Court that was playing word games where compelled papers are at issue.

In the end, the Court has been moving away from the overexpansive view of the word *witness* propounded in *Boyd* and has sharpened a distinction between compelled words—testimony—and physical evidence. This distinction maps onto one common understanding of the word *witness.* Witnesses testify; blood does not. The word *witness* comes from the Old English *witnes,* meaning "knowledge" (related to the Old English *witan,* "to know").[125] Except in a poetic sense, we do not usually conceive of blood as "knowing" anything. But if this is the key to understanding the privilege, why not exclude the defendant's compelled pre-trial testimony (words) but allow in the fruits (physical evidence) that the defendant's out-of-court compelled testimony might lead to?

What's the Big Idea?

What basic rationales underlie the Fifth Amendment? Many discussions by judges and scholars have obscured the privilege behind clouds of eulogy. Over a century and a half ago, Bentham noted that the privilege had long been shielded by an "assumption of the propriety of the rule, as a proposition too plainly true to admit of dispute."[126] In his widely influential 1968 Robert S. Marx Lectures, Judge Friendly urged a thorough examination of the policies of the privilege: the task was "indispensable to any reconsideration of the proper scope of the fifth amendment and peculiarly necessary because of the extent to which eloquent phrases have been accepted as a substitute for thorough thought."[127]

None of the rationales typically given for the self-incrimination clause can satisfactorily explain the current scope of the privilege and its relation to the rest of our legal and moral system.[128] Sometimes, the idea behind a given rationale is simply wrongheaded. At other times, the animating idea is valuable but proves too much or too little (or both) and thus cannot explain why the clause goes as far as it now does but no further.

One frequently mentioned rationale for the privilege is the "psychological cruelty" of the so-called cruel trilemma: without the privilege, the defendant would be forced to choose among self-accusation, perjury, or contempt.[129] But our justice system has no such scruples about compelling self-damaging answers from a civil litigant both in pretrial discovery and on the witness stand. Nor does our system object to forcing people to testify in criminal cases against friends and family members—except spouses—even though such compelled witnessing can be an extremely painful experience: today a mother may be forced, under penalty of contempt, to testify against her son and send him to the gallows.[130] Thus, as a descriptive theory, the psychological cruelty argument simply does not hold water. To make matters worse, it benefits only guilty defendants: there is no trilemma if one is innocent and says so. No other criminal procedure provision of the Bill of Rights is designed to give *special* protection from conviction to guilty defendants.[131]

Courts have also made much of the argument that the Fifth Amendment protects a special zone of mental privacy.[132] But here, too, the treatment of civil litigants and witnesses belies this rationale; they are often called to testify concerning intensely private, highly embarrassing matters—in divorce cases, for example. Even in criminal cases, immunity trumps the privilege. A witness given immunity can be forced to testify about anything in his private mental enclave. This treatment stands in dramatic contrast to the true privacy privileges of wife-husband, priest-penitent, doctor-patient, lawyer-client, and so on, for which no such trumping immunity exists.

Related to the notion of protecting mental privacy is the more convincing argument that the privilege helps to protect First Amendment values. But the scope of the privilege on this rationale is overbroad; its literal wording applies not just to political and religious groups but to murderers and rapists as well, whose cases lie far from the core of the First Amendment.

A different possible rationale taps into ideas about parity and symmetry. At the time of the Founding, a defendant was not even allowed to take the stand and testify under oath *for* himself.[133] Why, then, should the government have been allowed to force the defendant to take the stand and testify under oath *against* himself?[134] (Put another way, this disparity might seem to violate the minimal idea of parity underlying the compulsory process clause: the government could compel the defendant to be a witness, but he could not "compel" himself to be a witness.)[135] But this logic is obsolete today. The Court has held that a defendant enjoys a constitutional right to testify on his own behalf.[136] In any event, this rationale could not explain why fruits should be excluded, because no antidefendant fruits asymmetry has ever existed. Defendants in America have always enjoyed a general right to introduce physical evidence or to put on third-party witnesses, even if they learned of these things or persons from the government itself. Indeed, today parity cuts *against* broad Fifth Amendment claims: if the government is now obliged to supply a defendant with any exculpatory evidence and information it has, why shouldn't the defendant be obliged to supply the government with any inculpatory evidence and information he has?[137]

Another foundation of the clause might be "noninstrumentalization"—the notion that government impermissibly disrespects a person when it uses him as the means of his own destruction.[138] But noninstrumentalization proves too much. The government "uses" persons as witnesses all the time—whether they will or no. In general, the obligation to serve as a witness when necessary to enforce the laws is part of the duty of citizenship; generally, the law is entitled to every person's evidence.[139] If the government cannot use a person against himself in a criminal prosecution, why may it do so in a civil prosecution against him? And doesn't *Schmerber* legitimate dramatic instrumental use of a person against himself?[140] Though decided by the slimmest of margins in 1966, *Schmerber* is an absolutely central case today—the rock on which a great many cases and a considerable amount of crime detection policy have been built. Can anyone now imagine even a single Justice voting that government may not use an arrestee by forcing him to submit to photographing, fingerprinting, and voice tests whose results may be introduced in a criminal court? And if these instrumental uses are okay, why is using testimonial fruits so different on instrumentalization grounds?[141]

Occasionally, courts and scholars invoke such notions as preferring an accusatorial over an inquisitorial system[142] or achieving a "fair balance" between individuals and the state[143] to explain the privilege. These phrases, however, are more like slogans that simply restate the rule than carefully considered rationales. At times, the fair balance idea collapses into a sporting theory of justice—the idea that we should boost the odds for criminals just to keep the game interesting, above and beyond the valuable and important "handicap" that the government must prove its case beyond reasonable doubt.[144] And the aversion to inquisitorial schemes cannot explain why the privilege applies only in criminal but not civil cases. What's more, these notions fail to explain the key case of *Schmerber:* Is it not arguably imbalanced or inquisitorial when a prosecutor may suck blood from her adversary's very veins with needles that invade his body, and then use his own blood to destroy him at trial in a capital case, and then reinject those veins with lethal poison?

Also flawed is the related notion that the government must shoulder its entire burden of proof, or at least its prima facie case, without any help from the defendant.[145] The moral intuition underlying this "look ma, no hands" idea is fuzzy—especially in light of the government's heavy burden of proof—and once again, the idea runs afoul of *Schmerber* and its progeny. In many contexts, government *can* oblige a defendant to "help" in nontestimonial ways: by showing up at trial, by allowing witnesses to point at him, by making voiceprints, by giving up his very blood, and so on.[146]

Courts have also, rightly, shown considerable concern for deterring improper police practices, including physical brutality. But does the current scope of the privilege accomplish this goal? Although the more egregious forms of interrogation abuse such as beatings have stopped,[147] the practices detailed by Simon indicate that intimidation is alive and well in the police station. Far from civilizing[148] the interrogation process, the current interpretation of the Fifth Amendment has driven it underground. Open interrogation of suspects under direct judicial supervision would serve the goal of deterring police abuse far better, as would a better-constructed Fourth Amendment remedial regime for unreasonable seizures of persons.[149]

In addition, courts have stated that the privilege protects an innocent defendant from a bad performance on the stand.[150] But as we have seen, the broad scope of the current privilege actually harms the innocent defendant by denying her the Sixth Amendment right to compulsory process. Regarding her own performance, the scope of immunity is again too broad; the problem could be solved simply by allowing the defendant to refuse to testify at trial for the jury to hear but eliciting information pretrial that could generate admissible fruit.

Finally, and relatedly, courts and commentators have stressed that coerced statements are unreliable and that the privilege therefore serves the goal of reliability.[151] This is indeed a worthy goal, and courts have increasingly emphasized it over the past three decades. But if this is the touchstone, again the scope of immunity today is too broad. Why exclude the physical fruits of confessions when these are quite reliable and often highly probative pieces of evidence?[152]

In short, the various rationales repeatedly wheeled out to explain the privilege do not fit with the current scope of immunity.[153] Small wonder, then, that the self-incrimination clause—virtually alone among the provisions of the Bill of Rights—has been the target of repeated analytic assault over the course of the twentieth century from thoughtful commentators urging constitutional amendments to narrow it or repeal it altogether.[154]

In part, the current confusion about the rationale of the privilege stems from historical complexity and uncertainty. In the past six centuries the privilege has reflected several different fundamental ideas. Recent scholarship has displaced the earlier heroic, teleological accounts of the privilege's development.[155] It now appears that the privilege evolved from a maxim of canon law imported from the Continent: *nemo tenetur prodere seipsum*, "no one is obliged to produce himself."[156] Originally, this meant that the duty to reveal all sins at confession, as a condition of absolution, did not entail having to come forward and accuse oneself in court.[157] But once a prosecution was initiated and one was accused and called on as a witness, one had to answer truthfully.[158]

The sixteenth- and seventeenth-century incarnation of the privilege, closely related to the medieval version, involved protections against religious intolerance and open-ended fishing expeditions. In England, prerogative courts such as the Star Chamber and the High

Commission and ecclesiastical courts used the oath *ex officio*.[159] In this procedure, a person could be plucked from the street and forced to swear an oath that he would answer any questions the court might decide to ask him before any charge had been leveled against him or any probable cause had been shown to justify singling him out.[160] To make matters worse, the purpose of these indiscriminate procedures was often to identify and punish those whose only possible offense was theological disagreement with the Crown. During the sixteenth and seventeenth centuries, the battles over the oath *ex officio* concerned the subject-matter jurisdiction of ecclesiastical courts and the quality of the charge needed before the oath could be given.[161]

The privilege in a more modern form was half-heartedly invoked in late-seventeenth-century heresy and sedition trials, but, contrary to Wigmore's account, the privilege was not firmly established at that time.[162] Rather than emerging in the seventeenth century to protect defendants in sedition and heresy trials, the modern privilege actually grew legs in the late eighteenth century in ordinary criminal trials, both in England and in America.[163] It is probably no coincidence that it was just at this time that defense lawyers came to be widely used in criminal trials. Now that they had lawyers, criminal defendants could afford to be silent rather than having to conduct their own defenses; for their part, the lawyers must have enjoyed being able to control their cases without interference from their clients' risky testimony.[164]

The privilege in anything like the form we know it today was slow to catch on in America, even after the ratification of the Bill of Rights, and references to the privilege during the ratification debates were few. One reason is that routine pretrial procedure involved questioning of an accused by a magistrate, and the accused was expected to answer.[165] If he did not and insisted on standing mute in the face of accusations, this refusal to answer could be laid before a later criminal jury for whatever inferences they might draw.[166] In the mid-nineteenth century, police departments emerged and began to take over certain pretrial investigatory functions, relying on informal coercion. The distinction between informal confession at the hands of the police and compelled self-incrimination during formal proceedings was maintained until the 1897 case of *Bram* (briefly) and the 1966 case of *Miranda* (permanently) merged the two.[167]

Amid this tangled history and unconvincing catalogue of traditional rationales for the clause, three key questions about the scope of the clause stand out. First, why does the privilege apply in a "criminal case" but not in a civil case? Second, why does the privilege simply dissolve once immunity is granted, whereas no true privacy privilege—spousal, priest-penitent, doctor-patient, attorney-client, and the like—likewise dissolves in the presence of immunity? Third, why does the Fifth Amendment bar only compulsory "witness[ing]" rather than "furnishing evidence"? Any adequate theory must explain these three central features of the clause. No current theory does.[168]

The Solution

Current Fifth Amendment doctrine is a quagmire. But there is a way out—a road to firm, high ground. To clear up the confusion, I advocate a solution remarkably like the early scope of the privilege, one that borrows a page from current pretrial civil discovery.

Under this solution, the government would be able to compel all persons to testify truthfully in a wide variety of proceedings before the commencement of, or outside, a formal "criminal case" or trial. These venues include grand jury rooms, legislative hearings, civil cases, criminal cases in which someone else is on trial, and depositions organized by prosecutors. The penalty for refusing to answer would be contempt,[169] and the penalty for lying would be perjury.[170] In the case of criminal depositions, this compulsion would take place under judicial oversight, as in the civil discovery system, but with extra protection: the magistrate would physically preside, rather than oversee by remote control. Defense and prosecution lawyers and a court reporter would typically be present.[171] In high-profile cases, and perhaps ordinary cases as well, the magistrate could preserve a grand jury–like secrecy by closing the hearing to the public and sealing the deposition.[172] The prosecution would not be able to introduce compelled out-of-court testimony "in" a "criminal case" unless the defendant knowingly and intelligently consented at trial, with the judge looking on. But virtually all physical evidence and third-party testimony that the defendant's statement led to would be admissible.[173] The defendant could also be subpoenaed to provide anything in his possession, except possibly his intimate personal papers, upon pain of contempt. In a criminal trial the subpoenaed items could be introduced, but the fact that the defendant produced them could not.[174]

The textual argument is remarkably clean. A defendant cannot be forced to be a "*witness* against himself"—to testify, with his own words introduced against him—at trial "*in* [his own] *criminal case.*" *Witness* here is used in its natural sense, meaning someone whose testimony, or utterances, are introduced at trial. Witnesses are those who take the stand and testify, or whose out-of-court depositions or affidavits are introduced at trial in front of the jury. Indeed, this is exactly how the word *witness* seems to be used in the companion Sixth Amendment and in the treason clause of Article III.[175] Physical evidence, on the other hand, can be introduced at trial whatever its source—even if that source is a compelled pretrial utterance. A witness testifies but physical evidence does not. A thing is not a witness. Moreover, if person *A* takes the stand to testify against defendant *B,* this is not the same as forcing *B* to be a witness *against himself,* even if *B*'s compelled pretrial statement led the police to learn of *A*'s existence and information. Although our suspect has indeed been forced to testify pretrial, that testimony occurred outside his own criminal case, beyond the earshot of the jury. Unless these words are introduced at trial, a suspect is not a *witness* against himself *in* a criminal *case.*

This clean reading makes sense of all the words of the self-incrimination clause and shows how they fit together (and with kindred words of the Sixth Amendment), but it also does much more than that. It flushes out the heretofore elusive rationale of the self-incrimination clause, as best read: reliability. Compelled testimony may be partly or wholly misleading and unreliable; even an innocent person may say seemingly inculpatory things under pressure and suspicion and when flustered by trained inquisitors. But physical fruit is far more sturdy and reliable evidence, so it should be brought before the jury. Of course, government investigations and inquisitions implicate issues beyond reliability—of bodily autonomy, of personal privacy and dignity, of freedom of thought and conscience, and so on—but as we shall see, these concerns are often best addressed via other constitutional clauses and principles outside the self-incrimination idea.

This clean reading also solves many of the common-sense conundrums plaguing current doctrine. Indeed, this reading achieves many of the same results that Judge Friendly argued for in his wise and influential lectures on the self-incrimination clause.[176] But whereas Friendly's elaborate analysis led him to propose a six-pronged constitutional amendment of more than three hundred words to achieve his sensible results, we can now reach similar conclusions through a more elegant and parsimonious textual analysis of the fifteen words of the existing clause.

"Person"

Under my reading of the clause, the problem of the innocent defendant noted earlier would be solved. There would be no war between the Fifth Amendment privilege and the Sixth Amendment right to compulsory process to obtain witnesses. An innocent defendant could use *compulsory* process (Sixth Amendment) to *compel* (Fifth Amendment) the guilty party to be a *witness* (Fifth and Sixth Amendments) against himself, upon pain of contempt and under penalty of perjury. In short, the guilty could be made to sing and to be subject to withering questioning by defense counsel. The guilty witness's compelled testimony could not be introduced against him in any subsequent criminal trial, unless he authorized admission at trial. But officials would otherwise be free to prosecute, even on the basis of leads (fruits) generated by the compelled testimony.

The Canadians already have a similar rule in cases where the defense calls a witness who claims he might incriminate himself by answering. The witness is required to testify, but the prosecution cannot use his testimonial admissions—the words themselves—against him in a future proceeding.[177] However, Canada does allow the prosecution to use the fruits of his testimony against him.[178]

Some might claim there is a textual problem with this interpretation because the Fifth Amendment says "in *any* criminal case."[179] But the key "person" this clause is designed to protect is the "person" on trial—the defendant in *his own* criminal case. A witness required to testify at someone else's criminal trial with testimonial immunity is in basically the same position as a suspect required to give an immunized deposition for his own trial, or to testify in a civil case, in a legislative hearing, before a grand jury, or in any other proceeding.[180]

This testimonial immunity has several advantages over other sorts. Transactional immunity would thwart legitimate law enforcement against the guilty witness, and as a practical matter, so could use plus use-fruits immunity. Under the latter regime, prosecutors would need to prove that they had obtained evidence from independent sources, and, as we have seen, the costs of such a system in terms of lost evidence and administrative burdens can be high. Testimonial immunity, by contrast, would in no way hinder enforcement efforts against the immunized witness: the government loses nothing that it already had or might get independently. On the contrary, by immunizing the witness, an innocent defendant would be *helping* the police, generating leads that the police would be free to follow to convict the real culprit. The government therefore would have no excuse for denying the innocent defendant's constitutional right of compulsory process.

Because previous courts defined the Fifth Amendment too broadly, they ended up betraying the explicit Sixth Amendment right to compel witnesses. If the Fifth Amendment is restored to its proper scope, a defendant would indeed enjoy a kind of Sixth Amendment parity with the prosecutor. Both could subpoena; both could immunize. As we shall see in Chapter 3, this Sixth Amendment right is absolutely essential, for it is truly at the heart of our criminal procedure. It is nothing less than the right to mount a defense—a right of obvious importance to all defendants and of transcendent significance for truly *innocent* defendants.[181] As the Supreme Court put the point in its landmark case, *Washington v. Texas:*[182] "The right to offer the testimony of witnesses, and to compel their attendance, if necessary, is in plain terms *the right to present a defense,* the right to present the defendant's version of the facts as well as the prosecution's to the jury *so it may decide where the truth lies.*"[183]

Some might argue that the right to compel a guilty witness to take the stand would not benefit the innocent defendant very much. The witness would simply lie. Those who framed the Fifth Amendment, however, thought differently. Earlier generations believed that perjury was a mortal sin, resulting in eternal damnation: better to admit murder than commit perjury under oath.[184] The power of oaths several centuries ago is abundantly clear from the Constitution itself, which requires oaths in several of its most important provisions, and from landmark opinions of the Marshall Court stressing oaths.[185]

True, times have changed. Perjury has largely lost its religious connotations and is feared mainly for its possible secular sanction. Even today, however, perjury will sometimes be a more severe penal threat than the underlying crime, and if the Court were to embrace testimonial immunity, legislatures might choose to increase the maximum punishment for perjury. What's more, as noted above, the witness need not confess all on the stand for his testimony to be vital to an innocent defendant. Simply forcing a witness to tell his story can be invaluable. The innocent defendant then would have the opportunity to demolish it with questions and other evidence that might otherwise be excluded for lack of foundation. Prosecutors today, for example, get considerable mileage out of a suspect's lies. Alibis, denials, and explanations "can be checked and rechecked until a suspect's lies are the greatest evidentiary threat to his freedom."[186]

"Compelled"

In-Court Compulsion. Compared with the current morass, the compulsion line under a testimonial immunity regime would be easier to enforce. Pretrial, a suspect under this regime would be obliged to comply with all judicially authorized depositions, inquests, and subpoenas. If he does not, he could be made much worse off: held in contempt and punished. At trial, the judge would exclude the defendant's compelled pretrial testimony, unless the defendant affirmatively authorizes its introduction as evidence. And for the reasons identified above, courts could continue to follow the nice compulsion rule laid down in *Griffin* concerning in-court inferences about in-court silence.[187] The self-incrimination clause, as best read, is designed to protect a truly innocent defendant who might be made to look guilty on the stand by a clever prosecutor skilled in technical courtroom procedure and forensics. To infer guilt from mere in-court silence would seem to betray the innocent but unpersuasive defendant whom the clause seeks to protect.

Prosecutors could probably encourage the defendant to take the stand at trial or to authorize introduction of pretrial statements with bribes, such as recommendations of reduced jail time. The baseline of compulsion would be established by the burden-of-proof rules at trial, the definition of elements of the offense, the statutory sentence authorized, and the *Griffin* rule itself. These would fix a Coasean starting point from which defendant and prosecutor could bargain.[188] In contrast to the situation at the Founding,[189] today the Court has recognized the defendant's right to testify under oath; the innocent defendant is able to calculate the risk that his testimony will be misinterpreted, and this screening will help make the testimony that the defendant voluntarily authorizes to be admitted in court more reliable.

Under this logic, the "silence penalty" imposed by the Sentencing Guidelines should pass constitutional muster. *Griffin* is neatly distinguishable: there is a world of difference between using (then-unreliable) silence to prove guilt before guilt has been independently established and using silence once guilt has already been otherwise proved. Put another way, by the time the Guidelines are applied, they penalize moral culpability on the underlying offense, rather than silence per se. If the Guidelines' common-sense morality is to be upheld on this theory, however, the logic of the self-incrimination clause must sound in reliability, as we shall see in more detail below. After a successful appeal, a defendant may have a right to insist that his earlier-induced statements be excluded from the guilt-determination phase of the retrial—because, in law, he reverts back to presumptive innocence and *Griffin* thus applies. (In effect, his earlier-induced testimony is protected by the rule of testimonial immunity.) But in this second trial, as in the first, the Sentencing Guidelines' silence penalty remains in effect, constituting a lawful Coasean bribe to induce the defendant to (again) waive his "starting point" right of silence.

Out-of-Court Compulsion: Government Employment. Currently, the government, when acting as an employer, is caught between a rock and a hard place. It must choose either to act sensibly as an employer or to act efficiently in its sovereign capacity as law enforcer.[190] Instead, the government should be put in the same position as any other employer. It should be able to fire stonewalling employees and otherwise to act as a normal employer without detriment to its law enforcement function. The only way to guarantee no detriment is to allow all fruit in, thereby avoiding the burdens of Chinese walls, "canning," *North*-style acquittals, and so on.

But what about the out-of-court testimony itself? When could *it* come in? The issue here is cloudier—and the stakes are much lower once fruits may come in—but one clear rule would be that the limits on the power of the government-as-employer over its employees should be the limits on the power of normal employers. (Private standards of coercion, such as laws against extortion, would apply.) Under this theory, courts could hold that no impermissible Fifth Amendment compulsion exists from reasonable employment decisions because no one is compelled to work for the government in the first place. If statements made under threat of dismissal are reliable enough to come in when dismissal is threatened by a private employer, why not for a public employer, too?[191] (Note that in asking "How much pressure is too much pressure?" we now have a touchstone: reliability.) Any action beyond these limits should be construed as impermissible coercion, with the result that the coerced statement itself—but not the fruits—would be excludable. This, in effect, would treat coercion beyond responsible employment sanctions exactly the same as coercion in depositions, hearings, and the like. Deposition coercion is backed by contempt and imprisonment—powers no private party enjoys—and so the coercion in depositions is clearly the coercion of a "sovereign." The same should be true when a government employer acts more coercively than a reasonable private employer would; in effect, leveraging its sovereign power in the employment context is an "unconstitutional condition."[192]

Out-of-Court Compulsion: Required Records.   In required records cases the Court has adopted a balancing approach, unwarranted by constitutional text, in order to avoid the substantial burdens imposed by, and the broad logic underlying, *Kastigar's* use plus use-fruits immunity. That form of immunity would have practically foreclosed any prosecution of Bouknight for child abuse[193] and prevented the police from discovering the identity of, and therefore prosecuting, the hit-and-run driver in *Byers*.[194] The Court responded by creating exceptions to the privilege in the *Shapiro-Byers-Bouknight* line of cases. But the need for such exceptions shrinks dramatically if one gets at the root of the problem: the scope of immunity.

Under the testimonial immunity solution, required records, just like any other compelled, incriminating statement, would generally receive full Fifth Amendment protection. They themselves could not be introduced "in" a "criminal case"—that is, at trial—but any fruits they led to could be introduced.[195] Thus, the body of the child in a case like *Bouknight* would have to be produced and could be introduced in the trial of his abuser, but not the fact that the defendant's information led to him. The hit-and-run driver could still be prosecuted. The quandary the Court currently faces—possibly making the government worse off as criminal law enforcer whenever it needs records for legitimate noncriminal purposes—would thus be elegantly solved.[196]

•

Out-of-Court Compulsion: Police Interrogation. A deposition approach would limit abusive police tactics. The basic insight uniting pre–Warren Court voluntariness cases like *Brown v. Mississippi* and Warren-era landmarks like *Miranda* and *Escobedo* would be preserved and strengthened: we need to rein in unsupervised police officers who might be tempted to abuse suspects.[197] The best way to do this is to shift interrogation from police stations to magistrates' hearing rooms. On the civil discovery side, we generally do not try to get damning admissions from defendants by using third-degree tactics. We use subpoenas and depositions with lawyers, loosely supervised by judges.[198] *Miranda* failed to *require* the use of lawyers, magistrates, and recorders—and from a civil libertarian perspective, this has been its undoing. *Miranda* also failed to create strong incentives for suspects to talk and to tell the truth—and from a crime control perspective, this has been its undoing. The deposition model would combine both perspectives: the suspect would be protected from abuse and intimidation but must answer truthfully.

The question of how to treat confessions that are obtained by police outside the formal deposition-like process remains.[199] Fortunately, a deposition solution would make the problem much less pressing because the stakes would shrink: a civilized process would exist outside the police station to compel suspects to talk truthfully, and so the police would be less tempted to force the issue. In light of this civilized alternative, courts might well choose to police the police even more strictly than today, enforcing a prophylactic rule that no police station confession by a defendant is ever allowed in unless volunteered by a suspect in the presence of an on-duty defense lawyer or ombudsman, or unless the defendant consents to its introduction at trial.

Rooted in a legitimate concern about unsupervised police compulsion, this strict regime would create powerful incentives to conduct interrogation before magistrates rather than in police stations.

On the other hand, more relaxed schemes are also compatible with the testimonial immunity approach. For example, each suspect in custody could be told that he must be brought before a magistrate and a lawyer within a short time (say, five hours) and that he has an absolute right to remain silent until then; but he should also understand that if he stands mute until then, a later jury can be told of his premagistrate, prelawyer silence and might view more skeptically any story he later tries to offer at trial. The range of possible police station schemes compatible with testimonial immunity is hardly unique or embarrassing. Rather, it reflects the fact that the self-incrimination clause historically addressed formal testimonial compulsion in judicial settings, and so applying the clause to the informal compulsion of the modern police station requires creative adaptation of Founding principles.

And however we regulate the police station itself, nice problems will arise concerning suspects' statements and silences before station house custody commences—at the scene of the crime, on the street corner, in the squad car, and elsewhere. The wide variety of these encounters may well mock any effort at comprehensive rule making. But in keeping with our treatment of employment compulsion, we should accept one global rule of compulsion: reasonable adverse inferences from suspicious silence outside courtrooms need not always be treated as Fifth Amendment "compulsion."[200]

"In Any Criminal Case"

Textually, the Fifth Amendment speaks to witnessing *within* the criminal case, not beyond. Therefore, the key question is what "witnessing" is excludable "in" a "criminal case"—that is, at trial.[201] This question is the same as what the scope of immunity should be. The *Kastigar*[202] rule for "true" Fifth Amendment violations—use plus use-fruits immunity—should be trimmed back and brought into line with Justice O'Connor's suggested approach in *Quarles*[203] for "mere" *Miranda* violations. Compelled testimony should be excluded from a criminal case—unless the defendant authorizes its introduction at trial—but not fruits. A rule excluding compelled testimony would be much easier to enforce than the *Kastigar* rule excluding fruits—a rule that has led to many difficult issues of proof, but-for causation, and never-neverland counterfactuals, as in the *North* case. A statement by the defendant is self-identifying, but other physical evidence and witnesses are not: they do not come with "courtesy of defendant" labels stating how the government got them or whether the chain of causation ran through the defendant's pretrial statements. The recurrent friction between different government authorities with the power to grant immunity (states, federal prosecutors, Congress, and so on) that led the Court in *Murphy*[204] to move toward *Kastigar* would be eliminated. If government *A* grants immunity, government *B* would be no worse off. Currently, *A* can to some extent veto *B*'s law enforcement by imposing *North*-like litigation burdens on *B*, requiring it to prove it got all its evidence independently. So the very same internal logic that drove the Court in *Murphy* from *Counselman* to proto-*Kastigar* should now drive it all the way home to a *Quarles*-like rule.

Testimonial immunity also has some important history on its side; it is consistent with many courts' view of the privilege before the *Counselman* decision in 1892. Prior to *Counselman*, case after case in state after state and in lower federal courts held that the privilege was satisfied by excluding compelled pretrial testimony but not the fruits of that testimony.[205] Before 1892, the leading American case was *People v. Kelly*, decided by New York's highest court in 1861.[206] *Kelly* involved a witness called by a grand jury and asked to answer incriminating questions. The court held that as long as the compelled testimony was excluded from any subsequent criminal trial against the witness, the privilege was satisfied.[207] In addressing the argument that the privilege required broader immunity, the court announced:

> [N]either the law nor the Constitution is so sedulous to screen the guilty as the argument supposes. If a man cannot give evidence upon the trial of another person without disclosing circumstances which will make his own guilt apparent or at least capable of proof, though his account of the transactions should never be used as evidence, it is the misfortune of his condition and not any want of humanity in the law. . . . [T]he statute makes it impossible that his *testimony* given on that occasion should be used by the prosecution on the trial. *It cannot, therefore, be said that in such a criminal case he has been made a witness against himself.* . . .[208]

This rule was widely followed among the states; in his opinion in *Kelly*, Judge Denio observed that "[i]f the case is so situated that a repetition of [the witness's admission] on a prosecution against him is impossible, as where it is forbidden by statute, I have seen no authority which holds or intimates that the witness is privileged."[209] Numerous immunity statutes providing for testimonial but not use-fruits immunity were upheld.[210]

Furthermore, testimonial immunity was Congress's idea of the scope of the privilege at the time of *Kelly*.[211] An 1857 act provided broad transactional immunity for anyone who "shall be required to testify before . . . Congress."[212] Senator Trumbull criticized the scope of immunity as too sweeping, allowing "the greatest criminal [to] escape."[213] Subsequent events confirmed Trumbull's fears,[214] and the act was pointedly amended in 1862 to read simply: "The testimony of a witness . . . shall not be used as evidence in any criminal proceeding against such witness."[215] Congressional debate over this bill "shows conclusively" that Congress believed that the Constitution required only testimonial immunity.[216] Senator Benjamin Wade described the scope of immunity under the new statute with crystal clarity:

> You may inquire; [a witness] may testify and may be compelled to testify [out of court], but whatever he says shall not be used as evidence against him in any court. That is all that a rascal ought to have at the hands of justice. . . .
>
> . . . [I]f his [out-of-court] testimony is given, though it cannot be used directly against him, it may lead to other testimony that may throw light on the subject, whereby in the concatenation of events he may be convicted of crime. Well, sir, I hope it will be so.[217]

This was Congress's understanding of the privilege at the time it proposed the Fourteenth Amendment, making the Bill of Rights applicable against the states and reglossing the federal provisions.[218] (This clear understanding and legislative history looms especially large in light of the absence of much clarity or legislative history underlying the initial adoption of the self-incrimination clause in the 1780s.)

The early and middle nineteenth century, the period in which the above cases were decided and narrow immunity statutes adopted, is the key period in the development of the modern privilege. Once defense lawyers began to be widely used in the late eighteenth and early nineteenth centuries, defendants at trial could keep quiet and let their lawyers speak for them—as is the case now.[219] As the privilege began to take hold in the pretrial phase of magistrate examination, the criminal justice system needed a way to find out what happened—to tap the suspect as a valuable testimonial resource.[220] Immunity statutes proved to be the answer, and they sprang up in abundance during this period.[221] This is also the period that saw the emergence of professional police charged with systematic investigation of crime. Thus, it was in the early and middle nineteenth centuries that courts and legislatures hammered out the true scope of the modern privilege.

Unfortunately, the U.S. Supreme Court in *Counselman* chose to follow those few cases that called for transactional immunity rather than the large number that supported testimonial immunity. Wigmore noted only three cases before *Counselman* that required immunity broader than testimonial;[222] all three of these involved state constitutional provisions that, unlike the federal Fifth, protected against being compelled to give "evidence" against oneself. The most influential of these was the Massachusetts case *Emery v. Commonwealth*.[223] The second followed *Emery* and involved a very broad protective immunity statute,[224] and the third was later questioned by the court that initially decided it.[225] Indefensibly, the U.S. Supreme Court in *Counselman* followed *Emery,* which was based explicitly and self-consciously on the peculiar wording of the Massachusetts Constitution, and rejected *Kelly,* which was based on a New York provision that tracked the Federal Constitution virtually word for word.[226] When *Kastigar* effectively overruled *Counselman,* the Supreme Court adopted a new standard—use plus use-fruits immunity—but offered no good reason for failing to return to *Kelly's* testimonial immunity.[227] In short, Fifth Amendment doctrine today is the unconvincing and half-hearted residue of an 1870s opinion from Massachusetts that explicitly relied on state constitutional phrasing that the Federal Fifth Amendment impliedly rejected.

Counselman also relied on the landmark *Boyd* case,[228] whose Fourth and Fifth Amendment mishmash has now been emphatically rejected. Indeed, *Boyd's* role as the godfather of *Counselman* is visible in two of *Boyd's* key—and now repudiated—passages. The first fused the Fourth and Fifth Amendments: "We have already noticed the intimate relation between the two amendments. They throw great light on each other. For the 'unreasonable searches and seizures' condemned in the fourth amendment are almost always made for the purpose of compelling a man to *give evidence* against himself, which in criminal cases is condemned in the fifth amendment."[229] The second also explicitly read the Fifth Amendment as if it prohibited compulsion to "furnish evidence" and implied that all criminal subpoenas of a defendant violated the Fifth.[230] But these two interpretations were decisively renounced by the Supreme Court in *United States v. Leon*[231] and *Fisher v. United States,*[232] respectively. In each of these cases, the Court used the same phrase: *Boyd* had not stood "the test of time."[233] And the *Schmerber* case likewise makes emphatically clear that, contrary to *Boyd* and *Counsel-*

man, a criminal defendant may indeed be required to "furnish evidence" against himself.[234]

Counselman also rejected the English rule, which was testimonial immunity. In the coerced confession context, which *Miranda* merged into the self-incrimination clause, this rule was firmly established in the 1783 case *The King v. Warickshall*.[235] In *Warickshall*, the defendant, charged with being an accessory after the fact for knowingly receiving stolen property, made a confession because of "promises of favour,"[236] which in those days was rightly considered to be a coerced confession.[237] In her confession, she revealed where the stolen goods were hidden, and so they were found in her mattress in her lodgings. The question to be decided was whether the stolen goods and their location could be admitted into evidence; the court held that they were admissible. The court stated with assurance: "[T]his subject has more than once undergone the solemn consideration of the Twelve Judges; and a majority were clearly of the opinion, That although confessions improperly obtained cannot be received in evidence, yet that any acts done afterwards might be given in evidence, notwithstanding they were done in consequence of such confession."[238] Coerced confessions, said the court, were unreliable, but the fruits here posed no reliability problem.[239] To exclude these fruits simply in order to prevent a suspect from being "made the . . . *instrument* of her own conviction" would be "novel in theory," "dangerous in practice," and "repugnant to the general principles of criminal law."[240] This was apparently the leading English case on point when the U.S. Bill of Rights was adopted in 1791.

Seventy years later, in *The Queen v. Leatham*,[241] the English judges made clear that a similar result applied to self-incrimination under formal immunity statutes: only testimonial immunity, not transactional or use plus use-fruits immunity, was required. In *Leatham*, decided under an immunity provision of the Corrupt Practices at Elections Act, the defendant's immunized testimony before election commissioners led to discovery of a preexisting letter that was introduced against him at his subsequent trial for bribery. The court held that only the defendant's statements should be excluded and that the letter was admissible. J. Crompton noted: "In the analogous case of confessions by persons accused of crimes, they cannot be used against such persons if obtained from them under the compulsion of a threat, or the inducement of a promise; but matters to which such a confession gives a clue may nevertheless be unexceptionally put in evidence. For instance, if stolen goods or a murdered body are or is found in a place indicated by the confession, this fact may be given in evidence."[242] Several judges mentioned the great difficulties involved in administering a rule of use plus use-fruits immunity. As Crompton put the point, a legislative grant of use-fruits immunity "would have introduced great inconvenience, giving rise in every case to the necessity for an inquiry, in all subsequent proceedings, as to whether or not the clue which led to them was obtained from something let fall by the defendant when before the Commissioners, and thereby opening as wide a field for investigation as can possibly be conceived."[243]

The problems noted by Crompton would be avoided by restoring the narrow scope of the privilege and allowing fruits to come in. This result could also be reached by simply expanding the Supreme Court's inevitable discovery doctrine, expounded in *Murray v. United States*.[244] The fruits could have come to light anyway, so the argument would go, and the presumption to that effect would be irrebuttable.

"Witness"

Schmerber[245] was right to emphasize the distinction between testimony and physical evidence, but later decisions have failed to follow its logic to the end. Only the defendant's compelled *testimony* should be protected by the amendment. The "witnessing" that the defendant has a right to exclude from the criminal trial includes both statements on the stand at trial and the introduction at trial of any earlier compelled depositions. This definition of *witness* closely tracks what seems to be the best definition of *witness* under the confrontation and compulsory process clauses of the Sixth Amendment.[246] Unlike some state constitutions, such as the Massachusetts Constitution of 1780, the Fifth Amendment does not prohibit the government from compelling a defendant to "furnish evidence against himself."[247] Compelled fruit is admissible, but compelled testimony is not.

The 1977 case of *Fisher v. United States* also fits nicely into this framework.[248] Obliging a suspect to hand over incriminating words or things already in existence can be distinguished from obliging him to be a *witness*—to testify in response to clever questions put by a prosecutor. As we shall see, testimony extorted by clever prosecutors can raise distinct reliability concerns—prosecutors tricking suspects into misleading and hasty concessions that look like confessions—that are not generally present when a suspect is merely obliged to hand over an already extant object (with testimonial immunity for the act itself of handing over).[249]

Two borderline questions noted earlier remain concerning defendants' bodies and diaries. First, what, if any, protections should a defendant have if the prosecution would like to use his body, rather than his communications? The answer lies in the Fourth Amendment, not in the Fifth. The use of a defendant's body as physical evidence is not testimonial, and therefore it is not covered by a privilege that protects a person from "witnessing" against himself. But the Fourth Amendment guards against "unreasonable searches and seizures" of "persons," and its protections should be applied in these situations.[250] Properly construed, the requirement of "reasonableness" invites judges to engage in balancing the state's and the individual's interests;[251] factors to be considered should include the gravity of the offense charged, the invasiveness or humiliation of the examination or act, and the importance of the evidence to the prosecution's case.[252] (Unlike the Fifth Amendment, the Fourth Amendment approach would protect a person's body even in civil cases—indeed, especially in civil cases.) Under this approach, courts are free to distinguish sensibly between, say, a painful and intrusive stomach pumping and a quick and virtually painless taking of a blood sample.[253]

Second, what protection should diaries enjoy? Unlike bodies, diaries are clearly communicative and testimony-like. At a minimum, the search for and seizure of diaries should be governed by a Fourth Amendment reasonableness test. This test should be informed by the probability that a search for a diary will be intrusive, the broad freedom of thought principles of the First Amendment, and the special treatment the Fourth Amendment accords to "papers."[254] What's more, reading a person's diary (even if lawfully obtained) in open court, civil or criminal, can be seen as an additional invasion of privacy—an incremental "search" of a man's soul, an additional "seizure" of a woman's most intimate secrets—that once again calls for a careful judicial inquiry into the reasonableness of this public reading.[255] Above and beyond these Fourth Amendment concerns is a key Fifth Amendment concept—reliability. Writers of diaries often fantasize or write in a personal shorthand easily misinterpreted. Though not compelled testimony in exactly the same way that forcing the witness to take the stand is compelled testimony, diaries may raise sufficiently distinct reliability issues to justify treating them differently from all other voluntarily created documents that the government wants to search for or subpoena.[256] Thus we can see why the Court has intuited that diaries might differ on Fifth Amendment grounds from, say, voluntarily created business records.[257]

The Big Idea(s)

The self-incrimination clause has long been a mandate in search of a meaning, and the scope of immunity permitted under it has varied widely over the centuries. The rule of testimonial immunity has powerful advantages, especially when compared with transactional and use plus use-fruits immunity. It safeguards defendants *and* emphasizes truth-finding.

How, one might ask, is such a positive-sum solution—reducing the risk of *both* false convictions *and* false acquittals—even possible? As statisticians have long understood, one can simultaneously reduce both false negatives and false positives only by bringing more information into a system. That is precisely what testimonial immunity does—by bringing in fruit and facilitating civilized pretrial questioning. Our current system throws out too much information, and in the end, this hurts both truth-seeking prosecutors *and* innocent defendants.

But why does it make sense for the self-incrimination clause to distinguish between compelled testimony and compelled fruit?

First and foremost, fruits and physical evidence are more reliable than coerced testimony itself.[258] This analysis is similar to the logic underlying the substantive criminal law doctrine of corpus delicti. Truth is a preeminent criminal procedure value in the Bill of Rights: most procedures were designed to protect innocent defendants from *erroneous* conviction.[259] Especially when pressured, people may confess—or seem to confess—to crimes they did not commit. As Blackstone put the point in his bestselling *Commentaries*, out-of-court confessions "are the weakest and most suspicious of all testimony; ever liable to be obtained by artifice, false hopes, promises of favor or menaces; seldom remembered accurately, or reported with due precision; and incapable in their nature of being disproved by other negative evidence."[260] A leading modern commentator, Judge Friendly, echoed Blackstone's concern and noted that a prime motive for extending the privilege to informal proceedings must have been "the truly dreadful risk of the false confession. . . . [T]here is thus good reason to impose a higher standard on the police before allowing them to use a confession of murder than a weapon bearing the confessor's fingerprints to which his confession has led. . . ."[261]

Though the prospect of an unreliable confession (or perceived confession) occurring on the witness stand itself may seem to some unlikely in a criminal trial today, we must remember that from 1789 until well into this century, many innocent defendants in noncapital cases could not afford lawyers and were not furnished lawyers by the government. If forced to take the stand, they might be bullied or bamboozled by a professional prosecutor into assenting to untrue or misleading propositions that would—*wrongly*—seal their fate in the minds of the jury. While the concern about a slipup on the stand applies to other witnesses as well, slipups by the defendant are particularly damaging in jurors' minds.[262]

In a post-*Gideon*[263] world the defenseless defendant scenario is less likely, but even after *Gideon,* many defendants enjoy only nominal assistance of counsel. Moreover, even a good lawyer cannot always save an innocent but unpersuasive-sounding client from being demolished on the stand. As the Supreme Court observed a century ago in one of its earliest self-incrimination opinions: "It is not every one who can safely venture on the witness stand *though entirely innocent of the charge against him.* Excessive timidity, nervousness when facing others and attempting to explain transactions of a suspicious character, and offenses charged against him, will often confuse and embarrass him to such a degree as to increase rather than remove prejudices against him. It is not every one, however honest, who would, therefore, willingly be placed on the witness stand."[264]

More recently, the Supreme Court's repeated emphasis on trustworthiness has led it to sharpen the difference between testimony and physical evidence; the logical culmination of this trend is testimonial immunity. We need not say every coerced statement is unreliable, or every physical fact reliable; the Fifth Amendment lays down a bright-line rule, and as with any rule the rationale need not explain every instance of the rule's application. It is enough that *as a category,* a criminal defendant's compelled testimony is particularly troubling on reliability grounds.[265] On the other hand, voluntary testimony is likely to be more reliable because innocent defendants have the opportunity to screen themselves on the basis of whether they might be misunderstood.

Focusing on reliability answers our three basic questions that any theory of the clause must confront. First, why does the privilege apply only in a "criminal case" and not in civil ones? The answer lies in the higher degree of certainty required for a criminal conviction. We insist on proof beyond a reasonable doubt in criminal but not civil cases precisely because we are so much more concerned about erroneous *criminal* convictions. For the same reason, we are particularly concerned with unreliable evidence being introduced against a criminal defendant. (This also helps explain why corpus delicti is a *criminal* doctrine.)[266] Second, why can immunity overcome the privilege and "compel" a witness to speak? Because the fruits, which can be introduced in a criminal trial, will be more reliable than the speaker's immunized words, which must be excluded. Finally, why does the Fifth Amendment concern "witnessing" rather than furnishing evidence?

Again, pieces of physical evidence—a gun, the defendant's own body, tax records—are more reliable than forced words.

Although testimonial immunity begins with reliability, it does not end there. Government interrogation and investigation implicates other constitutional values, and testimonial immunity respects these values. For example, a distinction between testimony and physical evidence indirectly promotes First Amendment values. A rule excluding from criminal cases only defendants' compelled utterances (and perhaps intimate personal papers such as diaries) would lead to acquittals for most eighteenth-century thought crimes—including blasphemy, heresy, and sedition[267]—but it would not be nearly so big a stumbling block to prosecution of murderers and rapists, whose crimes generate nontestimonial fruits like knives and bodies.[268] Thus we do justice to both the Fifth Amendment's literal application beyond the thought crime and to its obviously weaker intuitive appeal in cases of violent crime.

Related to the First Amendment freedoms of thought and conscience is a certain narrow but important protection of "mental privacy" and "noninstrumentalization." A criminal defendant's compelled utterances may often reveal interior mental states—of guilt, conscience, joy, and so on. These compelled words and thoughts may reflect a defendant's inner self—his soul—and are far more likely to emerge in criminal interrogation than in the typical civil case. Under testimonial immunity, government at trial may not directly use a person's compelled inner life as the means of that person's own destruction. The government may directly use only tangible things—fruits—typically focusing on what happened rather than the personal meaning the defendant wishes to attach to these events. In this limited but important sense, testimonial immunity in effect protects a person from being compelled in a criminal case to be a witness against his own inner "self." The government is entitled to, and may use, every man's evidence, but not his soul. A straightforward focus on reliability reaches the same result. Reports of interior mental states are easily misunderstood, notoriously imprecise (depending on a person's mood when reporting), and hard to verify. "How did you feel when you killed her?" is a very different kind of question from "Where is her body buried?"

The "psychological cruelty" of a compelled self-incrimination now appears in a very different light. Conventional accounts focus on *guilty* defendants faced with a "cruel" choice of contempt, self-accusation, or perjury. As noted earlier, we should reject this misplaced effort to shield evildoers from the consequences of their crimes. But once we see that compelled testimony from an *innocent* defendant may be misleading, and may destroy a man who has done no wrong, a different cruelty emerges: the cruelty of forcing someone who knows he is innocent but unpersuasive to take the stand, knowing that his *truthful* testimony may well hang him because a clever prosecutor can twist his words, and make him look guilty before the jury. A desire to protect the *innocent* defendant from *erroneous* conviction—and from the added injury, insult, and cruelty of being forced to cut his own throat with an honest but unpersuasive performance—is wholly consistent with the deep structure of our Bill of Rights.

An added advantage of testimonial immunity is that no "emergency exception" is needed to prevent imminent harm. The need to get fruits in emergency situations—a loaded gun in *Quarles*[269] or *Innis,*[270] or a child in *Bouknight*[271] or *Brewer*[272]—will not create an exception that impermissibly allows compelled testimony itself to be introduced at trial. Justice O'Connor wisely warned against creating a "finespun new doctrine on public safety exigencies incident to custodial interrogation, complete with the hair-splitting distinctions that currently plague our Fourth Amendment jurisprudence."[273]

Finally, the use of depositions and pretrial judicial examination would curb the temptation to police abuse. Questioning would be accomplished in a relatively civilized setting, as in civil litigation, rather than in the rough-and-tumble atmosphere of interrogation at the police station, with its attendant intimidation, sleeplessness, and other physical and psychological pressures. The process would be judicially supervised; refusals to answer and outright lies would be punished with judicial contempt or adverse inferences, not with fists banging on desks and shouted four-letter words. These depositions and hearings would act as the modern equivalent of the nineteenth-century questioning of the accused by a magistrate. Fourth Amendment standards would constrain both the government's right to demand answers in general—the government must justify its decision to single a person out for detention (seizure) and interrogation (search)—and the government's right to ask any particular question. Irrelevant questions, questions for which no foundation had been laid, intrusive or embarrassing questions, repetitive questions—all these should be subject to a general Fourth Amendment test of reasonableness.[274]

The Founding-era history of the self-incrimination slogan in America was bound up with concerns about torture, and this chapter's overall framework attacks the paradigmatic problem of torture on several fronts. While torture can be lawless and unregulated, leaving a suspect's body and mind subject to the whims of examiners, a deposition approach civilizes and controls the process of evidence-gathering. While torture produces unreliable confessions, this chapter's big ideas begin with reliability. While torture is cruel, a holistic constitutional account provides a check by focusing on unreasonable or intrusive Fourth Amendment seizures of the person. (And the fact that even criminal witnesses and civil witnesses and parties—and everyone else, too—must be protected against torture proves that the root antitorture idea is largely a Fourth Amendment idea and not a Fifth Amendment idea.) Finally, torture has at times been particularly likely to occur in cases involving religious and political opponents of the government. In response, testimonial immunity reminds us of the First Amendment values indirectly protected when a defendant's words cannot be introduced at trial.

While testimonial immunity may at first glance seem like a startling break from current interpretations, in fact it is merely an extension of any one of four current doctrines or trends. First, it is a logical extension of *Schmerber's*[275] distinction between physical evidence and testimony. Second, the Court could replace *Kastigar*[276] by following the same reasoning that it followed in *Murphy*[277] to begin replacing *Counselman*[278] with *Kastigar:* intersovereign friction would be eliminated. Third, Justice O'Connor has pointed the way in *Quarles,* where she suggested always allowing fruits in for mere *Miranda* violations.[279] And finally, an extension of the inevitable discovery doctrine would simply presume that fruits have an independent source and thus can be introduced at trial.

Fifth Amendment jurisprudence, like that of the Fourth Amendment, needs to regain coherence. In Fourth Amendment case law, *Boyd's*[280] (con)fusion of the Fourth and Fifth Amendments led to a constitutionally flawed exclusionary rule, motivated by the mistaken notion that the Fourth, like the Fifth, requires that certain items be excluded from a criminal case.[281] In Fifth Amendment case law, *Boyd's* (con)fusion has led to the mistaken notion that the Fifth, like the Fourth, is about *things*—"effects" or fruits—and not just words. Instead, the privilege requires immunity that is absolute but narrow. Fact gathering should be accomplished under circumstances that are both more civilized and more apt to produce the truth. Instead of the current wide divergence between civil and criminal discovery practice, the two should be brought closer together. Finders of fact in criminal cases should not be deprived of reliable, highly probative evidence. A legal system that ignores the truth is simply not doing its job, and neither is a court that cannot make the Constitution cohere.

3 Sixth Amendment First Principles

In all criminal prosecutions, the accused shall enjoy the right to a speedy and public trial, by an impartial jury of the State and district wherein the crime shall have been committed, which district shall have been previously ascertained by law, and to be informed of the nature and cause of the accusation; to be confronted with the witnesses against him; to have compulsory process for obtaining witnesses in his favor, and to have the Assistance of Counsel for his defence.

The Sixth Amendment is the heartland of constitutional criminal procedure, yet the legal community lacks a good map of its basic contours, a good sense of its underlying ecosystem, a good plan for its careful cultivation. Amid all the amendment's tightly configured clauses, scholars, lawyers, and judges have often lost their way. The result, at times, has been bad constitutional law and bad criminal procedure.

In this chapter I offer a general framework for understanding the Sixth Amendment's first principles—for seeing how its many clauses fit together and cohere with other constitutional clauses and principles outside the amendment. To illuminate the internal architecture of the Sixth Amendment, I shall organize my account around three clusters of rights. First is the basic right to a *speedy* trial, a right embodied in a single clause that, as we shall see, in fact protects a cluster of distinct interests, including (a) a physical liberty interest in avoiding prolonged pretrial detention; (b) a mental liberty and reputational interest in minimizing unjust accusation; and (c) a reliability interest in assuring that the accuracy of the trial itself is not undermined by an extended accusation period.

After this speedy trial cluster comes a cluster of rights to a *public* trial—a trial of, by, and before the people. In a republican government, a trial should be a *res publica*, a public thing, the people's thing. Included in this cluster are the rights to (a) a trial held in public, (b) featuring an impartial jury of the people, (c) who come from the community where the crime occurred.

Finally comes the cluster of *fair* trial rights, encompassing notice and the opportunity to hear and be heard. Put slightly differently, this last cluster safeguards the right to know, and defend oneself against, an accusation of criminal wrongdoing. Textually, this cluster encompasses the rights to (a) be informed of the nature and cause of accusation; (b) be confronted with prosecution witnesses; (c) compel the production of defense witnesses; and (d) enjoy the assistance of counsel in defending against the accusation.

The deep principles underlying the Sixth Amendment's three clusters and many clauses (and, I submit, underlying constitutional criminal procedure generally) are the protection of innocence and the pursuit of truth. The *speedy* trial right protects the innocent man from prolonged de facto punishment—extended accusations that limit his liberty and besmirch his good name—before he has had a fair chance to defend himself. If government accuses an innocent man and then refuses to suspend its accusation, it must give him the right, speedily, to clear himself at trial and regain his good name and full liberty. And if government holds the accused in extended pretrial detention, courts must ensure that the accuracy of the trial itself will not thereby be undermined—as might occur if an innocent defendant's prolonged detention itself causes the loss of key exculpatory evidence.

So too, the *public* trial right protects the innocent man from an erroneous verdict of guilt. Witnesses for the prosecution may be less willing to lie or shade the truth with the public looking on; and bystanders with knowledge of the underlying events can bring missing information to the attention of court and counsel. A defendant will be convicted only if the people of the community (via the jury) believe the criminal accusation—believe both that he did the acts he is accused of, and that these acts are indeed criminal and worthy of the community's moral condemnation. This last aspect—passing judgment on a defendant's normative guilt or innocence—is an especially important part of the public trial idea.

Finally, the *fair* trial right also protects the innocent man from an erroneous verdict of guilt, though its safeguards highlight factual innocence ("I didn't do it") more than normative innocence ("I did it, but I did not thereby offend the public's moral code"). Counsel, confrontation, and compulsory process are designed as great engines by which an innocent man can make the truth of his innocence visible to the jury and the public.

In General: Framing The Issues

To say, as I do, that the Sixth Amendment is generally designed to elicit truth and protect innocence might at first seem either dangerous or trivial.[1] If my reading of the amendment protects *only* innocent men and women, it would indeed be dangerous—surely the amendment protects all accused persons, the guilty along with the innocent, in affirming rights to speedy, public, and fair trials. If, alternatively, my reading of the amendment concedes this obvious point, it might seem to border on the trivial: if the amendment protects both the guilty and innocent, how can it be said, in any deep or interesting way, to be about innocence? Who could be against the (trivial) idea that innocent people have rights too—the same rights as the guilty?

The above dilemma, I submit, is a false one. My account of the amendment is neither totalitarian nor trivial. Many parts of the amendment, rightly read, do not protect only *innocents*, but they do protect only *innocence;* they protect the guilty only as an incidental by-product of protecting the innocent because of their innocence.[2] Put another way, although the guilty will often have the same rights as the innocent, they should never have more, and never because they are guilty.[3]

These last points, too, might seem trivial to ordinary Americans— they reflect common sense—but they sharply conflict with various doctrines of modern constitutional criminal procedure that many judges and well-trained lawyers take for granted these days. These modern doctrines create what I shall call an upside-down effect, providing the guilty with more protection than, and often at the expense of, the innocent.[4]

For example, as we saw in Chapter 1, our Fourth Amendment case law at times has suggested that criminal suspects receive more privacy protection than presumptively law-abiding citizens:[5] exceptions to the so-called probable cause and warrant requirements are apparently easier to justify when the government is not seeking evidence from criminal suspects but is instead intruding on privacy interests of individual members of the general public.[6] Yet nothing in the text, history, or structure of the Fourth Amendment supports such an upside-down approach to privacy rights.[7] On the remedy side of the Fourth Amendment, case law is likewise upside down. The exclusionary rule creates huge windfalls for guilty defendants, but gives no direct remedy to the innocent woman wrongly searched.[8] The guiltier you are, the more evidence the cops find, the bigger the exclusionary rule windfall; but if the cops know you are innocent and just want to hassle you (because of your race, or politics, or whatever), the exclusionary rule offers exactly zero deterrence or compensation. Here, too, nothing in the Fourth Amendment's text, history, or structure supports such an upside-down and truth-suppressing remedial scheme.

As we saw in Chapter 2, current interpretations of the Fifth Amendment's self-incrimination clause are likewise upside down. Courts and commentators dwell on the so-called "cruel trilemma" of self-accusation, perjury, or contempt faced by some defendants. But this classic trilemma arises only if a person is in fact guilty. (Otherwise he need not directly accuse himself by speaking truthfully and commits no perjury when he asserts his innocence.) Why is the trilemma so "cruel" if one can avoid it simply by not committing crimes? By contrast, courts and commentators have often overlooked the distinctively cruel choice faced by some *innocent* defendants who, if forced to take the stand, might (say, because of nerves or an off-putting manner) hurt their own cause and be *erroneously* convicted.

This upside-down account of the cruel trilemma has had a huge effect in self-incrimination law. Its misplaced tenderness towards the guilty has led courts to needlessly exclude, in the name of self-incrimination clause values, reliable physical evidence of guilt—evidence that is in no sense Fifth Amendment "witness[ing]."[9] This exclusion is a windfall to the guilty without any offsetting benefit for the innocent. Even worse, an overbroad reading of Fifth Amendment self-incrimination has led courts to deny an innocent defendant her explicit Sixth Amendment right to compulsory process against a guilty witness who asserts his own right to avoid the cruel trilemma. Our innocent defendant knows who committed the crime, but today she cannot force him to take the stand in her own trial, even though her liberty and good name—perhaps even her life—are on the line.[10] Here too, nothing in the Constitution, rightly read, supports this upside-down and truth-suppressing effect.

In the first two chapters, I documented and critiqued these upside-down effects in current interpretations of the Fourth and Fifth Amendments, and here I propose to do the same for the Sixth Amendment. The Sixth Amendment speedy trial clause is my Exhibit A. Perhaps influenced by misguided Fourth and Fifth Amendment doctrines excluding reliable evidence of guilt, the Supreme Court, in the name of the speedy trial clause, has created the mother of all upside-down exclusionary rules. "The only possible remedy" for speedy trial violations, the Court has unanimously proclaimed, is dismissal of the case with prejudice—in effect, excluding all evidence of guilt forever.[11] At first blush, the Court's pronouncement seems plausible: if too much time has already elapsed, how can the government ever hold a constitutionally proper trial in the future? But as we shall see, this initial reaction is wrong in just about every way imaginable. As a matter of logic, there are many other possible remedies. As a matter of general remedial theory, dismissal with prejudice is rarely the remedy that best fits the legal rights and interests that have been violated. As a matter of history, some alternative remedies have deep roots in the common law underlying speedy trial. (The concept of dismissal with prejudice as the "only possible remedy" has no such roots.) As a matter of text and structure, dismissal with prejudice makes no sense as a response to many types of speedy trial violations. And as a matter of precedent, the modern Supreme Court has said and done many things that are logically inconsistent with what it has said and done about dismissal with prejudice.

The speedy trial dismissal remedy provides a windfall for the guilty while leaving the innocent defendant, who has suffered excessive detention or unjustified stigma owing to an extended accusation, uncompensated. (In this respect, dismissal resembles the Fourth Amendment exclusionary rule.) But dismissal is even more upside down than this in practice. Because judges (rightly) see the remedy as extreme, they are loath in any given case to admit that the speedy trial right was indeed violated. As a result, many innocent defendants are made affirmatively worse off, suffering greater violations of their explicit constitutional rights. (In this respect, dismissal resembles current doctrine under the Fifth Amendment self-incrimination clause.)

A sensible constitutional criminal procedure, I submit, must systematically right upside-down effects in current Fourth, Fifth, and Sixth Amendment doctrine. It must also begin to take constitutional text seriously. I have argued that the words of the Fourth Amendment really do mean what they say. They do not require warrants or probable cause for all searches and seizures, but they do require that all searches and seizures be reasonable. The words do not require exclusion of reliable evidence in criminal trials, but they do presuppose common law and other property and tort law remedies that secure Americans in their "persons, houses, papers, and effects." So too, I have argued that the words of the Fifth Amendment mean what they say. The words "same offence" in the double jeopardy clause really do mean "same offence," rather than "greater and lesser-included offences" or "same factual transaction" or any number of other things.[12] The self-incrimination clause really means that a criminal defendant must not be forced to be a "witness" against himself "in" a "criminal case"—by taking the stand at trial or having a compelled out-of-court affidavit or transcript introduced. But the clause does not say that if a person is forced to be a witness against himself before Congress, or in a civil case, or anywhere else outside his own criminal case, the fruits of that witnessing must be excluded from his criminal case. Unless the witnessing itself occurs inside his criminal case—in person or by affidavit or transcript—the words of the self-incrimination clause, and its innocence-protecting spirit, are satisfied.

A similar attention to the word "witness" will neatly solve many of the problems that currently beset Sixth Amendment confrontation clause doctrine. The modern Court has viewed the clause as implicated whenever hearsay comes into the criminal courtroom: If in-court *A* testifies about what out-of-court *B* said, the defendant's right to confront *B* is at stake.[13] But surely all hearsay cannot be unconstitutional. At common law, the traditional hearsay "rule" was notoriously un-ruly, recognizing countless exceptions to its basic preference for live testimony; and more recent statutes have proliferated exceptions. But the words and grammar of the confrontation clause are emphatically rule-ish: "In *all* criminal prosecutions, the accused *shall* enjoy the *right* . . . to *be confronted* with *the* witnesses against him"—no ifs, ands, or buts. And so the modern Court has put itself in a bind. If the clause does truly prohibit all hearsay, as its grammar might imply, it is utterly unworkable; but to make it workable—by recognizing commonsensical exceptions—is to offend its seeming grammar.

The obvious solution is to heed the word *witness* and its ordinary, everyday meaning. If I tell my mom what I saw yesterday, and she later testifies in court, I am not the witness; she is. Not all out-of-court declarants within the meaning of the so-called hearsay rule are "witnesses" within the meaning of the confrontation clause. In the Fifth Amendment self-incrimination clause, "witness" means a person who physically takes the stand to testify, or (to prevent government evasion of the spirit of the clause) a person whose out-of-court affidavit or deposition (prepared by the government for in-court use) is introduced as in-court testimony. In the Sixth Amendment the word "witness" means the same thing, and for the same reason. Once we see this, the Court's current confrontation clause conundrum vanishes. The clause means what it says, and the strict rule it lays down makes sense as a rule.

A sensible Sixth Amendment jurisprudence must begin with plain meaning, but it must not end there. Though the rules of the amendment make sense as rules, deeper principles lurk beneath the rules. The amendment does mean what it says; but sometimes it means even more. In many contexts, the *expressio unius* maxim is a sound one, but in the Sixth Amendment we must not apply the maxim woodenly.[14] The amendment recognizes that the *accused* has a right to a public trial, but perhaps the public trial right is also a right of, well, the public itself—the people. Likewise, the amendment vests the *accused* with a right to a jury, but surely the people themselves have a jury right too. Article III says that "[t]he Trial of all Crimes . . . shall be by Jury,"[15] whether an accused who pleads not guilty wants one or not;[16] and nothing in the words or history of the Sixth Amendment reveals any purpose to repeal that clear command.[17] More generally, of course, the Ninth Amendment explicitly tells us not to infer by *expressio unius* that a "right[] . . . [of] the people" has been surrendered.[18] And this explicit reminder seems especially apt when we deal with what are quite literally rights of *the people*—rights, that is, of the public and populace at large.[19]

But the Ninth Amendment reminder must radiate more broadly than this when we read the Sixth Amendment, lest we reach absurd results. The confrontation clause says that the accused has a right to observe and examine the government's *witnesses,* but surely the accused must also have a right to observe and examine the government's *physical evidence,* although the amendment does not explicitly say so. The compulsory process clause affirms the defendant's right to *forcibly subpoena* a witness; but surely the Constitution must also protect the defendant's right to present friendly witnesses who *volunteer* to testify on his behalf, although the amendment again does not explicitly say so.[20] If the defendant has a Sixth Amendment right to present exculpatory *witnesses* to the jury, surely he must also have a right to present exculpatory *physical evidence,* although, here too, the amendment does not explicitly say so.

If we insist on being textualists and only textualists, we can hide behind the explicit texts of the Ninth Amendment and the due process clause[21] to fill in the obvious textual gaps in the Sixth Amendment. But this hypertextual strategy misses how the rules of the Sixth Amendment themselves should influence sensible due process analysis. Behind the words of the Sixth Amendment rules are indeed "postulates which limit and control,"[22] "emanations" and "penumbras,"[23] spirit and structure as well as text—in short, Sixth Amendment principles as well as Sixth Amendment rules. And the first principles underlying the rules are, I submit, the protection of innocence and the commitment to truth-seeking trials. These first principles, of course, explain why it seems so obvious that a defendant must have a right to defend himself in certain ways not explicitly covered by the words of the confrontation and compulsory process clauses.

Protecting the innocent, pursuing the truth, and respecting the text—these, I claim, are the basic elements of a sensible Sixth Amendment jurisprudence (and, more generally, a sensible jurisprudence of constitutional criminal procedure). To see more clearly how this jurisprudence might work, and what it would entail in the Sixth Amendment, we need to get specific.

In Particular: Speedy Trial

The Supreme Court has said and done a great deal about the speedy trial clause in the last three decades: (1) It has repeatedly identified three major and distinct interests protected by the clause—an interest in avoiding prolonged pretrial detention, an interest in minimizing the anxiety and loss of reputation accompanying public accusation, and an interest in assuring the ultimate fairness of a long-delayed trial.[24] (2) It has made clear that the "major evils" of pretrial restraints on liberty and loss of reputation occasioned by accusation "exist quite apart from actual or possible prejudice to an accused's defense."[25] (3) It has held that the clause, by its plain meaning, simply does not apply to the time period between the commission of a crime and the date when a person is "accused" by the government (typically via arrest or indictment).[26] (4) Likewise, it has held that when a person ceases to be "accused"—because the government formally drops charges while retaining the right to reindict later—this nonaccusation period does not count against the government for speedy trial clause purposes.[27] (5) It has held that if delay during the preaccusation period (and presumably the nonaccusation period during which formal charges are dropped altogether) compromises the defendant's ability to defend herself fairly at trial, the "primary guarantee" against injustice comes from "the applicable statute of limitations," but due process principles may also prevent the trying of egregiously stale charges.[28] (6) It has noted that the judicial remedy of dismissing a case with prejudice for speedy trial clause violations is "unsatisfactorily severe . . . because it means that a defendant who may be guilty of a serious crime will go free, without having been tried. Such a remedy is more serious than [the Fourth Amendment] exclusionary rule."[29] (7) Nevertheless, it has also said, repeatedly and unanimously, that dismissal with prejudice—that is, dismissal with no possibility of refiling charges later—is "the only possible remedy" for speedy trial clause violations.[30]

What's wrong with this picture? What's wrong, I submit, is that proposition (7) simply does not follow from, and is in fact logically and practically inconsistent with, propositions (1)–(6). The first six propositions are sound, with firm roots in constitutional text, history, and structure, and in common sense. But proposition (7) betrays all this.[31]

Precedential Logic and Remedial Theory

Consider first some basic premises of general remedial theory as applied to propositions (1)–(6). If, as proposition (1) holds, there are indeed three distinct legal interests underlying the speedy trial clause, it would be odd that, remedially, one size fits all—that only one possible remedy (and an admittedly drastic one at that) exists. Each legal interest has a unique size and shape, and its own uniquely apt remedy package. Remedies should fit rights, and if rights (or "legal interests") do not come in a one-size-fits-all package, neither should remedies.

If Andy is arrested on the day of the crime and held in jail pretrial, let's stipulate that Andy's speedy trial right to be free from prolonged pretrial detention will be violated unless he is brought to trial within, say, a month of his incarceration.[32] But if Bill is accused of the same crime on the same day and is free on his own recognizance pending trial, a delay of more than a month between accusation and trial would not necessarily be unconstitutional. A wholly distinct interest—an interest in minimizing Bill's reputation loss and anxiety caused by public accusation—is at stake, and *that* interest will not be violated unless the accusation period stretches out for, say, one year. The fair-trial legal interest is different still. If Cindy is never even accused of the crime until eighteen months after the event, the speedy trial clause would not generally demand a trial immediately after indictment even though the evidence in Cindy's trial may well be more stale than in Andy's and Bill's trials.

But this point about speedy trial rights has dramatic implications for speedy trial remedies. If our incarcerated defendant Andy demands a speedy trial on day 30, and the prosecutor is unable to proceed to trial forthwith, a judge could simply order Andy released on his own recognizance, giving the prosecutor (in our hypothetical) eleven more months. Thus, the government will never have violated the speedy trial clause in this situation; Andy's case will become just like Bill's.[33] But suppose instead that our trial judge fails to do the right thing on day 30, and she wrongly keeps Andy in detention for, say, five more months and only then releases him from jail. Suppose further that a trial is held four months after release—ten months after the crime, arrest, and initial detention—and that the extra five months of unjustified detention have not irreversibly compromised Andy's ability to defend himself fairly at trial.[34] Has the speedy trial clause been violated in this scenario? Of course, by hypothesis. Andy's legal interest in avoiding undue pretrial detention was violated by five extra months in jail. *But the trial itself did not violate the speedy trial clause, nor did the date of the trial.*[35] The constitutional wrong here is *detention*, not the *trial* or its *timing*; if the judge had released Andy on day 30, the trial could have been held ten months after the crime, arrest, and initial detention without any violation of the speedy trial clause. Andy's case would have been no different from Bill's. Without this timely release, Andy's overlong detention is a constitutional violation regardless of when, or even whether, a trial later takes place. (This is a key implication of proposition (2) as laid down in the *Marion* case.)[36] Undue detention is an unjustified trespass—an unreasonable seizure of the person. This trespass, this unreasonable seizure, is a special outrage if Andy is in fact innocent—if the government would have dropped the charges against him anyway, rather than going to trial, or if the government would have lost the case against him at trial.[37] Dismissal with prejudice is a huge windfall to Andy if guilty—it makes him unjustifiably better off than a guilty Bill—but fails to fully remedy the constitutional wrong perpetrated against Andy if innocent.

As a remedy, dismissal with prejudice is thus an inapt, misfitting remedy for the legal interest violated. It is perverse and upside down. (Indeed, it simply magnifies the perversity of the Fourth Amendment exclusionary rule's approach to unreasonable searches and seizures generally, giving the guilty a windfall and the innocent a brushoff.) A constitutionally apt enforcement and remedial regime for Andy's liberty rights will call for injunctive and habeas suits, and framework statutes, to prevent or limit ongoing violations of his bodily liberty; after-the-fact compensatory and (in egregious cases) punitive damages for any unconstitutional detention time actually served; and sentencing offsets (if Andy is ever convicted) for time served to avoid double punishment.[38]

Next, consider the case of Bill—accused the day of the crime but never detained pretrial. If, one year later, Bill moves for an immediate trial and the trial judge grants his motion, no speedy trial right will ever have been violated. But suppose, instead, that our trial judge wrongly denies Bill's motion and he does not get his trial until five months later, seventeen months after initial accusation. Suppose further that the extra five months of undue anxiety and reputation loss that Bill suffers because of the overlong accusation in no way compromise his ability to defend himself fairly at trial.[39] Has the speedy trial clause been violated in this scenario? Of course, by hypothesis. Bill's legal interest in his good name and peace of mind was violated by five extra months of accusation. *But the trial itself did not violate the speedy trial clause, nor did the date of the trial.*[40] The constitutional wrong here is *overlong accusation and stigma,* not the *trial* or its *timing.* If the judge had dismissed Bill's accusation after one year, with explicit leave to the prosecutor to reindict whenever she was ready to proceed to trial forthwith, the Sixth Amendment accusation period would have been tolled, and the government-created stigma created by pending accusation would have lasted no more than one year. (This is the clear meaning of proposition (4) as laid down in the *MacDonald* and *Loud Hawk* cases.)[41] In this scenario, upon reindictment five months later, a trial could have been held seventeen months after initial accusation, without any violation of the speedy trial clause. Bill's case would have been no different from Cindy's.[42] Without this tolling of accusation via dismissal and reindictment, Bill's loss of his good name for five unjustified months is a constitutional violation regardless of when, or even whether, a trial later takes place. (Again, this follows from proposition (2) as laid down in *Marion.*)[43] Besmirching an innocent man's good name while denying him a quick chance to clear himself is a kind of verbal assault—a reputational mugging.[44] Of course, if Bill is in fact *guilty* as charged, he may lack good ground for complaint. In effect, truth of the accusation may be a defense that renders Bill's injury moot.[45] (And so, the constitutional violation of guilty Bill's reputation interest during the extra five months might be a species of harmless error.)

As with Andy's case, a dismissal with prejudice here would be perverse and upside down. The guilty man gets a windfall and the innocent one gets nothing for five unconstitutional months of mud on his name. A constitutionally apt enforcement and remedial regime for Bill's reputation right will call for timely judicial orders to either prosecute now or drop (for now) the pending accusation, with leave to reindict later—orders that would prevent or limit ongoing assaults on reputation; a requirement (at least for federal defendants) that any delayed trial be preceded by a fresh grand jury reindictment;[46] and after-the-fact compensatory and (in egregious cases) punitive remedies for innocent defendants who have suffered false and prolonged assaults on their good names.

Consider finally the case of Cindy—accused eighteen months after the crime, and free on her own recognizance until her trial, say, three months later. Suppose at trial Cindy seeks to dismiss her case with prejudice. She claims that her right to defend fairly has been irreversibly harmed by the long time period between crime and trial. Critical exculpatory evidence that was once available has now been lost in the mist of time; key defense witnesses have died or moved, or their memories have faded. But if these things happened in the first eighteen months, preindictment, Cindy's speedy trial claim is a clear loser. Under propositions (3) and (4) as laid down in *Marion, MacDonald,* and *Loud Hawk,* the clause applies only to "accused" persons, and simply has no relevance to a preaccusation (and presumably any tolled nonaccusation) period.[47] Even if all the evidence loss occurred in the final three (accusation period) months, Cindy should not yet be home free. If the clause applies only to evils in the accusation period, doesn't logic suggest that it should apply only to evils caused by *accusation itself?*[48] In other words, doesn't it apply only to harms that occur *when and because* one is "accused"? If so, Cindy should need to show that the accusation itself helped cause the loss of evidence. If not, Cindy's speedy trial claim should be no different from the claim of a comparably situated defendant—call her Denise—indicted twenty-one months after the crime, with the government ready, willing, and able to proceed forthwith. But since Denise has no good speedy trial claim—all this delay occurred preindictment, and thus outside her accusation period—Cindy should have no good speedy trial claim either.[49] Because no speedy trial right is violated in Cindy's and Denise's cases, no issue of speedy trial remedy—of possible dismissal with prejudice—should properly arise.

Beyond any applicable statute of limitations protection, Cindy and Denise may also try to invoke the broad innocence-protection principle underlying the due process clause. Unlike the clear words and logic of the speedy trial clause, which focus only on the accusation period and the distinctive harms caused by accusation, due process principles can focus on the threat to innocence posed by evidentiary staleness over the entire period between the crime and the trial. (This is the meaning of proposition (5), derived from the *Ewell, Marion,* and *Lovasco* cases.)[50] But in the absence of intentional governmental misconduct—purposefully delaying indictment for mere tactical advantage, in the hope, say, that a key alibi would die—Cindy and Denise are unlikely to win dismissal with prejudice under the due process clause. Their main protection will come from another innocence-protecting due process principle—the *Winship* principle that the government must prove its case beyond reasonable doubt.[51] Cindy and Denise will be free to argue at trial that the staleness of the case should raise reasonable doubt in the minds of the jury. Because the government bears a heavy burden of proof, added uncertainty caused by long lapses of time often helps defendants.[52]

In the hypotheticals discussed thus far, dismissals with prejudice under proposition (7) would seem to undercut the logic underlying propositions (1)–(6).[53] Contrary to proposition (7), dismissal with prejudice is not the "only possible" remedy, or even an apt one in many situations. But is it *ever* appropriate, as a constitutional mandate? Let's consider again defendants Andy, Bill, and Cindy.

Suppose, in Andy's case, that unconstitutionally prolonged pretrial detention—detention beyond the permissible one-month period—itself caused irreversible loss of evidence and the like, to Andy's detriment, and fundamentally weakened his ability to present key exculpatory evidence and make his defense at trial. Here, Andy might plausibly claim that any trial would itself be unfair, and that the unfairness was related, both causally and analytically (i.e., both factually and legally), to a constitutionally unspeedy accusation period. He was in jail too long only because he was *accused* too long, and he has irreversibly lost access to key evidence because of his incarceration, and not merely because of the passage of time.[54] In such a case, dismissal with prejudice might be an apt remedy.

But note here how this remedy has now been pegged to *innocence protection* and *truth-seeking:* Because of the government's own constitutional violation, reliable exculpatory evidence and the like have vanished. Even here, dismissal with prejudice is a severe sanction. A lesser fair-trial remedy[55] might let Andy's lawyers tell the jury his sob story of government-created impediments to his efforts to locate key evidence and witnesses, and let the jury draw whatever inferences it chooses, with Andy benefiting from *Winship*'s command to resolve all reasonable doubt in his favor.[56] But if instead dismissal with prejudice occurs, it occurs precisely to protect a possibly innocent Andy *because of his possible innocence.*[57]

It's hard to think of a similar scenario for (accused but undetained) Bill. It might be argued that the longer Bill's name is unconstitutionally tarred by an overly extended accusation, the harder it will be to find a fair jury, and thus trial fairness itself is at stake. But prospective jurors rarely know about indictments in run-of-the-mill cases; are dismissible for cause unless they promise to base their verdict solely on the evidence presented at trial; and are told that accusation itself is not evidence. (That, after all, is one of the core meanings of the legal presumption of innocence.) What's more, the possibility of continuances and venue transfers make it highly unlikely that any harm to a fair trial caused by Bill's overlong accusation will truly be irreversible.[58] (To avoid subjecting Bill to additional stigma during a continuance caused by an already overlong accusation period, his indictment could be formally dropped during a continuance period, after which a prosecutor would need to seek a new indictment.)[59]

Finally, consider Cindy's case. Suppose that she can show that prosecutors intentionally delayed indictment solely for tactical advantage, in order to impede her efforts to put on a strong defense at trial. Suppose further that as a result of this strategy she has indeed forever lost certain key exculpatory evidence or testimony. If so, due process principles might justify dismissal with prejudice, but once again, dismissal would be designed to protect Cindy because of her possible innocence.[60] Dismissal would punish government misbehavior, but on a very different logic from that of the Fourth Amendment exclusionary rule. The exclusionary rule punishes government for trying to *introduce* reliable evidence, whereas due process dismissal with prejudice would punish government for, in effect, trying to *suppress* a defendant's reliable evidence.[61]

The foregoing analysis has been based on general remedial logic, in the light of propositions (1)–(6) in current case law. Several big ideas about the speedy trial clause have done much of the work. For starters, the clause focuses distinctively and exclusively on harms created during and by criminal accusation. Next, these harms take three distinct shapes, implicating physical liberty, reputation and peace of mind, and reliable trials. Finally, dismissal with prejudice is never an apt response to physical liberty and reputation harms. Rather, dismissal is appropriate only in cases of reliable trial harm—in cases where the trial itself poses an unacceptable risk that, because of the government's own prolongation of accusation, an innocent man may be erroneously convicted.[62]

What remains is to root these big ideas about speedy trial clause rights and remedies in constitutional text, history, and structure.

Text, History, and Structure

Rights. The Sixth Amendment proclaims that "[i]n all criminal prosecutions, the accused shall enjoy the right to a speedy . . . trial." By its terms, this clause seems to apply only when the government has "accused" a person and initiated a "criminal prosecution[]." Elsewhere the amendment's district clause speaks of the time when "the crime shall have been committed," but contains no language suggesting that this is the moment when the *speedy trial* clock starts ticking. On the contrary, the tense of the district clause's "shall have been committed" plainly contrasts with the tense of the speedy trial clause's "shall enjoy," suggesting that the speedy trial right comes into play after the crime, not alongside it. Indeed, the amendment also proclaims that "[i]n all criminal prosecutions, the accused shall enjoy the right . . . to be informed of the nature and cause of the *accusation*." This modified repetition of the word *accused* strongly confirms that the Sixth Amendment as a whole is *accusation-based*. It is hard to imagine what the "nature and cause" clause could possibly mean prior to governmental accusation; and since this clause is syntactically interwoven with the very word *accused* in the speedy trial clause, plain grammar reinforces plain meaning: "accused" must mean "accused." Common sense provides further support: prior to accusation, how can we know precisely which statutorily defined crime the government must prove at a speedy trial? As the Court put the point in *Marion*, "[t]he framers could hardly have selected less appropriate language if they had intended the speedy trial provision to protect against pre-accusation delay."[63]

History and structure confirm the point. The *Marion* Court found "nothing in the circumstances surrounding the adoption of the Amendment indicating that it does not mean what it appears to say."[64] On the contrary, at the time of the Founding, leading common law commentators and landmark English legislation addressing trial timing had identified pretrial detention—detention triggered by governmental accusation rather than the commission of the crime simpliciter—as a key concern.[65] The Eighth Amendment's prohibition of "[e]xcessive bail" reflects a similar concern, thus reinforcing our reading of the Sixth.[66] Even more dramatic reinforcement for an accusation-based reading of the Sixth Amendment comes from the Fifth Amendment's requirement of grand jury indictment for any serious federal crime.[67] Precisely because criminal accusation itself creates distinctive risks to the "accused," the accusation process requires special safeguards; no person will be forced to run the risks of accusation unless a large panel representing the people—a grand jury—has decided to subject him to those risks. All this helps confirm our logical inference that the speedy trial clause protects a person not merely *after* he has become "accused," but *because* he has become "accused"—protects him, that is, from the distinctive risks of accusation itself.

What are those risks? Here too, a close examination of the Fifth Amendment can help illuminate the Sixth: "No person shall be held to answer for a capital, or otherwise infamous crime, unless on a presentment or indictment of a Grand Jury." Note the word *held*. The word is not merely metaphoric but also literal. Upon criminal accusation one's physical body is vulnerable to physical detention, pretrial. Note also the word *person*: "No *person* shall be *held* . . . " This embodied reference immediately follows two embodied references in the Fourth Amendment, protecting Americans' physical "persons" from being "searched" or "seized" unreasonably,[68] and it immediately precedes a dramatically physical reference in the Fifth Amendment's double jeopardy clause to the "life or limb" of "any person."[69] (Together, these four tightly clustered references are the only times the words *persons* and *person* appear in the Bill of Rights.) Precisely because one's very body may be held upon accusation of criminal wrongdoing, the speedy trial clause demands that a *trial* occur *speedily* after *accusation*. At such a trial, of course, an innocent man can, in the words of the Fifth Amendment, "answer" his "indictment"—can, in the words of the Sixth Amendment, make "his defence" against the "criminal . . . accusation." And if the innocent man prevails at this speedy, public, and fair trial, he immediately gets his "person" back and wins release from the cell in which he may be "held" during the accusation period.

But public accusation threatens more than a person's body; it also assaults his good name. The text of the speedy trial clause, after all, is not limited to those accused persons held in pretrial detention, but rather extends to "accused" individuals in "*all* criminal prosecutions." So, to make full sense of the text, we must focus on the harms inherent in every criminal accusation. Every criminal accusation, of course, is an attack on the accused's reputation—a charge of "criminal" wrongdoing in the words of the speedy trial clause, of "infamous" misconduct in the analogous words of the grand jury clause. At common law, a false accusation of criminal behavior was viewed as defamation per se.[70] (Note the obvious etymological link between de*fam*ation and accusations of in*fam*ous crime.) And as with pretrial detention, each additional day of accusation was a fresh assault, a new injury. Here too, the innocent man would want a *trial* to *speedily* follow *accusation,* so that he could offer his "answer" and put on his "defence." And if the innocent man can prevail at this speedy, public, and fair trial, he puts an end to the accusation of infamy and wins back his good name.

Of course, the innocent man might also lose at trial. If so, the detention (if any) of his body and the necessary assaults on his soul during the accusation period may merely be a foretaste of the injuries and indignities that may be heaped upon him after conviction. And here we see the final injury inherent in accusation itself: accusation puts a person on a path of peril. Formally, accusation and indictment shove a person onto a legal road whose destination can never be certain even for the innocent man. At the end of this road may hang a noose, as the Fifth Amendment reminds us in no less than three grim phrases: "*capital* . . . crime," "jeopardy of *life* or limb," and "deprived of *life,* liberty or, property." As we shall see, much of the rest of the Sixth Amendment was designed to reduce the risk that a noose would be wrapped around an innocent neck; and so it would be structurally odd if the speedy trial clause of that same amendment ignored this risk. On the contrary, it makes sense to read the clause as prohibiting situations where an extended accusation period itself could substantially increase the likelihood of an innocent man's being erroneously convicted. Again, the risk to innocence under the clause must not come from the mere passage of time—the standard evidentiary staleness issue addressed by statutes of limitations—but must somehow be traceable to an extended *accusation*.[71]

To insist that the speedy trial clause focuses not on ordinary evidentiary staleness but only on threats after and because of accusation does not leave defendants in egregiously stale cases constitutionally naked. The broad language of the due process clause is not limited by the language and logic of accusation; and so it can properly be deployed to address long delays between *crime* and trial.[72] The due process clause must supplement the speedy trial clause in at least one other respect. Although a defendant may seek to waive his right to a speedy trial, the speedy trial clause does not, by its terms, confer on him a general constitutional right to an *un*speedy trial. In general, a defendant has no constitutional right to stop the trial train (perhaps with the hope that governmental evidence will, over time, fade faster than his own defense evidence). But if the government seeks to go to trial so quickly that a defendant truly cannot assemble his defense, at some point due process will demand delay, lest an innocent man suffer an *undue* risk of erroneous conviction. Though this due process right goes beyond the text of the speedy trial clause, its innocence-protecting logic vindicates the deep structure of that clause, of the Sixth Amendment as a whole, and of constitutional criminal procedure generally.[73]

Remedies. Having consulted text, history, and structure to deduce the proper nature of speedy trial rights, we must now look to the same sources for guidance on speedy trial remedies.

The bodily liberty interest. Consider pretrial detention. The Founders' first line of defense came from the glory of the common law, the Great Writ of habeas corpus. Judges must issue this writ to end or soften the conditions of unduly oppressive pretrial detention. The aptness of the Great Writ to address the specific problem of pretrial detention was the centerpiece of the celebrated English Habeas Corpus Act of 1679.[74] This document stood alongside Magna Charta and the English Bill of Rights of 1689 as a towering common law lighthouse of liberty—a beacon by which framing lawyers in America consciously steered their course.[75]

We should not then be surprised that the only provision in the entire Constitution addressing the technical issue of remedies with any specificity was an Article I clause safeguarding the Great Writ.[76]

But even though habeas must be the first line of defense, it cannot be the only gun in our remedial arsenal. If, in Andy's case, a judge properly issues a writ on day 30, ordering Andy's release, habeas here is less a *remedy* than a *prevention* of any violation from ever occurring.[77] If, instead, a judge issues the writ only weeks or months later, habeas can limit the violation of bodily liberty and prevent fresh assaults, but it does not remedy the wrong done by detention after day 30 but before the writ issues. Habeas does not make Andy whole.

Here is where after-the-fact compensatory and punitive damages come in. Consider, for example, the Framers' clearly established regime for vindicating the Fourth Amendment—for remedying past wrongs and deterring future wrongs. Suppose a constable in the early Republic unconstitutionally arrested John Doe, without a warrant, without good reason, but with, say, a statute that conferred sweeping and arbitrary arrest powers on all constables. This arrest was, of course, a trespass against Doe's person. Doe could sue the constable in trespass, seeking compensatory and punitive damages for the outrage upon his person. The constable, in turn, would plead governmental authority: a statute authorized the trespass and in effect trumped the tort suit. In a world without a written Constitution, the constable's answer might have been a winner. Government (the argument would go) may do things that private persons may not; and so if the government authorizes its agent to pick your pocket, it's not called trespass—it's called taxes. But the Framers gave Americans a world with a written Constitution, and in Doe's case this would make all the difference. In response to the constable's invocation of lawful governmental authority, Doe would deny that the authority was indeed lawful. If the statute sought to authorize *unreasonable* seizures of persons—without good cause, without standards—the statute was itself unconstitutional under the Fourth Amendment. It was null and void—ultra vires—and thus no good defense. If a court agreed with Doe that the statute was unconstitutional under the Fourth Amendment, the constable's defense would fall, and Doe could win compensatory and (in the case of egregious conduct) punitive damages. And this was so even if the constable had acted in the good faith, but erroneous, belief that the authorizing statute was wholly constitutional.

As I have shown in Chapter 1, this was the clear Founding paradigm for vindicating the Fourth Amendment. More recent trends have updated this paradigm. In the landmark 1971 *Bivens* case, for example, the citizen was allowed to sue abusive federal officials for compensatory and punitive damages directly under the Fourth Amendment itself, without the need to plead and prove a predicate common law trespass.[78]

This clear paradigm of Fourth Amendment remedies has obvious implications for Sixth Amendment remedies. How is Andy any different from John Doe? How is a jailer unconstitutionally holding Andy in violation of the Sixth Amendment any different from a constable unconstitutionally seizing Doe in violation of the Fourth Amendment? If Doe can sue in trespass and win against the constable under the Fourth, why can't Andy sue in trespass and win against the jailer under the Sixth? If, today, a *Bivens* suit for damages lies directly under the Fourth, why not under the Sixth too?

Indeed, we can sharpen the point even finer. Isn't Andy's detention, if unconstitutional under the Sixth, also necessarily a Fourth Amendment violation too? The Fourth Amendment, of course, prohibits all *"unreasonable . . . seizures* [of] *persons."* Unreasonableness here surely encompasses seizures of persons for unreasonably long time periods.[79] And surely a seizure of a person that violates another provision of the Constitution—here, the Sixth Amendment—must be viewed as constitutionally unreasonable within the meaning of the Fourth Amendment.

At first, treating Sixth Amendment violations like Fourth Amendment violations might seem to support dismissal with prejudice by analogy to the so-called Fourth Amendment exclusionary rule. But we are seeking here principles from constitutional text, history, and structure, and none of these supports the Fourth Amendment exclusionary rule. The text of the Fourth Amendment says nothing about criminal exclusion; indeed, it nowhere distinguishes between government-initiated criminal cases (where exclusion now holds sway) and government-initiated civil cases (where exclusion is not now and never has been the rule). The Fourth Amendment's text, by contrast, does clearly presuppose tort law and property law—trespass rules and the like—protecting Americans in their "persons, houses, papers, and effects." No English court at the Founding had ever excluded reliable evidence on proto–Fourth Amendment grounds; nor has any English court since. Though most state constitutions featured state counterparts to the federal Fourth Amendment, no court in America—state or federal—ever excluded evidence on search-or-seizure grounds prior to 1886. By contrast, both English courts in the 1760s and early American courts, in landmark cases known to all lovers of liberty, awarded liberal tort remedies against abusive government searchers and seizers.

When exclusion finally came to America in 1886, it came not as a *remedy* for a past *Fourth* Amendment wrong, but rather as a kind of *prevention* of a threatened *Fifth* Amendment harm: to introduce as evidence, in a criminal case, a man's illegally obtained private papers would be tantamount to making him an involuntary *witness* against himself *in a criminal* case.[80] (And now we can see why exclusion—on *Fifth* Amendment grounds—applied only in criminal but not civil cases.) By a gradual and not always self-conscious process of extension, this rule for illegally seized diaries and private papers came to be applied to a great deal of other illegally seized "fruit."[81] As I have explained in detail in Chapters 1 and 2, this fusion of the Fourth and Fifth Amendments, though intriguing, was wrong from the outset and has now been decisively rejected by the Supreme Court.[82] Without it, the so-called exclusionary rule has no text, history, or structure to stand on.

What's more, even at the height of the exclusionary rule, an exception for unconstitutional seizures of persons was always recognized. Even if the government kidnapped a suspect in violation of every norm of civilized conduct and every Fourth Amendment principle in the book, it could nonetheless hold him for criminal trial. As a unanimous 1952 Court, per Justice Black, put the point in *Frisbie v. Collins:* "This Court has never departed from the rule announced in [1886] that the power of a court to try a person for crime is not impaired by the fact that he had been brought within the court's jurisdiction by reason of a 'forcible abduction.' . . . There is nothing in the Constitution that requires a court to permit a guilty person rightfully convicted to escape justice because he was brought to trial against his will."[83] If we substitute "after an overlong accusation period" for "by reason of a 'forcible abduction'" and "against his will" in this quote, we can see strong precedential support, even within the exclusionary rule tradition, for rejecting Sixth Amendment dismissal with prejudice.[84] Perhaps the implicit logic of *Frisbie* was that holding and using the defendant's body itself would not be testimonial witnessing in violation of the Fifth Amendment; or perhaps the Court simply saw the particularly dramatic upside-down effect that a judicial release order might entail and balked at the root idea of exclusion. (Release would be a huge windfall to the guilty, but would fail to make the innocent kidnap victim whole.) In any event, this case law confirms the need to develop tort remedies to vindicate the rights of innocent detainees. And so we return to the Framers' remedial paradigm that, as a general matter, held constables liable. If constables, why not jailers?

Our jailer, however, has an ace up his sleeve. Whereas our constable could point only to an unconstitutional statute, our jailer can point, in effect, to a court order authorizing Andy's pretrial detention. This court order is, by hypothesis, unconstitutional, but was issued by a court with jurisdiction. And at common law (crafted by judges) court orders (issued by judges) had special powers: an officer carrying out a *substantively* incorrect, but *jurisdictionally* authorized, court order could hide behind the order and escape liability. In the Fourth Amendment context, for example, a constable who executed a warrant that a judge had wrongly—indeed, unconstitutionally—issued (say, a warrant unsupported by probable cause, or authorizing an objectively unreasonable search) could hide behind the warrant. Our jailer would argue for like immunity.

Nor could Andy sue the judge who ordered this overlong detention because, once again, the judge's actions, even though substantively unconstitutional, were jurisdictionally authorized. The typical remedy for an incorrect judicial act is an appeal to a higher court, but this generally satisfactory remedy rings hollow in a few atypical situations where the real constitutional injury—here, day upon extra day of unconstitutional detention—is inflicted while an appeal is pending.[85]

In a world without a written Constitution, this remedial shell game—jailers hiding behind judges, judges hiding behind immunity and appeals, and appeals coming too late to vindicate the real legal interest at stake—would be bad enough; but in a world with a written Constitution it makes even less sense. The Constitution declares rights directly against the government itself. This is the lesson of *Bivens*,[86] and so when government, through its agents—judicial or executive or some combination—violates those rights, the government itself should be held liable for damages. Rights against government itself should be vindicated by remedies against government itself. As I have argued elsewhere, when government violates the express limits on its powers imposed by We the sovereign People in our Constitution, government, properly speaking, is neither "sovereign" nor "immune" and cannot in justice or logic invoke "sovereign immunity."[87]

And so, by analogy to and extension of constitutionally proper Fourth Amendment remedies for illegal seizures, we can deduce constitutionally proper Sixth Amendment remedies for illegal detention: Andy should be allowed to sue the detaining government for compensatory and (in cases of intentional or egregious violations) punitive damages. At the Founding, suits against the government itself were recognized de facto. A citizen would sue a government agent in his personal capacity, but everyone knew that the real party in interest was the government itself; as we saw in Chapter 1, the government would typically be forced to indemnify officials who were merely carrying out government policy.[88] Precisely because officials would be indemnified, the Founding generation understood that it was not unfair to hold officials strictly liable for constitutional torts, even if they acted on the good faith (but erroneous) belief that their behavior was fully constitutional. Thus, the Framers did not recognize, and would have rejected, the twentieth-century notion of "good faith immunity."

Once we see the logic of the Framers' ingenious remedial system—de facto government strict liability for constitutional torts—we can see how the system fails in certain unusual cases. If a series of governmental actors together violate a citizen's constitutional rights, but no one of them commits an actionable common law tort, the citizen has no one to sue, and the Framers' ingenious system of common law remedies fails its central purpose: to assure full remedies for every constitutional right.[89] And it was precisely this recognition that properly led the Court in *Bivens* to infer a damage action directly under the Constitution in a case where a constitutional violation had occurred without a predicate common law violation. But the *Bivens* Court stopped halfway and recognized a cause of action only against officers and not the government itself. If a right derives directly from the Constitution, and runs directly against the government itself, then the damage remedy should run directly against the government itself. Following *Marbury*'s logic, for every right against government there should be a remedy against government, de facto or de jure.[90] And the Sixth Amendment speedy trial right is most definitely a right against government *as such*. Only the government, after all, can conduct a trial, speedy or no; and private persons are not generally allowed to "hold" others against their will, unless they have been so authorized by the government.

A proper *Bivens*-like scheme to remedy unconstitutional pretrial detention would dramatically avoid the upside-down effect of dismissal with prejudice. Under an apt scheme a guilty Andy would never recover more than an innocent Andrea and might sometimes recover less. Suppose that Andy and Andrea have each suffered six months of pretrial detention, the last five of which were constitutionally unspeedy. Each was entitled to habeas release on day 30 but wrongly denied it. Between them, the judge and the jailer—both agents of the state—violated Andy's and Andrea's constitutional rights, even if neither official committed an actionable common law wrong. If Andrea's criminal case goes to trial and Andrea wins acquittal, let's say that she should get $50,000 in her later *Bivens*-like suit against the government.[91] But suppose that Andy, unlike Andrea, is later brought to trial and convicted, and receives a ten-year sentence, with a six-month set-off for pretrial time already served, and nine and one-half years to go.[92] If Andy brings a *Bivens*-like suit against the government, is he, too, entitled to $50,000— or, indeed, to anything? Admittedly, he wrongly served five months pretrial; but had he not been so detained, he would be serving five extra months posttrial. In terms of his liberty-deprivation interest, the unconstitutionality does not appear to have caused any incremental deprivation of liberty, but only accelerated the deprivation. And so here, perhaps, we have a kind of harmless error, ex post.

Tricky problems arise in intermediate cases. Suppose Andy is criminally tried, convicted, sentenced to six months, and released on the basis of time already served. At face value this, too, is an arguable case of harmless error, *ex post;* Andy's unconstitutional pretrial detention accelerated his loss of liberty but did not add to it. But suppose the six-month sentence was a judicial sham; had Andy not already served six months pretrial, he would simply have been released after conviction.[93] If so, unconstitutional pretrial detention really did rob him of months that he would never have lost, and his case looks more like Andrea's. *Bivens*-like courts must thus be alert to shams, but however they decide these cases, one thing is sure: a guilty Andy should never recover more than an innocent Andrea, and might sometimes justly recover less. And the reason for this is that the deep logic of the Sixth Amendment, and of constitutional criminal procedure generally, is to protect innocence.

The reputation interest. Similar principles apply to the reputation interest. As with habeas in the context of bodily liberty, the Constitution's first line of defense is prevention: judges must simply quash indictments that linger too long and thus stain the "accused['s]" reputation without giving him his "speedy . . . trial" to "answer" the "infamous" "indictment" of his character and "defen[d]" against the charge of "criminal" conduct. If quashing occurs in time—before one year in Bill's case—no violation of the reputation right will ever have occurred. If, however, judges fail to quash in time, quashing only prevents new assaults on reputation without making the accused whole.

And here, once again, is where after-the-fact, *Bivens*-like tort damages against the government should come in. If Bill suffers seventeen months of pretrial mud on his name, when the Constitution allows only twelve, Bill's constitutional rights have been violated by the government itself. Obviously Bill cannot sue the grand jurors who indicted him—they, like judges, were acting in a judicial capacity, even if they acted erroneously. Besides, Bill's cognizable injury is not the indictment itself, but the delay in giving him his day in court to clear his name. Nor could Bill, at common law, successfully sue the prosecutor or the judge; the indictment speaks in the name of the government, not the prosecutor personally, and the judge who wrongly delays trial is nevertheless acting within his jurisdiction. But even if no one person has violated Bill's common law rights, together various governmental agents have combined to violate his constitutional rights. Here too, a right against the government itself calls for a like remedy.

And here too, an innocent person should never recover less, and, indeed, should typically recover more than a guilty one. If Billy Jo, after seventeen months of accusation, the last five of which were unconstitutional, goes to trial, makes her defense, and wins, she should be compensated for the five extra months of stigma she endured unconstitutionally. (She is not, however, entitled to recover for the first year of accusation, since this was lawful. Similarly, she is not constitutionally entitled to reimbursement for all out-of-pocket legal fees if she wins: indictment and trial themselves are not unconstitutional, even though they inflict great harm.) By contrast, consider the case of guilty Bill, who likewise suffered seventeen months of accusation, but who is convicted at trial. The delay of his trial did heap five months of unconstitutional mud on his name, but had the trial occurred five months earlier, Bill would have been convicted earlier, with even more mud on his name. And so, here too, we see a kind of constitutional harmless error, ex post.[94]

A similar analysis applies if we substitute a pretrial "anxiety" or "peace of mind" interest for the reputational interest we have been studying. Strong support for this right-side-up remedial effect— where the innocent sometimes benefit more than the guilty—comes from one sensible corner of current Fourth Amendment law. In the 1983 *Place* case and the 1984 *Jacobsen* case, the Court dealt with certain governmental intrusions that, according to the Court, could detect only the presence of contraband but could not reveal any other private information.[95] These intrusions, said the Court, might make criminals nervous, but did not compromise any *legitimate* interest in privacy. Though the Court's particular approach—labeling these searches nonsearches[96]—was not particularly helpful, its deep instinct was sound: the searches were *reasonable*, and thus constitutional. And the reason these searches were reasonable is that, although they could ruin a drug runner's day, they posed little threat to the privacy interests of law-abiding folk. Lawbreakers *as such* have no *legitimate* interest in privacy, and are at times entitled to less peace of mind than are the law-abiding.[97]

The reliable trial interest. Consider, finally, the reliable trial interest underlying the speedy trial clause: an extended accusation period must not create an undue risk that the trial itself will result in the erroneous conviction of an innocent man.

Once again, the first line of defense, by analogy to habeas in the physical detention context, should be prevention. Indeed habeas itself *is* the first line of defense: judges who see that extended pretrial detention might cause irreversible loss of key exculpatory evidence must order the timely release of the detainee, or soften the conditions of confinement, to prevent the anticipated loss from ever occurring.

What happens, however, if this first line of defense fails, and evidence has already been irreversibly lost because of the defendant's constitutionally overlong detention? At this point, prevention now means preventing an unreliable trial from occurring—dismissing with prejudice if necessary. Such a dismissal fails to remedy a *past* bodily liberty or reputation violation, but it does prevent a *future* reliable trial violation. The wrong here is the *trial itself,* if it poses an undue threat of an erroneous conviction owing to the government's past lapses.[98]

Dismissal with prejudice is indeed an exclusionary rule of sorts, but one designed to protect innocence. And *that* kind of exclusionary rule draws strong structural support from other constitutional provisions. As we have seen, the Fourth Amendment, rightly read, contains no exclusionary rule; but the Fifth contains several, all of which are designed to protect innocence and/or to prevent vexation and oppression at trial itself. The self-incrimination clause excludes items from a criminal trial—a defendant's compelled statements—but as we saw in Chapter 2, this exclusionary rule is designed to reduce the risk of erroneous convictions of innocent defendants.

Consider next the double jeopardy clause, which excludes a second trial—dismisses with prejudice, in effect—if a defendant has already been acquitted or convicted of the same offense. If the defendant has already been *acquitted,* a second trial would indeed pose an intolerable risk to innocence. If a second trial is okay, why not a third? If a third, why not a fourth, and so on? Eventually, the government may be able to wear an innocent defendant down and find one statistically aberrant jury that would erroneously convict. Under this heads-we-win-tails-let's-do-it-over regime, the obvious innocence-protecting spirit of *Winship* would be undermined.[99] If, by contrast, a defendant has already been *convicted* of the very same offense, what purpose could a second trial have, other than to vex him?[100]

Alongside the double jeopardy clause's textual protections against multiple prosecutions for the "same offence," the due process principle prohibits innocence-threatening and vexatious multiple prosecutions more generally. The due process principle of collateral estoppel is a cousin of the double jeopardy idea of *autrefois acquit:*[101] if a defendant prevails on any factual issue in one criminal case, the government may not try to force him to prove it all over again in a second criminal case. Thus, although kidnapping and bank robbery are plainly different offenses, if a defendant is acquitted of kidnapping on the theory that the police simply nabbed the wrong man in a case of mistaken identity, the government would be barred from later trying him on a bank robbery charge growing out of the same episode. So too, a due process cousin of the double jeopardy idea of *autrefois convict* will bar vexatious multiple prosecutions for different offenses, where the government can point to no legitimate reason for forcing a defendant to undergo two traumatic trials rather than one single consolidated trial.[102]

The underlying principle of all these constitutional exclusionary rules outside the Sixth Amendment is to protect innocence and/or prevent a trial that would *itself* be vexatious and oppressive. Structural analysis suggests that the same should be true for the Sixth Amendment itself.

Dismissal with prejudice as "the only possible remedy?" How, in the end, are we to explain the modern Court's ahistorical embrace of dismissal with prejudice as the "only possible remedy?"[103] The perverse gravitational pull of the so-called Fourth Amendment exclusionary rule is no doubt part of the story. However, as the Court itself has noted, the exclusionary rule ordinarily blocks certain items of evidence but does not prevent the government from using other evidence to prove guilt.[104] Dismissal with prejudice, by contrast, altogether bars prosecution of the guilty. And in the one corner of exclusionary rule precedent where exclusion would indeed mean dismissal altogether—*Frisbie* and its progeny—the Court has emphatically resisted exclusion's gravitational pull.[105]

More generally, our modern system of constitutional criminal procedure seems to welcome broad, upside-down exclusions of reliable evidence—under the *Kastigar* gloss on the self-incrimination clause,[106] as "fruits" of coerced confessions and other "poisonous trees,"[107] and under the *Massiah* doctrine,[108] for example. Leading scholars of criminal procedure have applauded this system; and criminal defense attorneys have grown up under it. But virtually all of these upside-down exclusions rest on misreadings of constitutional text, history, and structure. Criminal defense attorneys may treat an upside-down world as inevitable—the only possible approach—but of course this is a terribly convenient view for them. They are paid to get their clients off, their clients are often guilty, and upside-down exclusion can help even guilty clients win—indeed, can especially help guilty clients win. Precisely because this at first seems so perverse, as nonlawyers intuit, it's convenient and comforting for lawyers to tell themselves that the Constitution compels this, and that there is no other way.

Scholars should know better, but too few of those who write in criminal procedure do serious, sustained scholarship in constitutional law generally, or in fields like federal jurisdiction and remedies.[109] As a result, discourse in constitutional criminal procedure has evolved separately, cutting itself off from larger themes of constitutional, remedial, and jurisdictional theory. Standard constitutional law modalities of text, history, and structure are often slighted,[110] and remedial lessons elsewhere in constitutional law ignored. Elsewhere in constitutional law, dismissal and exclusion are not the "only possible remedies." When freedom of speech or of the press is at stake, or equal protection, or due process, a Section 1983/*Ex parte Young*/*Bivens*[111] model—featuring before-the-fact prevention via injunctions and after-the-fact compensation and deterrence via damages—reigns as the dominant remedial approach. This is the general remedial model I have tried to adapt to the knotty speedy trial issues at hand.

After-the-fact damages are at times attacked as simply allowing the government to buy off constitutional rights with money, to cynically treat violations of sacred constitutional rights merely as the cost of doing business, to wrongly transform all constitutional rights into takings-clause-like "liability" rights.[112] This criticism is simply mistaken and rests on a misunderstanding of basic remedial theory.

The first line of defense must always be prevention—here, by scheduling speedy trials; by issuing writs of habeas corpus to prevent undue detention; by quashing lingering indictments that stigmatize; by preventing irreparably unfair trials from ever occurring; and so on. And if an *in-court* trial right has been violated in a way that might have led to an unjust and erroneous conviction of guilt,[113] and in a way that a new trial could avoid, a sound remedial model would of course *not* say: "Too bad, Mr. Gideon, you were denied your express right to counsel, and you were thereby convicted of a felony, quite possibly erroneously. Here's a few bucks, good luck in prison." Rather, the state must try to run the trial over again, this time without the constitutional violation. This rerunning of trials is merely an adaptation of the first line of defense—prevention—and a reflection of the value our Constitution rightly places on innocence protection.

But if a constitutional violation has already occurred *out of court,* a court cannot really prevent it: a court can rerun a trial but it cannot turn back the clock of time and rerun the world outside the court. A court cannot give Andy back the five months he was unlawfully held pretrial or make the five unconstitutional months of mud on Bill's name vanish *nunc pro tunc.* After-the-fact damages cannot metaphysically undo these harms, *but neither can dismissal with prejudice.*[114] Nothing can, metaphysically. But our general law of remedies does countenance after-the-fact damages to compensate, as best we can, for the past injury done, and to deter—to prevent—future injury.

Indeed, the permissibility of punitive damages shows how the takings clause objection is precisely inapt. When government takes a piece of property and pays a fair price for it, no punitive damages are ever awarded. Indeed, no right has ever been violated—the right is simply to after-the-fact compensation.[115] And so a judge should never enjoin a taking when the government stands ready to pay, cash in hand. By contrast, here we are focusing on rights that have been violated, where before-the-fact injunctions should have issued. Punitive damages are at times appropriate precisely to deter—to prevent—future violations. Indeed, the very concept of punitive damages originally entered into Anglo-American law in landmark proto–Fourth Amendment cases.[116] The Framers' remedial system for constitutional wrongs was based solidly on punitive damages, not exclusions as the "only possible remedy."

Until speedy trial discourse takes account of all this, glib judicial pronouncements about dismissal should not command the respect of thoughtful students of the Constitution.

In Particular: Public Trial

The next cluster of clauses in the Sixth Amendment focuses on the public, the people, and the community: "[T]he accused shall enjoy the right to a speedy and public trial, by an impartial jury of the State and district wherein the crime shall have been committed, which district shall have been previously ascertained by law. . . ." Both syntactically and substantively, these words reach back to the speedy trial clause and also push beyond it. The result is a distinctly republican vision of innocence protection and truth-seeking.

The Gallery: A Public Trial

Textually, the right to a "public trial" tightly intermeshes with the right to a "speedy . . . trial," and the two rights share much in common. As we have seen, the speedy trial right was crafted with the innocent man as the paradigm—a man falsely "accused" of "infamous" and "criminal" misconduct who would naturally want a "speedy" trial to "answer" the indictment and make his "defence." For the same reasons an innocent man might naturally want a "speedy" trial, he might want a "speedy *and public*" trial: he has nothing to hide, and indeed wants only to clear his name in open court, with the bracing cleanser of publicity helping to wash the mud off his name. When he wins, as he deserves to, he wants the world—the public—to know, so that he can get back his good name in civil society. In a case of malicious prosecution—say, trumped-up charges against a vocal government opponent—a public trial can expose corruption for all to see. In a case of mistaken identity, a public trial may reduce the risk of future mistakes. And if a defendant committed the acts he is charged with, but believes them justified, he should want the community to hear and understand his reasons.

Guilty defendants as a whole, by contrast, may be less enthusiastic about public trials, just as they may be less enthusiastic about speedy ones. An *un*speedy trial may help many a guilty defendant; and so too with a *secret* trial, where bribery may be easier. But, as we have seen, the Constitution does not in general confer on the defendant a right to an *un*speedy trial; and the same holds true for an *un*public trial. Indeed, the words that the Court has used in the speedy trial context apply a fortiori to the public trial right: "[T]here is a societal interest in providing a speedy trial which exists separate from, and at times in opposition to, the interests of the accused."[117] Begin with the text. Though the Sixth Amendment says the "accused" shall enjoy a right to a "public trial," it does not say that the accused has a right to a secret or private trial. Historically, virtually all criminal trials in England and America have been open to the people.[118] In his celebrated *Commentaries on the Constitution*, Joseph Story noted that the Sixth Amendment "does but follow out the established course of the common law in all trials for crimes. *The trial is always public.*"[119] And so, to return to the text of the Sixth Amendment, the right of public trial is indeed a right of the "accused" and only the "accused" in the sense that he may waive trial altogether by pleading guilty.[120] But *if* he pleads not guilty, and thus demands a trial, he must get a *public* trial, whether he will or no; for a trial from which the people are excluded is, in the Anglo-American tradition, not a trial at all.[121]

Structural analysis helps to identify some of the special purposes served by "public" trials in America. The phrase *the people* appears in no fewer than five of the ten Amendments that make up our Bill of Rights,[122] and so we would do well to take seriously the republican and populist overtones of its etymological cousin, *public,* in a sixth—*the* Sixth—Amendment. Ours is a system of re*public*an governments, state and federal—of governments of, by, and for the people.[123] Here, the people rule—not day to day, but ultimately, in the long run. All governmental policy and governmental policy makers can, in time, be lawfully replaced by the sovereign people via ordinary elections and constitutional conventions. This ultimate right of the public to change policy and policy makers creates a strong presumption that governmental action in all three branches will be open to public scrutiny. As Justice Blackmun put the point:

> Judges, prosecutors, and police officials often are elected or are subject to some control by elected officials, and a main source of information about how these officials perform is the open trial. And the manner in which criminal justice is administered in this country is in and of itself of interest to all citizens. In *Cox Broadcasting Corp. v. Cohn,* . . . it was noted that information about the criminal justice system "appears to us to be of critical importance to our type of government in which the citizenry is the final judge of the proper conduct of public business."[124]

The people, however, do not need to wait until Election Day to make a difference; their very presence in the courtroom can help discourage judicial misbehavior. As Sir Matthew Hale wrote in his widely influential treatise, "if the judge be PARTIAL, his partiality and injustice will be evident to all by-standers."[125] Or as Sir William Blackstone wrote in his even more widely influential treatise: "[Objections to evidence] are publicly stated, and by the judge are openly and publicly allowed or disallowed, in the face of the country; which must curb any secret bias or partiality, that might arise in his own breast."[126] The ability of the public to judge the judge should tend to protect innocent defendants from judicial corruption or oppression, but public scrutiny is bad news for many a guilty defendant, who might prefer an incompetent judge, or one "partial" to the defendant's cause—an old political friend, perhaps, or a new financial one.[127]

So too, the public right to monitor witnesses at trial was designed to help the truth come out, and truth of course helps innocent defendants more than guilty ones, as a rule. If, at trial, a bystander happens to have relevant information bearing on a key point, he can bring the matter to the attention of court and counsel.[128] In part because of this, witnesses who testify are less likely to perjure themselves in front of a public gallery—or at least this was the theory underlying the common law's commitment to public trials. In 1685, Solicitor General John Hawles put the point as follows: "[T]he reason that all trials are public, is, that any person may inform in point of fact, though not subpoena'd, *that truth may be discovered* in civil as well as criminal cases. There is an invitation to all persons, who can inform the court concerning the matter to be tried, to come into the court, and they shall be heard."[129] Truth was also Blackstone's theme: "This open examination of witnesses *viva voce*, in the presence of all mankind, is much more conducive to the clearing up of truth, than [a] private and secret examination. . . . [A] witness may frequently depose that in private, which he will be ashamed to testify in a public and solemn tribunal."[130]

In short, the public trial was designed to infuse public knowledge into the trial itself, and, in turn, to satisfy the public that truth had prevailed at trial. A public trial would protect innocence but would make life more difficult for the guilty. All these values have been turned upside down by modern doctrines that—in the name of the Constitution, no less—exclude evidence the public knows to be true. Put differently, even if a judge can prevent the jury from learning of some fact, she often cannot prevent the larger public from, at some point, learning of it. And the gap between public truth and truth allowed in the courtroom can demoralize the public, whose faith in the judicial system is a key goal of the public trial ideal.[131] In the wise words of Professor Nesson:

> [A] verdict of not guilty or not liable will only undermine the legal system's projection of behavioral norms if the public has an independent basis for believing that the defendant did in fact commit the wrongful act. . . . Supporters of the [exclusionary] rule who argue that the rule sets few criminals free . . . fail to appreciate the demoralizing message conveyed to the public when the assertion of an evidentiary rule that impedes the search for truth is permitted to override the substantive norm embodied in criminal law.[132]

Thus, various modern exclusionary rules are not merely indefensible as a matter of text, history, and structure, and remedially inapt to boot. These modern upside-down rules also do violence to the elaborate adjudicatory architecture of the truth-seeking, confidence-enhancing, innocence-protecting, public trial envisioned by the Sixth Amendment.

The Jury: Trial by the People

Closely linked to the public trial idea is the jury trial idea. Here too, the relevant legal interests are not merely the accused's but also the people's. Here too, public participation in the criminal justice system was designed to enhance public legitimacy of the criminal justice system, to pursue truth, and to protect innocence.

No idea was more central to our Bill of Rights than the idea of the jury. The only right secured in all state constitutions penned between 1776 and 1787 was the right of jury trial in criminal cases;[133] and even though the original Constitution omitted a general Bill of Rights, it did expressly protect criminal juries in Article III.[134] In the Bill of Rights itself, three separate amendments explicitly safeguarded juries—grand, petit, and civil[135]—and several other amendments tightly intermeshed with the jury idea.[136]

At root, jury trials were, in Thomas Jefferson's words, "trials by the people themselves."[137] And this right of trial by the people was not merely a right of the accused, but a right of the people—of the jurors too. To be sure, the Sixth Amendment says that the *accused* shall enjoy the right of "public trial, by an impartial jury." But, once again, the accused is nowhere given a right to a *non*jury trial. The undiminished language of Article III is clear and emphatic: "The *Trial* of *all Crimes . . . shall* be by *Jury*."[138] And so, just as a secret trial is no trial at all, a judge sitting without a criminal jury—at least at the federal level—is no court, and thus cannot try anything. The accused, and only the accused, can decide to plead guilty and thus waive trial altogether; but if he insists on standing trial, both judge and jury must be present. This, at least, is the theory of our Constitution, and of the Supreme Court throughout the nineteenth and early twentieth centuries,[139] though it has been rejected by the modern Court.[140]

An analogy to federal legislative bicameralism helps illustrate the point: a federal judge sitting without a jury is simply not a federal court capable of trying criminal cases, just as the Senate sitting without the House is not a federal legislature capable of passing laws.[141] Though this bicameral analogy rings odd in modern ears, it is precisely the one many supporters of a Bill of Rights had in mind in debates over the ratification of the federal Constitution. Here are the words of a leading Anti-Federalist pamphleteer: "It is essential in every free country, that common people should have a part and share of influence, in the judicial as well as in the legislative department. . . . The trial by jury in the judicial department, and the collection of the people by their representatives in the legislature . . . have procured for them, in this country, their true proportion of influence. . . ."[142] So too, another leading Anti-Federalist defined the jury as *the democratic branch of the judiciary power*—more necessary than representatives in the legislature."[143] Thomas Jefferson emphatically agreed: "[I]t is necessary to introduce the people into every department of government. . . . Were I called upon to decide whether the people had best be omitted in the Legislative or Judicial department, I would say it is better to leave them out of the Legislative."[144]

Just as the House could monitor and expose—check—any partiality or corruption in the Senate, so the jurors on the lower bench could check a corrupt or partial set of judges on the upper bench. According to Jefferson: "[W]e all know that permanent judges acquire an Esprit de corps, that being known they are liable to be tempted by bribery, that they are misled by favor, by relationship, by a spirit of party, by a devotion to the Executive or Legislative. . . . It is left therefore to the juries, if they think the permanent judges are under any biass whatever in any cause, to take upon themselves to judge the law as well as the fact. They never exercise this power but when they suspect partiality in the judges. . . ."[145] Even Alexander Hamilton, who disagreed with Jefferson about a great deal, and pooh-poohed the need for an explicit Bill of Rights,[146] agreed that juries discouraged corruption. In discussing the civil jury in *The Federalist No. 83*, Hamilton wrote: "The strongest argument in its favor is that it is a security against corruption. As there is always more time and better opportunity to tamper with a standing body of magistrates than with a jury summoned for the occasion, there is room to suppose that a corrupt influence would more easily find its way to the former than the latter. . . . The temptations to prostitution which the judges might have to surmount must certainly be much fewer, while the co-operation of a jury is necessary, than they might be if they had themselves the exclusive determination of all causes."[147] In short, like the people in the gallery box, the people in the jury box at a public trial could detect and deter judicial misconduct. A guilty defendant looking to bribe his way out or pull a few strings might well prefer a closed bench trial, and so might a judge and prosecutor on the take. But the Constitution did not permit the defendant, even with the agreement of judge and prosecutor, to oust the people from their rightful places in both the gallery box and the jury box.

For the Framers, however, the criminal jury was much more than an incorruptible fact finder. It was also, and more fundamentally, a political institution embodying popular sovereignty and republican self-government. Through jury service, citizens would learn their rights and duties, and actively participate in the governance of society. In the words of the prominent Anti-Federalist essayist "Federal Farmer": "[The people's] situation, as jurors and representatives, enables them to acquire information and knowledge in the affairs and government of the society; and to come forward, in turn, as the centinels and guardians of each other."[148] Jury service was both a duty and a right— a badge of first-class citizenship, no less than the right to vote. Indeed, throughout American history and constitutional discourse, the right to vote and the right to serve on juries have stood as fraternal twins, joined arm in arm. After all, in deciding guilt or innocence, jurors vote—that is what they do—and historically, ordinary voters have been eligible to serve on juries.[149] Tocqueville put it well:

> The jury system as understood in America seems to me as direct and extreme a consequence of the . . . sovereignty of the people as universal suffrage. They are both equally powerful means of making the majority prevail. . . . [T]he jury is above all a political institution [and] should be made to harmonize with the other laws establishing the sovereignty. . . . [F]or society to be governed in a settled and uniform manner, it is essential that the jury lists should expand or shrink with the lists of voters. . . . [In general] [i]n America all citizens who are electors have the right to be jurors.[150]

This populist vision of the people's right to vote and serve on juries may at times trump a given defendant's desires. Juries at the Founding were supposed to represent the polity—the people—not the defendant; and subsequent constitutional amendments have made clear that our polity now includes those once excluded—blacks and women, for example. Both the plain and the deep meaning of these amendments is that the right to vote—on juries, too—may not be abridged on the basis of race or sex or class or age.[151] And this right is paramount even if a defendant prefers otherwise, and wants a jury that looks like him rather than like America. Here the recent Supreme Court has been on just the right track, striking down race-based exclusions from jury service even when a defendant seeks these exclusions via peremptory challenges.[152]

The role of the criminal jury, however, involves even more than reliable fact-finding and republican self-government. It also involves normative judgment. In this last respect, the criminal jury wields more power than its civil counterpart. Criminal trials are unavoidably morality plays, focusing on the defendant's moral blameworthiness or lack thereof. And the assessment of his moral culpability is, under the Sixth Amendment, a task for the community, via the jury, and not the judge—but with an innocence-protecting twist. No judge can ever find a defendant guilty "as a matter of law," no matter how clear the defendant's factual and moral guilt to *the judge*.[153] No man who claims innocence can be condemned as guilty unless the community, via the jury, pronounces him worthy of moral condemnation. (And once acquitted by a jury, the defendant is, under the clear logic of both the Sixth Amendment and the double jeopardy clause, forever quit of the charge.)[154] But a judge who finds a defendant innocent "as a matter of law" may set him free, even if the jury disagrees.

A careful comparison of the Sixth and Seventh Amendments' descriptions of the jury's role is illuminating. The Seventh explicitly highlights the role of the civil jury in finding "fact[s]";[155] the Sixth does not. To be sure, at the Founding, the dominant view among well-trained lawyers was that a jury, when rendering a general verdict, could take upon itself the right to decide both law and fact.[156] So said Chief Justice Jay for a unanimous Supreme Court in 1794.[157] But, on the civil side, several doctrinal devices in 1791 enabled judges to avoid or overturn general verdicts,[158] and these devices have only grown in number and power over the last two hundred years—nonsuits, demurrers, summary judgments, directed verdicts, special verdicts, special interrogatories, new trials, J.N.O.V.s, and so on. But parallel devices did not exist in criminal cases in 1791, and few have emerged since: every criminal jury verdict is a general verdict in which the jury decides law and fact "complicately," to use an eighteenth-century term. And no criminal jury verdict of acquittal can ever be overturned. By contrast, note how the Seventh Amendment explicitly permits limited "re-examin[ation]" of civil jury verdicts.[159]

The District: Trial by the Community

This role of moral judgment is subtly accented by the little-discussed district clause of the Sixth Amendment. Under the Sixth, but not the Seventh, the jury must generally be drawn from "the . . . district wherein the crime shall have been committed." At first blush, this seems like a simple venue provision, designed merely for ease of litigation: the case should be tried where the crime occurred because that's where the witnesses and physical evidence are. There is much to be said for this simple view, and it nicely meshes with both the general truth-seeking mission of the Sixth Amendment and the specific logic of a gallery to monitor witnesses and bring new facts to light.[160] But if mere litigation convenience was the *only* issue, why didn't the Seventh Amendment likewise call for civil jury trial in "the State and district wherein the cause of action shall have arisen?" What's more, many defendants might find a jury from the crime district quite inconvenient and uncongenial—imagine, for example, a traveling salesman tried for a crime that took place in a state and district far from his home and friends. Finally, we should note that, technically, the district clause regulates the place from which jurors are chosen, rather than the place that they must sit at trial.[161]

Underlying the district clause is also, perhaps, the idea that a crime—unlike a civil wrong—constitutes a moral rupture, a distinct breach of the peace of the place where the crime occurred.[162] A crime is committed not merely against the victim but against the community. And an apt judicial response to this crime, this moral rupture, requires not merely good fact-finding but moral judgment—moral judgment by the community via the jury.[163]

But here, too, how can the jury judge well on behalf of the community if, because of upside-down exclusion rules, it is denied reliable information that is known to the general community?[164]

In Particular: Fair Trial

Finally, let us turn to the Sixth Amendment's closing cluster of clauses, protecting nothing less than a defendant's right to put on his defense—to show he didn't do it. Here too, truth-seeking and innocence protection loom large.

Nature and Cause of Accusation

> [T]he accused shall enjoy the right . . . to be informed of the nature and cause of the accusation.

The need for this fundamental right is obvious: if a defendant doesn't even know what he is charged with having done, how can he show he didn't do it? Only slightly less obvious is the way in which this fundamental right is especially valuable for the wholly innocent defendant. An "accusation," after all, typically focuses on allegations about the defendant's past conduct: what he did, when, where, why, how, with whom, to whom, and so on. If the government is in fact on the nose in its accusation, the accusation itself may tell the guilty defendant only what he already knows. But if the accusation is way off base—say, in a case of mistaken identity—it may tell the innocent defendant a great deal about where the government went wrong, and how he might go about showing this at trial or before.

Confrontation

> [T]he accused shall enjoy the right . . . to be confronted with the witnesses against him.

This clause builds on several of the clauses we have already examined. Like many other intermeshing Sixth Amendment ideas, confrontation is designed to promote the truth. First, like the public trial clause, the confrontation clause may discourage deliberate perjury by prosecution witnesses, who might be ashamed to tell their lies with the defendant in the room and afraid that their lies will not stand up to open scrutiny. Second, by simply allowing a defendant to hear a witness's story, the clause may help an innocent defendant to figure out where the witness might be mistaken (perhaps in all good faith). In this respect, the confrontation clause echoes and amplifies the themes of its "nature and cause" neighbor: unless a defendant knows what the government is alleging, how can he show he didn't do it, or show where the government went wrong? Third, the clause enables the defendant not merely to hear the witness's story but to directly question and cross-examine it—to show the jury and the public where the holes are—and to invite the witness herself to supplement or clarify or revise the story, so that the jury and the public may hear the *whole* truth. In this last respect, the confrontation clause links arms with its other neighbor, the compulsory process clause, which also affirms a defendant's right to present truthful evidence before the jury and the public.

In light of the obvious linkages between public trial and confrontation, we should not be surprised that Blackstone discussed the ideas together (in a chapter on trial by jury), or that he stressed truth-seeking:

> The oath administered to the witness is not only that what he deposes shall be true, but that he shall also depose the *whole* truth. . . . And all this evidence is to be given in open court, in the presence of the parties, their attorneys, the counsel, and all bystanders, and before the judge and jury. . . .
>
> This open examination of witnesses *viva voce,* in the presence of all mankind, is . . . conducive to the clearing up of truth. . . . Besides, the occasional questions of the judge, the jury, and the counsel, propounded to the witnesses on a sudden, will sift out the

truth much better than a formal set of interrogatories previously penned and settled: and the confronting of adverse witnesses is also another opportunity of obtaining a clear discovery, which can never be had upon any other method of trial.[165]

Modern Supreme Court case law has exuberantly echoed Blackstone here, defining the "Confrontation Clause's very mission" as promoting "the accuracy of the truth-determining process in criminal trials";[166] and labeling cross-examination the "greatest legal engine ever invented for the discovery of truth."[167]

Though the text and purposes of the confrontation clause seem clear enough, modern Supreme Court case law on the clause is surprisingly muddled in logic and exposition. The results, on the whole, are sensible enough, but the Court has had difficulty believing that the clause could really mean what it says. If witness *A* takes the stand at trial and testifies about what her best friend *B* told her about the defendant, the Court has worried that this hearsay might impede the defendant's right to directly confront his true accuser: the out-of-court declarant, friend *B*.[168] On the other hand (the Court has reasoned), it would be utterly impractical to try to exclude all hearsay from criminal trials; surely, it makes sense to allow in *some* forms of hearsay.[169] And so the Court has balanced. But the words of the confrontation clause do not seem to balance; they seem to state a bright-line rule. Thus the Court has decided the words cannot possibly mean what they say— they merely state a principled *preference* for live testimony.[170]

This interpretive strategy runs rampant in modern constitutional criminal procedure. Though the Fourth Amendment's words do not explicitly require warrants and probable cause for every search and seizure, the Court has at times assumed they do so impliedly.[171] But since these implied rules, if taken literally, make no sense in many cases, the Court has balanced, at times treating the Amendment as merely creating a *preference* for warrants—just as the Sixth (on the Court's account) creates a *preference* for live testimony. The problem, of course, is that the word "preference" nowhere appears in the Fourth and Sixth Amendments, or in their accompanying history.

Consider next the Fifth Amendment's double jeopardy clause. Though its words bar retrial after acquittal or conviction on the "same offence," the Court has decided that "same" really cannot mean "same"—i.e., identical. Rather, it must mean "greater and lesser-included"—the so-called *Blockburger* test.[172] But sometimes literal application of this *Blockburger* test would lead to absurd results. Imagine a case where the government convicts a defendant of attempted murder. After conviction, the victim dies from her injuries. Shouldn't the government now be allowed to prosecute for murder (with a set-off for any earlier punishment to avoid double counting)? The Court has made clear that reprosecution can occur on these facts[173]—here too, it has balanced. But if the double jeopardy clause really does state a bright-line rule, by what right do judges balance it away?

Finally, consider the Fifth Amendment self-incrimination clause. Though the words of the clause speak only of "witness[ing]," the Court has insisted that the clause bars physical and other fruit of compelled out-of-court statements.[174] But sometimes it makes good sense to require records, of business activity and the like, and then later use those records to help detect crime. And so here, too, in its required records cases, the Court has simply balanced.[175] Yet the text of the clause seems more rulelike than this.

The solution to all these problems, I have suggested, begins with taking the text seriously. The words of the Fourth Amendment, properly read, do not require or prefer warrants. The word "same" in the double jeopardy clause means what it says.[176] The self-incrimination clause does not bar fruit, but only certain types of "witness[ing]." The rules in the Fourth and Fifth Amendments make sense as rules. Of course, at times we must go beyond the letter of these rules to protect their spirit and to thwart governmental shams and evasions of fundamental rights. But we cannot properly understand the true principles underlying these rules until we understand the rules proper, and take them seriously as rules.[177] As it turns out, this approach, which helps sort out the Fourth and the Fifth Amendments, also works well in the Sixth, and indeed, neatly solves the Court's current confrontation clause conundrum.

The place to begin is the text—in particular, the word *witness*. Hasn't the Court wrongly conflated the word *witness* in the confrontation clause with the somewhat different idea of "an out-of-court declarant"—or, more elaborately still, "an out-of-court declarant whose utterance is introduced for the truth of the matter asserted"—under the hearsay rule?[178] In ordinary language, when witness *A* takes the stand and testifies about what her best friend *B* told her out of court, *A* is the witness, not *B*. Imagine, for example, that *B* were later asked whether she had ever before been a witness in a criminal prosecution. Surely *B* could say no; indeed, she may not even know that witness *A* paraphrased her words on the stand.[179]

Of course, sometimes words in a legal document mean something different from the same words in ordinary language. However, in a

Constitution ratified by, subject to, and proclaimed in the name of, the people, it would be unfortunate if words generally could not be taken at face value.[180] At any rate, surely a careful ordinary citizen reading the confrontation clause and pondering the word *witness* might look to see how the word is used elsewhere in the Constitution itself.[181]

Consider, then, the treason clause of Article III, Section 3, one of a handful of clauses in the original document identified by the Federalist Papers as in the nature of a traditional bill of rights:[182] "No Person shall be convicted of Treason unless on the Testimony of two Witnesses to the same overt Act, or on Confession in open Court."[183] Imagine that a defendant is on trial for treason, with his life in the balance, and witness *A* testifies that she saw defendant's overt act, and that friend *B* told *A* that *B* also saw the same act. *A* is of course a witness; but should out-of-court friend *B* count as a witness too, within the meaning of the treason clause? I should hope not. Indeed, it is hard to imagine a more patent (and, if permitted, potent) evasion of the words and the spirit of the treason clause's requirement of *two* witnesses. And so, here at least, *witness* most clearly does not mean any out-of-court declarant.

Consider next the Fifth Amendment self-incrimination clause: "No person . . . shall be compelled in any criminal case to be a witness against himself." The core rule here seems clear enough: a defendant cannot be forced to take the stand in his own case. Thus, the core meaning of *witness* resonates with ordinary language, applying to those who take the stand and testify in open court, but not to all out-of-court declarants.

But the self-incrimination clause shows that we need to refine our definition of *witness* to vindicate the obvious intent of the rule. Consider the following question: is a person who "testifies" by videotaped deposition, or who prepares a written deposition or affidavit intended for court use and then used in court, a witness? In ordinary language, this question might be a close one, but a quick look at the self-incrimination clause tells us that the obvious answer is yes. The government may not force the criminal defendant to take the stand and answer questions—that is the plain meaning of the clause. But suppose, in the middle of the trial, the government temporarily "adjourns" the proceedings. The prosecutor, with the help of the bailiff, forcibly takes the defendant into the next room and forces him, upon pain of contempt, to answer questions. The next morning, the prosecutor introduces a videotape of this interrogation, or a written transcript of it, or an affidavit or a deposition signed (again, under penalty of contempt) by the defendant. Surely this is an obvious violation of the core rule against self-incrimination, at least in spirit. But also, I believe, in letter; we should treat an affidavit or transcript, prepared for in-court use and introduced in court as testimony, as *witnessing*. And of course the same thing is true if the compelled interrogation yielding the deposition occurred the day before the trial, or a year before, rather than during the trial itself.

Now turn to the Constitution's next use of the word *witness*, in the confrontation clause itself. The core meaning, here too, is clear enough: when a witness in court takes the stand, the defendant must have a chance to look him in the eye and confront him with questions. And so, if the defendant were banished from the courtroom when witness *A* took the stand, the violation would be flagrant. But suppose a ham-fisted government tried to move the mountain rather than Mohammed: in the middle of the trial, proceedings are "adjourned," and the prosecutor, jury, and judge all troop into the next room to hear witness *A*'s story, while defendant Mohammed is obliged to stay put. This too, is an obvious violation. But now suppose instead that a more clever government adjourns the trial, walks into the next room and gets witness *A* to tell his story, and *A* immediately leaves the jurisdiction. When the trial resumes the next day, the prosecutor introduces a video transcript of witness *A*'s story, or a written affidavit or deposition, as testimony. Surely this sneakiness violates the core rule of the confrontation clause, at least in spirit. But also, I submit, in letter. As in the self-incrimination clause, we must properly read the word *witness* to encompass videotapes, transcripts, depositions, and affidavits when prepared for court use and introduced as testimony. And of course this is also true if the deposition was taken before the trial, rather than during it.[184]

The case of depositions differs in key ways from the case where witness *A* takes the stand and recounts what her best friend *B* said. Our deposition was given in a formal, solemn setting, and typically under oath or affirmation; and so a jury might give it great weight on that account, treating it as equal to sworn testimony in the courtroom itself. (This was especially true in the Framers' world, where great weight was placed on oaths.)[185] By contrast, a jury would be much more likely to discount friend *B*'s tale, since *B* took no oath and may have been speaking loosely, without knowledge of the grave legal stakes at issue. Second, a deposition purports to be a precise rendition of the deponent's testimony, once again encouraging a jury to treat it as equivalent to in-court testimony. By contrast, a jury would be less likely to view *A*'s account as a precise repetition of *B*'s words. Third, in depositions, the government has manipulated the process to get witness testimony, qua testimony, with all the formal trappings, while excluding the defendant. Government administers the oath, asks the questions, and transcribes the answers, while purposefully excluding the accused. No similar manipulation occurs when friend *B* talks to her best friend *A*, perhaps even before the crime has occurred, or the government has appeared on the scene. In light of all this, it makes sense to say that a deponent is a "witness" in a way that friend *B* is not.

Our reading of the word *witness* fits its ordinary, everyday meaning and closely follows the logic of the core rules of the self-incrimination and confrontation clauses. It also has several other virtues. For starters, it perfectly fits the history behind the confrontation clause, a history born of revulsion against trial by affidavit.[186] Note how Blackstone presented the confrontation right as designed to avoid the unfairness of government-prepared depositions:

> This open examination of witnesses *viva voce*, in the presence of all mankind, is much more conducive to the clearing up of truth, than the *private and secret examination taken down in writing before an officer* . . . where a witness may frequently *depose* that in private, which he will be ashamed to testify in a public and solemn tribunal. There an *artful or careless scribe* may make a witness speak what he never meant, by dressing up his *depositions* in his own forms and language; but here he is at liberty to correct and explain his meaning, if misunderstood, which he can never do after a *written deposition* is once taken. Besides, [cross-examination] will sift out the truth much better than a *formal set of interrogatories previously penned* and settled.[187]

In one of its earliest and most quoted expositions on the clause, the Supreme Court echoed Blackstone: "The primary object of the [confrontation clause] was to prevent depositions or *ex parte* affidavits . . . being used against the prisoner in lieu of a personal examination and cross-examination of the witness."[188]

What's more, our reading of "witness" in the confrontation clause nicely meshes with the best reading of "witness" in its fraternal twin, the compulsory process clause.[189] A defendant should be able to oblige witnesses to take the stand at trial; but she should also be allowed to oblige pretrial depositions and affidavits, "canning" testimony to be later introduced in court in situations where the witness might not be available at the time of the trial. (Imagine an alibi on his deathbed, pretrial.) When the shoe is on the other foot, the government has the power, pretrial, to subpoena a dying eyewitness[190] and "can" her deposition (with the defendant looking on, and able to cross-examine); and as we shall see, the compulsory process clause should give the accused subpoena parity.[191] (Note also how this "canning" may help the accused preserve evidence during a long accusation period, thus protecting one of the interests that we saw earlier in the speedy trial context.)

In addition, the very existence of the compulsory process clause powerfully undercuts any possible fairness concern about our straightforward reading of "witness" in the confrontation clause. If witness *A* testifies about what out-of-court friend *B* said, and the defendant wants to challenge *B*'s memory or truthfulness directly, face-to-face, the defendant can always use his own compulsory process right to subpoena *B* and interrogate him on the stand, for all to see.[192]

Happily, our reading of the confrontation clause squares with the results of almost all modern Supreme Court cases.[193] The Court has rightly seen that the word *witness* must go beyond those who take the stand in the flesh. But the Court, at least in its language, has failed to crisply distinguish between general out-of-court declarations—one friend talking to another, often even before the government is involved—and governmentally prepared depositions.[194] In its results, however, the Court has intuitively sensed this difference.

Of course, just because garden-variety hearsay that the government tries to introduce at trial clears the confrontation clause hurdle does not mean it is automatically admissible. The flexible hearsay rules, with their flexible exceptions, will typically stand as additional nonconstitutional barriers—much like nonconstitutional statutes of limitations in the speedy trial context. And under an evolving hearsay doctrine, courts can focus directly on reliability, without having to bend the words or the rulelike grammar of the confrontation clause. Beyond this reliance on ordinary rules of evidence, if certain hearsay is horrendously unreliable—in a way the jury could not appropriately discount for—the truth-seeking and innocence-protecting principles of the due process clause and the Sixth Amendment more generally could come into play.

And here we see the final reason for objecting to the Court's shotgun wedding of the hearsay rule and the confrontation clause.[195] Sometimes hearsay will be reliable, and will help *a defendant prove her innocence.*[196] It would be highly unfortunate if we read the Constitution as a document opposed to hearsay as such. For on such a reading, an innocent defendant might face tough sledding in trying to introduce certain reliable hearsay to prove his innocence, despite his right to put on the stand witnesses in his own favor.[197]

To the clause undergirding that right, the confrontation clause's fraternal twin, we now turn.

Compulsory Process

> [T]he accused shall enjoy the right . . . to have compulsory process for obtaining witnesses in his favor.

Underlying this clause is nothing less than the right of the accused to offer "his defence" at his "public trial"—to show the jury and the world that he is not guilty of the "infamous" and "criminal" conduct of which he stands "accused."[198] In the words of the Supreme Court, "The right to offer the testimony of witnesses, and to compel their attendance, if necessary, is in plain terms *the right to present a defense . . . to the jury so it may decide where the truth lies.*"[199] This defense can begin with vigorous questioning of government witnesses and evidence under the letter and spirit of the confrontation clause; but it reaches full bloom in the defendant's compulsory process clause right to present witnesses and evidence of his own. The clause explicitly speaks only of compelling witnesses, but surely the rights to present witnesses who volunteer, and to present physical evidence, follow a fortiori. If the accused, in order to show his innocence, is generally empowered to drag a human being, against her will, into the courtroom to tell the truth, surely he must also enjoy the lesser-included rights to present other truthful evidence that in no way infringes on another human being's autonomy. These lesser-included rights are plainly presupposed by the compulsory process clause;[200] the entire innocence-protecting and truth-seeking structure of the Sixth Amendment, and of constitutional criminal procedure generally, makes no sense without them. (And here we see again the difference between, on one hand, a plain-meaning approach sensitive to letter and spirit and, on the other hand, wooden literalism.)

At least three interesting sets of questions arise concerning the scope of the compulsory process clause. First, does a defendant have a right to knowingly put on perjured testimony if he thinks he can get away with it, fooling (at least for now) the jury and perhaps even the public? Second, exactly how much compulsion is a defendant entitled to use? Suppose a state enforces its subpoenas by fining those who defy. If a reluctant defense witness opts to pay the fine rather than testify, can a defendant insist that she be "compelled" even more—say, held in contempt? Or, if that is not enough, may a defendant insist that the government threaten to boil the witness in oil? Third, exactly whom may the defendant compel as a "witness?" Does the clause give a defendant a right to compel a recalcitrant husband to testify about marital conversations with his wife, or a reluctant doctor to testify, without patient consent, about a patient's private medical condition? What if the government has in place a general spousal or doctor-patient privilege scheme that would prevent the prosecution from compelling analogous witnessing?

In light of all that we have seen, the first question seems easy. A major purpose of the Sixth Amendment, in its public trial and confrontation clauses, is to deter and detect perjury and other frauds upon the court: the amendment seeks truth, not lies. A witness who breaks her oath may be punished for perjury; and a defendant or attorney who conspires with the witness may likewise be punished for soliciting or suborning this perjury. The Sixth Amendment gives the accused a right to show he did not engage in "infamous" conduct, not a right to perpetrate infamous conduct in the courtroom itself.[201]

The answers to our second and third questions are related: A defendant should be given compulsion parity with the government. Whatever compulsion the government could use against a given recalcitrant witness, a defendant can use. If the government cannot compel a doctor to testify against his patient because of a general doctor-patient privilege, a defendant cannot so compel this doctor.

The constitutional virtues of this test are many. It offers a clean, easy-to-administer rule. It borrows from general themes elsewhere in constitutional law—of nondiscrimination and virtual representation—in areas like equal protection, and interstate privileges and immunities.[202] The idea is to enable defendants to benefit from the balance that the state tries to strike when its own evidence-seeking self-interest is at stake. In general, the government will want to give itself broad subpoena power. Without such power, government in a great many cases cannot hope to carry its heavy *Winship* burden of proof. And so when a government chooses to deny itself a certain coercion technique (threats to boil a reluctant witness in oil), or even all coercion against certain highly valued social relationships of intimacy and trust (like the one between wife and husband), this self-denial proves that the government really does see a "compelling interest" against compulsion.

Though the words of the compulsory process clause do not, on their face, demand a parity reading, the established Anglo-American right that the clause meant to declare was clearly defined in terms of subpoena parity. The landmark English Treason Act of 1696 gave defendants "the like Processe . . . to compel their Witnesses . . . as is usually granted to compel Witnesses to appear against them."[203] Some early American formulations echoed this. Thus, William Penn's 1701 Pennsylvania Charter of Privileges declared that defendants "shall have the same Privileges of Witnesses . . . as the Prosecutors";[204] and the New Jersey State Constitution of 1776 gave accused persons "the same privileges of witnesses . . . as their prosecutors are or shall be entitled to."[205] The precise federal formulation, using the language of "compulsory process," derives, it seems, from Blackstone's influential *Commentaries,* and here too, the parity idea is explicit: the accused must enjoy "the same compulsive process to bring in his witnesses for him, as was usual to compel their appearance against him."[206] The first Congress, which drafted the confrontation clause in 1789, statutorily implemented its rule in 1790 in words that, once again, explicitly sounded in parity: "[A capital defendant] shall have the like process of the court . . . to compel his . . . witnesses to appear at his . . . trial, as is usually granted . . . to appear on [behalf of] the prosecution."[207]

In its sparse compulsory process case law, the Court has repeatedly struck down asymmetric witness rules and noted the asymmetry,[208] but in one important corner of law, the government today can compel witnessing where defendants cannot. When government prosecutes defendant A, it will often need the testimony of A's (perhaps junior) partner-in-crime B in order to carry its *Winship* burden and make its charges stick. But when the government subpoenas B, B may claim his self-incrimination privilege. (Otherwise, the government could simply force B to testify in A's case, and then turn around and prosecute B, using a transcript of B's prior testimony against himself.) But the government may nonetheless compel B, even in the teeth of B's self-incrimination claim, so long as government gives B minimal Fifth Amendment immunity. According to the modern Court in the *Kastigar*[209] case, this immunity must guarantee that the government will not use B's testimony, or any fruits derived from the testimony, in any later criminal case against B. The government may still prosecute B, but it must prove that everything in its case is wholly independent of B's earlier compelled testimony. This, of course, can be a hard thing to prove, as the special prosecutor in the Oliver North case can attest.[210]

But now suppose that the government decides not to compel B's testimony via minimal Fifth Amendment *(Kastigar)* immunity but that defendant A wants to oblige B to take the stand. A believes that B's truthful testimony would in fact prove A's innocence. B did it, not A. A subpoenas B, but B resists, claiming his self-incrimination privilege. A now demands that the government give B *Kastigar* immunity so as to overcome B's privilege, and compel B to testify. What result?

Under current doctrine, A would lose.[211] Otherwise, every defendant could give his partners in crime an "immunity bath," and the government will be much worse off when it tries to prosecute the criminal partners in later cases. The government, again, would have to prove that nothing in its case was in any way influenced by the defendant's prior compelled testimony, and this can be very hard to prove—especially when witnesses testify as expansively as they can to maximize their future immunity.

Note, however, what has happened. Defendant A is being denied his express right to compel B to witness—in testimony that might indeed prove A innocent. The minimal idea of subpoena parity underlying the compulsory process clause is violated here: government can "compel" B to testify (via *Kastigar*) but the defendant may not. B's Fifth Amendment rights seem to be at war with, and to prevail against, A's Sixth Amendment rights, even though A is of course (for now) the one who is on trial, perhaps with his very life at stake.

The problem here, however, has been created by the Court, not the Constitution. The Court has simply misread the word *witness*—again that key word—in the self-incrimination clause. And once we read that clause correctly, the compulsory process clause springs free from its current shackles. As explained in Chapter 2, *Kastigar* is wrong. So long as the government never introduces B's transcript as testimony in a later criminal case against B, B will never have become an involuntary *witness* against himself in his own case. Fruits of prior testimony are allowable; *fruits* are not *witnessing*. And so the government may compel B's testimony in A's case merely by giving B "testimonial" immunity— B's testimony cannot itself be introduced against B. Under this rule, if the government decides *not* to immunize and compel B, A can do so. A can indeed enjoy compulsion parity, but the government need never fear immunity baths. When A immunizes and compels B, the government is never worse off than it would have been without immunity. Indeed, it is better off, for now it can use any leads or fruits generated by B to prosecute B. Through the compulsory process clause, innocent A can in fact help the truth come to light and bring guilty B to justice. Instead of being at war with each other, the Fifth and the Sixth Amendments can now work together, in a way that promotes truth and protects innocence.

Happier still, Fifth Amendment testimonial immunity would also powerfully reinforce Sixth Amendment speedy trial clause values. Currently, many a defendant may languish pretrial while the government first tries to convict an accomplice, who can then be obliged to testify against the defendant without the high cost of *Kastigar* immunity. With testimonial immunity in place, the government could instead prosecute the defendant *A* and his alleged accomplice *B* together in a speedy joint trial, with two juries empaneled. If either *A* or the government seeks to oblige *B* to take the stand, *B*'s jury can be dismissed—this is, in effect, testimonial immunity—but *A*'s jury can hear all. And the prosecutor or *B*, of course, could similarly compel *A* to testify, with *A*'s jury excused, if *A* pleads the Fifth. On this reading, the Constitution coheres, with testimonial immunity rules tightly intermeshing with speedy trial values and compulsion parity ideas.

Of course, even compulsion parity does not entirely even the scales between prosecution and defendant. Beyond its power to "compel" witnesses, government can "encourage" them to volunteer, by covering their expenses, or promising them greater immunity than is required to "compel" them under the self-incrimination clause. Government can also spend vast sums of money to investigate crime. Most defendants lack a parity of resources to "encourage" and "investigate" other witnesses. The parity underlying the compulsory clause is in this sense a narrow one; it is a parity of subpoena-like compulsion power.[212]

But the idea that parity is the touchstone only for compulsion can at times help defendants, especially innocent defendants. Consider a case where a defendant is not seeking to compel a balky witness but trying to put on the stand a voluntary witness or to introduce some physical evidence. Assume that, under a general evidence rule in place in the jurisdiction—a rule applicable against prosecutors and defendants—this evidence is inadmissible. By hypothesis, the evidence rule passes a parity test, but the defendant can respond that parity applies only to compulsion. Here, the defendant can argue that because no unwilling human being is being coerced, the test should be a more general Sixth Amendment and due process test of innocence protection and truth-seeking: unless the evidence is so unreliable, in the context of other evidence in the case, that it cannot properly be assessed by the jury and the public, a defendant should be able to get it in.[213] He has a general right to make his defense—to show he didn't do it—lest we unduly increase the risk of erroneously convicting an innocent man.

It remains, finally, to ponder more carefully the plight of the innocent man who seeks to compel a witness who hides behind a general privilege—say, a doctor who refuses to testify about private medical facts concerning her patient unless the patient consents. Unlike, say, a government-informer privilege, this one passes the parity test. Nevertheless, our defendant responds: "I am innocent. And this doctor has evidence—reliable evidence—that can prove my innocence to the jury and to the public."

Though there appears to be little support for the defendant's plea in the history of the compulsory process clause, its English roots, or its early implementation in America, it still tugs at our hearts. But perhaps its very emotional power is its own undoing; for at a minimum, the defendant (or his counsel) can make this speech to the jury, and argue that the unavailability of the evidence should raise reasonable doubts.[214]

Alternatively, we might say that compulsion parity is necessary to vindicate the compulsory process clause, but not sufficient.[215] If, however, we reject this approach and embrace compulsion parity as both necessary and sufficient, we are admitting that truth and innocence protection are not the *only* important values—we as a society also care about other things, including preserving fragile and socially beneficial relationships of trust like the bonds between wife and husband, doctor and patient, priest and penitent.

But such a recognition does not demolish my general claims here about the huge importance of truth-seeking and innocence protection in the Sixth Amendment and in constitutional criminal procedure generally. After all, if innocence protection were the only value, to be maximized at all costs, we would simply refuse to allow anyone to be convicted, in order to eliminate any possibility of an erroneous conviction of an innocent man.

Moreover, the existence of true privacy privileges—doctor-patient, spousal, and priest-penitent, for example—surely does not support broad upside-down exclusionary rules of constitutional criminal procedure, like the Fourth Amendment *Boyd/Weeks/Mapp*[216] rule and the Fifth Amendment *Kastigar* rule. To begin with, privacy privileges are simply not constitutional criminal procedure. Indeed, like Voltaire's Holy Roman Empire they are often none of the above. First, these privileges have typically not been entrenched as textual *constitutional* mandates, and so if their precise contours prove inconvenient, they can be easily adjusted. Second, they are most definitely not *criminal:* they apply in all courtrooms, civil and criminal. By contrast, the Fourth Amendment exclusionary rule applies only in criminal and not civil cases; and the *Kastigar* rule likewise bars fruits only in criminal cases but not civil ones. Third, privacy privileges are not truly *procedural.* They are rooted in substantive norms, protecting valuable social relations—bonds of trust and privacy that would be destroyed by the public witnessing *itself.*

Exclusionary rule rhetoric at times tries to sound the same themes, but this rings hollow. The underlying Fourth Amendment protects privacy, but the introduction in court of, say, drugs or stolen goods *itself* works no new *privacy* violation.[217] (If it did, exclusion would be required in civil cases, too.) Of course, friends of the Fourth Amendment exclusionary rule argue it will *deter* future violations, but that is very different from privacy privileges where exclusion is itself the *right*, not an analytically misfitting *remedy*. The analytic misfit of ordinary Fourth Amendment exclusion is that exclusion is neither necessary nor sufficient to deter. It is not sufficient because it fails to focus on cops who know a citizen is innocent, and predictably find no evidence in the course of hassling her. Once we realize, as did the Founders, that we must provide deterrent remedies for innocent citizens, we can put an analytically proper remedy in place, and exclusion is no longer necessary to deter. And, not coincidentally, our proper remedial scheme will be right side up, making innocent citizens whole and denying guilty defendants windfalls. In short, the Framers understood deterrence much better than do exclusionary rule fans.[218]

What's more, true privacy privileges respect the deep norms underlying a public trial; they simply mark the border between the public and the truly private. As the word *priv*ilege implies, these immunities shield *private* communications that have never before been made public. And so when these privileges are observed, we do not suffer the public demoralization that now occurs, when publicly available information is simply shut out of the public courtroom.[219] The public trial ideal promises that anyone who seeks to offer reliable evidence can "draw nigh, and will be heard." The exclusionary rule betrays this ideal; but many privacy privileges do not—they do not bar members of the public from coming to court and volunteering their information.

Counsel

> [T]he accused shall enjoy the right . . . to have the Assistance of Counsel for his defence.

This last right is a big one, ramifying in many directions. Here I shall briefly discuss only three. First, when does the right attach? Second, does it encompass the right to state-provided counsel? Third, what are the ethical limits of counsel's role in assisting the accused in making her defense? In pondering these questions, we shall see how the clause neatly interlocks with other clauses in the Sixth Amendment; here, too, innocence protection and truth-seeking are, or should be, central.

Given the explicit words of the counsel clause, and the overall architecture of the Sixth Amendment, the "right . . . to have the Assistance of Counsel for [one's] defence" is triggered when and because a person is "accused" of "criminal" wrongdoing. As we saw in our discussion of the speedy trial clause, the Sixth Amendment is *accusation-based*, because accusation itself subjects a person to distinct risks.[220] One risk is the threat of prolonged pretrial detention—a threat triggered by arrest or indictment. To prevent this evil, an accused may need to file a habeas writ; to compensate for any past violation and deter any future one, an accused may need to bring a *Bivens*-like action. And these are things that lawyers are (or at least should be) good for. Filing writs and the like requires familiarity both with broad substantive law—the rights of free men and women—and technical procedural law: where to file, with what words, before whom, and so on. And so for pretrial detainees, the right to counsel simply makes real one of the core legal interests guaranteed by the speedy trial clause.

Even for an "accused" not subject to arrest or pretrial detention, the formal accusation itself of course triggers another threat to liberty. Formally, indictment sets the stage for trial; once indicted, even a person who honestly pleads not guilty risks erroneous conviction. In order to defend himself, an accused needs to understand the accusation—this is the obvious logic of the "nature and cause" clause. But indictments can at times be laced with technical legal language that an accused person— especially, perhaps, if wholly innocent (say, in a case of mistaken identity)—may not understand. Here, too, the "Assistance of Counsel" can help breathe life into the promise of an earlier Sixth Amendment clause.

Consider, finally, the trial itself, when the accused at last gets a chance to clear his name before the jury and the world—to poke holes in the government's case and to present his own, revealing the truth and showing his factual or normative innocence. But this trial may be filled with technical lawyer's law—for example, the rules of evidence. And so without expert legal assistance, the accused may well be unable to exercise his all-important rights to cross-examine government witnesses and to present his own evidence and witnesses—rights at the heart of the confrontation and compulsory process clauses. Once again, we see how the Sixth Amendment's last clause merely makes real the promise of its earlier provisions.[221]

Of course, there may well be occasions prior to criminal accusation when general, innocence-protecting principles will trigger an analogous right of counsel, but there is no blanket rule requiring counsel before accusation.[222] Consider, for example, the immemorial practice of excluding defense lawyers from the grand jury inquest.[223] An arrest may trigger the risk of extended pretrial detention, but a grand jury summons does not. A trial is governed by technical rules of evidence, but a grand jury is not. Thus, the Sixth Amendment analysis we have developed explains both why a person has a general right of counsel after and because of accusation, and why she has no blanket right before, even if she is paying the bill.

But what about those "accused" persons who cannot pay the bill for the "Assistance of Counsel?" Are they entitled to counsel at government expense? The text of the counsel clause can be read either way. But structural arguments strongly support the modern Court's view that indigent defendants have a right to the assistance of counsel at government expense.[224] As we have seen, in many respects the last clause of the Sixth Amendment simply implements the rights guaranteed by its earlier clauses, and these clauses protect rich and poor alike. The appointment of counsel requires government to act "affirmatively," but so does the compulsory process clause, which requires government to act affirmatively to enforce subpoenas. Government payment of defense counsel costs money, but so does convening an impartial jury, holding a public trial, informing the accused of the "nature and cause" of charges, and so on.

At first, history might seem to strongly undercut our textual and structural analysis. The very Congress that proposed the Sixth Amendment provided, in its statutes, for appointed counsel in capital cases but not elsewhere.[225] But this history should not be overread. The legal theory was not that indigents in noncapital cases would simply have to do without the "Assistance of Counsel." Rather, it was that the judge himself could act as counsel and provide a defendant legal assistance.[226] Because judges were of course paid by the government, this too was a form of government-provided "counsel" for indigent defendants.

But this was a plainly inadequate form, especially because some of the rights in the Sixth Amendment are based on a healthy suspicion of judges. And the need for expert legal advice has only grown over the last two centuries, as criminal law—both substantive and procedural—has become increasingly complex.

Even if the history of the First Congress were (wrongly) deemed to trump text and structure in the Sixth Amendment context, the indigent's right to appointed counsel could also be derived from the innocence-protecting spirit of the due process clause. The flexibility of the clause, focusing explicitly on how much process is due, can easily accommodate evolving historical developments. Twentieth-century America is considerably wealthier than was eighteenth-century America; and this in turn bears on whether additional procedural safeguards, though costly, are nonetheless due—reasonable, apt, fair.[227] In today's world, an indigent defendant without counsel runs an undue risk of being convicted, even if wholly innocent.

The importance of innocence and truth also helps answer our final question, concerning the appropriate ethical boundaries of counsel's role. As we have seen, a guilty defendant has no general right, under the Sixth Amendment or anything else, to perjure himself, or knowingly introduce false evidence, or commit other infamous acts in the courtroom itself. The point here is not merely that if he does commit a fraud upon the Court and is found out, he may be punished. Rather, it is that he may not do it even if he knows he can "get away with it" or is willing to "run the risk." This "get away with it" mentality—that a person has a "right" to commit perjury (or to murder witnesses, for that matter) so long as he can cover his tracks, or is willing to "do the time"—reflects a Holmesian "bad man" view of the law. But our Sixth Amendment is structured around a good man, wrongly charged. The "bad man" view is built on lies and concealment; but the Sixth Amendment was written to promote truth and openness—publicity.

All of this has huge implications for the proper role of counsel. If the accused has no right to defraud the court, surely he has no right to the "assistance" of counsel in perpetrating his frauds. Bribing judges, lying on the stand, putting on false witness, fabricating evidence, threatening prosecution witnesses—none of these is part of a lawful Sixth Amendment "defence," and so counsel must avoid aiding any of these acts. Counsel, under the Sixth Amendment, is provided to enforce the law's letter and spirit, not to evade them.

Thus, the Sixth Amendment's structure rejects the ideas that a lawyer owes some unbending duty of loyalty to the accused, and that a lawyer must never act against his client.[228] Rather, counsel's obligations of client loyalty are limited by the truth-seeking architecture of the Sixth Amendment. To be sure, effective "Assistance of Counsel" cannot occur if a lawyer is merely the spy of the system. And so, the attorney-client relationship is shielded by a privacy privilege akin to the husband-wife, doctor-patient, and priest-penitent privileges. But the attorney-client privilege is also different. Spouses, doctors, and priests may simply stay out of the courtroom, and keep their private information out of the public trial. The lawyer, by contrast, plays a hugely public and active role; simple nonfeasance is not feasible, and so he must take care to avoid becoming an active agent of fraud.

In its landmark ruling in the 1986 case *Nix v. Whiteside*, the Supreme Court held that "under no circumstances may a lawyer either advocate or passively tolerate a client's giving false testimony. This, of course, is consistent with the governance of trial conduct in what we have long called 'a search for truth.'"[229] The logic of *Nix* is that perjury must be prevented, and not merely by the adversary system of prosecutorial cross-examination and the subsequent threat of perjury prosecution. Defense counsel herself must not assist this fraud, and merely putting a witness on the stand and asking questions counts as impermissible assistance. In short, at times a lawyer cannot ask questions and let the jury decide, even if this strategy maximizes her client's chance for victory. "Plainly, [counsel's duty of loyalty] is limited to legitimate, lawful conduct compatible with the very nature of a trial as a search for truth."[230]

This logic, however, raises unsettling questions about extremely vigorous cross-examination of *truthful* witnesses, a tactic that most American defense lawyers today view as obviously appropriate and perhaps required by legal ethics.[231] Consider a bank robbery case in which the accused tells his lawyer that he, in fact, committed the crime and that the security guard saw him. If the guard takes the stand as a prosecution witness, how vigorously may defense counsel cross-examine her? Does the Sixth Amendment oblige, permit, or prohibit questions on cross-examination to show that the guard's eyesight is not great, that she had only a few seconds to observe the robber, and that she failed to immediately pick out the defendant in a lineup? A critic of this cross-examination might view it as the moral equivalent of fraud: Isn't counsel implicitly suggesting, through his questions, that the security guard is mistaken—a fact that counsel knows is false? Counsel, however, has a strong response: "My questions do not necessarily imply that my client is in fact innocent but only that the government has failed to provide proof beyond a reasonable doubt. The guard's eyesight and shaky identification do raise reasonable doubt, and so the implicit theory of the case underlying my admittedly vigorous questions is utterly truthful. Even if my client is in fact guilty, the government's proof is still weak, and this weakness should be emphasized to the jury and the public, in keeping with the true spirit of Sixth Amendment innocence protection." Counsel's line here is a fine one—between asking questions that imply factual innocence and asking questions that merely imply reasonable doubt—but, in principle, a workable one.

But now consider a date rape case where the defendant, once again, tells his lawyer that he did it. May the lawyer try to demolish the victim when she takes the witness stand, impugning her motives, questioning her honesty, bringing up her past sexual history? In at least four ways, this case seems different, and the vigorous cross-examination at issue may actually tend to undermine the spirit of the Sixth

Amendment. First, counsel, by his questions, is implicitly saying that the witness is not merely possibly mistaken, but is in fact a liar—indeed, a perjurer.[232] In ordinary morality, there is a big difference between asking someone "are you sure?" and calling her a liar. In any other context, this knowingly false public accusation of dishonesty would be actionable, but when this reputational mugging occurs in a courtroom it is immune from defamation laws. Counsel can thus "get away with it" in a Holmesian "bad man" sense; but as we have seen the Sixth Amendment is built on a very different worldview. (Indeed, as we saw in the speedy trial context, the amendment was designed to shield Americans from baseless reputational assaults, especially when defamation actions are unavailing because of courtroom immunities.) Second, savaging a truthful witness's honor and character powerfully discourages truthful witnesses from coming forward—in precise violation of the spirit of the public trial clause. Outright extortion, bribery, or physical intimidation of a would-be witness is clearly illegitimate; but is a brutal verbal assault carried out in a public courtroom and built on lies really so different? (And let us not forget that this cruel verbal assault takes aim at a woman who has already suffered a savage physical assault from the lawyer's client.) Third, in trying to paint the rape victim as a liar, a lawyer typically must "playact" and posture in ways that implicitly argue to the jury and the public not merely that reasonable doubt about guilt exists, but that the accused is in fact not guilty. And the implicit representation is a knowing falsehood—a lie.[233] Fourth, and related, the emphasis on reasonable doubt in the bank robbery case closely tracks the core purpose of counsel in the Sixth Amendment, based on lawyers' special familiarity with legal rules, like the *Winship* principle. Anyone can insult, bully, playact, posture, and mislead—that is not why the Sixth Amendment calls for lawyers. Rather, lawyers contribute something special to a trial precisely because they understand the importance of procedural rules like *Winship*.

It is no answer to all this to simply point to, and hide behind, the "adversary system" as a justification for trying to demolish a rape victim on the witness stand. As we have seen, the entire premise of the Sixth Amendment, and of the confrontation clause in particular, was that the truth will likely out in a vigorous exchange. But the question now at hand is precisely *what the ground rules of that exchange should be* so as to vindicate this premise and maximize the possibility that the truth will indeed out. If perjury is beyond the pale—even when one could get away with it within an adversary system—perhaps certain forms of cross-examination (and other lawyers' tactics) should themselves be cross-examined. And because any ethical restrictions on misleading cross-examination would constrain prosecutors as well as defense counsel, such restrictions in the long run may prove a net plus to innocent defendants.[234]

These final speculations will no doubt strike many American lawyers, steeped in gladiatorial ethics and a sporting theory of justice, as outright heresy. But perhaps this reaction is itself only a sign of how far we have strayed from the Sixth Amendment's first principles. This amendment speaks to and about lawyers with more directness than any other clause in the Constitution, and yet many lawyers today misread its letter and spirit. And so our current lack of a good map of the amendment may mean not merely bad constitutional law and bad criminal procedure, but perhaps bad legal ethics too.

4 The Future of Constitutional Criminal Procedure

We live in interesting times, and the times are especially interesting for those of us who work in the field of constitutional criminal procedure. In the three preceding chapters I have sought to explore the foundations of the field—to lay bare, and elaborate upon, the "first principles" of the Fourth, Fifth, and Sixth Amendments. These chapters, in earlier incarnations, have already begun to provoke heated controversy over some of my specific doctrinal claims.[1] (As I said, we live in interesting times.) In this brief concluding chapter, I shall try to pull the camera back, highlighting some of the general features of my "first principles" project. In the process, I hope to say a few words about the past and present of constitutional criminal procedure, and a few more words about its future—in courts, in Congress, in classrooms, and in conversations everywhere in between.

Where Are We, and How Did We Get Here?

The Past

As a subfield of constitutional law, constitutional criminal procedure stands as an anomaly. In many other areas of constitutional law, major Marshall Court opinions stand out and continue to frame debate both in courts and beyond. In thinking about judicial review and executive power, we still look to *Marbury v. Madison*;[2] in pondering the puzzle of jurisdiction stripping, we go back to *Martin v. Hunter's Lessee*;[3] in reflecting on the scope of Congress's enumerated powers and related issues of federalism, we re-examine *McCulloch v. Maryland*;[4] in considering vested property rights, we return to *Fletcher v. Peck*[5] and *Dartmouth College v. Woodward*;[6] and so on. But no comparable Marshall Court landmarks dot the plain of constitutional criminal procedure.

It is often thought that the explanation for this anomaly lies in another Marshall Court landmark, *Barron v. Baltimore*.[7] Most criminal law, the argument goes, is state law: murder, rape, robbery, and the like are generally not federal crimes. Under *Barron*, the constitutional criminal procedure rules of the Bill of Rights did not apply against states, and so the Marshall Court predictably heard few cases raising issues of constitutional criminal procedure.

Barron is indeed part of the story, but only part. For the federal government was very much in the crime-fighting business in the first century of the Bill of Rights. For constitutional scholars, perhaps the most vivid example of early federal criminal law comes from the infamous Sedition Act of 1798; but we must also not forget the territories. Perhaps *the* most central and sustained project of the federal government in its first century was the "Americanization" of this continent through territorial expansion, organization of territorial governments, and eventual admission to statehood of these territories.[8] In the territories, the federal government did indeed enforce garden-variety criminal laws against murder, rape, robbery, and so on. And the Bill of Rights very much applied to these criminal cases, even under *Barron*. Territorial law was, constitutionally speaking, federal law.

But—and this is the key point—for virtually the entire first century of the Bill of Rights, the United States Supreme Court lacked general appellate jurisdiction over federal criminal cases.[9] This little-known fact helps explain why, for example, the Sedition Act prosecutions in the late 1790s—which raised the most important and far-reaching constitutional issues of their day—never reached the Supreme Court for ultimate judicial resolution.[10]

By the time Congress decided to give the High Court general appellate review over federal criminal cases in 1891, the sun was already setting on the Territorial Era. Thus, the criminal cases the Supreme Court heard under the new jurisdictional regime were indeed a skewed lot, with disproportionately more federal customs violations, tax evasions, and bootleggings than murders, rapes, and robberies. It was this era, of course, that gave birth to the controversial exclusionary rule.

Then came the Warren Court, which overruled *Barron* and began applying the Fourth, Fifth, and Sixth Amendments directly against states, under the banner of selective incorporation. With many, many more state criminal cases filling its docket, the Warren Court proceeded to build up, in short order, a remarkable doctrinal edifice of Fourth Amendment, Fifth Amendment, and Sixth Amendment rules—the foundations of modern constitutional criminal procedure.

But these foundations were none too sure. On a lawyerly level, some of the Warren Court's most important criminal procedure pronouncements lacked firm grounding in constitutional text and structure. Key rulings ran counter to early case law both in lower federal courts and in state courts construing analogous provisions of state constitutions. Precisely because so few Marshall Court cases existed, this break with Founding-era understandings was less visible. On key issues, the Warren Court seemed to contradict itself, laying down sweeping rules in some cases that it could not quite live by in other cases. On a political level, many of the Warren Court's constitutional criminal procedure pronouncements did not sit well with the American electorate. The guilty too often seemed to spring free without good reason—and by this time the guilty regularly included murderers, rapists, and robbers, not just federal income tax frauds and customs cheats. In a constitutional democracy, the People, in the long run, usually prevail. Federal judges may be, at times, "insulated" and "countermajoritarian," but majorities elect Presidents, and Presidents, with the advice and consent of elected Senators, pick federal judges.

And so, with Earl Warren's retirement and Richard Nixon's election on a "law and order" platform, the counterrevolution began. But the foundations of this counterrevolution are also none too sure. Like the Warren Court, the Burger and Rehnquist Courts have at times paid little heed to constitutional text, history, and structure and have mouthed rules one day only to ignore them the next. If the Warren Court at times was too easy on the guilty, the Burger and Rehnquist Courts at times have been too hard on the innocent.

The Present

Where does all this leave us today? At a crossroads. On at least four different levels, I submit, the present is a particularly ripe moment for a fundamental rethinking of constitutional criminal procedure, and for a choice among competing visions.

Consider first the level of *Supreme Court doctrine*. At this level, constitutional criminal procedure is, to put it bluntly, a mess. For more than a quarter of a century, the Burger and Rehnquist Courts have busily reshaped Warren Court doctrine in this field. But often, the Court has chosen to proceed by indirection. Warren Court landmarks are distinguished away rather than overruled;[11] old cases are hollowed out from within, but the facade remains—or does it? And so *United States Reports* now swells with language bulging this way and that, at virtually every level of generality and specificity.

But the problem runs even deeper. For starters, many of the contradictions came from the Warren Court itself. The Warren Court told us that the Fourth Amendment requires warrants and probable cause for all searches and seizures.[12] But in *Terry v. Ohio*, Chief Justice Warren himself, writing at the peak of his reign, told us that frisking is a "search" that does *not* require warrants *or* probable cause.[13] Indeed, *Terry* quoted the amendment as simply banning *unreasonable* searches and seizures and declined even to recite its language about warrants and probable cause.[14] The Warren Court told us that the Constitution requires exclusion of illegally obtained evidence.[15] But in *Terry*, the Court warned against a "rigid and unthinking application of the exclusionary rule."[16] The Warren Court told us that the exclusionary rule derived from a synergy between the Fourth Amendment and the Fifth Amendment self-incrimination clause.[17] But in *Schmerber v. California*, Justice Brennan—the playmaking guard of Earl Warren's team—sharply separated the Fourth and Fifth Amendments.[18] In so doing, Justice Brennan and the Court clearly held that a man could indeed be obliged to furnish evidence—his very blood, no less—against himself in a criminal case. And the logic of that clear holding, as we saw in Chapters 1 and 2,[19] left both the exclusionary rule and broad theories of self-incrimination exclusion dangling in midair, with no principled support, constitutionally speaking.

So too, the Burger and Rehnquist Courts have failed to live up to their articulated principles. The post-Warren Court has admitted that the exclusionary rule lacks constitutional footing[20] but has kept the rule nonetheless. The Court has failed to build up alternative remedial schemes that would protect innocent people from outrageous searches and seizures and would also deter future government abuse. In *Los Angeles v. Lyons*, decided in the heyday of the Burger Court, the majority simply looked the other way when Los Angeles police officers engaged in obviously brutal, possibly racist, and at times deadly choke holds of presumptively innocent citizens.[21] The post-Warren Court has, at times, admitted that warrants are not the ultimate Fourth Amendment touchstone; reasonableness is.[22] But in *Zurcher v. Stanford Daily News*, the Court worshiped the warrant and blessed the most constitutionally unreasonable of searches—paper searches of antigovernment newspapers.[23] The *Stanford Daily News* was not even alleged to have been engaged in criminal wrongdoing, and yet it, too, got the back of the judicial hand.

When judges either must strain against dominant doctrine to explain easy cases (like *Terry* and *Schmerber*) or actually get easy cases wrong (like *Lyons* and *Zurcher*), they have obviously taken a wrong turn somewhere. Hence a desperate need for returning to, and rethinking, first principles.

Consider next the level of *Supreme Court personnel*. We now stand at a generational changing of the guard. With the retirements of Justices Brennan, Marshall, and White in the early 1990s, none of those who shared the bench with Chief Justice Earl Warren now sits. Two-thirds of the current High Court never even sat with Chief Justice Warren Burger.[24] Very few of the current Justices have much of a *personal* stake—as an author or dissenter—in the elaborate doctrinal structures that have been built up and then whittled down in constitutional criminal procedure. The swing Justices today are highly intelligent and relatively nonideological.[25] They just want to do what is right—and so here again, there is a desperate need for a clear statement of what are, or should be, the first principles in the field. Again, precedent alone cannot guide the way—even for those Justices who steer by precedent as their polestar—because precedent in this field is so regularly contradictory or perverse.

Now turn to the level of *congressional and national political conversation*. Here, too, we are in the midst, it seems, of a generational changing of the guard. After a half-century of Democratic domination, the House fell into Republican hands in 1994. At first, it might seem implausible that a bare majority of the House and Senate could radically rewrite criminal procedure policy. Intrabranch filters like the committee system and the filibuster rule can slow things down and force slim majorities to yield to strong minorities; and of course there is always the possible presidential veto to consider. But even if a mere majority cannot unilaterally prevail in enacting law, it can often unilaterally define a national agenda—holding hearings to shine a national spotlight on certain issues while pushing other issues off the stage. When the Democrats controlled, they did not schedule many hearings on affirmative action or on the exclusionary rule—wedge issues that might have splintered the Democratic coalition of minorities, liberal elites, and the working class. But with Republicans in charge, the exclusionary rule and other issues of criminal procedure have indeed leaped onto the agenda, and many different proposals now jostle for attention.[26] Political debate about criminal procedure was certain to heat up even more in 1996, with presidential, congressional, and state campaigns waged in the wake of the ballyhooed "trial of the century," in which many believe that a guilty man got away with murder. But which, if any, of the various proposed reforms now swirling about would actually move America in the right direction? Yet again, we see the need for an overall framework of analysis and vision of proper first principles.

Finally, let us consider the level of *academic scholarship*. On this level, too, we stand near a generational changing of the guard in constitutional criminal procedure. Those who in their youth led cheers for the Warren Court are moving toward, or have already passed into, their retirement years. Dramatic trends are at work in the academy generally. In constitutional law, textualism and originalism have staged a comeback; economic analysis has reconfigured many curricular fields; critical race theory and feminism insistently urge us to ask "the race question" and "the gender question" everywhere; and so on. How will a new generation of constitutional criminal procedure scholars reshape the academic orthodoxies we have inherited?

In the preceding three chapters I have put forth my vision of how constitutional criminal procedure must be reshaped. In what follows, I shall try to summarize and explain some of the key elements of this vision.

Where Should We Go from Here?

Constitutional Methodology

To begin with, we must distinguish *constitutional* criminal procedure from criminal procedure generally. Not all sensible rules of criminal procedure can or should be constitutionalized.[27] The Constitution—when read in light of its text, history, and structure, its doctrinal elaboration in precedent, the need for principled judicial standards, and so on—simply may not speak to some issues. This is, of course, one of the reasons we have legislatures—to make sensible policy where the Constitution permits choice. Legislative solutions can be adjusted in the face of new facts or changing values far more easily than can rules that have been read into the Constitution.

Consider, for example, the so-called exclusionary rule. I have attacked this as a rule of *constitutional* criminal procedure. This rule is, quite simply, not in our Constitution. I have not claimed that the Constitution prohibits exclusion, only that it does not require it. In some times, and in some places, a legislative scheme of exclusion might be sensible—a two-by-four between the eyes to get the attention of mulish police. I have emphasized the costs to innocent victims of such exclusion schemes, but a legislature certainly could decide that the benefits outweigh the costs for now. If the facts change over time—if, say, police are now generally more sensitive to Fourth Amendment issues than they were in 1961—a legislature is free without embarrassment to change the law. A court, however, is not likewise free to rule one day that the Constitution requires exclusion as a matter of principle and then to disregard that very principle the next day.

A critic might object that the Supreme Court has never really said that the Constitution requires exclusion as a matter of principle but only that exclusion is one apt remedy to deter. And, the critic might argue, a court is free to fashion flexible remedies one day and adjust them the next. Such a critic, however, would be wrong about both Supreme Court case law and constitutional remedial theory. In about twenty cases, decided over almost a century, the Supreme Court practiced exclusion in the name of a *requirement* of the Fifth Amendment self-incrimination clause, in tandem with the Fourth Amendment.[28] Exclusion was not merely a judicially fashioned, empirical, pragmatic, and deterrence-based *remedy* for an antecedent Fourth Amendment violation. It was also, and more importantly, a *right* under the self-incrimination clause: introducing illegally obtained evidence at trial would *itself* violate the Fifth Amendment. The paradigm here was a diary wrongfully seized from a criminal defendant and then read against him at trial: reading the diary in court was itself seen as akin to compelling a defendant to "witness" against himself, in violation of self-incrimination principles. Only this argument from principle explains some of the most basic features of the Supreme Court's case law. Only this provides the justification for exclusion as a constitutional mandate. Only this explains why exclusion applies in criminal cases but not civil cases. Only this explains why illegal arrests are different from illegal searches. Only this explains so-called "standing" rules.

But, I have argued, this argument from principle rests on an incorrect reading of the Constitution. Today, the Supreme Court agrees.[29] But if so, then exclusion must fall. The critic's deterrence/remedy gambit fails as a matter of *constitutional* law. Once we admit—as the Supreme Court now does[30]—that a Fourth Amendment violation is complete at the time of the search and that no new violation occurs when evidence is admitted at trial, we are admitting that exclusion is not logically linked to the scope of the violation. Judicial remedies must fit the scope of the right. For example, a court is not free, as a matter of constitutional law, to play the "Leavenworth lottery": Because the government violated the constitutional rights of *A*, judges spin the wheel and spring some lucky (but unrelated) convict *B* from Leavenworth. This scheme might indeed deter—and a legislature might have the power to enact this into law—but courts have no such power as a matter of traditional remedial theory. And with the Fourth-Fifth fusion argument having been shattered by *Schmerber, Fisher,* and *Leon,*[31] exclusion is analytically indistinguishable from the "Leavenworth lottery."

As these last points suggest, the Constitution is not some ventriloquist's dummy that can be made to say anything the puppeteer likes. Yet it is remarkable how little attention many leading scholars and distinguished judges have paid to the text of the Constitution while busily making criminal procedure pronouncements in its name. Perhaps this is because so much of the debate, both academic and judicial, took shape in the early to mid-1960s, when textual argument in constitutional law often drew smirks from sophisticated lawyers. But most of the major Warren Court pronouncements did draw, at least in part, on text, and stood on the shoulders of that giant of constitutional textualism, Justice Hugo Black. Exclusion in *Mapp* was required by the words and spirit of the Fourth *and* Fifth Amendments, said Justice Black in providing the critical fifth vote[32]—echoing repeated invocations in Justice Clark's opinion for the Court (at least six, by my count).[33] Incorporation of the Bill of Rights against the states, reminded Justice Black in *Duncan,* simply followed the words and spirit of the Fourteenth Amendment as a whole, including its privileges or immunities clause.[34] Warrants and probable cause, said the Warren Court, were required because the text of the Fourth Amendment implicitly said so; its words made no sense otherwise.[35] Florida could not try Gideon without a lawyer, Justice Black wrote for the Court, because the Sixth Amendment's words provided for a "right of counsel" and the Fourteenth Amendment's words incorporated fundamental rights against states.[36] Miranda must go free, said the Court, because he was in effect compelled to be a witness against himself in a criminal case in violation of the words and spirit of the Fifth Amendment.[37] And so on.

What's more, sophisticated constitutional lawyers today no longer scoff at textual argument. Unlike Coach Lombardi on winning, we do not consider text "the *only* thing," but we do think it is relevant—it is *something*—that the Fourth Amendment's text fails to require warrants and probable cause for all searches and seizures; and that this failure makes lots of sense. Surely it is relevant that the Fourth Amendment says nothing about exclusion and that if it did, it surely does not distinguish between civil and criminal cases. Surely it is relevant that the Fourth Amendment's words about the people's right to be secure in "their persons, houses, papers and effects" conjure up tort law, which does protect these interests. Surely it is relevant that, when Oliver North is forced to testify before Congress and his words are never admitted against him in his criminal trial, but testimonial fruits do come in, North has never been *compelled* to be a *witness* against himself *in a criminal* case. Surely it is relevant that the Sixth Amendment speaks only to rights of the "accused." Surely it is relevant that, if I testify about what my mom told me one day, my mom is not in any ordinary-language sense a "witness" within the wording of the confrontation clause. Surely it is relevant that in other clauses featuring the word "witness"—such as the treason clause[38]—the Constitution uses the word in its plain-meaning sense.

Textual argument is, as I have said, a proper starting point for proper constitutional analysis. Sometimes, plain-meaning textual arguments in the end must yield to the weight of other proper constitutional arguments—from history, structure, precedent, practicality, and so on.[39] And so the astonishing thing is not that someone might find the above-catalogued textual points to be outweighed at times by other arguments. Rather, the astonishing thing is that these textual points are almost never made, or even seen. This is true even when the text, carefully read, explains most or all of the leading cases in a given area, or when the text resonates with obvious common sense. In virtually every other area of constitutional law, such a state of affairs is unimaginable. I think it cannot last much longer in the area of constitutional criminal procedure. The field may have evolved as an insular ecosystem unto itself, but global changes in constitutional law discourse must soon affect the atmosphere here, too.

Similar points can be made about constitutional history and structure. English common law antecedents of the Fourth, Fifth, and Sixth Amendments, as well as early state and federal cases, certainly belong in a proper conversation about *constitutional* criminal procedure. The fact that English courts have *never* excluded evidence on Fourth Amendment–like grounds, and that *no* American court, state or federal, *ever* did so during the first century after Independence surely deserves some mention. So, too, with the fact that England has never excluded "fruits" of immunized testimony or coerced confessions, and the fact that the English rule reigned as the dominant one in Congress and in American courts prior to the Supreme Court's 1892 *Counselman* case for testimonial immunity,[40] and until the 1960s for coerced confessions. Similarly, it must matter that early courts never claimed that the "only" remedy for speedy trial violations was dismissal with prejudice.

Structurally, we must pay close attention to how different parts of our Constitution fit together, textually and practically. Textually: Shouldn't "reasonableness" under the Fourth Amendment be read in light of other constitutional values—of property, privacy, equality, due process, free speech, democratic participation, and the like—affirmed in other amendments? Shouldn't Seventh Amendment juries play some role in determining Fourth Amendment reasonableness, just as they play a role in determining reasonableness generally in tort law? Why should preclusive ex parte warrants be worshiped in the Fourth Amendment when they so obviously present genuine Fifth Amendment due process problems of notice and opportunity to be heard? Wouldn't it be nice if the word *witness* could have the same meaning in the treason clause, the self-incrimination clause, the confrontation clause, and the compulsory process clause? Practically: Hasn't an overbroad reading of the Fifth Amendment self-incrimination clause betrayed the accused's explicit Sixth Amendment right to compel witnesses in his favor? Hasn't that overbroad reading also obstructed the defendant's explicit Sixth Amendment right to a speedy trial? Thus, hasn't our Fifth Amendment doctrine ended up helping guilty defendants while hurting innocent ones?

As these last points make clear, proper methodology of constitutional criminal procedure does not blind itself to practical effects. Indeed, though the preceding chapters have always sought to respect text, history, and structure, they have also sought to make good common sense, motivated by the simple idea that constitutional criminal procedure should protect the innocent, and not needlessly advantage the guilty.

The Substance of Process

This commonsensical point, I submit, is the essence of our Constitution's rules about criminal procedure, and so I shall repeat it: the Constitution seeks to protect the innocent. The guilty, in general, receive procedural protection only as an incidental and unavoidable byproduct of protecting the innocent *because* of their innocence. Lawbreaking, *as such*, is entitled to no legitimate expectation of privacy, and so if a search can detect only lawbreaking, it generally poses little threat to Fourth Amendment values.[41] By the same token, the exclusionary rule is wrong as a constitutional rule precisely because it creates windfalls for guilty defendants but gives no direct remedy to the innocent woman wrongly searched. If you are guilty of heinous crimes and the police find mountains of incriminating evidence, you may get a huge exclusionary rule windfall; but if the cops know you are innocent and just want to harass you—say, because of your race—the exclusionary rule offers absolutely no compensation or deterrence whatsoever.[42]

Truth and accuracy are vital values. A procedural system that cannot sort the innocent from the guilty will confound any set of substantive laws, however just. And so to throw out highly reliable evidence that can indeed help us separate the innocent from the guilty—and to throw it out by pointing to the Constitution, no less—is constitutional madness. A Constitution proclaimed in the name of We the People should be rooted in enduring values that Americans can recognize as *our* values. Truth and the protection of innocence are such values. Virtually everything in the Fourth, Fifth, and Sixth Amendments, properly read, promotes, or at least does not betray, these values.

If anyone believes that other nice-sounding, but far less intuitive, ideas are also in the Constitution, the burden of proof should be on him. Here are two examples: (1) "The Constitution requires that government must never profit from its own wrong. Hence, illegally obtained evidence must be excluded." (2) "No man should be compelled to be an instrument of his own destruction. Hence, reliable physical fruits of immunized testimony should be excluded." These sound nice, but where does the Constitution say *that?* And are we truly willing to live by these as constitutional rules? The first would require that the government return stolen goods to thieves and illegal drugs to drug dealers. But this has *never* been the law. The second would prevent coerced fingerprinting and DNA sampling. This, too, is almost impossible to imagine in practice.[43] By contrast, the innocence-protection rock on which I stand, and the specific Fourth, Fifth, and Sixth Amendment derivations therefrom, are things that we can all live by, without cheating.

Light from Afar

My vision of constitutional criminal procedure borrows from and builds on insights elaborated in other scholarly fields. Consider, for example, how much we constitutional criminal proceduralists can learn from what might at first seem a most unlikely source: tax scholarship. In developing a now-classic framework of analysis, Professor Stanley Surrey brought into view the "upside-down" effect of certain tax subsidies: by subsidizing certain private activity via tax deductions rather than direct governmental outlays, the federal government effectively gave greater subsidies to high-bracket taxpayers than to low-bracket taxpayers. In light of the purposes underlying some subsidies, argued Professor Surrey, this distributional pattern of benefits was perverse—"upside down" in Professor Surrey's famous phrase.[44]

Professor Surrey understood that both direct expenditures and tax deductions could subsidize and create incentives, but with very different distributional consequences. A similar focus on distribution helps explain one of the many ways in which the exclusionary rule is so perverse—upside down, if you will. Both tort law and evidentiary exclusion seek to create incentives—both seek to deter misconduct—but with very different distributional patterns. Under proper tort law, the guilty man never recovers more simply because he is guilty;[45] but the exclusionary rule rewards the guilty man, and only the guilty man, precisely because he is guilty. This is the "bite" of the rule, the lever by which it moves the police to repent and reform. Under the self-incrimination clause, fruits-immunity similarly rewards the guilty without helping the innocent. Indeed, it rewards the guilty in ways that hurt the innocent. Constitutional criminal procedure must cleanse itself of these and other similarly "upside-down" rules.

It is often claimed that the exclusionary rule and fruits-immunity never truly "reward" the guilty. Had the government not searched illegally or compelled the testimony, the argument goes, the government would not have the fruit, and so exclusion of the fruit never creates a windfall for guilty defendants but only restores the status quo ante.[46] But this glib argument ignores what I have called the "causation gap," encompassing all the possible ways in which the fruit might very well have come to light anyway. Courts have given too little rein to such antiexclusionary doctrines as inevitable discovery; and where eventual fruits discovery is only probable, or possible, rather than inevitable, permanent exclusion creates huge windfalls for many guilty defendants.

With issues of incentives, deterrence, distribution of reward, and causation so obviously important, it should be plain that criminal procedure scholars can also learn important lessons from tort law scholarship. The text of the Fourth Amendment presupposes tort law, and the Founders repeatedly invoked the idea of punitive damages to "deter"— their word—unreasonable searches and seizures. Originalism and functionalism converge here, for the Founders understood deterrence far better than many sophisticated modern-day scholars. Consider, for example, the following passage from Professor William J. Stuntz in favor of the exclusionary rule: "Thus, the difficulty with [tort] damages boils down to this: no one knows how to value damages for illegal searches with any accuracy. . . . Overdeterrence is a special concern. . . . Underdeterrence, however, is also a serious problem."[47]

Now, Bill Stuntz is a friend of mine—and there is no one in the field whose work I respect more—but there are so many things wrong with his functionalist defense of the exclusionary rule that it is hard to know where to start. Here, and elsewhere, Professor Stuntz acts as if the choice is tort law *or* exclusion—but nobody (and surely not Professor Stuntz) really thinks so. No one proposes that tort and tortlike remedies be abolished. To do so would be insane—like declaring open season on those whom the cops know to be innocent, but do not like and want to hassle. Exclusion alone could never be sufficient.

But if so, the wrinkles of tort law must be ironed out regardless of whether we keep or scrap exclusion. For the Webster Bivenses of the world—innocent citizens hassled by government—it will always be "damages or nothing"[48] and courts will need to fashion sensible rules about damage remedies here just as they do everywhere else in tort law. And if at the end of the day there is, as Professor Stuntz believes, a real risk of overdeterrence, how does that argue for *adding*—not, I repeat, substituting—whatever additional deterrence comes from exclusion?

But Professor Stuntz's problems are only beginning. Suppose that we really did have to choose between tort law and exclusion. Tort law risks overdeterrence and underdeterrence—but so does the exclusionary rule. (So does *any* solution.) The underdeterrence of exclusion is obvious. For starters, it has no bite—no bark, even—when cops want to hassle someone they know to be innocent, from whom they expect to find no evidence. But even when police expect to and do find evidence, the exclusionary rule underdeters by allowing government to get the drugs off the street or return the stolen goods to their rightful owner, to use the evidence in a civil suit against the searchee, or to use the evidence in a criminal suit against anyone else. Exclusion also can greatly overdeter, as we have seen, by preventing government from *ever* using critical evidence (or its fruit) against the searchee, even though that evidence (or its fruit) might otherwise have come to light.

Perhaps Professor Stuntz thinks that the exclusionary rule's unavoidable overdeterrence and underdeterrence will somehow cancel each other out, leaving us with something that Goldilocks would call "just right." But like the story of the three bears, this is pure fantasy. Tort law, by contrast, is logical and realistic—tort law remedies can be squarely tailored to fit the tortious wrong of unreasonable search and seizure. Unlike exclusion, tort law is thus not inherently mismatched and is far more likely to reach the right amount of overall deterrence. Punitive-damage multipliers can always be cranked up or down to achieve a given overall level of deterrence, whereas exclusion cannot be adjusted at the margins without raising serious "Leavenworth lottery" issues.

Let us now summarize, on purely functional grounds, the contrast between tort law and exclusion. The upside-down exclusionary rule skews benefits towards the guilty; tort law is right-side up. The precise amount of deterrence from exclusion turns on a whole range of accidental contingencies: whether a search seeks evidence as such, whether a search uncovers evidence, whether that evidence may be used in other ways (civilly, or against other criminal defendants), whether other evidence will suffice to convict the target, and whether the unavoidable causation gap will be big or small. Tort law, by contrast, focuses on the invasion of the search itself—its intrusiveness, its outrageousness, its violence, and so on. Put a different way, exclusion is simply not linked, analytically speaking, to the scope of the violation, which occurs before a criminal trial, not during it. Tort law focuses precisely on the scope of the violation. Professor Stuntz thinks that Fourth Amendment doctrine should focus more on police violence.[49] I agree—but the exclusionary rule simply does not work here. Whether the cops punched me in the nose is almost never analytically—or even causally—linked to whether they found evidence in my house.[50] Exclusion would thus achieve the right amount of overall deterrence only by the wildest of coincidences, like the broken watch that tells the correct time twice a day. Finally, tort law payment comes from the wrongdoing government, whereas the visible sight of grinning criminals freed by exclusion localizes savage "demoralization costs" on identifiable crime victims. This last phrase, of course, comes from Professor Michelman's classic analysis of the just compensation clause, a clause that, as I have shown, resembles the Fourth Amendment in some ways.[51]

The "demoralization costs" concept reminds us that beyond tort law, narrowly defined, lies the broad field of law and economics generally. Here too, constitutional criminal proceduralists have much to learn. Perhaps the biggest lesson is the importance of ex ante incentive effects.[52] Overprotection of some rights may trigger strategic reactions that will lead to predictable underprotections elsewhere. The exclusionary rule tempts judges to deny that Fourth Amendment violations occurred; something similar occurs under the draconian rule requiring dismissals with prejudice for all Sixth Amendment speedy trial clause violations. If all searches really do require warrants and probable cause, judges will strain to deny that some intrusions really are "searches." If we prevent the government from freezing a suspect's story in place early on in a civilized deposition, we may drive interrogation underground into far more potentially abusive forums; we will also encourage surprise searches, sting operations, and other serious intrusions.

Precisely because courts overprotect the guilty by excluding testimonial fruit, they undermine other defendants' explicit right to compel incriminating testimony from third-party witnesses—a right of surpassing importance to *innocent* defendants. More generally, if doctrine creates an overly intricate matrix of trial rights, the government may react by trying to hold fewer trials, thereby forcing some defendants into harsher plea bargains. In general, plea bargaining may tend to punish guilty and innocent alike—or to advantage those with powerful lawyers—rather than to sift the innocent from the guilty. For many innocent defendants, less may be more: less trial procedure may mean more trials, and thus more chance to prove their innocence.

Just as less can sometimes be more, "different" can at times be the "same": Some of the Founders' basic vision must be "translated" into our legal culture.[53] Entity liability is one example; since the locus of government decision making has shifted over two hundred years from the individual constable to the police department, so should the locus of de jure liability for constitutional torts. By contrast, various exclusionary rules are bad translations because they impose upside-down effects that were anathema to the Framing generation and are hateful to the general citizenry even today.

Administrative law is in some ways a modern-day translation of tort law—with workers' compensation boards and OSHA rules displacing common law negligence suits. Similar translations may make sense in constitutional criminal procedure. Administrative compensation schemes with "right-side up" recovery patterns may sensibly supplement, and perhaps in places supplant, individual (and more cumbersome) tort suits. Citizen review panels within police departments can serve functions akin to common law–style juries. Speedy trial framework statutes can regularize pretrial process. The list could go on. In the preceding chapters, I have perhaps devoted less attention to administrative schemes than they deserve. But my relative deemphasis must not be mistaken for hostility.

If *constitutional criminal procedure* must attend to *constitutional* law, it also must attend to *criminal* law and *procedural* law. Criminal procedure must work to vindicate rather than undermine sensible norms of substantive criminal law. At one specific level, my framework links the criminal procedural rule against compelled self-incrimination based on a fear of false confession with the sensible substantive criminal law doctrine of corpus delicti. At a more general level, my procedural vision seeks to vindicate substantive norms by emphasizing accuracy and truth-finding in adjudication. Process should be arranged to separate those who did violate the substantive law from those who did not. If some substantive criminal laws—drug laws, perhaps—are bad policy, then let us change them directly rather than trying to offset or neuter them with procedural gimmicks that will also obstruct our efforts to enforce uncontroversially sensible criminal laws, like those against murder, rape, and robbery. At times, however, some procedural rules will have a differential impact on different crimes.[54] For example, a rule excluding compelled testimony but admitting compelled fruit casts a happy substantive shadow: it will help political and religious dissenters without giving much aid and comfort to murderers. Blasphemy and libel tend not to generate physical fruit, but murder results in dead bodies, bloody knives, and the like. Criminal proceduralists must carefully attend to the ways that procedure can affect substantive enforcement policy for good or for ill. At the most general level, things do not "cancel out" if we exclude half the evidence, catch half the truly bad guys, and then simply double the punishment for those unlucky enough to get caught. The social norms underlying sensible substantive laws are best reinforced with high detection, and quick (though not necessarily severe) punishment. "War on crime" rhetoric needs to be channeled away from savage penal policies toward strategies that lead to high detection and quick, reliable adjudication.

Laws against murder, rape and robbery remind us of the importance of *victims*. Feminist theory is especially important here, given that women are more likely to be victims than to be criminal defendants.[55] And in asking the "race question" we must also remember that racial minorities are often the victims of crime, too. In thinking about feminism and critical race theory more generally, we should also ask about the race and gender of those doing the searching, seizing, questioning, and adjudicating: police, prosecutors, judges and juries. All of these issues, I submit, are central to the idea of a truly *constitutional* criminal procedure.

Will judges, scholars, lawmakers, and citizens hearken to my call for a reconceptualization of the field? It is far too early to tell, but by nature I am an optimist. Some will no doubt oppose my vision—but others, I hope, will rally to the banner I have tried to raise. Debate will be vigorous—perhaps even heated—but vigorous debate is healthy in a vibrant democracy. As I said, we live in interesting times.

Reinventing Juries:
Ten Suggested Reforms

No idea was more central to our Bill of Rights—indeed, to America's distinctive regime of government of the people, by the people, and for the people—than the idea of the jury. Yet no idea today has suffered more abuse—from benign neglect to malignant hostility to cynical manipulation and strategic perversion—than the idea of the jury. (And lawyers, judges, and law professors, alas, bear much of the blame for all this.) In this brief Appendix, I offer a few ideas about how to restore juries to their rightful place in our constitutional order.

Juries at the Founding

My first claim—the centrality of the jury to the Founders —is a huge one, but easy to prove.[1] The only right secured in all state constitutions drafted between 1776 and 1787 was the right of jury trial in criminal cases. The criminal jury was one of only a handful of rights explicitly affirmed in the Philadelphia Convention (in Article III); and the convention's only discussion of whether to add a more elaborate bill of rights took place in response to concerns about protecting civil juries. When the convention imprudently omitted such a bill, Anti-Federalists pounced on the omission during the ratification debates, and jury-protection clauses topped their wish lists. Of the six state ratifying conventions that floated amendment ideas in 1788, five put forth two or more explicit jury proposals.

A close look at our Bill of Rights confirms all this. Three amendments explicitly protect the jury: the Fifth Amendment safeguards criminal grand juries, the Sixth further protects criminal petit juries, and the Seventh preserves civil juries. These three clauses are only the most visible tip of the jury iceberg. Let's start with the First Amendment and its ringing defense of freedom of speech and of the press. As the 1730s Zenger trial had made clear and the 1790s imbroglio over the Alien and Sedition Acts would confirm, freedom of the press was tightly linked to jury trial in the 1780s. Indeed, the "no prior restraint" doctrine that intertwined with freedom of the press had its deepest roots in jury trial ideas. A prior restraint could issue from a judge via an injunction and have bite in contempt proceedings that excluded a jury; nonprior restraints, like libel judgments, could have bite only if the government could persuade a jury of the publisher's peers to rule against him.

Now consider the Second Amendment. Like the jury idea, the Second Amendment tried to empower ordinary citizens—"the people." Indeed, the "militia" and the "jury" were cousins. Both were local bodies, composed of ordinary citizens. Both were collective, republican institutions. Militia service and jury service were twin duties of good citizenship; and roughly speaking, those adult male citizens eligible to serve on one were also eligible to serve on the other. Both the militia and the jury reflected suspicion of paid, professional central officialdom—a central standing army on the one hand, and judges, prosecutors, and bureaucrats on the other. (And the Third Amendment, of course, simply continued this suspicion of a paid, professional standing army.)

As we saw in Chapter 1, the civil jury was at the heart of the Fourth Amendment. Modern case law has turned this amendment upside down. At the Founding, warrants were not required; they were *disfavored: "No* warrant shall issue but upon . . ." And they were disfavored precisely because (like a prior restraint) they issued from paid government bureaucrats and cut the jury out of the loop: the whole purpose of a warrant was to cut off the citizen target's ability to sue the searcher or seizer in a civil jury trespass action. In short, the Fourth and Seventh Amendments were tightly linked: the preferred vehicle for litigating the Fourth Amendment was a tort suit brought by a citizen and tried before a Seventh Amendment jury of fellow citizens. And in this tort suit, the key Fourth Amendment issue would be whether the government's search or seizure had been "reasonable"—a standard tort question (like negligence) to be shaped over the long run by juries in tandem with judges.

We have already noted the Fifth Amendment's explicit grand jury clause; but let us now note two more Fifth Amendment jury ideas. First, see how the double jeopardy clause snugly safeguards the role of the criminal jury. Article III and the Sixth Amendment require that a criminal case be tried by a jury; and the double jeopardy clause generally prevents appellate judges from reversing that jury's verdict of acquittal. In effect, the double jeopardy clause operates much like the second clause of the Seventh Amendment, which generally prevents appellate judges from overturning a *civil* jury's verdict. (This connection was well understood by the Framers.)[2] Next, consider the majestic Fifth Amendment phrase, "due process of law." This grand phrase traces back to Lord Coke, who defined it, in words well known to all eighteenth-century lawyers, as "indictment or presentment of good and lawful men"—that is, a grand jury.[3]

Passing over the Sixth and Seventh Amendments—the tip of our iceberg—we come to the Eighth, addressing bail and punishments. How, one may well ask, is the jury relevant here? Aren't bail hearings and sentencing hearings often held by judges sitting alone, without juries? Exactly so—but from another perspective, this proves my point. Precisely because judges acting without juries were suspect, the Bill of Rights had to put special limits on them, limits in the Eighth Amendment. (So, too, in the Fourth Amendment warrant clause and in the First Amendment rule against prior restraints.)

Well-trained modern lawyers have been taught that the Ninth Amendment—if it is about anything—is about individual rights like privacy; and that the Tenth Amendment—if it means much at all—means states' rights and federalism. Here, as elsewhere, well-trained lawyers would do well to read the text. Both amendments explicitly speak of "the people"—of Ninth Amendment "rights . . . retained by the people" and Tenth Amendment "powers . . . reserved . . . to the people." The Preamble, of course, triumphantly trumpets the right and power of "We the People" to collective self-governance; and no phrase appears in more of our first ten Amendments than the phrase "the people." The core idea conjured up by this phrase is not privacy, not federalism, but popular sovereignty—the idea of the people's control over their mere agents in government.[4] And this idea, in large measure, underlies the American idea of jury trial, trial "by the people themselves," as Thomas Jefferson exuberantly put the point in 1789.[5]

This concludes my whirlwind tour of the Founders' Constitution and the Bill of Rights. I plead guilty to selective emphasis—but I hope I have nevertheless said enough to win provisional assent to my first huge claim: that the jury idea was absolutely central to the Founders' Bill of Rights, and their distinctive constitutional idea of popular self-government. Let me now move to my second huge claim: that the current state of affairs betrays the jury and the people, and that lawyers, judges, and law professors must bear much of the blame.

First, a few words of clarification. No, I am not arguing that we can, or should want to, go back to everything that was said and done in 1789. Much of our Constitution has changed. Amen! Or perhaps I should say "Amend!" for the most distinctive changes have occurred through constitutional amendments redefining "We the self-governing people" to include blacks, women, the poor, and the young. But nothing in these glorious amendments—the Fifteenth, Nineteenth, Twenty-Fourth, and Twenty-Sixth—moots the jury idea. Rather, as we shall see, these new amendments reaffirm popular self-government and demand only that *all* the people should count, and vote—count and vote, I shall argue, in juries, too.

Nor am I ignoring larger forces at work over the last two centuries—nationalism, bureaucratization, technological complexity, and increasing specialization of labor. The jury idea must make its peace with these forces, but a just peace calls for creative accommodation rather than unconditional surrender. Take nationalization, for example. At the Founding, the jury—like much of the Bill of Rights—reflected localist suspicion of central authority. The American Revolution, born in local rebellion against imperial oppression, cast a long localist shadow. But in the Civil War era, the national government emerged as liberty's last best hope, and a new banner unfurled: "Freedom National!" A new Bill of Rights arose—the Thirteenth, Fourteenth, and Fifteenth Amendments—exemplifying this new nationalism. But in many ways this new nationalism only strengthened the old jury idea. The Fourteenth Amendment was drafted to reverse *Barron v. Baltimore*[6] and apply the principles of the Bill of Rights—including many of its jury ideas—against the states;[7] and as I noted in passing, the Fifteenth Amendment created a national guarantee that states allow blacks to vote, in juries and elsewhere. Similar adaptations of the jury idea will be needed to accommodate bureaucratization and specialization of labor, as we shall see. But here too, the core populist idea of the jury trial must be retooled,[8] not retired.

Finally, in placing much of the blame on lawyers, judges, and law professors, I admit the importance of both materialism and idealism. Material incentives matter, and so do ideas. Over two centuries, lawyers—both prosecutors and defense attorneys—have had strong incentives to aggrandize their own roles in litigation at the expense of the jury. But their motives have been *parti*al and *parti*san; the *parti*es have wrested control from the *whole* people, embodied in the jury idea. The deepest constitutional function of the jury is to serve the people, not the parties—to serve them by involving them in the administration of justice and the grand project of democratic self-government. Alas, over the years, short-term convenience of litigants has won out against the long-run values of public education and participation. Judges, of course, are charged with protecting these enduring constitutional values; but they too have perverse and partisan incentives here. The jury was to check the judge—much as the legislature was to check the executive, the House to check the Senate, and the states to check the national government. On this materialist account, prosecutors, defense attorneys, and judges have, over the centuries, contrived to carve up among themselves things that rightfully belong to the jury—to all of us, as citizens.

And why have we failed—as jurors, as citizens—to fight off these creeping assaults? Here, too, a material incentive analysis is helpful. Prosecutors and judges are professional repeat players; defense attorneys are paid; whereas the people at large lack tight organization. The benefits of jury service are widely dispersed—they redound to fellow citizens as well as the individual jurors. But the individual juror bears all of the cost—the hassle, the inconvenience, the forgone wages—of jury service. Jury service is not just a right but a duty; predictably few of us have militantly insisted that we perform this duty, just as few of us insisted in the Reagan years that we pay our fair share of the intergenerational tax burden.[9]

Here is where law professors come in. For one socially useful role of the not-for-hire academic should be to articulate long-run systematic values that the partisans and the temporary, self-interested agents will predictably slight. We have, for example, a rich academic law and economics literature decrying special-interest rent seeking—the honey subsidies, the grazing fee giveaways, and so on—but we lack an equally vigorous literature championing the common good over the special interests in jury law. Law professors have, in general, been better capitalists than democrats.

In the classroom, the big idea of the jury is carved up into a few trivial ideas scattered across the curriculum. Civil procedure devotes a week or so to the Seventh Amendment, but this hardly shows the jury in its best light. Fundamentally, the jury is, in Tocqueville's phrase, a *political* institution, not a procedural one. It exists to promote democracy for the jurors, not efficient adjudication for the parties. Criminal procedure professors typically discuss a *defendant's* right to a criminal jury; but what about the people's right—and duty—to serve and vote on a jury? In criminal procedure, antijury warrants typically become the heroes of the Fourth Amendment story; celebration of judge-fashioned exclusionary rules drowns out serious discussion of the jury-driven tort suit at the

Amendment's core; and the only thing said about the grand jury (typically) is that a clever prosecutor can get it to indict a ham sandwich. And what about classes in constitutional law proper? The jury goes almost unmentioned. Prior restraint is taught as a *press* rule; the "judicial department" means judges; and "democracy" means legislatures. Federalism, legislative bicameralism, presentment—all this and much more is studied, but the big idea of the jury almost never is. One is reminded of the line in *Casablanca* when the smuggler played by Peter Lorre suggests that Humphrey Bogart's character despises him: "I probably would," Bogart's saloon keeper replies, "if I gave you any thought."

Outside the classroom, there is still more cause for shame. When academics have publicly weighed in on jury debates in this century, it has too often been on the wrong side—trivializing the jury, mocking it, coming up with new theories for whittling away its power. As a Yale man, I am happy to say that the worst offenders here have been prominent men from Harvard—Felix Frankfurter, Erwin Griswold, and Charles Fairman, to name a few[10]—but other schools (including my own) have not lagged far behind.

I have painted with an extremely broad brush in sketching out this scathing indictment of lawyers, judges, and law professors. True, some have stood up against this constitutional betrayal—but too few. My own hero is the great Hugo Black, who had an abiding faith in the Constitution, the jury, and the people. (And for all this, he was mocked by sophisticated cynics in the academy—wise fools!) Unlike most of his fellow Justices, Black had practiced as a trial lawyer; it is unfortunate that the one Court that has the most power to save or kill the jury has so little familiarity with the institution, now that circuit riding is ancient history.

Juries Today

In these few remaining pages, I shall offer ten admittedly broad and tentative suggestions for reinventing juries today—preserving the Founders' big idea in our modern world. Ten is an arbitrary number to be sure, but who am I to quarrel with God and Moses on Sinai, the ratifiers of the federal Bill of Rights in 1791, or David Letterman, for that matter? Because my individual proposals are linked by a single vision, it is best to set out up front some of the basic features of that vision.

First, we must see the big idea of the jury generally, above and beyond the Fifth, Sixth, and Seventh Amendments. Grand juries, petit juries, and civil juries do differ from one another, but they are all juries of sorts. Adjectives should not obscure nouns. Also, we must see how this big idea connects up to other constitutional ideas. In particular, three closely related constitutional analogies strike me as especially fruitful: the legislative analogy, the bicameral analogy, and the voting analogy.

At the Founding, analogies between legislatures and juries abounded. In the words of a leading Anti-Federalist pamphleteer: "It is essential in every free country, that common people should have a part and share of influence, in the judicial as well as in the legislative department. . . . The trial by jury in the judicial department, and the collection of the people by their representatives in the legislature . . . have procured for them, in this country, their true proportion of influence. . . ."[11]

Closely related was the idea of bicameralism: just as the legislature featured two equal branches, one upper and one lower, so too with the judiciary. The judges constituted the upper branch of the bicameral judicial department; the juries, the lower branch.[12] If we take these analogies seriously, certain jury issues will appear in a new light.

Most important is the light cast by the voting analogy. Jurors vote in juries, and ordinary voters have in America typically been eligible to serve as jurors. As Tocqueville put the point:

> The jury system as understood in America seems to me as direct and extreme a consequence of the . . . sovereignty of the people as universal suffrage. They are both equally powerful means of making the majority prevail. . . . [T]he jury is above all a political institution [and] should be made to harmonize with the other laws establishing the sovereignty. . . . [F]or society to be governed in a settled and uniform manner, it is essential that the jury lists should expand or shrink with the lists of voters. . . .
>
> [In general, i]n America all citizens who are electors have the right to be jurors.[13]

In recent opinions, the Supreme Court has begun to reaffirm this Tocquevillian vision, analogizing voting and jury service.[14] The analogy has broad implications, shifting analysis from a litigant's right to be tried by a jury to a citizen's right to serve and vote on a jury. As a result of this shift, a defendant's racially based peremptory challenges do not protect his own legitimate right to be tried by a jury he deems to be fair; rather, they threaten the people's right to serve and vote on juries free from racial discrimination. Race-based peremptory challenges, even in the hands of a defendant, violate the Fifteenth Amendment; and gender-based challenges violate the Nineteenth.[15]

With these general remarks framing the issue, let us now turn to my top ten list (in no particular order) of suggested jury reforms.

No Excuses

Citizens should not easily escape the duty, and "repeat-player regulars" (lawyers and judges) should not easily deny citizens the right, to serve on juries. Consider first citizen efforts to shirk jury duty. In part, the shirking problem arises because those who do serve are too often treated shabbily in a process run by—and for the convenience of—repeat-player regulars. Reforms on this front should solve part of the problem, but not all of it. Specialization of labor is another culprit: specialization breeds inequality of citizens, and the jury idea is rooted in equality. Less abstractly, specialization means that many citizens may not want to give up a week of their careers—and the big bucks they can make in that week—to shoulder their equal share of duties of citizenship.

A sensible system, I suggest, would require each citizen to devote, say, one week a year to jury service—note the analogy to the modern Swiss militia. Each citizen could "time shift"—declare well in advance *which* week is most convenient—but except for genuine emergencies, citizens should be obliged to serve when their week comes up.[16] We should turn specialization of labor to the service of democracy by, for example, providing professional specialized day care (or day care vouchers) to enable homemakers—mainly women, today—to take their turns in the project of collective self-governance.

And how should this obligation be enforced? Stiff fines are one option. If you shirk your week, you must pay two weeks' salary. (Flat fines, by contrast, would be functionally regressive and create incentives to shirk for high-salary citizens.) More radically (and problematically), we could relink jury service and voting: if you want to opt out of the responsibilities of collective self-government, fine—but you may not then exercise any of its rights. You have two choices: to be a citizen, with democratic rights and duties, or a subject, ruled by others. On this view, you are not *entitled* to vote outside juries if you are unwilling to serve and vote inside juries. If you are not willing to engage in regular focused deliberation with a random cross section of fellow voters, you should not be governing the polity, just as you may not vote in the Iowa caucuses unless you attend and hear the arguments. Citizens not only have freedom to speak to fellow citizens on issues of public concern: they have duties to listen. As a practical matter these duties are generally unenforceable, but the jury provides a forum to force citizens who might never engage each other—they live in different neighborhoods, work in different worlds, attend different schools, worship in different churches—to listen to each other, and to deliberate collectively.

Two obvious objections arise. First, isn't the no-serve, no-vote rule a type of in-kind poll tax, outlawed by the Twenty-Fourth Amendment?[17] Perhaps, but note that unlike a flat fee, a personal service poll tax bites the wealthy as much as the poor, and thus avoids class discrimination—the real mischief that the Twenty-Fourth Amendment was designed to redress. If requiring Iowa's citizens to listen before they vote in caucuses does not violate the amendment, requiring them to serve on juries may not be so different.

A second objection runs like this: "If jury service is ultimately designed to reconnect the citizens with each other and the polity, we must remember that voting also reconnects. We should be encouraging voting, not discouraging it, and so the no-serve, no-vote rule undermines its long-run goal." For me, this is a weighty, and perhaps dispositive, objection, but I also fear that too many citizens see voting as private and not public: "I'm entitled to vote on any basis I see fit, and don't have to explain or justify myself to fellow citizens. Voting is private and self-regarding—what I do in the ballot booth is like what I do in the bedroom—it's nobody else's business." I think this view is deeply wrong. We have secret-ballot rules to cure second-best problems of force and fraud that would occur if thugs could monitor your vote,[18] not because voting is inherently private or self-regarding. Perhaps too many people today are voting for the wrong reasons—and relinking voting to jury service may help remind them of the true, public-regarding nature of these rights.

Once we solve the shirking problem and enforce the *duty* to serve, we must deal with the flip side of the coin: the efforts of repeat-player regulars to deny the citizen her *right* to serve. Excuses for cause should be extremely limited: if you are the brother-in-law of the plaintiff, you are excused; but you may not be excused merely because you happen to have ideas—what self-governing citizen shouldn't have ideas? Put simply, a juror should have an open mind but not an empty mind. It is sad that in order to try Oliver North, you couldn't know who he was.[19] Too often, juries come up with stupid results because we let the parties pick stupid jurors in stupid ways.

The bicameralism analogy is quite helpful here: the same standard for recusal should apply to judge and juror. Indeed, if anything, juror bias is less problematic, because the juror is only one of twelve, and must openly articulate reasons to persuade her peers,[20] whereas a biased judge can single-handedly manipulate the proceedings in ways hard to detect and reverse. (And our juror will sit one week a year, our judge, fifty.)

At the federal level, repeat-player regulars should not be able to conspire to excuse criminal jurors en masse by agreeing to a bench trial. Article III demands that the trial for *"all crimes shall be* by jury" and "shall" and "all" meant just that to the Framers. So said unanimous Supreme Courts in the nineteenth century, but since the New Deal, the Court has wrongly allowed defendants who plead not guilty to be tried by judges alone.[21] The bicameralism analogy here has bite: an Article III judge sitting without a criminal jury is not a criminal court with jurisdiction, just as the Senate sitting without the House is not a legislature. (Whether this Article III mandate should be imposed on state criminal proceedings is, of course, a different question.)[22]

Preempting Peremptories

By and large, the first twelve persons picked by lottery should form the jury. The jury—and not just the venire—should be as cross-sectional of the entire community of the whole people as possible. Peremptory challenges should be eliminated: they allow repeat-player regulars—prosecutors and defense attorneys—to manipulate demographics and chisel an unrepresentative panel out of a cross-sectional venire.[23]

The suggestion here closely builds on my first one. Juries should represent the people, not the parties. Democracy is well served if juries force together into common dialogue a fair cross section of citizens who might never deliberate together anywhere else.

All the broad principles outlined earlier—the big idea of the jury generally, the legislative analogy, the bicameral analogy, the voting analogy—cut against peremptories. We do not let a defendant handpick a personalized designer legislature to fashion the norms governing his conduct; or the prosecutor who pursues him; or the grand jury that indicts him; or the judge who tries him; or the appellate court that reviews his case. We do not *try*—and I'll resist the temptation to wisecrack here—to pick the most stupid persons imaginable to serve in our legislatures, or on our judiciary. When ordinary citizens vote, they have never been subject to the sort of reverse literacy test reflected in a joke that made the rounds in 1994: "Knock knock. . . . Who's there? . . . O. J. . . . O. J. who? . . . Congratulations, you're on the jury!" And in voting, we are especially uneasy about depriving citizens of the right to vote on the basis of discretionary and low-visibility judgments that may mask racial or sexual prejudice and stereotyping.

Three big arguments support peremptories. First is the idea of legitimacy: the parties will better respect a decision reached by a body they helped to select. But what about the legitimacy of the verdict for the rest of society—We the People who see weird juries, chosen in weird and expensive ways, generate weird outcomes? And the trial judge, appellate court, legislature, and grand jury are legitimate even though the defendant didn't handpick any of them or have any peremptory challenges. And so here we have a good example of repeat-player regulars dressing up their power grab against the jury in the name of principle.

Next is the prophylactic argument from voir dire: we must allow a defense counsel to probe jurors with incisive questions at voir dire; and counsel needs peremptories to vigorously exercise this right, lest counsel offend a juror for whom no provable grounds exist for a "for cause" dismissal. But since I propose getting rid of almost all "for cause" dismissals and thus most voir dire, the prophylactic argument collapses.

Finally, there is the argument from the long history of peremptories. But the Supreme Court has repeatedly made clear that no constitutional right to peremptories exists:[24] they are as much a relic of an imperfectly democratic past as the now dead (or at least dying) "key man" system for generating venires. Peremptories at the Founding, I suspect, were typically exercised as a polite way of dismissing folks with personal knowledge of the parties. In a largely homogeneous community, peremptory challenges would rarely skew the demographics of the eventual jury.[25] But after the Fifteenth and Nineteenth Amendments, we must be vigilant to prevent racial and gender discrimination wrapped in the inscrutable cloak of the peremptory challenge. To take the voting analogy and Reconstruction seriously, we should choose to vindicate the more modern constitutional right to vote free from discrimination over the more ancient *non*constitutional right to exclude jurors on the basis of unarticulated prejudice.

Regularizing Juries

My next suggestion should follow naturally. We should try to regularize juries—empower them in ways that make them less vulnerable to encroachments of the repeat-player regulars, without turning them into professionals themselves. First, a single jury, once constituted, should be able to try several cases in a row. If you can hear four quick cases in your week a year, great! The grand jury hears more than one indictment; the judge sits on more than one case; and the legislature decides more than one issue in a session. In England, at least, a typical seventeenth- or eighteenth-century jury did sit for several cases seriatim.[26]

Deliberation among fellow citizens will be enhanced;[27] the burden of jury service will be more evenly distributed—one week for everyone; and more trials can take place if we get rid of all the wasteful preliminaries like elaborate voir dire and peremptories. Remembering the big idea of juries generally, perhaps we should have a single jury hear both civil and criminal cases in its week. Note finally, that though we are regularizing the jury, we have not professionalized it: one week a year will not turn citizens into government bureaucrats, though it will give citizens regular practice in the art of deliberation and self-government.

We should also pay jurors for their time. Again, one week a year will not turn them into professionals, but payment at a fair flat rate will enable a broad cross-section to serve. The legislative and bicameral analogies suggest payment; judges and legislators are paid for their time. At first the voting analogy seems to cut the other way: we do not pay voters to vote. But the time spent going to polls and voting—one hour perhaps—is much less than the week a year involved in jury service. To decline to compensate citizens for their sacrifice—or to pay them $5 per day as is done in many California courts—is in effect to impose a functionally regressive poll tax that penalizes the working poor who want to serve and vote on juries but who cannot afford the loss of a week's pay. Payment should come from the government, not private employers. All jurors are equal as jurors and should be paid equally. One person, one vote, one paycheck.

Most controversially, we should sometimes allow juries to hire support staff, if necessary. In a world of increasing complexity and specialization of labor, few can do an important job well without support. If legislators and judges can have staffs, why not grand juries?[28] We trivialize juries when we insist that they—and only they—must stay in the eighteenth-century world of generalists. Because juries are single-shot entities rather than continuing bodies, they have predictably lost out to ongoing repeat players over two centuries. Perhaps a permanent staff with undivided loyalty to the jury itself—with mandatory term limits to prevent the staff from entrenching itself and using the jury as a ventriloquist's dummy to advance its own agenda—should be considered.

Respecting Juries

My next proposals are far more modest. Some judges do not allow jurors to take notes. This is idiocy. Judges take notes, grand jurors take notes, legislators take notes—what's going on here? If juries today come up with stupid results sometimes, don't put the blame on them alone. Why shouldn't juries be told at the *outset* of a case—in plain English, not legalese—what the basic elements of the charged offenses are, so they can be thinking of them, and checking them off in their notebooks, as the trial unfolds? If judges are allowed to ask questions from the bench, should not juries at least be allowed to forward questions to the judge to be asked, if not substantively inappropriate?[29] More generally, we must try to design the system to welcome jurors. They are the ones paying for these proceedings, and they are entitled to be treated with respect. Instead, all too often, they are treated rudely by court regulars, made to wait in cramped and uncomfortable quarters, treated as if their time had no value, shuttled around without explanation, and so on. We should use juries to reconnect citizens with each other and with their government. After serving on a jury, a citizen should, in general, feel better—less cynical, more public-regarding—about our system, but our current regime, run for the convenience of the regulars, too often has exactly the opposite effect.[30]

Educating the People

Once we start thinking about the jury from the perspective of democracy rather than adjudication—from the viewpoint of the citizenry rather than the litigants—other possibilities open up. Let us again hear Tocqueville's words:

> To regard the jury simply as a judicial institution would be taking a very narrow view of the matter, for great though its influence on the outcome of lawsuits is, its influences on the fate of society itself is much greater still. The jury is therefore above all a political institution, and it is from that point of view that it must always be judged. . . . [The jury] should be regarded as a free school which is always open and in which each juror learns his rights. . . . I do not know whether a jury is useful to the litigants, but I am sure it is very good for those who have to decide the case. I regard it as one of the most effective means of popular education at society's disposal.[31]

If this is the big idea, why not take advantage of new technology to advance it? Jury deliberations can be videotaped.[32] Even if these deliberations can never be introduced to impeach the jury's verdict—just as *The Brethren*[33] is inadmissible evidence to overturn a Supreme Court case—the videotape can be used (perhaps after some time delay in sensitive cases) as high school teaching materials about democracy in action. For those who find the legislative analogy useful, think of how much C-SPAN broadcasts of legislative debates and hearings have contributed to public education.

Indeed, we might even go a step further. Opponents of the jury often attack it for being a "black box" and for failing to "give reasons." But inscrutability and muteness are not the essence of juries—one of the historic functions of grand juries, for example, was to issue reports and presentments, as we shall see. If a criminal petit jury or civil jury would like to explain its reasons beyond a terse "guilty" or "judgment for plaintiff," perhaps we should allow the jury to employ a "jury clerk"—akin to today's judicial clerk—to help compose a statement of reasons that will enhance public understanding and education.[34]

Safety in Numbers

For the Framers, a criminal jury meant "twelve men, good and true." Today, in light of the Fifteenth, Nineteenth, Twenty-Fourth, and Twenty-Sixth Amendments, we must update all this: "men" must include women, too, and "good and true" jurors include the black, the poor, and the young. But twelve should still mean twelve.

Almost no one on the Supreme Court ever thought otherwise until recently. But when the criminal jury right was incorporated against the states, via the Fourteenth Amendment, in 1968, the Court signaled a willingness to water down this clear historical rule to accommodate state traditions of smaller juries.[35] Today—in state courts at least—criminal juries of fewer than twelve jurors are permitted.[36] And this lax rule has now made its way into the federal courts on the civil side, where six-person juries have been blessed by the Supreme Court as satisfying the Seventh Amendment.[37]

The Court has noted that the number twelve does not explicitly appear in the Constitution.[38] And there is nothing magic about twelve—just as there is nothing sacred about a top ten list. But both have a fair amount of history behind them, and once we move off twelve, where shall we stop? If eleven is enough, why not ten? If ten, why not nine? By mathematical induction, we could in theory unravel down to one; and clearly something has gone wrong. If the number is at some point arbitrary, why not stick with one that has history clearly on its side?

And here are two more fundamental reasons for twelve over six—which is where the current Court seems ready to draw the line.[39] First, if jury service is a positive good—a democratic plus—isn't twelve twice as good as six? More citizens will participate and be educated at Tocqueville's school. Second, if we want individual juries to be cross-sectional, to draw citizens from different backgrounds together in common deliberation, we should want *each jury* to be of substantial size. A minority perspective is less likely to be represented on a jury of six than on one of twelve. And so the deep inclusionary and cross-sectional spirit of later amendments (Fifteen, Nineteen, Twenty-Four, and Twenty-Six) confirms our Founding vision of safety in large numbers. If anything, if twelve is not sacred, we should consider increasing the size of juries. Once again, the big idea of juries generally supports this: grand juries typically have twenty-three members. (The legislative analogy is also helpful here—most legislatures have more than twelve members.) Of course, at some point a jury could become so large that genuine deliberation and dialogue would suffer;[40] but twelve hardly seems to mark this upper bound.

(Super-) Majority Rule?

But all this leads to another controversial—and I admit highly tentative—suggestion. Perhaps, even in criminal cases, we should move away from unanimity toward majority or supermajority rule on juries.

Founding history is relatively clear. A criminal jury had to be unanimous. But like the number twelve, this clear understanding was not explicitly inscribed into the Constitution, and the modern Supreme Court has upheld state rules permitting convictions on 10–2 votes.[41]

Beyond this precedent, four main arguments support my suggestion that nonunanimous verdicts should be constitutionally permissible. First, unlike the jury size issue, once we depart from the Framers' clear starting point, we do not slide all the way down a slippery slope. Six was not a particularly principled jury number, but majority rule has unique mathematical properties, and surely no one could think that a defendant could be convicted by a *minority* vote. Majority rule thus sets a principled lower bound for any reform. Second, at the Founding, unanimity may have drawn its strength from certain metaphysical and religious ideas about Truth that are no longer plausible: some may have thought that all real Truths would command universal—unanimous—assent.[42] Third, most of our analogies tug toward majority rule—legislatures generally use it; voters abide by it; appellate benches follow it (even in criminal cases); and grand juries are governed by it[43]—or supermajority rule: in the impeachment context, the House, acting as a kind of grand jury, votes by majority rule, but the Senate, acting as a kind of petit jury, must summon a two-thirds vote to convict.[44]

Last, and most important, all my other suggested reforms put tremendous pressure on unanimity. Unanimity *within* a jury at the Founding was nestled in a cluster of other rules that now must fall. Blacks, women, and the poor were excluded from voting and from jury service. Key man systems rounded up the usual suspects—a set of relatively homogeneous citizens—to serve. Peremptory challenges could further trim off outliers on a distributional curve. But if everyone now gets to serve on a jury and we eliminate all the old undemocratic barriers, preserving unanimity might also be undemocratic, for it would create an extreme minority veto unknown to the Founders. In practice this minority veto could disempower juries by preventing an intolerably large percentage of jury cases from ever reaching a final verdict.

Even at the Founding, perhaps unanimous jury verdicts existed in the shadow of a jury custom of majority rule. Juries would discuss the matter and vote on guilt; and even if the minority were unconvinced about guilt, they would in the end vote to convict after they had been persuaded that the majority had listened to their arguments in good faith. This custom might be hard to institutionalize today, but it bears some resemblance to legislative "unanimous consent" rules. A single lawmaker may often slow down proceedings—force her colleagues to deliberate more carefully on something that matters to her—but in the end she may not prevent the majority from implementing its judgment. Perhaps the same should hold true for juries. Recall once again Tocqueville: "The jury system [and] universal suffrage . . . are both equally powerful means of making the majority prevail."[45]

In allowing juries to depart from unanimity, we must try to preserve the ideal of jury deliberation and self-education—jurors should talk to and listen to each other seriously and with respect. Friends of unanimity argue that it promotes serious deliberation—everyone's vote is necessary, so everyone is seriously listened to. But unanimity cannot guarantee *mutual* tolerance—what about the eccentric holdout who refuses to listen to, or even try to persuade, others? ("You can't make me, so there!") Conversely, nonunanimous schemes can be devised to promote serious discussion. Jurors should be told that their *job* is to talk and listen to others with different ideas, views, backgrounds, and so on. So too, judges can advise jurors that their early deliberations should focus on the evidence and not their tentative leanings or votes—and that no straw poll should be taken until each juror has had a chance to talk about the evidence on both sides. Institutionally, perhaps we might try a scheme where on Day 1, a jury must be unanimous to convict; on Day 2, 11–1 will suffice; on Day 3, 10–2, and so on, until we hit our bedrock limit of, say, two-thirds (for conviction) or majority rule (for acquittal). To discourage jurors in the (early) majority from freezing out and waiting out the (early) minority, and to encourage the (early) minority to make arguments rather than filibuster, jurors should be told that the whole purpose of our sliding vote scheme is to give a sole holdout on Day 1 a fair chance to pick up a convert by Day 2, and so on.

Jury Review

So far, I have focused more on criminal juries than civil. Tocqueville, however, found civil juries even more educational for the citizenry than criminal ones. At the Founding, a key role for all juries was to protect citizens from government abuse—and the paradigmatic Seventh Amendment case was one brought by an aggrieved citizen against an abusive government official. We should revive this grand tradition, especially in Fourth Amendment cases. As I have argued in Chapter 1, Seventh Amendment juries should play a part in helping to define which searches and seizures are "reasonable" within the meaning of the Fourth Amendment. The Constitution comes from the people, and the people should have some role in administering it and saying what it means.[46] Often, legislators and judges will properly lay down rules establishing the per se reasonableness or the per se unreasonableness of certain types of searches and seizures, much as they lay down rules establishing per se negligence and per se nonnegligence (safe harbors) in tort law. But sometimes reasonableness will call for a contextual, common-sense assessment that defies broad categorization, and sometimes a jury will be the best body to make this common-sense and democratic assessment. And so here too, the bicameralism analogy is useful. Just as judges can review actions of government for unconstitutionality—*Marbury*-style judicial review[47]—sometimes juries can too, as when assessing the mixed fact and law question of Fourth Amendment reasonableness.[48]

Why Not Administrative Grand Juries?

So asks my friend Ron Wright, in a recent issue of the *Administrative Law Review*.[49] Professor Wright's inspiring idea is to find niches in administrative agencies where citizen input, citizen advisory panels, citizen oversight groups, and so on, would be desirable and workable. I shall not go into detail here, but I shall simply note how Ron's work is in the best tradition of the creative accommodation I am urging. The Founders knew not the modern administrative state, but they did try to build citizen involvement into every branch of government they did know: a lower legislative branch of rotating citizen-legislators (or so they thought), criminal prosecutions that would involve grand juries, and bicameral judicial trials featuring juries in both civil and criminal cases. Now that a massive administrative branch has arisen, fidelity to deep constitutional structure should lead us to try to find room here, too, for the people.[50]

Preserving Presentments

In his celebrated 1790 Lectures on Law, Founder James Wilson described the grand jury as "a great channel of communication, between those who make and administer the laws, and those for whom the laws are made and administered. All the operations of government, and of its ministers and officers, are within the compass of their view and research. They may suggest publick improvements and the modes of removing publick inconveniences: they may expose to publick inspection, or to publick punishment, publick bad men, and publick bad measures."[51]

In exposing corruption and wrongdoing, grand juries used the devices of presentments and reports, bringing to light abuses that the citizenry at large had a right to know about, even if no indictable offense had occurred. In an elegant student note, my sometime coauthor Renée Lettow suggests reviving the tradition of grand jury presentments, giving a cross-sectional deliberative body of citizens a more active and visible role than that of prosecutorial rubber stamp.[52] She has stated her case well, and it, too, belongs on a short list of potential jury reforms.

Underlying Lettow's arguments—and Wright's too, for that matter—is the vision I have tried to conjure up here: what I have called "the big idea of the jury" and "popular sovereignty." The vision is a demanding one—and at times, an expensive one. Some of my proposed reforms may, in the short run, cost money. Public education is always costly, in the short run. But in the long run—at least in a government of the people, by the people, and for the people—public ignorance is always more expensive, as the Founders of our Constitution well understood.

Notes

1. Fourth Amendment First Principles

1. *See, e.g.,* Silas J. Wasserstrom, *The Incredible Shrinking Fourth Amendment,* 21 Am. Crim. L. Rev. 257, 257–59 (1984) (describing the warrant requirement, the probable cause requirement, a broad definition of "searches and seizures," and the exclusionary rule as the basic elements of modern Fourth Amendment case law).

2. The Fifth Amendment prescribes grand juries for "infamous *crime,*" bars double jeopardy for "the same *offense,*" and prohibits compelled self-incrimination "in any *criminal* case." U.S. Const. amend. V (emphasis added). The Sixth Amendment guarantees "the *accused*" a host of procedural rights in "all *criminal* prosecutions," and the Eighth Amendment bars "cruel and unusual *punishments.*" *Id.* amends. VI, VIII (emphasis added). Punishment is quintessentially, even if not exclusively, a criminal law concept.

3. I am not the first modern scholar to observe this point. *See, e.g.,* Richard A. Posner, *Rethinking the Fourth Amendment,* 1981 Sup. Ct. Rev. 49, 49–58; *see also* Bradford P. Wilson, *Enforcing the Fourth Amendment: A Jurisprudential History* 9–19 (1986) (providing historical support for a tort-law remedial model in Fourth Amendment cases).

4. My approach cannot make perfect sense of all that the modern Court has said and done. No approach can. As the leading champion of stare decisis on the current Court has noted, when precedents conflict we must choose among them, and such a choice must, to some extent, be shaped by factors other than precedent. *See* Church of the Lukumi Babalu Aye, Inc. v. City of Hialeah, 113 S. Ct. 2217, 2248 (1993) (Souter, J., concurring in part and concurring in the judgment).

My approach does, however, strive to keep faith with—indeed to build an overall framework uniting—many of the finest judicial utterances on the amendment found in modern volumes of *U.S. Reports* and authored by a wide range of Justices. For example, in trying to take constitutional text and history seriously, I follow the lead of Justices Black and Scalia. *See, e.g.,* California v. Acevedo, 111 S. Ct. 1982, 1992 (1991) (Scalia, J., concurring in the judgment); Coolidge v. New Hampshire, 403 U.S. 443, 509 (1971) (Black, J., concurring and dissenting). In writing that the ultimate touchstone of the amendment is not a warrant or probable cause, but reasonableness, I echo Chief Justice Rehnquist and Justices Black, Harlan, White, Scalia, and Kennedy. *See Acevedo,* 111 S. Ct. at 1992 (Scalia, J., concurring in the judgment); National Treasury Employees Union v. Von Raab, 489 U.S. 656, 665 (1989) (Kennedy, J.); Robbins v. California, 453 U.S. 420, 437–38 (1981) (Rehnquist, J., dissenting); Cady v. Dombrowski, 413

U.S. 433, 439 (1973) (Rehnquist, J.); *Coolidge*, 403 U.S. at 509 (Black, J., concurring and dissenting); Chimel v. California, 395 U.S. 752, 772–73 (1969) (White, J., dissenting); Cooper v. California, 386 U.S. 58, 62 (1967) (Black, J.); *cf. Coolidge*, 403 U.S. at 492 (Harlan, J., concurring) (citing the work of Telford Taylor critiquing the warrant requirement). In pointing out that, historically, warrants were disfavored devices, because they immunized government searchers and seizers from later liability, I build on the work of Justices White and Scalia. *See, e.g., Acevedo*, 111 S. Ct. at 1992 (Scalia, J., concurring in the judgment); Payton v. New York, 445 U.S. 573, 607–8 (1980) (White, J., dissenting). In reiterating that ex parte warrants were intended to be limited devices, used only against a locus of wrongful or dangerous activity, and only after meeting the explicit standard of probable cause, I track the views of Justice Stevens. *See, e.g.,* Zurcher v. Stanford Daily, 436 U.S. 547, 577–83 (1978) (Stevens, J., dissenting); Marshall v. Barlow's Inc., 436 U.S. 307, 326–28 (1978) (Stevens, J., dissenting). In suggesting that the seriousness of a crime is relevant in assessing reasonableness, I openly embrace what Justice Jackson admitted made consummate common sense. *See, e.g.,* Brinegar v. United States, 338 U.S. 160, 183 (1949) (Jackson, J., dissenting); McDonald v. United States, 335 U.S. 451, 459–60 (1948) (Jackson, J., concurring). In advocating a broad definition of searches and seizures and special sensitivity in free expression cases, I embrace the instincts of Justice Stewart. *See, e.g.,* Katz v. United States, 389 U.S. 347, 350–53 (1967) (Stewart, J.); Stanford v. Texas, 379 U.S. 476, 482–85 (1965) (Stewart, J.). In calling for candid discussion of the racial issues posed by search and seizure policies, I salute the honesty exemplified by both Chief Justice Warren and Justice Marshall. *See, e.g.,* Florida v. Bostick, 111 S. Ct. 2382, 2390 n. 1, 2394 n. 4 (1991) (Marshall, J., dissenting); United States v. Sokolow, 490 U.S. 1, 12 (1989) (Marshall, J., dissenting); Terry v. Ohio, 392 U.S. 1, 14–15 and n. 11 (1968) (Warren, C.J.). In registering grave doubts about the exclusionary rule, I extend the arguments of Chief Justice Rehnquist and Justices White, Blackmun, and O'Connor. *See, e.g.,* Immigration & Naturalization Serv. v. Lopez-Mendoza, 468 U.S. 1032, 1040–50 (1984) (O'Connor, J.); United States v. Leon, 468 U.S. 897, 905–13 (1984) (White, J.); New York v. Quarles, 467 U.S. 649, 664–72 (1984) (O'Connor, J., concurring in the judgment in part and dissenting in part); California v. Minjares, 443 U.S. 916, 916–28 (1979) (Rehnquist, J., dissenting from the denial of a stay); United States v. Janis, 428 U.S. 433, 443–60 (1976) (Blackmun, J.). In stressing the need for injunctive relief to address systematic police brutality, I embrace opinions authored by Justices Marshall and Blackmun. *See, e.g.,* City of Los Angeles v. Lyons, 461 U.S. 95, 113–37 (1983) (Marshall, J., dissenting); Rizzo v. Goode, 423 U.S. 362, 381–87 (1976) (Blackmun, J., dissenting). In championing civil damage actions against wayward officials, I build on the views of Justices Brennan and Harlan. *See, e.g.,* Bivens v. Six Unknown Named Agents of Fed. Bureau of Narcotics, 403 U.S. 388, 389–97 (1971) (Brennan, J.); *id.* at 398–411 (Harlan, J., concurring in the judgment). In championing the role of the civil jury in deciding reasonableness, I resonate with Chief Justice Rehnquist and Justice Scalia. *See, e.g., Acevedo*, 111 S. Ct. at 1992 (Scalia, J., concurring in the judgment); *Minjares*, 443 U.S. at 926 (Rehnquist, J., dissenting from the denial of a stay); *see also* Antonin Scalia, *The Rule of Law as a Law of Rules*, 56 U. Chi. L. Rev. 1175, 1180–86 (1989) (providing a similar discussion of the civil jury).

5. I emphasize that my package of criticisms and alternatives is offered as a whole. Because I believe my package has internal analytic integrity, I would resist partisan or ideological efforts to pick and choose, using part of my analysis while ignoring the rest. For example, "conservatives" might be tempted to use this chapter to gut the exclusionary rule further while ignoring the need to build up civil remedies. But this "conservative" move would break faith with constitutional text and history. Compared with my package, it would also leave the people less "secure in

their persons, houses, papers, and effects." This would be a perversion of my purpose. "Liberals," by contrast, might be tempted to beef up both civil remedies and exclusion. But any effort to prop up or expand the exclusionary rule would also break faith with the amendment's text and history. What's more, it too would leave the people less secure in their persons, houses, papers, and effects by (first) rewarding crimes against persons and property; (second) generating bad law, as judges strain to keep material evidence in by claiming searches were constitutional, in precedents that may then become stumbling blocks against recovery by law-abiding civil plaintiffs; and (third) rendering the Fourth Amendment contemptible in the eyes of most Americans.

6. *See, e.g.*, Mincey v. Arizona, 437 U.S. 385, 390 (1978); Coolidge v. New Hampshire, 403 U.S. 443, 454–55 (1971); Johnson v. United States, 333 U.S. 10, 14–15 (1948).

7. Most proponents of the warrant requirement appear to concede that this implicit command should yield in the face of extreme urgency or necessity—as should, the proponents argue, even explicit constitutional commands.

8. Yet another possible reading would be to infer that a search or seizure pursuant to a warrant supported by probable cause, particular description, and the other warrant clause requirements is per se reasonable. Although I once suggested as much, *see* Akhil Reed Amar, *The Bill of Rights as a Constitution*, 100 Yale L.J. 1131, 1179–80 (1991), I now confess error. The requirements set out in the warrant clause are an absolute minimum, but the text nowhere says that warrants must issue whenever these requirements are met, or that warrants may issue when these requirements are met, even if the search or seizure would otherwise be unreasonable. The global reasonableness command applies to all searches and seizures, and in some circumstances, this command will have independent bite, precluding the issuance of a warrant even when the warrant clause requirements are satisfied. For an example and discussion, see text at note 87 below.

9. The following are the state predecessors of the Fourth Amendment, in order of enactment: Va. Const. of 1776 (Declaration of Rights) §10; Pa. Const. of 1776 (Declaration of Rights) art. X; Del. Const. of 1776 (Declaration of Rights) §17; Md. Const. of 1776 (Declaration of Rights) art. XXIII; N.C. Const. of 1776 (Declaration of Rights) art. XI; Vt. Const. of 1777, ch. 1, §XI; Mass. Const. of 1780, pt. I, art. XIV; N.H. Const. of 1784, pt. I, art. XIX; Vt. Const. of 1786, ch. 1, §XII. The language from Pennsylvania, Vermont, Massachusetts, and New Hampshire most closely anticipated the eventual language of the federal Fourth Amendment.

10. *See* Jones v. Root, 72 Mass. (6 Gray) 435, 436, 439 (1856) (upholding a warrantless seizure of liquors); Rohan v. Sawin, 59 Mass. (5 Cush.) 281, 284–85 (1850) (holding that a warrant is not required for arrest under either the national or the Massachusetts Constitution); Mayo v. Wilson, 1 N.H. 53, 60 (1817) (stating that New Hampshire's counterpart to the Fourth Amendment "does not seem intended to restrain the legislature from authorizing arrests without warrant, but to guard against abuse of warrants issued by Magistrates"); Wakely v. Hart, 6 Binn. 316, 318 (Pa. 1814) ("[I]t is nowhere said, that there shall be no arrest [i.e., seizure] without warrant. To have said so would have endangered the safety of society.").

11. *See, e.g.*, State v. Brown, 5 Del. (5 Harr.) 505, 506–7 (Ct. Gen. Sess. 1853); Johnson v. State, 30 Ga. 426, 429–32 (1860); Baltimore & O. R.R. Co. v. Cain, 81 Md. 87, 100, 102–3 (1895); Reuck v. McGregor, 32 N.J.L. 70, 74 (Sup. Ct. 1866); Holley v. Mix, 3 Wend. 350, 353 (N.Y. Sup. Ct. 1829); Wade v. Chaffee, 8 R.I. 224, 225 (1865). These cases, from the original thirteen states, were all cited in United States v. Watson, 423 U.S. 411 (1976). *See id.* at 420.

12. *See* 4 William Blackstone, *Commentaries on the Laws of England* 286–92 (1765); 2 Matthew Hale, *The History of the Pleas of the Crown* *85, *88–92 (Professional Books

Ltd. 1987) (1736); 1 *id.* *587–88; 2 William Hawkins, *A Treatise of the Pleas of the Crown* 74–86 (Professional Books Ltd. 1973) (1721).

13. *See* Act of May 2, 1792, ch. 28, §9, 1 Stat. 264, 265 (repealed 1795).

14. 423 U.S. 411, 414–24 (1976).

15. Justice Powell justified an arrest exception on policy grounds as well as historical grounds: arrest warrants should not be required because they can grow "stale." *See id.* at 431–32 (Powell, J., concurring). But so can search warrants; thus, the double standard remains unjustified. Indeed, the policy argument boomerangs because, as a category, search warrants, which identify a place where goods are *now* believed to be, rather than a person believed to have *already committed* a crime, are more likely to grow stale than arrest warrants.

16. Telford Taylor, *Two Studies in Constitutional Interpretation* 28–29 (1969) (footnotes omitted).

17. *Id.* at 57.

18. *See* Chimel v. California, 395 U.S. 752, 762–63 (1969).

19. *See* Taylor, *supra* note 16, at 24–25; Eric Schnapper, *Unreasonable Searches and Seizures of Papers*, 71 Va. L. Rev. 869, 903 (1985) ("It must either be sworn that I have certain stolen goods, or such a particular thing that is criminal in itself, in my custody, before any magistrate is authorized to grant a warrant to any man to enter my house and seize it." (quoting a 1765 English pamphlet by the Father of Candor)).

20. *See* Taylor, *supra* note 16, at 44–45, 62, 98–99.

21. *See* Entick v. Carrington, 19 Howell's State Trials 1029, 1073 (C.P. 1765) (Camden, C.J.) ("I wish some cases had been shewn, where the law forceth evidence out of the owner's custody by process. . . . [A] search for evidence is disallowed upon the [principle that] the innocent would be confounded with the guilty.").

22. The amendment also applies, of course, to arrest warrants and other warrants authorizing "seizure" of the "person." Here I consider only search warrants. For more discussion of search warrants for "mere evidence," *see infra* note 24 and text at note 86.

23. Though silly, this was apparently the rule announced in Gouled v. United States, 255 U.S. 298 (1921), *see id.* at 308–11, which stood until overruled in Warden v. Hayden, 387 U.S. 294 (1967), *see id.* at 300–10.

24. Thus, the facts of *Gouled*, which involved a search warrant, should have led the Court to rein in search warrants for mere evidence in the possession of innocent third parties. Because the *Gouled* Court seemed to think that searches generally required warrants, *see Gouled*, 255 U.S. at 308, it apparently misframed its "mere evidence rule" as a silly ban on all searches for mere evidence, rather than as a sensible ban on all ex parte warrants for wholly innocent evidence held by an unsuspecting third party. *See infra* text at note 86. In fact, the key language of *Gouled* is ambiguous—the Court repeatedly speaks of the law applicable to "search warrants," *see id.* at 308–11. Later courts would have done well to read its rule as limited to search warrants.

Nor does the early landmark case of Entick v. Carrington, 19 Howell's State Trials 1029 (C.P. 1765), support a broad ban on warrantless searches for mere evidence, for the facts of that case also involved a warrant, and Lord Camden's key phrase declared only that the law does not "force[] evidence out of the owner's custody *by process*," *id.* at 1073 (emphasis added). Professor Taylor has noted that there has never been a general rule in England against seizures of purely evidentiary material. *See* Taylor, *supra* note 16, at 61; *see also id.* at 53 ("Camden was simply observing . . . that neither statute nor common law authorized the use of *search warrants* to obtain evidence of crime." (emphasis added)); *infra* note 86.

25. *See* Act of July 31, 1789, ch. 5, §24, 1 Stat. 29, 43 (repealed 1790).

26. *See* Act of Mar. 2, 1799, ch. 22, §68, 1 Stat. 627, 677 (repealed 1922); Act of

Feb. 18, 1793, ch. 8, §27, 1 Stat. 305, 315; Act of Aug. 4, 1790, ch. 35, §§31, 48, 64, 1 Stat. 145, 164, 170, 175 (repealed 1799). The 1790 act is discussed in United States v. Villamonte-Marquez, 462 U.S. 579, 584 (1983) (upholding boarding and inspection, without warrants or probable cause, of ships in U.S. waters with access to the open seas).

27. Act of July 31, 1789, ch. 5, §24, 1 Stat. 29, 43 (repealed 1790).

28. Act of March 3, 1791, ch. 15, §§25, 29, 1 Stat. 199, 205–6.

29. *See* Gelston v. Hoyt, 16 U.S. (3 Wheat.) 246, 310 (1818) (Story, J.) ("At common law, any person may at his peril, seize for a forfeiture to the government; and if the government adopt his seizure, and the property is condemned, he will be completely justified. . . ."); 2 Hawkins, *supra* note 12, at 77 ("And where a Man arrests another, who is actually guilty of the Crime for which he is arrested, it seems, That he needs not in justifying it, set forth any special Cause of his Suspicion, but may say in general, that the Party feloniously did such a Fact, for which he arrested him . . . ." (citation omitted)).

30. *See, e.g.,* Entick v. Carrington, 19 Howell's State Trials 1029, 1067 (C.P. 1765); Money v. Leach, 97 Eng. Rep. 1075, 1082–83 (K.B. 1765); Wilkes v. Wood, 19 Howell's State Trials 1153, 1166 (C.P. 1763), 98 Eng. Rep. 489, 498.

31. 16 U.S. (3 Wheat.) 246, 310 (1818). For further illustrations of the ex post defense, see Johnson v. Tompkins, 13 F. Cas. 840, 845, 849 (C.C.E.D. Pa. 1833) (No. 7416) (Baldwin, Cir. J.); Rohan v. Sawin, 59 Mass. (5 Cush.) 281, 284–85 (1850); Wakely v. Hart, 6 Binn. 316, 318–19 (Pa. 1814).

32. *See, e.g.,* Gerard V. Bradley, *Present at the Creation? A Critical Guide to* Weeks v. United States *and Its Progeny,* 30 St. Louis U. L.J. 1031, 1041–45 (1986).

33. *See* Warden v. Hayden, 387 U.S. 294, 298–300 (1967).

34. *See, e.g.,* United States v. Matlock, 415 U.S. 164, 169–71 (1974).

35. *See, e.g.,* Illinois v. Rodriguez, 497 U.S. 177, 183–86 (1990).

36. *See id.* at 183, 186.

37. *See, e.g.,* Arizona v. Hicks, 480 U.S. 321, 328 (1987) (holding that merely looking at a turntable is not a "search"). Perhaps merely looking without touching is not a "seizure," but it surely should count as a "search" for one who believes in plain meaning, as does Justice Scalia, the author of *Hicks. See infra* note 39.

A far more egregious example comes from the Court's so-called open-field doctrine, whereby trespassing on a person's property, climbing over her fences and peering into her barns is somehow not a search; nor, apparently, is hovering over an enclosed backyard with a helicopter. *See* United States v. Dunn, 480 U.S. 294, 297–98, 300–301 (1987); California v. Ciraolo, 476 U.S. 207, 215 (1986).

38. *See* Dow Chem. Co. v. United States, 476 U.S. 227, 238 (1986); United States v. Karo, 468 U.S. 705, 716 (1984).

39. Or with the naked eye. The *Oxford English Dictionary* includes the following definition, among others, of the verb *search:* "to look scrutinizingly at" 14 *Oxford English Dictionary* 806 (2d ed. 1989). The dictionary then proceeds to feature examples from O. W. Holmes ("He searched her features through and through.") and Augusta Wilson ("While he drank, his eyes searched her face, and lingered admiringly on her beautiful hand."). *Id.*

40. The example is intentionally gendered. *See* infra text at notes 185–86.

41. Thus, Justice Scalia's repudiation of the warrant requirement in California v. Acevedo, 111 S. Ct. 1982 (1991), *see id.* at 1992 (Scalia, J. concurring in the judgment) frees him to adopt a more straightforward definition of *search* than the one his acceptance of the requirement shoehorned him into in *Hicks, see supra* note 37.

42. Katz v. United States, 389 U.S. 347, 360 (1967) (Harlan, J., concurring). Although the phrase comes from Justice Harlan's concurring opinion, later Court opinions have taken it to distill the essence of the *Katz* majority. *See, e.g.,* Terry v. Ohio, 392 U.S. 1, 9 (1968).

43. *See, e.g.,* National Treasury Employees Union v. Von Raab, 489 U.S. 656, 675 n. 3 (1989) (airline passenger search); New Jersey v. T.L.O., 469 U.S. 325, 337–43 (1985) (public school search); Delaware v. Prouse, 440 U.S. 648, 660 (1979) (annual auto safety inspection); United States v. Martinez-Fuerte, 428 U.S. 543, 564–66 (1976) (border crossing search); United States v. Biswell, 406 U.S. 311, 316 (1972) (inspection of pervasively regulated business). In *T.L.O.,* the warrantless search was arguably both selective and intrusive; a fortiori, unintrusive and nondiscriminatory searches in public schools would seem permissible.

44. As we have seen, the warrant clause does plainly presuppose a search for items akin to contraband or stolen goods. *See supra* text at notes 19–24. But the possession of these items may be unknowing and wholly innocent; and the search warrant, strictly speaking, does not run against a criminal suspect, but against a place. *See* Taylor, *supra* note 16, at 60. As Professor Taylor notes, a search warrant is quasi-in-rem. *See id.* Most important, the first clause of the Fourth Amendment explicitly addresses *all* searches and seizures, not just criminal ones.

45. It will not do to point to the greater trial protections accorded criminal defendants over civil litigants (proof beyond reasonable doubt, and so on). As we shall see in Chapter 3, these procedural rights do not even begin to attach until one becomes "accused" in some way; and many searches and seizures, even of criminal suspects, occur well before this point.

46. *See* Terry v. Ohio, 392 U.S. 1, 30–31 (1968).

47. Consider, for example, grand jury and legislative subpoenas, *see* Oklahoma Press Publishing Co. v. Walling, 327 U.S. 186, 208–9 (1946); automobile searches, *see* Carroll v. United States, 267 U.S. 132, 147–53 (1925); and prison searches, *see* Hudson v. Palmer, 468 U.S. 517, 522–30 (1984).

48. Although the text of the Fourth Amendment speaks of the reasonableness of the underlying search or seizure, the modification shifts the focus to the reasonableness of bypassing the warrant. The textual and historical basis for this shift is shaky. Searches under warrants that meet all the conditions of the warrant clause are not per se reasonable. *See supra* note 8; *infra* text at note 87. Nor are they somehow "preferred"—a word nowhere in the Fourth Amendment. As we shall see, the Framers most clearly did not prefer an ex parte warrant regime to the civil jury regime that warrants were designed to displace. *See infra* text at notes 60–85.

49. For a more charitable explanation of how judges came to stand the Fourth Amendment on its head, *see* Taylor, *supra* note 16, at 44–46.

50. *See id.* at 26–27.

51. 19 Howell's State Trials 1153 (C.P. 1763), 98 Eng. Rep. 489.

52. The leading historical account of the Fourth Amendment found only a single reference to the writs of assistance in debates leading up to the amendment, and that reference came from the pen of Mercy Otis Warren, the sister of the colonial lawyer James Otis, who argued the writs of assistance case. For details, see Amar, *supra* note 8, at 1176 n. 208. *Cf.* Wasserstrom, *supra* note 1, at 285 n. 149 (citing evidence questioning the importance of Otis's speech).

53. John Wilkes, a flamboyant member of Parliament, published an anonymous attack on the majesty and ministry of King George III in a 1763 pamphlet, *The North Briton Number 45*. The pamphlet enraged the ministry, which issued a general search and arrest warrant against the pamphlet's publishers and printers. No names were listed in the warrant; it authorized henchmen to round up the usual suspects and gave the henchmen discretion to decide who those suspects were. Wilkes's house was broken into; his private papers were rifled, read, and seized; and he was arrested and imprisoned in the Tower of London. After winning release on habeas corpus, Wilkes and some of the other fifty or so search targets brought hugely successful civil damage suits against the offending agents. The *Wilkes* case was a cause

célèbre in the colonies, where "Wilkes and Liberty" became a rallying cry for all those who hated government oppression. Americans across the continent named cities, counties, and even children in honor of Wilkes and the libertarian judge, Lord Camden. Witness, for example, Camden, New Jersey; Camden, South Carolina; Camden, Maine; Camden Yards in Baltimore, Maryland; Wilkes-Barre, Pennsylvania; Wilkes County, Georgia; Wilkes County, North Carolina; and of course, John Wilkes Booth. For more on Wilkes, *see* Pauline Maier, *From Resistance to Revolution,* 162–69 (1972); Raymond W. Postgate, *That Devil Wilkes* (1929); George Rudé, *Wilkes and Liberty* (1962); and Pauline Maier, *John Wilkes and American Disillusionment with Britain,* 20 Wm. & Mary Q. 373 (1963).

54. Consider, for example, Massachusetts Governor William Shirley's efforts in 1753 to issue gubernatorial warrants. *See* Tracey Maclin, *The Central Meaning of the Fourth Amendment,* 35 Wm. & Mary L. Rev. 197, 221 (1992).

55. *See, e.g.,* Shadwick v. City of Tampa, 407 U.S. 345, 347–54 (1972) (upholding a nonlawyer-clerk-as-magistrate scheme); Coolidge v. New Hampshire, 403 U.S. 443, 449–53 (1971) (imposing some limits on who could issue warrants, but falling far short of banning all nonjudicial warrants).

Actually, my description may not quite be fair to police chiefs, who probably have more direct, routine contact with the citizenry subject to search and seizure than do warrant clerks, who typically hear only the cops' side of the story.

56. *See* Bernard Bailyn, *The Origins of American Politics* 68 (1968).

57. *See* William E. Nelson, *Emulating the Marshall Court: The Applicability of the Rule of Law to Contemporary Constitutional Adjudication,* 131 U. Pa. L. Rev. 489, 489 (1982) (book review).

58. *See, e.g.,* Act of July 31, 1789, ch. 5, §24, 1 Stat. 29, 43 (repealed 1790); Taylor, *supra* note 16, at 24–25.

59. *See infra* text at notes 67–68, 225–31.

60. *See infra* text at notes 79–85.

61. U.S. Const. amend. IV (emphasis added).

62. Taylor, *supra* note 16, at 41.

63. *See* 2 Bernard Schwartz, *The Bill of Rights: A Documentary History* 665, 733–34, 841–42, 913, 968 (1971) (recording the proto–Fourth Amendments proposed in Pennsylvania, Maryland, Virginia, New York, and North Carolina).

64. *Id.* at 1027; *see also* Entick v. Carrington, 19 Howell's State Trials 1029, 1039 (C.P. 1765), 95 Eng. Rep. 807, 812 (labeling overbroad warrants "unreasonable or unlawful" (reporting the oral argument of the plaintiff's counsel)).

This seems a good place to attack the widespread canard that the ultimate wording of the Fourth Amendment need not be taken seriously, because it was a result of happenstance, not careful consideration. The final language of the amendment, the story goes, was initially proposed by New York Congressman Egbert Benson and voted *down* by the first Congress. Later, Benson, as chairman of the style committee, stubbornly rewrote the amendment in his pet language and slyly slipped it past an inattentive House. *See, e.g.,* Maclin, *supra* note 54, at 208–9 (repeating the canard and labeling it "undisputed history").

The canard is triply troubling. First, it is quite possible that Benson's initial proposal *passed,* and that the House reporter Thomas Lloyd misrecorded the vote—as he did on several other occasions, involving other provisions of the Bill of Rights. *See, e.g.,* Edward Dumbauld, *The Bill of Rights and What It Means Today* 35 n. 6, 41 n. 28, 42 n. 32 (1957). Scribal error is highly consistent with everything serious historians know about Lloyd. *See* James H. Hutson, *The Creation of the Constitution: The Integrity of the Documentary Record,* 65 Tex. L. Rev. 1, 35–38 (1986). Contrary to the canard, the House and Senate treated the final wording of their proposed amendments with great care, as is obvious from many other textual fine-tunings. *See* 2 Schwartz, *supra* note 63, at 1145–67. Second, the canard fails to do justice to the Constitution's textuality and to its text—a text adopted by supermajorities of both houses and ratified by a supermajority of states. Third, if the lack of an explicit warrant requirement were simply a drafting accident in the first Congress, we still could not easily account for the widespread absence or explicit rejection of the warrant requirement everywhere else—in common law treatises, state constitutions, early state cases, early federal cases, founding era deliberations generally, state ratifying conventions, and so on.

65. *See* Wilkes v. Halifax, 19 Howell's State Trials 1406 (C.P. 1769); Entick v. Carrington, 19 Howell's State Trials 1029 (C.P. 1765), 95 Eng. Rep. 807; Money v. Leach, 19 Howell's State Trials 1001 (K.B. 1765), 97 Eng. Rep. 1075; Beardmore v. Carrington, 19 Howell's State Trials 1405 (C.P. 1764), 95 Eng. Rep. 790; Wilkes v. Wood, 19 Howell's State Trials 1153 (C.P. 1763), 98 Eng. Rep. 489; Huckle v. Money, 19 Howell's State Trials 1404 (C.P. 1763), 95 Eng. Rep. 768.

66. *Wilkes,* 19 Howell's State Trials at 1154–55, 98 Eng. Rep. at 490.

67. *Leach,* 19 Howell's State Trials at 1026, 97 Eng. Rep. at 1087 (quoting the plaintiff's allegations (emphasis added)).

68. *See* Bernard Bailyn, *The Ideological Origins of the American Revolution* 123 (1967); Gordon S. Wood, *The Creation of the American Republic, 1776–1787,* at 10, 299 n. 66 (1969); Alan H. Scheiner, Note, *Judicial Assessment of Punitive Damages, The Seventh Amendment, and the Politics of Jury Power,* 91 Colum. L. Rev. 142, 150 n. 40 (1991).

69. *Pennsylvania and the Federal Constitution 1787–1788,* at 154 (John B. McMaster and Frederick D. Stone eds., 1888). This essay has recently been reprinted, *see Essay of A Democratic Federalist, reprinted in* 3 *The Complete Anti-Federalist* 58, 61 (Herbert J. Storing ed., 1981).

70. *Pennsylvania and the Federal Constitution 1787–1788, supra* note 69, at 782; 2 *Documentary History of the Ratification of the Constitution* 526 (Merrill Jensen ed., 1976).

71. *Essays by Hampden, reprinted in* 4 *The Complete Anti-Federalist, supra* note 69, at 198, 200.

72. *Notes on* Erving v. Cradock, *in* Josiah Quincy, Jr., *Reports of Cases Argued and Adjudged in the Superior Court of Judicature of the Province of Massachusetts Bay Between 1761 and 1772,* at 553, 557 (1865).

73. *Essays by a Farmer (I), reprinted in* 5 *The Complete Anti-Federalist, supra* note 69, at 5, 14.

74. *Genuine Information of Luther Martin, in* 2 *The Complete Anti-Federalist, supra* note 69, at 27, 70–71. Publius's discussion of the civil jury directly responds to this passage, *see* The Federalist No. 83, at 500 (Alexander Hamilton) (Clinton Rossiter ed., 1961).

75. *Notes of Samuel Chase (IIB), in* 5 *The Complete Anti-Federalist, supra* note 69, at 82, 82.

76. 2 Schwartz, *supra* note 63, at 733.

77. *Id.* at 733–34. For further, more subtle, linkages between what would become the Fourth and Seventh Amendments, see the back-to-back references to these ideas in Letter from James Madison to George Eve (Jan. 2, 1789), *in* 2 Schwartz, *supra* note 63, at 997; *Letters of Centinel (I), reprinted in* 2 *The Complete Anti-Federalist, supra* note 69, at 136; *Letters from the Federal Farmer (IV), reprinted in* 2 *The Complete Anti-Federalist, supra* note 69, at 249; *Essays of Brutus (II), reprinted in* 2 *The Complete Anti-Federalist, supra* note 69, at 375; *An Old Whig (V), reprinted in* 3 *The Complete Anti-Federalist, supra* note 69, at 37; *Objections of a Son of Liberty, reprinted in* 6 *The Complete Anti-Federalist, supra* note 69, at 34–35.

78. Act of March 3, 1791, ch. 15, §38, 1 stat. 199, 208.

79. *See* Michigan v. Tyler, 436 U.S. 499, 508 (1978); Camara v. Municipal

Court, 387 U.S. 523, 532 (1967). In some cases where the Court has required a warrant, might a badge have sufficed?

80. Cooper v. Boot, 99 Eng. Rep. 911, 916 (K.B. 1785); *see also* Johnson v. Tompkins, 13 F. Cas. 840, 845 (C.C. E.D. Pa. 1833) (No. 7416) (Baldwin, Cir. J.) (describing the immunity from trespass liability conferred by "lawful warrant" as "an incontestable principle of the law"). The word *warrant*, as used in the Fourth Amendment, thus fused together preclearance with immunity. On the possibility today of requiring forms of judicial preclearance that would not necessarily immunize, *see infra* text at notes 189–92.

81. Reed v. Rice, 25 Ky. (2 J.J. Marsh.) 44, 46 (1829).

82. Robinson v. Richardson, 79 Mass. (13 Gray) 454, 457 (1859).

83. 1 Thomas Cooley, *A Treatise on the Constitutional Limitations Which Rest upon the Legislative Power of the States of the American Union* 618 (8th ed. 1927); Thomas Cooley, *A Treatise on the Constitutional Limitations Which Rest upon the Legislative Power of the States of the American Union* *303 (1st ed. 1868) [hereinafter Cooley, First Edition].

84. Payton v. New York, 445 U.S. 573, 607–8 (1980) (White, J., dissenting) (joined by Burger, C.J., and Rehnquist, J.); *see also* Carroll v. United States, 267 U.S. 132, 156 (1925) (recognizing that a properly issued judicial warrant "protects the seizing officer against a suit for damages").

85. 4 Blackstone, *supra* note 12, at 288. For further support, *see* Michael Dalton, *The Countrey Justice* 300–306 (photo. reprint 1972) (1622); 2 Hawkins, *supra* note 12, at 82–83; 2 Hale, *supra* note 12, at 119; 1 Richard Burn, *The Justice of the Peace and Parish Officer* 295 (7th ed. 1762). For representative restatements of the basic principle in American law, see Bell v. Clapp, 10 Johns. 263, 265–66 (N.Y. 1813); William E. Nelson, *Americanization of the Common Law*, 92 (1975); Cooley, First Edition, *supra* note 83, at *307. As stated by Justice James Wilson in his famous Lectures on Law: "With regard to process issuing from the courts of justice, . . . though the writ be illegal, the sheriff is protected and indemnified in serving it. From this general rule, however, one exception must be taken and allowed. He must judge, at his peril, whether the court, from which the process issued, has or has not jurisdiction of the cause." *The Works of James Wilson* 552 (Robert G. McCloskey ed., 1967); *see also id.* at 568, 684 (containing similar language).

86. For more analysis, see the extraordinarily thoughtful remarks of Justice Stevens in Zurcher v. Stanford Daily, 436 U.S. 547, 577–83 (1978) (Stevens, J., dissenting). For a statutory response to *Zurcher* that is attentive to some of Justice Stevens' concerns, see the Privacy Protection Act of 1980, Pub. L. No. 96-440, 94 Stat. 1879 (codified at 42 U.S.C. §§2000aa, 2000aa-5 to 2000aa-7, 2000aa-11, 2000aa-12 (1988). *Cf.* 18 U.S.C. §3144 (1988) (stating that a "judicial officer may order the arrest" of a material witness upon showing that "it may become impracticable to secure the presence of the person by subpoena"). And for an earlier recognition of similar concerns, see Robinson v. Richardson, 79 Mass. (13 Gray) 454 (1859):

> [I]t cannot be doubted [that the Massachusetts Fourth Amendment counterpart and prototype] was intended strictly and carefully to limit, restrain and regulate the granting and issuing of warrants . . . to the general class of cases, in and to the furtherance of the objects of which they had before been recognized and allowed, . . . and certainly not so to vary, extend and enlarge the purposes for and occasions on which they might be used. . . .
>
> . . . Certainly no person ought to be compelled to disclose any facts or information to be given as evidence . . . until he has at least had an opportunity of urging his objections [before] some competent judicial tribunal. . . .

Id. at 457–58. Therefore, a state statute allowing search warrants for discovering concealed property or assets of a debtor's estate was held unconstitutional. Further important analysis and documentation may be found in Cooley, First Edition, *supra* note 83, at *305–7. Consider also Entick v. Carrington, 19 Howell's State Trials 1029 (C.P. 1765). As we have seen, *see supra* note 24, it appears that Lord Camden was speaking only of ex parte warrants for "mere evidence" and not of warrantless searches or subpoenas, in which the target could challenge the intrusion in a subsequent judicial proceeding. *See Entick,* 19 Howell's State Trials at 1064, 1066 (noting that an ex parte warrant "is executed against the party before he is heard or even summoned" and that "he has no power to reclaim his goods, even after his innocence is cleared by acquittal"). On the due process problems raised by ex parte *seizure* warrants, see United States v. James Daniel Good Real Property, 114 S.Ct. 492 (1993).

87. *Cf.* Winston v. Lee, 470 U.S. 753, 763–66 (1985) (holding that compelling the surgical removal of a bullet was, on the facts of the case, unreasonable, despite judicial authorization and probable cause). Once again, the example in the text is intentionally gendered. *See infra* text at notes 185–86.

88. 4 Blackstone, *supra* note 12, at 288.

89. *See* Wilkes v. Halifax, 19 Howell's State Trials 1406, 1407 (C.P. 1769). Wilkes had asked for even more. *See id.* at 1407.

90. For emphasis on the importance of the facial regularity of warrants, *see, e.g.,* Conner v. Commonwealth, 3 Binn. 38, 40, 43–44 (Pa. 1810); Grumon v. Raymond, 1 Conn. 40, 47–48 (1814); Ortman v. Greenman, 4 Mich. 291, 293 (1856); and Mangold v. Thorpe, 33 N.J.L. 134, 138 (1868). For the theory that would underlie any indemnification action and distinguish it from the general rule against contribution among tortfeasors, *see* Joseph Story, *Commentaries on the Law of Agency,* §339, at 347 (1839); and *infra* note 199. Ministerial execution—involving the ordinary amount of intrusion necessarily incident to the enforcement of a warrant—should be distinguished from especially unreasonable, intrusive, or abusive actions beyond those contemplated by the mere warrant itself.

91. *See, e.g., Grumon,* 1 Conn. at 47–48; *Ortman,* 4 Mich. at 293; *Mangold,* 33 N.J.L. at 138; 2 Hale, *supra* note 12, at 119; 2 Hawkins, *supra* note 12, at 82–83; *The Works of James Wilson, supra* note 85, at 552.

92. *See, e.g.,* New Jersey v. T.L.O., 469 U.S. 325, 340 (1985); Almeida-Sanchez v. United States, 413 U.S. 266, 269–73 (1973). *See generally* Wasserstrom, *supra* note 1, at 304–9 (discussing the probable cause requirement).

93. *Cf.* Taylor, *supra* note 16, at 49–50 (convincingly critiquing the efforts of Learned Hand and Felix Frankfurter to limit warrantless searches to the same scope as warranted searches).

94. Whiteley v. Warden, 401 U.S. 560, 566 (1971).

95. Albert W. Alschuler, *Bright Line Fever and the Fourth Amendment,* 45 U. Pitt. L. Rev. 227, 243, 263 (1984).

96. *See supra* notes 25–28.

97. *See supra* text at note 37–38. Consider also United States v. Place, 462 U.S. 696 (1983). When it held that a dog sniff was not a "search," *see id.* at 706–7, the Court was pointedly aware that a contrary result would require "probable cause," *see id.* at 707. Further evidence that the probable cause test drives Justices into strained and stingy definitions of *search* appears openly in Arizona v. Hicks, 480 U.S. 321 (1987), in which Justice O'Connor states that because "cursory inspection" without probable cause was "reasonable," it should not be labeled a "full-blown search," *see id.* at 333 (O'Connor, J., dissenting).

98. After quoting the Fourth Amendment, circuit judge and Supreme Court reporter William Cranch declared in an early case: "The cause of issuing a warrant of arrest, is a crime committed by the person charged. Probable cause, therefore, is a

probability that the crime has been committed by that person." United States v. Bollman, 24 F. Cas. 1189, 1192 (C.C.D.C. 1807) (No. 14,622).

99. One possible rejoinder to this last point might be that, although the probability for each individual citizen is quite low, the probability that some citizen will be carrying a gun into JFK today—or this year—is high enough to satisfy the strict 50 percent standard. This rejoinder is even more ominous. Government can always achieve a high enough overall probability of finding something if it searches *everyone* for *everything*. But such a total search, in many contexts, would hardly be reasonable. (Put another way, probable cause alone cannot be the heart of the amendment because it focuses on only one component—probability—of an overall search equation whose reasonableness also depends on other components, such as the sheer magnitude of search.) In the warrant context, the government's effort to cumulate probabilities is constrained by the particular description mandate. Once wrenched from its warrant context and adjoining safeguards, the probable cause requirement yet again reveals itself to be unhelpful or perverse.

100. See Camara v. Municipal Court, 387 U.S. 523, 535–38 (1967); Alschuler, *supra* note 95, at 252. For a thoughtful effort to provide historical support for this approach, see Joseph D. Grano, *Probable Cause and Common Sense: A Reply to the Critics of* Illinois v. Gates, 17 U. Mich. J.L. Ref. 465, 478–95 (1984). But even Grano's own evidence shows that probable cause was associated with individualized suspicion of wrongdoing. Given the limited and ex parte nature of traditional search warrants for items akin to contraband or stolen goods, individualized suspicion makes sense as a prerequisite for warrants, but it does not make sense as the test for all searching and seizing—outside the criminal context, for example.

101. See Marshall v. Barlow's, Inc., 436 U.S. 307, 320 (1978); *Camara*, 387 U.S. at 535–38. Justice Stevens has valiantly and persuasively attacked these newfangled warrants as wholly counter to the Fourth Amendment's text and spirit. See Michigan v. Clifford, 464 U.S. 287, 299, 302 (1984) (Stevens, J., concurring in the judgment); *Barlow's*, 436 U.S. at 325–28 (Stevens, J., dissenting) (joined by Blackmun and Rehnquist, JJ.).

102. On the undermining of the tort model, and what must be done now to undo the damage, *see infra* text at notes 196–221 on the twists and turns in the road to exclusion, see Silas Wasserstrom and William J. Mertens, *The Exclusionary Rule on the Scaffold: But Was It a Fair Trial?* 22 Am. Crim. L. Rev. 85, *passim* (1984).

103. The word *tort* might be thought anachronistic, as a late nineteenth-century word pulling together under one roof various earlier noncontractual civil causes of action—trespass, assault, trover, and so on. Yet Lord Chief Justice Charles Pratt (soon to become Lord Camden) uses the word over and over in Huckle v. Money, 95 Eng. Rep. 768 (C.P. 1763), *see id.* at 768–69; and Beardmore v. Carrington, 95 Eng. Rep. 790 (C.P. 1764), *see id.* at 791–93, two of the leading English cases presaging our Fourth Amendment. Nothing, however, turns on the word *tort* as opposed to the underlying causes of action it now encompasses—trespass, invasion of privacy, and so on.

104. These cases are collected *supra* note 65.

105. See Wilson, *supra* note 3, at 9–33. For a smattering of nineteenth-century cases, see Taylor, *supra* note 16, at 188 n. 71.

106. United States v. La Jeune Eugenie, 26 F. Cas. 832, 843–44 (C.C.D. Mass. 1822) (No. 15,551).

107. Commonwealth v. Dana, 43 Mass. (2 Met.) 329, 337 (1841).

108. See 1 Simon Greenleaf, *A Treatise on the Law of Evidence* §254a (Simon G. Croswell ed., 14th rev. ed. 1883).

109. See 4 John H. Wigmore, *Wigmore on Evidence* §§2183–84, at 626–39 (2d ed. 1923). Bradford P. Wilson has collected supporting material from fourteen states in

the late nineteenth and early twentieth century. *See* Wilson, *supra* note 3, at 68 n. 12. Subsequent to the U.S. Supreme Court's opinion in Boyd v. United States, 116 U.S. 616 (1886), a few states at the turn of the century began to drift away from the well-established rule against exclusion. *See* Wilson, *supra* note 3, at 72 n. 60.

110. *See, e.g.*, Wilson, *supra* note 3, at 45–112; Potter Stewart, *The Road to* Mapp v. Ohio *and Beyond: The Origins, Development and Future of the Exclusionary Rule in Search and Seizure Cases*, 83 Colum. L. Rev. 1365, 1372–77 (1983).

111. 116 U.S. 616 (1886).

112. *Id.* at 630, 633.

113. The most important cases here are Weeks v. United States, 232 U.S. 383, 393, 398 (1914); Silverthorne Lumber Co. v. United States, 251 U.S. 385, 392 (1920); Amos v. United States, 255 U.S. 313, 315–16 (1921); and Gouled v. United States, 255 U.S. 298, 306, 311 (1921).

114. Lochner v. New York, 198 U.S. 45 (1905).

115. The unexplained turning point was Agnello v. United States, 269 U.S. 20 (1925), which excluded unlawfully seized cocaine by fusing together the Fourth and Fifth Amendments, *see id.* at 33–35. Note, however, that at the time cocaine was subject to forfeiture but was not, perhaps, quite like stolen goods. *Cf. id.* at 23–24 (U.S. government argument describing cocaine as "a thing inherently vicious, used at the means of committing crime, analogous to burglars' tools or lottery tickets"). *See also* Osmond K. Fraenkel, *Recent Developments in the Law of Search and Seizure*, 13 Minn. L. Rev. 1, 4–5 and nn. 48–52 (1928) (citing five states declining to apply *Weeks* rule to contraband); State v. Pluth, 195 N.W. 789, 793–94 (Minn. 1923) (interpreting federal rule as not requiring exclusion of contraband because property would not be returned). Explicit, if cryptic, acknowledgment of the applicability of the exclusionary rule to contraband came in Trupiano v. United States, 334 U.S. 699, 710 (1948).

116. *See* Taylor, *supra* note 16, at 67.

117. *See* Schmerber v. California, 384 U.S. 757, 760–72 (1966). *Schmerber* is discussed at greater length in Chapter 2.

118. *See, e.g.*, United States v. Leon, 468 U.S. 897, 905–6 (1984); United States v. Doe, 465 U.S. 605, 610 n. 8 (1984); Andresen v. Maryland, 427 U.S. 463, 471–73 (1976); Fisher v. United States, 425 U.S. 391, 405–14 (1976). For a careful narrative of *Boyd's* demise, see Note, *The Life and Times of* Boyd v. United States *(1886–1976)*, 76 Mich. L. Rev. 184, 190–211 (1977) (authored by Stan Krauss). For more analysis, *see infra* Chapter 2.

119. *See* Taylor, *supra* note 16, at 52–53 (analyzing Entick v. Carrington, 19 Howell's State Trials 1029, 1073 (C.P. 1765)).

120. *See infra* note 122.

121. *See* People v. Kelly, 24 N.Y. 74, 83–84 (1861).

122. In other words, prior to trial, a suspect could be made to sing, with only a guarantee of "testimonial" rather than "use-fruits" or "transactional" immunity. Broader ideas of immunity derive from *Boyd* itself, via its kindred spirit, Counselman v. Hitchcock, 142 U.S. 547 (1892). The original view laid down by *Kelly* bears a striking resemblance to Justice O'Connor's proposed rule regarding "mere *Miranda*" violations. *See* New York v. Quarles, 467 U.S. 649, 665–69 (1984) (O'Connor, J., concurring in the judgment in part and dissenting in part). *Kelly* was widely followed in other states. For some kind words for *Kelly* and a catalog of like-minded cases, see 4 Wigmore, *supra* note 109, §2283, at 965–72. For much more analysis, *see infra* Chapter 2.

In England, the rule laid down by a 1783 case was that "when a coerced confession leads to recovery of stolen property, the confession will be suppressed but the property will be admitted in evidence." Gordon Van Kessel, *The Suspect as a*

Source of Testimonial Evidence: A Comparison of The English and American Approaches, 38 Hastings L.J. 1, 29 and n. 129 (1986) (citing The King v. Warickshall, 1 Leach 263, 264–65, 168 Eng. Rep. 234, 235 (1783)). Van Kessel also notes that there is no English exclusionary rule for search and seizure violations, if evidence is reliable: "It matters not how you get it; if you steal it even, it would be admissible." *Id.* at 32 (quoting Regina v. Leatham, 8 Cox Crim. Cas. 498, 501 (Q.B. 1861) (Crompton, J.)).

123. *See* Leonard W. Levy, *The Origins of the Fifth Amendment* 331–32 (1968).

124. *See* Henry J. Friendly, *The Fifth Amendment Tomorrow: The Case for Constitutional Change,* 37 U. Cin. L. Rev. 671, 679–80 (1968). As we shall see in Chapter 2, the best justification for the Fifth Amendment is that testimony compelled from a criminal defendant or suspect is inherently unreliable and poses an intolerable risk of convicting the innocent. But this logic surely argues against a rule excluding reliable physical evidence—a rule whose primary beneficiaries are overwhelmingly guilty.

The point here extends beyond the Fifth Amendment. As I explain in Chapters 3 and 4, the deep logic of the criminal procedure provisions of the Bill of Rights is not to protect truly guilty defendants—especially those who have committed violent crimes—from conviction, but primarily to protect truly innocent defendants from *erroneous* conviction.

125. Thus, the provision of the Fifth Amendment that does "run almost into" the Fourth is not the incrimination clause, but the just compensation clause. Both the Fourth Amendment and the just compensation clause transcend the civil/criminal distinction. Both paradigmatically speak to governmental grabbing of tangible things. Both are property-focused, in large part. Note the obvious textual parallels between "seizures" of "houses, papers, and effects" and "tak[ings]" of "private property."

126. U.S. Const. amend. V (emphasis added). *See generally infra* Chapter 2. And for a long list of Supreme Court cases documenting that exclusion derived from Fourth-Fifth fusion, *see infra* Chapter 4, note 28.

127. *Cf.* United States v. Janis, 428 U.S. 433 (1976) (refusing to exclude evidence in a civil prosecution).

128. Ker v. Illinois, 119 U.S. 436 (1886), and Frisbie v. Collins, 342 U.S. 519 (1952), both hold that illegal seizure and transfer of a suspect does not deprive a court of jurisdiction to try him as a criminal defendant. *See Ker,* 119 U.S. at 444; *Frisbie,* 342 U.S. at 522. Immigration and Naturalization Serv. v. Lopez-Mendoza, 468 U.S. 1032 (1984), reached a similar holding on explicitly Fourth Amendment grounds, *see id.* at 1039–40. For more discussion, *see infra* Chapter 3, text at notes 83–84.

129. *See* Holt v. United States, 218 U.S. 245, 252–53 (1910). For more discussion, *see infra* Chapter 2, text at notes 106–15.

130. *See* Agnello v. United States, 269 U.S. 20, 35 (1925) (suggesting, apparently on Fourth-Fifth fusion grounds, that introduction of evidence illegally obtained from *A* does not violate *B*'s "constitutional rights"); *cf.* Alderman v. United States, 394 U.S. 165, 171–76 (1969) (reaching a similar result on Fourth Amendment grounds).

131. My categorization and description of the standard slogans are themselves quite standard. *See, e.g.,* Randy E. Barnett, *Resolving the Dilemma of the Exclusionary Rule: An Application of Restitutive Principles of Justice,* 32 Emory L.J. 937, 938–39 (1983).

132. On the English rejection of exclusion over the centuries, *see* Van Kessel, *supra* note 122, at 28–34; on the Canadian rejection of blanket exclusion, see Polyvios G. Polyviou, *Search and Seizure* 328 (1982); and The Queen v. Collins, [1987] 1 S.C.R. 265, 280 (Can.); on the rejection of the American model (circa

1974) in other countries, see John Kaplan, *The Limits of the Exclusionary Rule*, 26 Stan. L. Rev. 1027, 1031 (1974).

133. *See* United States v. Janis, 428 U.S. 433, 447 (1976) ("In the complex and turbulent history of the [exclusionary] rule, the Court has never applied it to exclude evidence from a civil proceeding, federal or state."). *Janis* distinguished away One 1958 Plymouth Sedan v. Pennsylvania, 380 U.S. 693 (1965), which, in a quasi-criminal forfeiture action, excluded property "not intrinsically illegal in character," *id.* at 700. *Plymouth Sedan* does not support exclusion of "per se contraband"; and in any event, its explicitly *Boyd*-ish logic would not seem to survive *Schmerber supra* note 118.

134. *See supra* text at notes 106–9. It is also hard to attribute to the Fourteenth Amendment any design to impose a warrant or probable cause requirement on states in the process of making the federal Fourth applicable against state action; for this reason, my earlier discussion of warrants and probable cause largely ignored the Fourteenth Amendment. The "privileges" and "immunities" that "no state shall abridge" under the Reconstruction Amendment were indeed designed to encompass rights and privileges declared in the federal Fourth, but these rights were rights against unreasonable searches and overbroad warrants, not against warrantless searches per se. Because the federal Fourth closely tracked counterpart clauses in many state constitutions, it would be odd indeed if federalization of these state rules somehow suddenly turned them upside down.

Of course, the equal protection clause of the Fourteenth Amendment does attune us to the evil of discrimination—a key point in giving concrete meaning to the reasonableness command, *see infra* text at notes 183–88.

There is also a fascinating story to be told about how the fugitive slave experience may have increased fondness for warrants among some early abolitionists— but the telling of that tale must await another day.

135. It is no answer to say that the Fourth Amendment, as originally designed, was intended to protect only against intrusions by government, rather than by private thugs. First, if we look at the original design of the Fourth Amendment, we see that its text, history, structure, and early implementation do not support the exclusionary rule. *See supra* text at notes 103–9. The argument in this section seeks to refute modern-day policy arguments for exclusion, and surely it is fair on policy grounds to point out the modern-day threat posed by private violence unleashed by the exclusionary rule. As Professor Mary Becker has trenchantly noted, the focus only on government intrusions has often left women today especially vulnerable to private violence perpetrated by boyfriends, husbands, and men generally. Following the old line that "a man's house is his castle," modern-day policemen have too often declined to get involved to protect women against domestic abuse. *See* Mary E. Becker, *The Politics of Women's Wrongs and the Bill of "Rights": A Bicentennial Perspective*, 59 U. Chi. L. Rev. 453, 507–9 (1992).

Second, the Founding generation was acutely aware of the threat posed by unregulated private violence. Social contract theory, exemplified by Hobbes and Locke, focused precisely on how government—although threatening to liberty and security—might often be less threatening than unregulated private violence in the state of nature. Perhaps the primary duty of government was to protect loyal citizens against such violence. *See* Steven J. Heyman, *The First Duty of Government: Protection, Liberty, and the Fourteenth Amendment*, 41 Duke L.J. 507, *passim* (1992); *cf.* Entick v. Carrington, 19 Howell's State Trials 1029, 1074 (C.P. 1765) ("[T]yranny, bad as it is, is better than anarchy; and the worst of all governments is more tolerable than no government at all."). In assessing the "reasonableness" of any Fourth Amendment government intrusion, we should consider whether an incremental government intrusion will be more than offset by a likely diminution in intrusion from private violence. *See, e.g.,* National Treasury Employees Union v. Von Raab, 489 U.S. 656, 675 n. 3 (1989) (suggesting that governmental metal detectors at airports are reasonable if they reduce the threat posed by skyjackers). If the reality of private violence threatening the security of the citizens' "persons, houses, papers, and effects" may be considered in determining when Fourth Amendment rights are violated, why can't it also be considered in fashioning Fourth Amendment remedies?

Of course, in claiming that private violence may be relevant to Fourth Amendment analysis, I am not making the outlandish claim that the amendment itself creates a legal right against wholly private action. Nor am I claiming here that the amendment requires government action to protect against private violence; only that it permits such action, if reasonable. Likewise, I am not claiming that the Fourth Amendment requires introduction of evidence that will make us more secure against private violence, only that it permits introduction.

136. *See* Yale Kamisar, *"Comparative Reprehensibility" and the Fourth Amendment Exclusionary Rule,* 86 Mich. L. Rev. 1, 36 n. 151, 47–48 (1987); Yale Kamisar, *Remembering the "Old World" of Criminal Procedure: A Reply To Professor Grano,* 23 U. Mich. J.L. Ref. 537, 568–69 (1990).

137. In essence, I am suggesting that the Court's "inevitable discovery" doctrine be vastly widened. *See* Murray v. United States, 487 U.S. 533, 536–44 (1988). The civil damage action in general does not suffer from an equal causation gap. The citizen need only prove that the government committed an illegal intrusion; subsequent developments are often irrelevant. The classic argument for exclusion, by contrast, depends upon the additional assumption that, in the months or years after the search, the truth would not somehow have come to light. Nor should we unthinkingly say that because the government was a wrongdoer, all doubt should be resolved against it, for the truly guilty defendant is also a wrongdoer.

Admittedly, a civil damages model raises genuine valuation difficulties—how to translate into dollars constitutional interests in privacy, personhood, and property—that require crude approximations. But crude approximations must be made in an exclusionary rule system. How far should we trace the chain of but-for causation? To the introduction of civil evidence? Of *A*'s evidence in *B*'s trial? Of evidence that possibly, but not certainly, might have come to light anyway? And so on. In fact, as I explain in later chapters, a damages model is far less crude than exclusion, because it is tailored to the true legal interests, and thus it asks the right questions directly. *See infra* Chapter 3, note 114; Chapter 4, text at notes 47–51.

138. *See* Trupiano v. United States, 334 U.S. 699, 710 (1948); United States v. Jeffers, 342 U.S. 48, 53–54 (1951); One 1958 Plymouth Sedan v. Pennsylvania, 380 U.S. 693, 698–99 (1965).

139. The old common law rule of ex post defense, see *supra* text at notes 29–31, is not applicable here because the shirt is, by hypothesis, neither contraband nor a stolen good. But suppose it were. The old common law rule is, of course, nowhere frozen into the Fourth Amendment's text. I invoked it earlier simply to suggest that, if the amendment was understood by the Founders to require warrants and probable cause, it is odd that no one addressed the possible tension with the extant common law. The best modern-day reading of the old rule would say not that a successful search is necessarily reasonable but that a trespass action for the *seizure* cannot lie when one does not own the thing seized. Trespass could still lie for the prior unreasonable search, though proving unreasonableness might require showing that the searchers knew that one's possession of the contraband or stolen item was unknowing and wholly innocent. And since *Katz* and *Bivens,* of course, a suit may lie even if no technical trespass occurred. *See* Bivens v. Six Unknown Named Agents of Fed. Bureau of Narcotics, 403 U.S. 388, 393–94 (1971); Katz v. United States, 389 U.S. 347, 353 (1967).

140. *See* Douglas Laycock, *Modern American Remedies: Cases and Materials* 143 (2d ed. 1994); Daniel J. Meltzer, *Deterring Constitutional Violations by Law Enforcement Officials: Plaintiffs and Defendants as Private Attorneys General* 88 Colum. L. Rev. 247, 270 (1988); John C. Jeffries, Jr., *Damages for Constitutional Violations: The Relation of Risk to Injury in Constitutional Torts*, 75 Va. L. Rev. 1461, 1474–76 (1989); Posner, *supra* note 3, at 50–53; William J. Stuntz, *Warrants and Fourth Amendment Remedies*, 77 Va. L. Rev. 881, 900–901 (1991).

141. If this scheme seems contrived or wacky, I can only say that it is no more contrived than the exclusionary rule, and 90 percent less wacky. But *cf. infra* Chapter 4, text at note 30 (suggesting that only legislatures and not courts may craft ad hoc untraditional and inapt "remedial" schemes like the "Leavenworth lottery").

142. See Six (6) Mexican Workers v. Arizona Citrus Growers, 904 F.2d 1301, 1305 (9th Cir. 1990); State v. Levi Strauss & Co., 715 P.2d 564, 570–71 (Cal. 1986); Charles A. Wright, Arthur R. Miller, and Mary K. Kane, 7B *Federal Practice and Procedure* §1784, at 81–88 (2d ed. 1986).

143. Some might argue that medicine must taste bad to be good—that the beneficiary class of any Fourth Amendment scheme must be vile persons, else their recovery will not shock the government into complying with the Constitution. This, however, is not the theory of constitutional remedies outside the Fourth Amendment—under §1983, for example. The police department will surely not like to see its budget being depleted, even for socially beneficent purposes. For a discussion of why deterrence theory should focus on the governmental department rather than the individual officer or the government more abstractly, see Peter H. Schuck, *Suing Government* 102–9 (1983).

144. *See supra* note 135.

145. Of course, I do not here challenge or betray the defendant's legal presumption of innocence and its doctrinal entailments—for example, that the prosecutor must prove the defendant's guilt beyond reasonable doubt with reliable evidence. I merely claim that, as a factual matter, the subcategory of criminal defendants who seek Fourth Amendment exclusion of reliable evidence are likely to have committed the criminal acts charged (or something close)—as is also true of, say, the subcategory of criminal defendants who claim entrapment.

146. "The government undertook the responsibility of defending all actions arising from the warrant and the payment of all judgments. The expenses incurred were said to total £100,000." Nelson B. Lasson, *The History and Development of the Fourth Amendment to the United States Constitution* 45 (De Capo Press 1970) (1937).

147. Wilkes v. Wood, 19 Howell's State Trials 1153, 1167 (C.P. 1763), 98 Eng. Rep. 489, 498–99 (emphasis added).

148. *Essays by a Farmer (I), supra* note 73, at 14 (emphasis added).

149. *Pennsylvania and the Federal Constitution 1787–1788, supra* note 69, at 154 (emphasis added).

150. *See* Katz v. United States, 389 U.S. 347, 352–53 (1967).

151. *See* Bivens v. Six Unknown Named Agents of Fed. Bureau of Narcotics, 403 U.S. 388, 397 (1971).

152. In this paragraph, I self-consciously echo the wide-ranging and sophisticated observations in Lawrence Lessig, *Fidelity in Translation*, 71 Tex. L. Rev. 1165 (1993). In Lessig's terminology, my claim here is that switching to the criminal exclusion model rather than refurbishing the civil remedial model violates the principle of "conservativism." *See id.* at 1213–14.

153. *See supra* note 135.

154. *See* Boyd v. United States, 116 U.S. 616, 630, 633 (1886).

155. *See id.* at 627–28.

156. This point emerges strikingly in Silas J. Wasserstrom and Louis M. Seidman, *The Fourth Amendment As Constitutional Theory*, 77 Geo. L.J. 19, 30–31, 38, 43 (1988).

157. *See* Zurcher v. Stanford Daily, 436 U.S. 547, 555 (1978) (describing pre-1967 case law).

158. Again, it is no answer to point to the special procedural safeguards enjoyed by criminal defendants. *See supra* note 45.

159. McDonald v. United States, 335 U.S. 451, 459–60 (1948) (Jackson, J., concurring).

160. Brinegar v. United States, 338 U.S. 160, 183 (1949) (Jackson, J., dissenting).

161. *See* Welsh v. Wisconsin, 466 U.S. 740, 750–53 (1984); Payton v. New York, 445 U.S. 573, 585–600 (1980); United States v. Watson, 423 U.S. 411, 414–24 (1976); Warden v. Hayden, 387 U.S. 294, 298–99 (1967); Johnson v. United States, 333 U.S. 10, 14–15 (1948).

162. *See* Dalia v. United States, 441 U.S. 238 (1979); United States v. United States District Court, 407 U.S. 297, 314–24 (1972); Katz v. United States, 389 U.S. 347, 354–59 (1967).

163. *Katz*, 389 U.S. at 364–66 (Black, J., dissenting).

164. The *Katz* Court tried to downplay this concern. *See id.* at 355 n. 16. For sharp criticism, *see* Taylor, *supra* note 16, at 113–14.

165. *See* Taylor, *supra* note 16, at 85–89.

166. *See* United States v. Nates, 831 F.2d 860, 867 (9th Cir. 1987) (Kozinski, J., dissenting) ("Being subject to a secret search and then never being told about it is something I think most people would find especially offensive, and this then bears on the reasonableness of the procedure employed by the government.").

167. For a nice discussion of some possible distinctions, see James B. White, *The Fourth Amendment as a Way of Talking About People: A Study of* Robinson *and* Matlock, 1974 Sup. Ct. Rev. 165, 227–31. Alas, White then goes on (unsuccessfully in my view) to try to press warrants and probable cause into service as the appropriate regulatory devices. *See id.* at 231. *See also* Lewis v. United States, 385 U.S. 206, 210 (1966) (defendant assumes risk of defection when he thinks he is dealing with a fellow lawbreaker whom he invites into his house as a "necessary part of his illegal business"); William J, Stuntz, *Waiving Rights in Criminal Procedures*, 75 Va. L. Rev. 761, 791–95 (1989) (generalizing this insight).

168. Here, I break with Judge Posner, who seems to me to reduce the Fourth Amendment to mere tort law, and therefore (in his hands) a kind of crude cost-benefit analysis. *See* Posner, *supra* note 3, at 50, 56, 74–75.

169. For an exemplary application of this approach, see John H. Ely, *Democracy and Distrust* (1980), in which Ely uses the values underlying more specific constitutional clauses to inform more open-textured language of Ninth and Fourteenth Amendments, *see id.* at 87–101.

170. I include here the Fourteenth Amendment, which is very much part of our Bill of Rights today. *See* Amar, *supra* note 8, at 1136–37; Akhil Reed Amar, *The Bill of Rights and the Fourteenth Amendment*, 101 Yale L.J. 1193, 1266–84 (1992).

171. Telford Taylor saw this point early on. *See* Taylor, *supra* note 16, at 66–68.

172. 436 U.S. 547 (1978).

173. *See id.* at 567–68.

174. *See id.* at 570–71 and n. 1 (Stewart, J., dissenting). Justice Stevens also dissented in a brilliant opinion that his fellow Justices simply ignored. *See id.* at 577–83 (Stevens, J., dissenting). But his dissent largely sidestepped the special issues of press freedom posed by the case. Following Justice Stevens's insights, I have argued above that, as a general matter, ex parte warrants for mere evidence should not issue against parties believed wholly innocent. *See supra* text at notes 19–24, 86.

175. *Zurcher,* 436 U.S. at 564.

176. This approach, building on Justice Stewart's thoughtful analysis in Stanford v. Texas, 379 U.S. 476 (1965), *see id.* at 481–86, would have enriched Justice Kennedy's heartfelt intuition that permanently destroying books is a more constitutionally unreasonable seizure than temporarily closing a bookstore. *See* Alexander v. United States, 113 S. Ct. 2766, 2779 (1993) (Kennedy, J., dissenting).

177. Lo-Ji Sales, Inc. v. New York, 442 U.S. 319 (1979), which invalidated an open-ended warrant enforced by an on-site inspection, *see id.* at 325, 329, should not stand in the way of a sensibly administered scheme designed to reduce intrusiveness by bringing the in-camera review to the target, rather than requiring a mountain of sealed files to come to the judicial Mohammed. The system proposed in the text seems far more protective of privacy and privilege than the *Zurcher*-like search of an attorney's office approved in Andresen v. Maryland, 427 U.S. 463 (1976), *see id.* at 472–73.

178. Even if the testimonial diary is treated as the equivalent of the owner, a strict view of the Fifth Amendment's principles would allow a subpoena of the diary and evidential use of any fruits of the diary as long as the diary itself was not introduced as testimony in the courtroom. *See supra* text at notes 121–22. An even narrower view would allow both a subpoena and the introduction of the diary as testimony on the theory that, because the diary was written prior to any government compulsion, it is free from the inherent unreliability of government-compelled self-incrimination—unreliability that (according to this theory) is the only true concern of the Fifth Amendment. *See supra* note 124. On this view, even though compelled production of the diary involves both compulsion and testimony, it does not involve compelled testimony within the spirit of the Fifth. The logic of Fisher v. United States, 425 U.S. 391 (1976), seems to lean this way, but the Court took special care to reserve the issue of private papers and diaries, *see id.* at 401 n. 7, 414. For much more analysis, *see infra* Chapter 2.

179. In the most famous case following *Wilkes,* Lord Camden declared that "papers are the owner's . . . dearest property [and] will hardly bear an inspection; . . . where private papers are removed and carried away, the secret nature of those goods will be an aggravation of the trespass." Entick v. Carrington, 19 Howell's State Trials 1029, 1066 (C.P. 1765). *See also id.* at 1063 (stating that the Halifax warrant threatens "the secret cabinets and bureaus of every subject in this kingdom"). The special concern for *"private* papers" recurs in Wilkes v. Halifax, 19 Howell's State Trials 1406 (C.P. 1769), *id.* at 1408 (emphasis added); *see also* Beardmore v. Carrington, 19 Howell's State Trials 1405, 1406 (C.P. 1764), 95 Eng. Rep. 790, 793–94 ("Can we say that 1000 pounds are monstrous damages as against him, who has granted an illegal warrant to a messenger who enters into a man's house, and pries into all his secret and private affairs . . . ?").

180. *See generally* Schnapper, *supra* note 19.

181. *Cf.* Hurtado v. U.S., 410 U.S. 578, 588–91 (1973) (holding that the takings clause did not require the government to pay anything to indigent material witnesses incarcerated in order to assure their presence at trial, upholding a statute that authorized the payment of one dollar per day, and opining that the "ultimate fairness of the compensation" was irrelevant to the Fifth Amendment claim before the Court). For discussion of the often unreasonable seizures of material witnesses, see Ronald L. Carlson and Mark S. Voelpel, *Material Witnesses and Material Injustice,* 58 Wash. U. L.Q. 1, *passim* (1980); Comment, *Pretrial Detention of Witnesses,* 117 U. Pa. L. Rev. 700, *passim* (1969).

182. Whereas *Boyd* gave property the rights of persons, this approach would more sensibly accord persons the same solicitude given to property.

183. 392 U.S. 1, 14–15 and n. 11, 20 (1968). I thus applaud Professor Maclin's

recent efforts to restore race to a central place in the Fourth Amendment discourse but suggest that his emphasis on warrants and probable cause, and away from reasonableness, undercuts his larger purpose. *See* Tracey Maclin, *"Black and Blue Encounters"—Some Preliminary Thoughts About Fourth Amendment Seizures: Should Race Matter?* 26 Val. U. L. Rev. 243, *passim* (1991); *see also* Sheri L. Johnson, *Race and the Decision to Detain a Suspect*, 93 Yale L.J. 214, *passim* (1983) (emphasizing the importance of race in Fourth Amendment contexts).

184. For rich discussions of the importance of crime victims' race, see Stephen L. Carter, *When Victims Happen to Be Black*, 97 Yale L.J. 420, *passim* (1988); Randall L. Kennedy, McKlesky v. Kemp: *Race, Capital Punishment, and the Supreme Court*, 101 Harv. L. Rev. 1388, 1388–95, 1421–22 (1988).

185. *See supra* text at notes 40, 87.

186. *Pennsylvania and the Federal Constitution 1787–1788, supra* note 69, at 154.

187. Brinegar v. United States, 338 U.S. 160, 183 (1949) (Jackson, J., dissenting).

188. The same logic underlies Michigan Dep't of State Police v. Sitz, 496 U.S. 444 (1990), which upheld a sobriety checkpoint in contradistinction to random stops that leave too much discretion to officers, *see id.* at 452–55.

The remedial logic undergirding the Fourth Amendment is also relevant here. Especially in a system in which damages are used as central remedies, it makes little sense to oblige every taxpayer to pay, say, $100 in order for each to receive, say, $30 in Fourth Amendment damages. (The other $70, of course, gets lost in the system.) And the same is true for the takings clause—if a burden is widely shared, we tend to label it a "tax," not a "taking," and no compensation is due. So here, a search or seizure that is truly spread across the citizenry will often seem reasonable—or at least not to require a judicial as opposed to a political remedy. But when a search or a seizure or a taking falls unevenly—on only a few, or on a discrete subset of the general population—the issue is quite different.

Note that here, too, we see striking connections between the Fourth Amendment and the takings clause, and the internal coherence of Fourth Amendment rights and remedies.

189. For elaboration, see Stuntz, *supra* note 140, at 914–18.

190. Thus, the results of many "warrant requirement" cases need not necessarily be jettisoned, although their logic would need to be reconceptualized. This point may be especially important to those Justices who care most about precedent and stability.

My description of the modern-day police as paramilitary suggests the relevance of Second Amendment concerns about standing armies, as Professor Steiker has perceptively noted. *See* Carol S. Steiker, *Second Thoughts About First Principles*, 107 Harv. L. Rev. 820, 837–38 (1994). After noting that police officials are now more tightly organized—and thus dangerous—than in the 1780s, we should further ask whether violent criminals are also more organized and dangerous; threats to security come from both government and criminals, *see supra* note 135.

See also Bissonette v. Haig, 776 F. 2d 1384, 1392 (8th Cir. 1985) (involving siege at Wounded Knee, and proclaiming that "unauthorized action by a military officer can be 'unreasonable' under the Fourth Amendment even though the same thing, if done by a civilian official, would not"), *aff'd on rehearing*, 800 F. 2d 812 (8th Cir. 1986) (en banc), *aff'd for absence of quorum*, 485 U.S. 264 (1988).

191. *See supra* text at notes 79–85.

192. The lack of res judicata effect and the ex parte nature of the proceedings might raise "case" or "controversy" concerns were preclearance sought from Article III judges. But these Article III constraints would not apply to non–Article III magistrates.

193. *See* Katz v. United States, 389 U.S. 347, 350–53 (1967).

194. For example, in the so-called right-to-die case, could not Missouri's policy

have been seen as unreasonably seizing Nancy Cruzan, in effect chaining her to her death bed? *See* Cruzan v. Director, Missouri Dep't of Health, 497 U.S. 261, 288 (1990) (O'Connor, J., concurring) (invoking "Fourth Amendment jurisprudence"); Jed Rubenfeld, *The Right of Privacy*, 102 Harv. L. Rev. 737, 795 (1989) (suggesting that, when the government prevents life-support disconnection in right-to-die cases, the government is in effect affirmatively seizing and occupying the patient's body); *cf.* Winston v. Lee, 470 U.S. 753, 766–67 (1985) (holding that government-compelled surgery to remove bullet from a suspect for evidentiary purposes would be an "unreasonable" intrusion under the Fourth Amendment). And note the prominent invocation of the Fourth Amendment in Justice Douglas's opinion for the Court in Griswold v. Connecticut, 381 U.S. 479 (1965). *See id.* at 484–85.

195. *Cf.* Cass R. Sunstein, *Naked Preferences and the Constitution*, 84 Colum. L. Rev. 1689, 1704–27 (1984) (championing rationality review, and canvassing various doctrinal bases and analogues, but not the Fourth Amendment).

196. *Essays by a Farmer (I), supra* note 73, at 14.

197. *See* Wilkes v. Halifax, 19 Howell's State Trials 1406, 1407 (C.P. 1769); Lasson, *supra* note 146, at 45.

198. *See* Ronald H. Coase, *The Problem of Social Cost*, 3 J.L. & Econ. 1 (1960).

199. *See* Luther v. Borden, 48 U.S. (7 How.) 1, 87–88 (1849) (Woodbury, J., dissenting); David E. Engdahl, *Positive Immunity and Accountability for Positive Governmental Wrongs*, 44 U. Colo. L. Rev. 1, 17–18 (1972); *see also* Nelson, *supra* note 85, at 17–18 (noting the lack of government officer immunity, but not discussing indemnification).

200. *Essays by a Farmer (I), supra* note 73, at 14.

201. *See* Wilkes v. Halifax, 19 Howell's State Trials 1406, 1408–9 (C.P. 1769).

202. 5 U.S. (1 Cranch) 137, 162–63 (1803). For more elaboration of the claims in this paragraph, see Akhil Reed Amar, *Of Sovereignty and Federalism*, 96 Yale L.J. 1425, 1484–92 (1987).

203. For detailed discussion, see Schuck, *supra* note 143, at 55–121.

204. The First Congress provided a nice illustration in its statute regulating searches of distilleries and seizures of liquor. In suits against officers for abusive seizures, "the jury . . . shall assess reasonable damages for any prejudice or waste . . . which shall be paid out of the treasury of the United States." But "if it shall appear from the verdict of the jury that any prejudice or waste was sustained by the negligence of the officer, he shall be responsible therefor to the United States." Act of March 31, 1791, ch. 15, §38, 1 Stat. 199, 208.

205. For historical evidence of the importance of deterrence, see *supra* text at notes 146–49. Textually, the amendment proclaims that the right of the *people* against unreasonable intrusions *shall not be violated*.

206. Privacy Protection Act of 1980, Pub. L. No. 96–440, 94 Stat. 1879 (codified at 42 U.S.C. §§2000aa, 2000aa-5 to 2000aa-7, 2000aa-11, 2000aa-12 (1988)).

207. *See* 42 U.S.C. §2000aa (1988). The act also provides for attorney's fees and minimum damages. *See id.* §2000aa-6(f).

208. *See* 42 U.S.C. §1983; Will v. Michigan Dep't of State Police, 491 U.S. 58, 77–85 (1989) (Brennan, J., dissenting) (correctly arguing that the plain words of §1983, in combination with the Dictionary Act, recognize government liability for deprivations of constitutional rights). Of course, Justice Brennan's position lost (5–4) in *Will*, but stare decisis has not barred libertarian overrulings of other incorrectly decided §1983 cases—see, for example, Monell v. Department of Social Servs., 436 U.S. 658 (1978), which overruled in part Monroe v. Pape, 365 U.S. 167 (1961), *see Monell*, 436 U.S. at 663—and should not do so here, in light of the constitutional overtones of the remedial issue (stretching back to *Marbury*) and the broad judicial authority traditionally exercised over fashioning remedies.

209. Bivens v. Six Unknown Named Agents of the Fed. Bureau of Narcotics, 403 U.S. 388 (1971).

210. *See id.* at 398–411 (Harlan, J., concurring in the judgment).

211. *See* Amar, *supra* note 202, at 1484–92.

212. *Essays by a Farmer (I), supra* note 73, at 14.

213. *See* Wilkes v. Wood, 19 Howell's State Trials 1153, 1167 (C.P. 1763) (quoted *supra* text at note 147); Huckle v. Money, 95 Eng. Rep. 768, 768–69 (C.P. 1763); Beardmore v. Carrington, 19 Howell's State Trials 1405, 1406 (C.P. 1764), 95 Eng. Rep. 790, 794 ("It is an unlawful power assumed by a great minster of state. Can any body say that a guinea per diem is sufficient damages in this extraordinary case, which concerns the liberty of every one of the king's subjects? We cannot say the damages of 1,000 [pounds] are enormous.").

In *Huckle v. Money*, Camden declared:

> [I]f the jury had been confined by their oath to consider the mere personal injury only, perhaps 20 [pounds'] damages would have been thought damages sufficient; but the small injury done to the plaintiff, or the inconsiderableness of his station and rank in life did not appear to the jury in that striking light in which the great point of law touching the liberty of the subject appeared to them at the trial; they saw a magistrate over all the King's subjects, exercising arbitrary power, violating Magna Charta, and attempting to destroy the liberty of the kingdom, by insisting upon the legality of this general warrant before them; they heard the King's Counsel, and saw the solicitor of the Treasury endeavouring to support and maintain the legality of the warrant in a tyrannical and severe manner. These are the ideas which struck the jury on the trial; and I think they have done right in giving exemplary damages [of 300 pounds]. *Huckle*, 95 Eng. Rep. at 768–69.

214. *See* Colleen P. Murphy, *Integrating the Constitutional Authority of Civil and Criminal Juries*, 61 Geo. Wash. L. Rev. 723, 799–800 and n. 435 (1993); Leslie E. John, Comment, *Formulating Standards for Awards of Punitive Damages in the Borderland of Contract and Tort*, 74 Cal. L. Rev. 2033, 2039 (1986).

215. Remedial evolution must remain within the civil model to avoid the charge that judges have simply imported new principles into the Constitution in the guise of fashioning remedies. The Fourth Amendment clearly does presuppose full civil remedies—the only question is how to implement that requirement today. By contrast, the criminal exclusion model cannot be found underlying the Fourth Amendment. Its root norm that the guilty benefit more than the innocent is not only perverse but contrary to the substantive and remedial logic of the Bill of Rights. *See supra* note 124; *infra* Chapters 3 and 4.

The point here is severable from my arguments on behalf of a role for the civil jury. If a civil jury model were deemed unworkable for twenty-first-century America, faithful interpreters would be obliged, if at all possible, to substitute other civil remedial models—administrative and judicial—before conjuring up a wholly extra- and counterconstitutional scheme of criminal exclusion.

216. *See Huckle*, 95 Eng. Rep. at 768. Note also how the court in *Huckle* used certain aggregation techniques to resolve the claims of many other printers whose cases were similar to Huckle's. *See id.* at 769.

217. *But cf.* Farrar v. Hobby, 113 S. Ct. 566, 575 (1992) (holding that a civil rights litigant who was in it only for the money is not automatically entitled to attorney's fees under 42 U.S.C. §1988 if only nominal damages are awarded).

218. For the grim statistics, see Los Angeles v. Lyons, 461 U.S. 95, 115–16 and n. 3 (1983) (Marshall, J., dissenting).

219. 461 U.S. 95, 101–13 (1983).

220. Lest I be accused of Monday morning quarterbacking, let the record show that I sharply attacked *Lyons* in 1987, in the first paragraph of the first article I ever wrote as a law professor. *See* Amar, *supra* note 202, at 1425.

221. *See* Ronald F. Wright, *Why Not Administrative Grand Juries?* 44 Admin. L. Rev. 465, 510–11 (1992). Citizen review panels can thus be seen as an excellent example of "fidelity" in "translation" as American law becomes more bureaucratized, yet continues to pledge allegiance to the democratic and participatory ethos underlying the jury system at the Founding. On fidelity, see generally Lessig, *supra* note 152, *passim*.

222. *See* Kenneth C. Davis, *Discretionary Justice* 52–161 (1969); Kenneth C. Davis, *Police Discretion* 98–138 (1975); Anthony G. Amsterdam, *Perspectives on the Fourth Amendment,* 58 Minn. L. Rev. 349, 416–28 (1974); Kaplan, *supra* note 132, at 1050–55; Carl McGowan, *Rule-Making and the Police,* 70 Mich. L. Rev. 659, *passim* (1972).

223. *See* Wright, *supra* note 221, at 512–14.

224. Doctrine can be built up in a traditional common law fashion or in a more openly regulatory way. The former model is fact-specific, with the Court writing an opinion that says, "in this case, the search was unreasonable because . . . " The latter model is more rulelike: "In this entire subcategory, searches are per se unreasonable." Both models are, of course, ideal types, and a dialectic exists between them.

225. Of course, in a criminal case, the government prosecutor bears the burden of proof beyond reasonable doubt, whereas in a civil case, the citizen plaintiff typically bears the burden of proof, under a preponderance-of-evidence standard.

226. In certain contexts, judges might be able to declare a government action not a "search" or "seizure"—or not "unreasonable"—as a matter of law. Whereas the Sixth Amendment does not allow a directed verdict or JNOV against the citizen, the Seventh does, in order to limit the jury's role to finding facts and not declaring law. (Unlike the Sixth, the Seventh explicitly privileges only jury fact-finding.) For more analysis, *see infra* Chapter 3.

There is considerable evidence verifying the reasonableness role of the civil jury in search and seizure cases throughout the nineteenth century. Here I shall present only a smattering. *See* Simpson v. McCaffrey, 13 Ohio 509, 517 (1844) ("It is further a rule that the circumstances which would render a search reasonable are for the jury to judge." (quoting the statement of John C. Tidball and William Kennon, Jr., attorneys for the plaintiff)); Luther v. Borden 48 U.S. (7 How.) 1, 87 (1849) (Woodbury, J., dissenting) ("And if the sanctity of domestic life has been violated, the castle of the citizen broken into, or property or person injured, without good cause, in either case a jury of the country should give damages, and courts are bound to instruct them to do so, unless a justification is made out fully on correct principles."); Allen v. Colby, 47 N.H. 544, 549 (1867) ("The provision of the constitution against unreasonable searches and seizures cannot be understood to prohibit a search or seizure . . . when the jury under correct instructions from the court, have found that the seizure was proper and reasonable . . . ."); 2 Frederick Sackett, *Brickwood's Sackett on Instructions to Juries* §2449(a) (3d ed. 1908) ("The Court instructs the jury that an officer or private individual may arrest without a warrant, one whom he has reasonable ground to suspect of having committed a felony."). I am indebted to Alex Azar for much of the material in this paragraph.

227. For a brilliant and historically powerful celebration of the civil jury, see Note, *supra* note 68, at 148–60. And for intriguing efforts to integrate juries into an exclusionary rule scheme, see Ronald J. Bacigal, *A Case for Jury Determination of Search and Seizure Law,* 15 U. Rich. L. Rev. 791, *passim* (1981); and George C. Thomas III and Barry S. Pollack, *Saving Rights from a Remedy: A Societal View of the Fourth Amendment,* 73 B.U. L. Rev. 147, *passim* (1993). Finally, note how the jury satisfies

several of the concerns about current Fourth Amendment theory. *See* Wasserstrom and Seidman, *supra* note 156, at 48–50, 102–3, 107 (noting the fact-dependency of reasonableness, its value-laden quality, the unrepresentative nature of judges, and the lack of a need for legal expertise on many issues).

228. In a recent opinion, Justice Scalia at times seemed to veer close to this "frozen in amber" approach to Fourth Amendment reasonableness. *See* Minnesota v. Dickerson, 113 S. Ct. 2130, 2139 (1993) (Scalia, J., concurring). His earlier formulations strike me as less frozen and more attractive. *See e.g.*, California v. Acevedo, 111 S. Ct. 1982, 1992–94 (1991) (Scalia, J., concurring in the judgment); Scalia, *supra* note 4, at 1180–86.

229. *See* Amar, *supra* note 8, at 1183–91. More discussion of these issues appears in the Appendix.

230. For an example, see the extraordinarily lyric and powerful vision of an inclusive jury summoned up at the outset of Justice Kennedy's opinion for the Court in Powers v. Ohio, 111 S. Ct. 1364, 1366–70 (1991). For post-*Powers* cases promoting jury inclusivity, see Georgia v. McCullum, 112 S. Ct. 2348, 2351–54 (1992); and Edmonson v. Leesville Concrete Co., Inc., 111 S. Ct. 2077, 2080 (1991).

Excluding parts of the community from the jury box is akin to excluding them from the ballot box; the right to vote applies to voting in juries every bit as much as to voting for candidates and must not be abridged on the basis of race, sex, class, or age. *See* U.S. Const. amends. XV, XIX, XXIV, XXVI; Amar, *supra* note 8, at 1202–3. Jury exclusions brought about by private manipulation—venue transfers, peremptory challenges, and the like—are thus no less troubling than, say, white primaries. The voting analogy is explained in more detail in the Appendix.

231. Compare Thomas Jefferson's exuberant 1789 definition of jury trial as trial "by the people themselves." Letter from Thomas Jefferson to David Humphreys (Mar. 18, 1789), *in* 5 *The Writings of Thomas Jefferson, 1788–1792*, at 90 (Paul Leicester Ford ed., 1895).

To repeat: my proposed model does not place sole reliance on civil juries, and welcomes a vigorous role for judges in civil cases, based on constitutional reasonableness, especially if judges suspect systematic jury undervaluation of important constitutional values, or illegitimate prejudice against certain Fourth Amendment claimants. (For example, if the key issue is ex ante reasonableness, judges can disallow testimony of ex post success if they believe the prejudicial effect of this testimony would prevent juries from treating Adam and Bob equally. *See supra* notes 139–140 and accompanying text.)

2. Fifth Amendment First Principles

1. *See* John H. Langbein, *The Historical Origins of the Privilege Against Self-Incrimination at Common Law*, 92 Mich. L. Rev. 1047, 1084–85 (1994). This history is briefly canvassed *infra*, text at notes 155–67.

2. 142 U.S. 547 (1892).

3. 406 U.S. 441 (1972).

4. For a similar organizational strategy, see Bruce A. Ackerman, *Beyond Caro-lene Products*, 98 Harv. L. Rev. 713 (1985). And in the self-incrimination literature, see Peter Lushing, *Testimonial Immunity and the Privilege Against Self-Incrimination: A Study in Isomorphism*, 73 J. Crim. L. and Criminology 1690, 1697–1708 (1982).

5. The quandary of an innocent defendant who wishes to show that some-one else committed the crime is highlighted by Professor Peter Tague. *See* Peter W. Tague, *The Fifth Amendment: If an Aid to the Guilty Defendant, an Impediment to the Inno-cent One*, 78 Geo. L.J. 1 (1989).

6. This account is drawn from Peter Tague. *See id.* at 1–3.

7. As will be explained in more detail below, the type of immunity now required is "use plus use-fruits" immunity, which prevents the prosecution from using either the words of the testimony or any evidence (fruits) found as a result of the testimony. *See* Kastigar v. United States, 406 U.S. 441, 453 (1972).

8. *See* Webb v. Texas, 409 U.S. 95, 96, 98 (1972); Washington v. Texas, 388 U.S. 14, 22 (1967); 388 U.S. at 24–25 (Harlan, J., concurring). New Jersey's state constitutional precursor of the federal compulsory process clause explicitly gave defendants "the same privileges of witnesses . . . as their prosecutors are or shall be entitled to." N.J. Const. art. XVI (1776). This provision traces back to William Penn's 1701 Pennsylvania Charter of Privileges: "THAT all criminals shall have the same Privileges of Witnesses . . . as their Prosecutors." Pa. Charter, art. V (1701). Similarly, Sir William Blackstone's widely influential treatise defined the compulsory process principle as giving the defendant "the same compulsive process to bring in his witnesses for him, as was usual to compel their appearance against him." 4 William Blackstone, *Commentaries* *352 (emphasis deleted). Blackstone's formulation in turn built on the landmark Treason Act of 1696. *See infra* note 9. This Act gave defendants "the like process . . . to compel their witnesses . . . as is usually granted to compel witnesses to appear against them." 7 Will. 3, ch. 3, §7 (1696) (Eng.). James Madison's particular "compulsory process" phraseology in the Sixth Amendment appears to borrow directly from Blackstone. *See* Peter Westen, *The Compulsory Process Clause*, 73 Mich. L. Rev. 71, 97–98 and n. 114 (1974). On compulsory process parity more generally, *see id.* at 78, 95, 116, 128, 140 n. 331, 147–48, 158–59, 168, and 177–82. General privileges—spousal, priest-penitent, and so on—which put limits on the government as well as the defendant, raise different issues and thus lie beyond the scope of the discussion here. For much more discussion—including analysis of general privileges—*see infra* Chapter 3, text at notes 198–219.

9. Our legal forebears attempted to correct this sort of imbalance as early as the 1690s, when Parliament enacted the Treason Act. This landmark act granted the defendant in treason cases many of the same powers the prosecution had, including the right to legal representation and compulsory process to obtain witnesses. *See* Langbein, *supra* note 1, at 1056, 1067–68.

10. A perjury prosecution against the lying witness is of course possible, but perjury can be hard to prove beyond a reasonable doubt, and a perjury prosecution may be less important than the original case from the prosecutor's perspective.

11. Tague thinks that the prosecution "has no substantive reason" to refuse to grant immunity to the witness in single-culprit cases. *See* Tague, *supra* note 5, at 37, 53. The reasons seem obvious enough.

12. Most courts have refused to grant immunity even if the testimony is crucial to a defendant's case. *See, e.g.,* United States v. Heldt, 668 F.2d 1238, 1282–83 (D.C. Cir. 1981) (holding that a trial court should not grant immunity to defense witnesses who are actual or potential targets of prosecution). For academic commentary on the subject, see Westen, *supra* note 8, at 166–70 (arguing that courts have the constitutional ability to grant immunity or to force prosecutors to grant immunity) and Peter Westen, *Incredible Dilemmas: Conditioning One Constitutional Right on the Forfeiture of Another*, 66 Iowa L. Rev. 741, 762–75 (1981) [hereinafter Westen, *Incredible Dilemmas*] (providing more elaboration of this view). *See also* James F. Flanaghan, *Compelled Immunity for Defense Witnesses: Hidden Costs and Questions*, 56 Notre Dame L. Rev. 447, 461–63 (1981) (arguing against judicial grants of immunity for defense witnesses in multiculprit crimes on the practical grounds that in the eventual prosecution of the witness, the prosecutor would have difficulty proving that she gathered evidence without the aid of the witness's testimony).

13. Tague notes that every U.S. court that has considered the issue has so held. *See* Tague, *supra* note 5, at 5. For the reasons behind this view, *see id.* at 13–52.

14. *Id.* at 2.

15. *But see id.* at 40–43 (discounting this concern).

16. Or, at least, what we *should* pay jurors to do. In fact, some jurors, alas, are not paid at all for their efforts and most are paid far too little. For my proposed corrective, *see infra* Appendix.

17. *Cf. supra* Chapter 1, text at note 97 ("[U]njustified expansions of constitutional rights often lead to dangerous and unjustified contractions elsewhere."). For more discussion of this point, *see infra* Chapter 4, text at note 52. For a good illustration of this principle in the Fifth Amendment context, see Allen v. Illinois, 478 U.S. 364, 369–75 (1986) (holding that proceedings under one state's Sexually Dangerous Persons Act were not "criminal" despite the potential for moral stigma and incarceration in a maximum security institution). The *Allen* Court's characterization of the case as "noncriminal" eliminated the need to apply self-incrimination principles, which the Court thought undermined the reliability of fact-finding. 478 U.S. at 375. As we shall see, however, the self-incrimination clause, rightly understood, is not at war with reliability. Had the *Allen* Court properly construed the clause, it might have been more inclined to admit that the case before it was indeed criminal. Instead, a "broad" reading of the self-incrimination clause ended up eliminating the defendant's explicit constitutional right to other "criminal" procedure safeguards outlined in the Sixth Amendment.

18. During the debates over ratification of the Federal Constitution, several participants expressed fears that the Constitution failed to provide common law protection against torture to extract confessions. In Virginia, Patrick Henry warned that "Congress may introduce the practice of the civil law, in preference to that of the common law. They may introduce the practice of France, Spain, and Germany—of torturing, to extort a confession of the crime. . . . [T]hey will tell you that there is such a necessity of strengthening the arm of government, that they must have a criminal equity, and extort confession by torture, in order to punish with still more relentless severity." 3 *The Debates in the Several State Conventions on the Adoption of the Federal Constitution* 447–48 (Jonathan Elliot ed., 1886). George Nicholas retorted that Henry's argument about torture applied equally to the Virginia Constitution. *See* 3 *id.* at 450–51. At this point, George Mason, the drafter of Virginia's Bill of Rights, jumped into the fray and argued that his state's Bill of Rights did prohibit torture: "[O]ne clause expressly provided that no man can give evidence against himself; and . . . [Nicholas] must know that, in those countries where torture is used, evidence was extorted from the criminal himself." 3 *id.* at 452; *see also* 2 *id.* at 111 (recording remarks by Abraham Holmes in the Massachusetts debates linking torture and the Inquisition with the federal government's ability to compel a man to furnish evidence against himself). Leonard Levy has noted that references to the privilege are scarce in the literature and debates surrounding the ratification of the Constitution and the Bill of Rights. *See* Leonard W. Levy, *Origins of the Fifth Amendment: The Right Against Self-Incrimination* 430 (1968). The Framers occasionally acknowledged that the privilege served as a ban on torture, but "nothing can be found of a theoretical nature expressing [an additional] rationale or underlying policy for the right in question or its reach." *Id.*

19. 380 U.S. 609 (1965).

20. *See id.* at 614–15.

21. The innocent defendant may want to avoid taking the stand because he is likely to perform badly, being inarticulate and concerned that an experienced prosecutor, skilled in the artificial rules governing courtrooms, will be able to trip him up. The jury, our innocent defendant might also fear, will likely overreact to any real or perceived slipup on his part on the stand. In addition, he may be worried that his prior convictions will come in to impeach his credibility, wrongly inducing the jury

to think that he must also be guilty in the case at hand. The latter problem may be cured by a rule, such as Mont. R. Evid. 609, that prior convictions are not available to attack credibility. The former problem, however, cannot be cured so easily.

See generally Stephen J. Schulhofer, *Some Kind Words for the Privilege Against Self-Incrimination*, 26 Val. U. L. Rev. 311, 330–35 (1991) (defending *Griffin* on reliability grounds). Even if silence were mildly probative, a typical jury might draw far too large an adverse inference, and this also (by hypothesis) would be statistically unsound. In this situation, *Griffin's* rule overprotects—by disallowing instructions to the jury that an inference can be made—but a more carefully tailored instruction to "infer, but not too much" might be unworkable.

22. U.S. Sentencing Commn., Federal Sentencing Guidelines Manual §3.E1.1 (1993 ed.).

23. *Id.*

24. The Supreme Court denied certiorari in a recent case raising the issue of whether the sentencing reduction can be conditioned on defendant's admitting to *uncharged* conduct. Kinder v. United States, 112 S. Ct. 2290 (1992). The defendant agreed to a plea bargain but then was denied the sentencing reduction when he refused to admit to conduct to which he had not pled guilty. As Justice White pointed out in his dissent to the denial of certiorari, there is a circuit split on this question. *See* 112 S. Ct. at 2293 (White, J., dissenting).

In contrast, courts seem to agree that the sentencing reduction can be conditioned on the defendant's admitting to conduct for which he has been *convicted*. See, for example, United States v. Henry, 883 F.2d 1010 (11th Cir. 1989): "'[T]he guideline recognizes societal interest in . . . the increased potential for rehabilitation among those who feel and show true remorse for their anti-social conduct.' . . . To hold the acceptance of responsibility provision unconstitutional would be to say that defendants who express genuine remorse for their actions can never be rewarded at sentencing. This the Constitution does not require." 883 F.2d at 1011–12 (quoting United States v. Belgard, 694 F. Supp. 1488, 1497–98 (D. Or. 1988)).

But if we follow the seeming logic of *Griffin's* "no worse off" test, such a condition would also violate the privilege, and no court has explained how *Griffin* is to be distinguished away.

It might be claimed that intervening cases upholding plea bargaining have eroded *Griffin:* a defendant who pleads not guilty may be penalized more severely than—made worse off compared with—a defendant who pleads guilty. *Cf.* Brady v. United States, 397 U.S. 742, 749–54 (1970). Formally, however, pleading and witnessing are not the same thing; a plea bargain may benefit a defendant whether or not he would have taken the stand as a witness at trial. Thus, the plea-bargaining cases may not resolve the arguably distinct witnessing issues raised by the "silence penalty" in sentencing.

25. As we shall see in more detail, *see infra* notes 55–56, the Fifth Amendment protects against compelling statements outside a "criminal case" if those statements are later usable *inside* a criminal case—at a criminal trial.

26. *See* Lefkowitz v. Turley, 414 U.S. 70 (1973) (holding that a state could not cancel existing contracts of and deny future contracts to a contractor who refused to testify without immunity concerning state contracts); Gardner v. Broderick, 392 U.S. 273 (1968) (holding that a state could not discharge a police officer who refused to testify without immunity before a grand jury about the performance of his official duties); Uniformed Sanitation Men Assn. v. Commissioner of Sanitation, 392 U.S. 280 (1968) (announcing a similar holding in a companion case concerning sanitation workers).

27. *See* Stephen A. Saltzburg and Daniel J. Capra, *American Criminal Procedure* 456 (4th ed. 1992).

28. Some of the reasons that an innocent person might stand mute in a technical legal proceeding governed by artificial and unfamiliar rules would not apply to informal accusation in some noncourt settings. *See supra* note 21, *infra* text at notes 262–65.

29. Even Dean Griswold acknowledged the appropriateness of a private employer's firing someone who refused to answer questions about his job. *See* Erwin N. Griswold, *The Fifth Amendment Today* 57–58 (1955); *see also* Adamson v. California, 332 U.S. 46, 60 (1947) (Frankfurter, J., concurring) ("Sensible and just-minded men, in important affairs of life, deem it significant that a man remains silent when confronted with serious and responsible evidence against himself which it is within his power to contradict").

30. In essence, Fifth Amendment immunity raises "causation gap" issues analogous to those raised by the Fourth Amendment exclusionary rule. For more discussion of this causation gap, *see supra* Chapter 1, text at notes 136–37; *infra* Chapter 4, text at notes 45–46.

31. 425 U.S. 308 (1976).

32. *Id.* at 318 ("[Palmigiano's] silence was given no more evidentiary value than was warranted by the facts surrounding his case."). The Court felt that other constitutional protections, such as the Sixth Amendment right to counsel, were not required in the prison disciplinary context. *See* 425 U.S. at 315. In civil cases, we routinely allow adverse inferences to be drawn when a witness "takes the Fifth." But, it might be argued, in civil cases it is generally not the government that benefits from the inference; the beneficiary is the opposing private party, and the government merely adjudicates. By that logic, adverse inferences from silence in civil cases could be drawn in favor of private parties, but not in favor of the government when it is a party in a civil suit. Like the cases involving the government in its capacity as an employer, this puts the government in an unjustifiably weaker position than comparable private actors.

33. Again, a Fifth Amendment violation occurs at the point when compelled testimony is introduced in a criminal case. *See supra* note 25; *infra* note 55.

34. 335 U.S. 1 (1948).

35. Emergency Price Control Act of 1942, ch. 26, 56 Stat. 23 (repealed 1966).

36. 335 U.S. at 32–33. Chief Justice Vinson, possibly influenced by the wartime, emergency nature of the regulations, wrote for the Court: "[N]o serious misgiving that [the bounds imposed by the Fifth Amendment] have been overstepped would appear to be evoked when there is a sufficient relation between the activity sought to be regulated and the public concern so that the Government can constitutionally regulate or forbid the basic activity concerned, and can constitutionally require the keeping of particular records, subject to inspection by the Administrator." 335 U.S. at 32. He then noted that Congress unquestionably had the constitutional power to control commodity prices as a wartime emergency measure. 335 U.S. at 32.

37. 335 U.S. at 51 (Frankfurter, J., dissenting).

38. Counselman v. Hitchcock, 142 U.S. 547 (1892).

39. 390 U.S. 39 (1968). The other two cases were Grosso v. United States, 390 U.S. 62 (1968) (reversing a conviction for failure to pay an excise tax on wagers) and Haynes v. United States, 390 U.S. 85 (1968) (reversing a conviction for possession of an unregistered firearm).

40. 390 U.S. at 57.

41. 402 U.S. 424 (1971).

42. *See* Byers v. Justice Court, 458 P.2d 465, 477 (1969).

43. 402 U.S. at 427 n. 3.

44. *Id.* at 427 (emphasis added).

45. Baltimore City Dept. of Social Servs. v. Bouknight, 493 U.S. 549 (1990).

46. *Id.* at 559. The Court, however, did not categorically state that Bouknight would be denied all immunity: "We are not called upon to define the precise limitations that may exist upon the State's ability to use the testimonial aspects of Bouknight's act of production in subsequent criminal proceedings." *Id.* at 561. As we shall see below, this caveat in effect sidesteps the real issue in the case and under the clause generally: the scope of the immunity that must be given in a criminal case.

47. Kastigar v. United States, 406 U.S. 441 (1972).

48. *See* Miranda v. Arizona, 384 U.S. 436 (1966).

49. *See* David Simon, *Homicide: A Year on the Killing Streets* 199–220 (1991). Simon is a reporter for the *Baltimore Sun* who spent four years on the police beat before his research leading to *Homicide*. Simon concludes, "[I]f the . . . intent of the Miranda decision was, in fact, an attempt to 'dispel the compelling atmosphere' of an interrogation, then it failed miserably." *Id.* at 199.

50. *Id.* at 204–20.

51. Recently, several experienced homicide detectives in Detroit were publicly criticized and disciplined by their superiors for using the office copy machine in purported lie detector tests. The process worked as follows:

> [T]he detectives, when confronted with a statement of dubious veracity, would sometimes adjourn to the Xerox room and load three sheets of paper into the feeder.
> "Truth," said the first.
> "Truth," said the second.
> "Lie," said the third.
> Then the suspect would be led into the room and told to put his hand against the side of the machine. The detectives would ask the man's name, listen to the answer, then hit the copy button.
> Truth.
> And where do you live?
> Truth again.
> And did you or did you not kill Tater, shooting him down like a dog in the 1200 block of North Durham Street?
> Lie. Well, well . . .

Id. Occasionally, a confession would result.

52. *See* William J. Stuntz, *Lawyers, Deception, and Evidence Gathering*, 79 Va. L. Rev. 1903, 1905 (1993) ("Deception and advantage taking are . . . at the core of criminal investigation, even though legal ethics doctrine largely banishes them from the evidence-gathering process in civil cases."). Of course, I am not proposing to abolish all governmental "deception"—sting operations, undercover agents, and the like. I largely agree with Professor Stuntz that criminal law enforcement should not be constrained by all the rules applicable to civil litigation. But I shall argue that certain more "civilized" techniques, like depositions, should be available to criminal law enforcement officers.

53. Langbein, *supra* note 1, at 1055.

54. *Cf.* Paul G. Kauper, *Judicial Examination of the Accused: A Remedy for the Third Degree*, 30 Mich. L. Rev. 1224 (1932); Yale Kamisar, *Kauper's "Judicial Examination of the Accused" Forty Years Later: Some Comments on a Remarkable Article*, 73 Mich. L. Rev. 15 (1974).

55. Some have argued that the Fifth Amendment cannot mean what it says— that, contrary to its words, it must apply to compulsion *outside* a criminal case. Surely (the argument goes), we cannot allow a prosecutor to recess a criminal trial, walk across the street and compel—upon pain of contempt—a defendant to answer ques-

tions, and then walk back across the street, reconvene the trial, and introduce as evidence both a transcript and a videotape of the compelled statement. What is true of a compelled deposition across the street in the middle of the trial must be true of compulsion in pretrial legislative hearings, civil cases, grand jury inquests, and so on. (*Miranda* says that the same should hold for informal compulsion—backed by threatened police brutality rather than formal contempt—in the police station.)

All this is true—except the notion that we have somehow gone beyond the words of the Fifth Amendment. *But see* Henry J. Friendly, *The Fifth Amendment Tomorrow: The Case for Constitutional Change*, 37 U. Cin. L. Rev. 671, 677 (1968). In all our examples, compulsion may not exist within the criminal case; but the introduction of the compelled statement—the witnessing—does occur *in* a criminal case, and it is this introduction that violates the Fifth Amendment. This is why out-of-court compelled testimony accompanied by formal or informal immunity simply does not violate the amendment: unless the compelled statement is introduced at a criminal trial, a person has not been made a "witness" (via transcript and videotape) against himself *in* a "criminal case." Although courts and commentators have often been confused—and confusing—on this point, the foregoing appears to be the view of the current Court. *See* Larry J. Ritchie, *Compulsion That Violates the Fifth Amendment: The Burger Court's Definition*, 61 Minn. L. Rev. 383, 386, 430 (1977); *cf.* Michigan v. Tucker, 417 U.S. 433, 440–41 (1971) (declaring that to allow the in-court introduction of testimony created by out-of-court coercion would "practically nullif[y]" the Fifth Amendment privilege); Piemonte v. United States, 367 U.S. 556 (1961) (saying that once proper immunity is offered, no Fifth Amendment violation occurs when a person is forced, upon penalty of contempt, to incriminate himself outside his own criminal case); Brown v. Walker, 161 U.S. 591 (1896) (announcing a similar holding).

Put another way, deposition-like compulsion outside the courtroom is not bad; we use it all the time in civil cases. What is bad is *using* compelled testimony inside a criminal case—for reasons that, as we shall see later, have to do with the presumptive unreliability of certain types of compelled testimony. By contrast, unregulated police-station coercion is often bad in itself and calls for special rules.

56. In effect, the ability of the government to demand self-incriminating statements in legislative hearings and the like after offering the proper immunity means that—like its Fifth Amendment companion, the takings clause—the self-incrimination clause in some ways states a liability rule, not a property rule. *See generally* Guido Calabresi and A. Douglas Melamed, *Property Rules, Liability Rules, and Inalienability: One View of the Cathedral*, 85 Harv. L. Rev. 1089 (1972). Once we see this, we should see the centrality of the scope of immunity: it establishes the all-important fixed price at which the government may buy a person's testimony outside his own criminal case.

Another more nuanced and textual way to see the point is as follows: The clause is absolute, but strictly speaking it applies only to testimony *in* one's own criminal case. But because one must be able to "take the Fifth" outside criminal cases, *see supra* note 55, the clause must be enforced by a rule of exclusion *within* a criminal case. In effect, we have a kind of "liability rule" for "taking the Fifth" in grand jury rooms, civil cases, legislative hearings, and so on—enforceable by a specific performance or "property rule" of exclusion *within* the criminal case, an exclusion that the government may *not* "buy off" with money at a judicially fixed price, as with a pure liability rule. (For more discussion of this point, *see infra* Chapter 3, text at notes 113–16.) But to allow a person outside his own criminal case to ignore all requests to furnish self-incriminating testimony, even after proper immunity has been given, would plainly ignore the textual bounds of the Amendment, which is limited to *criminal* cases. In effect, it would give a person an absolute right to withhold all testimony, anywhere, anytime, and yet be free from pressure or compulsion. Such a rule is practically unworkable as well as textually implausible. *See Piemonte,* 367 U.S. at 556; *Brown,* 161 U.S. at 591.

57. *See infra* text at notes 205–10.

58. 142 U.S. 547 (1892).

59. *Id.* at 586 ("In view of the constitutional provision, a statutory enactment, to be valid, must afford absolute immunity against future prosecution for the offense to which the question relates.").

60. Although courts might require the convict's compelled statement to harm him in some way to satisfy the requirement that he be a witness "against himself," that requirement might be met easily. Certain avenues of postconviction collateral review—habeas corpus and writs of coram nobis—may in some situations be limited to the factually innocent, and a compelled postconviction confession might undercut a defendant's ability to pursue these postconviction avenues.

61. *See* Akhil Reed Amar and Jonathan L. Marcus, *Double Jeopardy Law After Rodney King,* 95 Colum. L. Rev. 1, 11–15 (1995).

62. *See* Barron v. Baltimore, 32 U.S. (7 Pet.) 243, 247–49 (1833); *see also* Feldman v. United States, 322 U.S. 487 (1944) (holding that a defendant's compelled testimony in a state proceeding could be used in federal court to convict the defendant of a federal crime); United States v. Murdock, 284 U.S. 141 (1931) (holding that the federal government need only immunize a witness from federal prosecution and that fear of state prosecution and use of federally compelled testimony will not excuse a refusal to answer).

63. 378 U.S. 1, 10–11 (1964) (quoting Ohio *ex rel.* Eaton v. Price, 364 U.S. 263 (1960) (Brennan, J., dissenting)).

64. 378 U.S. 52, 77 (1964).

65. *See id.* at 78–79.

66. *Id.* at 92–107 (White, J., concurring).

67. *Id.* at 106–7.

68. Here too, we see the "causation gap." *See supra* note 30.

69. 406 U.S. 441 (1972).

70. *See id.* at 453.

71. *See id.* at 456–59.

72. Although *Kastigar* uses the term *derivative use* to describe this type of immunity, *use-fruits* is more graphic and is used by leading criminal procedure scholars as well as by many circuits. *See, e.g.,* Saltzburg and Capra, *supra* note 27, at 484; United States v. Parker, 848 F.2d 61, 62 n. 1 (5th Cir. 1988); United States v. Ingraham, 832 F.2d 229, 238 (1st Cir.1987); United States v. Perry, 788 F.2d 100, 115–16 (3d Cir. 1986); *In re* Grand Jury Proceedings Larson, 785 F.2d 629, 630 n. 2 (8th Cir. 1986); Grand Jury Subpoena of Ford v. United States, 756 F.2d 249, 253 (2d Cir. 1985).

73. 406 U.S. at 446, 462.

74. *See supra* note 56; *see also* Baltimore City Dept. of Social Servs. v. Bouknight, 493 U.S. 549 (1990), where the Court dodged the only issue in the case: the scope of immunity, *see supra* note 46.

75. 406 U.S. at 460.

76. *See* Letter from William Treanor to Akhil Amar (December 23, 1994). Professor Treanor was a prosecutor in the Oliver North investigation.

77. *See* United States v. Schwimmer, 882 F.2d 22, 26 (2d Cir. 1989) (recommending the use of Chinese walls); U.S. Dept. of Justice, U.S. Attorneys' Manual §111.40 (1987) (suggesting that prosecution of an immunized witness should be handled by a lawyer unfamiliar with the substance of the witness's testimony).

78. *See* United States v. North, 920 F.2d 940, 942–43 (D.C. Cir. 1990) (amending United States v. North, 910 F.2d 843 (D.C. Cir. 1990)). An investigation is "canned" by completing all steps—such as interviewing witnesses, taking deposi-

tions, and searching for physical evidence—before immunized testimony is given. Thus the testimony could not have affected the investigation.

79. 920 F.2d 940 (D.C. Cir. 1990).

80. *Id.* at 942.

81. *Id.* at 942–43 (internal quotations and citation omitted).

82. Uses of immunized testimony are divided into two—largely artificial—categories: nonevidentiary and evidentiary uses. Nonevidentiary use generally involves exposure of a prosecutor to immunized testimony. The term is vague and mainly defined by lists of examples. One court has listed the following nonevidentiary uses: "assistance in focusing the investigation, deciding to initiate prosecution, refusing to plea-bargain, interpreting evidence, planning cross-examination, and otherwise generally planning trial strategy." United States v. McDaniel, 482 F.2d 305, 311 (8th Cir. 1973) (finding such uses impermissible). Although the *North* court did not reach the question of whether nonevidentiary use had occurred because the prosecution had not been exposed to the immunized testimony, the court suggested that nonevidentiary use was impermissible. *See* 910 F.2d at 856. Several courts have come to the opposite conclusion. *See* United States v. Serrano, 870 F.2d 1, 16–17 (1st Cir. 1989) (stating that *Kastigar* does not protect against all nonevidentiary uses of compelled testimony because the distinction between use plus use-fruits and transactional immunity would disappear otherwise); United States v. Mariani, 851 F.2d 595, 600 (2d Cir. 1988) (stating that the Fifth Amendment does not "foreclose the prosecution of an immunized witness where his immunized testimony might have tangentially influenced the prosecutor's thought processes"); United States v. Byrd, 765 F.2d 1524, 1530–31 (11th Cir. 1985) (stating that *Kastigar* does not protect against nonevidentiary uses of compelled testimony such as the decision whether to indict or whether to accept a plea bargain); United States v. Pantone, 634 F.2d 716, 730–31 (3d Cir. 1980) (holding that *Kastigar* does not prohibit a prosecutor's "mere access to immunized grand jury testimony").

Evidentiary uses—uses that would somehow contribute to the evidence presented at trial—are generally not permitted in *Kastigar*'s regime. The cases revolve around the definition of *evidentiary*. In *North*, the D.C. Circuit declared that use of the immunized testimony by witnesses to refresh their memories—a virtually irrebuttable presumption if they were exposed to the testimony—is evidentiary use. *See* 920 F.2d at 945–46. Again, several courts have disagreed. *See* United States v. Helmsley, 941 F.2d 71, 82 (2d Cir. 1991) (declining to apply the evidentiary use concept to a witness who may have been exposed to immunized testimony); United States v. Kurzer, 534 F.2d 511, 517 (2d Cir. 1976) (requiring the government to prove merely that the witness's decision to testify was not influenced by immunized testimony).

Different approaches to use immunity are discussed in Jerome A. Murphy, Comment, *The Aftermath of the Iran-Contra Trials: The Uncertain Status of Derivative Use Immunity,* 51 Md. L. Rev. 1011, 1030–31, 1045–46 (1992) (discussing cases that have differed from the *North* standard) and Gary S. Humble, *Nonevidentiary Use of Compelled Testimony: Beyond the Fifth Amendment,* 66 Texas L. Rev. 351 (1987). The *North* case provoked a legislative effort to overturn it. Senators Joseph Lieberman and Warren Rudman introduced a bill permitting "the use of testimony based on a witness's personal knowledge, regardless of whether the witness has been exposed to the defendant's compelled testimony, as long as such exposure is in no way attributable to the prosecution." Michael Gilbert, Note, *The Future of Congressional Use Immunity After* United States v. North, 30 Am. Crim. L. Rev. 417, 434–35 (1993) (citing S. 2074, 102d Cong., 1st Sess., 137 Cong. Rec. S18, 385 (1991)).

83. Yet again, we see a possible "causation gap." *See supra* notes 30, 68.

84. The Canadian regime is described *infra* text at notes 177-78, and note 244; the English approach is sketched out *infra* text at notes 241-43.

85. 417 U.S. 433 (1974).

86. *Id.* at 449.

87. 467 U.S. 649 (1984).

88. *See id.* at 672 (O'Connor, J., concurring in part and dissenting in part) ("Limitation of the *Miranda* prohibition to testimonial use of the statements themselves adequately serves the purposes of the privilege against self-incrimination.").

89. *Id.* at 673. Justice O'Connor emphasized the importance of examining the approaches of countries such as England, India, Scotland, and Ceylon in crafting our own rules regarding confessions and pointed out that the Court in *Miranda* had explicitly looked to those countries in developing the *Miranda* rule. She noted that in those countries, "nontestimonial evidence derived from all confessions 'not blatantly coerced' was and still is admitted." *Id.*

Note that in expressing concern that "entire investigations" not be lost, Justice O'Connor seemed worried about the possibility that, say, the gun might well have been found regardless of the antecedent *Miranda* violation. *See also* Henry J. Friendly, *Benchmarks* 279 (1967) (expressing concern that applying *Miranda* to fruits would "in effect confer immunity unless the prosecution can meet the burden of showing that its fruits would have been discovered anyway"). Yet again, we see the possible "causation gap." *See supra* notes 30 and 68.

90. Justice O'Connor stated:

Indeed, whatever case can be made for suppression evaporates when the statements themselves are not admitted, given the rationale of the *Schmerber* line of cases. Certainly interrogation which provides leads to other evidence does not offend the values underlying the Fifth Amendment privilege any more than the compulsory taking of blood samples, fingerprints, or voice exemplars, all of which may be compelled in an "attempt to discover evidence that might be used to prosecute [a defendant] for a criminal offense."

467 U.S. at 670–71 (O'Connor, J., concurring in part and dissenting in part) (quoting Schmerber v. California, 384 U.S. 757, 761 (1966)).

91. 470 U.S. 298, 304, 308–9 (1985). In *Elstad,* the "fruit" was itself a statement from the defendant, which the Court found voluntary and reliable even though it was the fruit of an earlier, *Miranda*-defective utterance.

92. *Id.* at 308.

93. *See, e.g.,* United States v. Gonzalez-Sandoval, 894 F.2d 1043, 1048 (9th Cir. 1990) (stating that "the reasoning of *Elstad* and *Tucker* applies as well to non-testimonial physical evidence obtained as a result of a *Miranda* violation"); United States v. Sangineto-Miranda, 859 F.2d 1501, 1514–18 (6th Cir. 1988) (admitting the fruits of mere *Miranda* violation because "the goal of the fifth amendment's exclusionary rule is to assure trustworthy evidence"); United States v. Bengivenga, 845 F.2d 593, 600–601 (5th Cir. 1988) (finding that a "mere violation of *Miranda*" does not trigger the exclusion of nontestimonial fruit); United States *ex rel.* Hudson v. Cannon, 529 F.2d 890, 894–95 (7th Cir. 1976) (holding, in reliance on *Tucker* and before *Quarles,* that fruits of a mere *Miranda* violation should not be excluded).

94. Note how various statements from Justice O'Connor's opinion explicitly speak of the logic underlying not merely *Miranda* but the privilege against self-incrimination itself. *See supra* notes 87–93 and accompanying text. *See also* 467 U.S. at 460 (O'Connor, J., concurring in part and dissenting in part) ("nothing in *Miranda or the privilege itself* requires exclusion of nontestimonial evidence") (emphasis added). Her invocations of *Schmerber* also sound in pure self-incrimination theory, as distinct from "mere" *Miranda* concerns. *See supra* note 90 and text at note 91.

95. 116 U.S. 616 (1886).

96. On the common law's special solicitude for private papers, see Entick v. Carrington, 19 Howell's State Trials 1029 (C.P. 1765). The idea of what was "private," however, was construed very broadly indeed in certain English cases and went far beyond diaries. *See, e.g.*, Regina v. Mead, 92 Eng. Rep. 119, 119 (K.B. 1703) (refusing to require the defendants, who were charged with executing an office of trust without taking an oath, to produce books showing the election of the corporation's officers because "they are perfectly of a private nature"); Rex v. Worsenham, 91 Eng. Rep. 1370, 1370 (K.B. 1701) (refusing to require the defendants in a forgery case, who were custom-house officers, to produce custom-house books because the books were "a private concern" and therefore requiring production would be "to compel the defendants, to produce evidence against themselves"); Chetwind v. Marnell, 126 Eng. Rep. 900, 900 (C.P. 1798) (noting that the plaintiff, in an action brought on a testator's bond that was suspected of being forged, would not be compelled to produce the bond for inspection, if it might be the means of convicting him of a capital felony); the Queen v. Granatelli, 7 Rep. State Trials (New Series) 979, 986 (C.C.C. 1849) (refusing to require a witness, in a prosecution for fitting out a vessel against a friendly power, to produce a sales agreement of the company for which he was secretary because it might incriminate him); *see also* Roe v. Harvey, 98 Eng. Rep. 302, 305 (K.B. 1769) (Mansfield, L.J.) ("[I]n a criminal or penal cause, the defendant is never forced to produce any evidence; though he should hold it in his hands, in Court."). None of these cases involved immunity statutes, and thus none focused on the precise scope of immunity necessary to overcome the self-incrimination privilege.

97. *See* Telford Taylor, *Two Studies in Constitutional Interpretation* 67 (1969).

98. *See* Lochner v. New York, 198 U.S. 45 (1905).

99. *See supra* Chapter 1, text at notes 110–30.

100. *See* William J. Stuntz, *The Substantive Origins of Criminal Procedure* 105 Yale L.J. 393 (1995).

101. One commentator states that excluding such evidence was the majority rule. *See* Charles Gardner Geyh, *The Testimonial Component of the Right Against Self-Incrimination*, 36 Cath. U. L. Rev. 611, 621 (1987).

102. *Compare* People v. Akin, 143 P. 795, 796 (Cal. Dist. Ct. App. 1914) (refusing to compel a physical examination for venereal disease); State v. Height, 91 N.W. 935, 940 (Iowa 1902) (same); State v. Newcomb, 119 S.W. 405, 409 (Mo. 1909) (same); Bowers v. State, 75 S.W. 299, 300 (Tex. Crim. App. 1903) (same); People v. McCoy, 45 How. Pr. 216, 217 (N.Y. Sup. Ct. 1873) (refusing to compel a physical examination for evidence of childbirth) *with* O'Brien v. State, 25 N.E. 137 (Ind. 1890) (holding that the results of a compelled physical examination for scars and identifying marks were admissible); State v. Miller, 60 A. 202 (N.J. 1905) (same); People v. Corder, 221 N.W. 309, 309–10 (Mich. 1928) (allowing evidence of a voluntary physical examination); Noe v. Monmouth, 143 A. 750 (N.J. 1928) (holding that compelling the physical examination of a driver for signs of intoxication was permissible).

103. *Compare* Cooper v. State, 6 So. 110 (Ala. 1889) (holding that a defendant cannot be compelled to make footprints to have his tracks compared to those found at the scene of the crime); Day v. State, 63 Ga. 668 (1879) (same); State v. Sirmay, 122 P. 748 (Utah 1912) (same) *with* United States v. Kelly, 55 F.2d 67 (2d Cir. 1932) (permitting the State to compel the defendant to give fingerprints); People v. Jones, 296 P. 317 (Cal. App. 1931) (same; finding that fingerprints are not testimonial); Magee v. State, 46 So. 529 (Miss. 1908) (allowing the State to compel a defendant to put his foot in a track found at the scene of a crime, because the compulsion posed no risk to truth finding).

104. *Compare* Blackwell v. State, 67 Ga. 76 (1881) (holding that the State cannot compel a defendant to show an amputated arm at trial); State v. Jacobs, 50 N.C.

(5 Jones) 256 (1858) (holding that the State cannot compel a defendant to show himself to the jury for purposes of ascertaining his race); Ward v. State, 228 P. 498 (Okla. Crim. App. 1924) (holding that the State cannot compel the defendant to put on a coat); Turman v. State, 95 S.W. 533 (Tex. Crim. App. 1898) (holding that the State cannot compel the defendant to put a cap on his head) *with* Ross v. State, 182 N.E. 865 (Ind. 1932) (finding it permissible to compel a defendant to grow a beard); State v. Oschoa, 242 P. 582 (Nev. 1926) (finding it permissible to compel a defendant to show his body to the jurors and to put on a shirt for them); State v. Ah Chuey, 14 Nev. 79 (1879) (holding that a compelled showing of a tattoo does not violate the privilege, because the privilege's purpose is to help find the truth); Sprouse v. Commonwealth, 81 Va. 374 (1886) (finding that requiring a forger to write his name does not violate the privilege).

105. *See* J. A. C. Grant, *Self-Incrimination in the Modern American Law,* 5 Temple L.Q. 368, 373–87 (1931); *see, e.g.,* Bruce v. State, 21 S.W. 681 (Tex. Crim. App. 1893). The court in *Bruce* stated: "[T]he ground upon which this testimony is said to be admissible is that in these cases the physical facts speak for themselves, and no [fears] or hopes of the prisoner could produce or effect a resemblance of his track, or of the wounds or clothing, and their resemblance aids the jury in their search after the truth." 21 S.W. at 682.

106. 384 U.S. 757 (1966).

107. *Id.* at 761 (footnote omitted).

108. 218 U.S. 245 (1910); *see* 384 U.S. at 763.

109. 218 U.S. at 252–53.

110. 384 U.S. at 764.

111. *See* Note, *The Life and Times of* Boyd v. United States *(1886–1976),* 76 Mich. L. Rev. 184, 196–98 (1977) (authored by Stan Krauss).

112. Boyd v. United States, 116 U.S. 616, 630 (1886).

113. *Compare* 384 U.S. at 760–65 (Part II: "The Privilege Against Self-Incrimination Claim") *with id.* at 766–72 (Part IV: "The Search and Seizure Claim"). In each part, *Boyd* is mentioned only once, and briefly. *See id.* at 763–64 (reading *Boyd* as a self-incrimination case about "papers"); *id.* at 768 (reading *Boyd* as a search and seizure case about warrants and thus as "not instructive" in the case at hand).

114. *Id.* at 775 (Black, J., dissenting).

115. U.S. Const. amend. IV (affirming the people's right to be secure in their "persons, houses, papers, and *effects*" (emphasis added)).

116. New York v. Quarles, 467 U.S. 649, 671 (1984) (O'Connor, J., concurring in part and dissenting in part) (quoting Friendly, *supra* note 89, at 280).

117. 467 U.S. at 670–71 (O'Connor, J., concurring in part and dissenting in part).

118. *See* United States v. Wade, 388 U.S. 218 (1967).

119. *See* Gilbert v. California, 388 U.S. 263 (1967).

120. *See* United States v. Dionisio, 410 U.S. 1 (1973).

121. *See* Pennsylvania v. Muniz, 496 U.S. 582 (1990).

122. 387 U.S. 294, 302–3, 306–7 (1967).

123. *See* Couch v. United States, 409 U.S. 322 (1973) (holding that a summons served on a taxpayer's accountant requiring him to produce the taxpayer's personal business records in his possession did not violate the taxpayer's Fifth Amendment rights); Bellis v. United States, 417 U.S. 85 (1974) (holding that neither a partnership nor its individual partners were shielded on self-incrimination grounds from the compelled production of partnership records); Fisher v. United States, 425 U.S. 391, 402–14 (1976) (holding that the defendant's Fifth Amendment rights were untouched because he was compelled to produce incriminating papers and not to give self-incriminating *testimony*); Andresen v. Maryland, 427 U.S. 463, 470–77 (1976) (holding that the introduction at trial of the defendant's business records did

not violate the Fifth Amendment because the statements were "voluntarily committed to writing" and were seized pursuant to a valid search warrant). For more discussion, see Note, *supra* note 111.

In one respect, the Court has qualified the general rule allowing introduction of subpoenaed documents or other physical evidence. The *Fisher* Court briefly observed that the act of producing documents itself might have "communicative aspects," such as indicating the taxpayer's belief that those were the documents described in the subpoena, that might be both "testimonial" and "incriminating" for purposes of the Fifth Amendment. *See* 425 U.S. at 410. But the Court did not attempt to lay down a rule for such cases. In United States v. Doe, 465 U.S. 605, 612–14 (1984) *(Doe I)*, the Court relied on this caveat in *Fisher* to uphold exclusion of existent documents subpoenaed from the defendant. The Court emphasized, however, that its holding was based on deference to factual findings made by the district court. *See* 465 U.S. at 613–14. Doe v. United States, 487 U.S. 201 (1988) *(Doe II)*, specified that the privilege applied in cases where producing the evidence would testify to the existence, possession, or authenticity of the things produced. *See* 487 U.S. at 209. Some of the complexities here are explained *infra* notes 174, 249.

124. *See Fisher,* 425 U.S. at 414 (bracketing the issue of private papers under the Fifth Amendment); *Doe I,* 465 U.S. at 610 n. 7 (repeating *Fisher's* Fifth Amendment caveat concerning private papers); 465 U.S. at 619 (Marshall, J., concurring in part and dissenting in part) (emphasizing n. 7 as leaving open the Fifth Amendment status of private papers). *But see* 465 U.S. at 618 (O'Connor, J., concurring) (arguing, contrary to n. 7, that "the Fifth Amendment provides absolutely no protection for the contents of private papers of any kind").

125. *Webster's Third New International Dictionary* 2627 (1971).

126. 5 Jeremy Bentham, *Rationale of Judicial Evidence* 229 (London, Hunt and Clarke 1827).

127. Friendly, *supra* note 55, at 679–81, 698.

128. Traditional rationales have long been under attack. Judge Friendly, David Dolinko, and others have convincingly shown that various traditional rationales for the privilege cannot support Fifth Amendment doctrine, at least as it now exists. *See* Friendly, *supra* note 55; *see also* Lewis Mayers, *Shall We Amend the Fifth Amendment?* (1959); David Dolinko, *Is There a Rationale for the Privilege Against Self-Incrimination?,* 33 U.C.L.A. L. Rev. 1063 (1986); Donald A. Dripps, *Foreword: Against Police Interrogation—And the Privilege Against Self-Incrimination,* 78 J. Crim. L. and Criminology 699 (1988). Other commentators criticizing the Fifth Amendment over the years have included such luminaries as John Henry Wigmore, Roscoe Pound, and Charles McCormick. *See* Friendly, *supra* note 55, at 672–74. Against them are ranged the arguments of Robert S. Gerstein, *Privacy and Self-Incrimination,* 80 Ethics 87, 90 (1970) (arguing that individuals should have absolute control over revelations of guilt and remorse); Robert S. Gerstein, *Punishment and Self-Incrimination,* 16 Am. J. Juris. 84, 88 (1971) (similar); Thomas S. Schrock et al., *Interrogational Rights: Reflections on* Miranda v. Arizona, 52 S. Cal. L. Rev. 1, 49 (1978) (claiming that the purpose of the privilege is to enhance autonomy by protecting the individual's right to choose how he "takes responsibility"); Schulhofer, *supra* note 21, at 330–33 (suggesting that the privilege protects innocent defendants from bad performances on the witness stand); and William J. Stuntz, *Self-Incrimination and Excuse,* 88 Colum. L. Rev. 1227, 1229 (1988) (arguing that the privilege should properly be construed as protecting "excusable perjury," not merely silence); *cf.* Saltzburg and Capra, *supra* note 27, at 446–48 (compiling justifications for the privilege and responses).

129. Murphy v. Waterfront Commn., 378 U.S. 52, 55 (1964); *see also* Miranda v. Arizona, 384 U.S. 436, 460 (1966).

130. Professor Luban argues that the law should recognize broader intrafamily

immunity from compelled witnessing. *See* David Luban, *Lawyers and Justice: An Ethical Study* 197 (1988). But the fact that Anglo-American law has never done this dramatizes the weakness of Luban's account as a descriptive matter. Normatively, a self-incrimination privilege seems much harder to justify than a family privilege: compelling an innocent mother to send her own son to prison or death seems ruthlessly callous, but compelling him to tell the truth and confess seems much less cruel. If he wanted to avoid this cruelty, he could have done so by not committing the crime; his dilemma arises only because he is a criminal.

131. This theme is explored in greater depth in Chapters 3 and 4. Provisions like the First Amendment do of course protect those guilty of "crimes" like heresy and seditious libel, but these provisions sound in substance, not criminal procedure. As a matter of substantive law, heresy should not be a crime at all; by contrast, the Fifth Amendment applies to things that should be criminal, like rape, murder, and arson. The Eighth Amendment protects the guilty from excessive punishment but not from convictions. The double jeopardy clause does protect the guilty via the plea of autrefois convict, but the clause and its underlying principles provide even more protection to the innocent via pleas of autrefois acquit and collateral estoppel. *See* Amar and Marcus, *supra* note 61, at 36–37. Moreover, autrefois convict bars only *multiple* convictions of the guilty—in effect, protecting against excessive punishment, *see id.* at 28–29, 36 and n. 184—but of course allows the government one unfettered shot at convicting the guilty on the basis of reliable evidence.

132. *See Murphy*, 378 U.S. at 55; Couch v. United States, 409 U.S. 322, 328 (1973); *see also* Gerstein, *Privacy and Self-Incrimination, supra* note 128, at 90–91 (arguing that the self-condemnation and remorse entailed by incriminating oneself should remain private). Justice O'Connor, however, has written that the privacy rationale does not apply to suspects in custodial interrogation: "Where independent evidence leads police to a suspect, and probable cause justifies his arrest, the suspect cannot seriously urge that the police have somehow unfairly infringed on his right 'to a private enclave where he may lead a private life.'" New York v. Quarles, 467 U.S. 649, 670 (1984) (O'Connor, J., concurring in part and dissenting in part) (citing *Murphy*).

133. Defendants were not *allowed* to testify under oath at trial in America until the mid-nineteenth century. *See generally* Joel N. Bodansky, *The Abolition of the Party-Witness Disqualification: An Historical Survey*, 70 Ky. L.J. 91 (1982).

134. *See* Theodore Barlow, *The Justice of Peace: A Treatise Containing the Power and Duty of That Magistrate* 189 (London, Lintot 1745) ("[I]t would be hard, and unequal to rack a Man's Conscience with the Religion of an Oath, and make his Discovery tend to his Condemnation, but not allow his Denial on Oath to have any Weight towards his Exculpation or Acquittal."), *quoted in* Langbein, *supra* note 1, at 1085 n. 157; *cf.* 3 John Henry Wigmore, *Treatise on the Anglo-American System of Evidence in Trials at Common Law* (3d ed. 1940). According to Wigmore, "In view of the apparent unfairness of a system which practically told the accused person, 'You cannot be trusted to speak here or elsewhere in your own behalf, but we shall use against you whatever you may have said,' it was entirely natural that the judges should employ the only makeweight which existed for mitigating this unfairness and restoring the balance, namely, [excluding unreliable] confessions." *Id.* §865(3), at 354.

135. *See* Westen, *supra* note 8, at 119–20 (using the compulsory process clause to buttress the defendant's right to testify); Peter Westen, *Order of Proof: An Accused's Right to Control the Timing and Sequence of Evidence in His Defense*, 66 Cal. L. Rev. 935, 985 n. 206 (1978) (similar). For more discussion *see infra* Chapter 3, text at notes 198–219.

136. *See* Rock v. Arkansas, 483 U.S. 44, 51–53 (1987) (holding that a defendant enjoys a right to testify on her own behalf under the Fifth, Sixth, and Fourteenth Amendments).

137. *See* United States v. Agurs, 427 U.S. 97 (1976); Brady v. Maryland, 373 U.S. 83 (1963); Abraham S. Goldstein, *The State and the Accused: Balance of Advantage in Criminal Procedure,* 69 Yale L.J. 1149, 1198 (1960).

138. On noninstrumentalization and government "usings," see generally Jed Rubenfeld, *The Right of Privacy,* 102 Harv. L. Rev. 737 (1989); Jed Rubenfeld, *Usings,* 102 Yale L.J. 1077 (1993); and Jed Rubenfeld, *Reading the Constitution as Spoken,* 104 Yale L.J. 119 (1995). On the noninstrumentalization idea in the self-incrimination context, see Luban, *supra* note 130, at 194 ("[M]aking me the active instrument of my own destruction signals the entire subordination of the self to the state."). As this Luban quotation indicates, individual variations of the noninstrumentalization idea often come equipped with a set of nice distinctions between active and passive use.

139. *See* 8 Wigmore, *supra* note 134, §2192, at 64 ("For more than three centuries it has now been recognized as a fundamental maxim that the public (in the words sanctioned by Lord Hardwicke) has a right to every man's evidence.") Frankly, it is hard to see how modern society could operate without this general presumption.

140. Schmerber v. California, 384 U.S. 757 (1966).

141. Other problems for noninstrumentalists: Doesn't the government use a suspect as the testimonial instrument of his own destruction when it secretly invades his house (with a warrant), wiretaps his conversations without his consent, and then uses his own words against him in a criminal trial? Or when it subpoenas the defendant to furnish extant documents written in his own hand and then uses those documents at trial? Or when it compels a defendant to authorize (with words) the release of his own bank statements and then uses the authorization and the bank statements to convict him? *See* Olmstead v. United States, 277 U.S. 438, 462 (1928); Andresen v. Maryland, 427 U.S. 463, 470–77 (1976); Fisher v. United States, 425 U.S. 391 (1976); Doe v. United States, 487 U.S. 201 (1988) *(Doe II).*

142. *See* Murphy v. Waterfront Commn., 378 U.S. 52, 55 (1964).

143. *See* 378 U.S. at 55.

144. *See In re* Winship, 397 U.S. 358 (1970). This valuable safeguard does benefit some guilty defendants but only as an incidental byproduct of achieving its direct aim of protecting *innocent* defendants from *erroneous* convictions.

145. *See* Williams v. Florida, 399 U.S. 78, 108 (1970) (Black, J., dissenting) (arguing that the Florida notice-of-alibi rule violated the Fifth Amendment and claiming that a criminal defendant has a "historical and constitutionally guaranteed right . . . to remain completely silent, requiring the State to prove its case without any assistance of any kind from the defendant himself"); *see also* Kevin R. Reitz, *Clients, Lawyers, and the Fifth Amendment: The Need for a Projected Privilege,* 41 Duke L.J. 572, 581–82 (1991) (asserting that defendant retains "the right to doubt the justness" of the state's criminal law enforcement and thus the right to refuse his aid). Reitz here confuses the First and Fifth Amendments. Of course a defendant has the right to doubt the state—and to say so vigorously and without penalty—but the claimed right to withhold information and reliable evidence without penalty simply does not follow.

146. Not surprisingly, Justice Black's dissent in *Williams,* setting out the "no help from defendant" theory, echoes his *Schmerber* dissent and indicates that Justice Black understood that to accept *Schmerber*—as do all the Justices today, presumably—is to reject the "no help" theory. *See Williams,* 399 U.S. at 111 (Black, J., dissenting) ("[A] criminal defendant cannot be required to give evidence, testimony, or any other assistance to the State to aid it in convicting him of crime." (citing *Schmerber,* 384 U.S. at 773 (Black, J., dissenting))).

I do not mean to suggest that the government has no initial burden to meet before it can pluck someone off the street and question him or require him to produce evidence. As we shall see *infra* text at note 274, fishing expeditions are prevented by the Fourth Amendment rule against unreasonable searches and seizures, which typically calls for reasonable suspicion before stopping and questioning, and probable cause before arrest.

147. *See* Simon, *supra* note 49, at 199 ("Miranda and its accompanying decisions . . . effectively ended the use of violence and the most blatant kind of physical intimidation in interrogations.").

148. Pun very much intended. I mean here to conjure up a "civilized" process akin to that used today in civil law countries and in civil pretrial discovery in the United States.

149. Some ideas for bolstering Fourth Amendment remedies are sketched out in Chapter 1, text at notes 196–221.

150. *Cf.* Murphy v. Waterfront Commn., 378 U.S. 52, 55 (1964); Wilson v. United States, 149 U.S. 60, 66 (1893).

151. *See, e.g.,* Michigan v. Tucker, 417 U.S. 433, 448–49 (1974); *Murphy,* 378 U.S. at 55; Griswold, *supra* note 29, at 10–19; Schulhofer, *supra* note 21; *see also* Withrow v. Williams, 113 S. Ct. 1745, 1753 (1993) (linking the "Fifth Amendment 'trial right'" and *Miranda* to "the correct ascertainment of guilt" and arguing that "*Miranda* serves to guard against 'the use of unreliable statements at trial'" (quoting Johnson v. New Jersey, 384 U.S. 719, 730 (1966))). *But see* Tehan v. United States *ex rel.* Shott, 382 U.S. 406, 415–16 (1966) (rejecting the innocence-protection rationale in the course of refusing to give *Griffin* retroactive effect).

152. In a thoughtful essay that properly focuses on innocence and reliability, Professor Schulhofer fails to discuss how these rationales argue against current Fifth Amendment fruits doctrine. *See* Schulhofer, *supra* note 21, at 330–33.

153. Professor Stuntz's argument that the Fifth Amendment protects "excusable perjury," *see* Stuntz, *supra* note 128, is flawed for several reasons. First, it is anachronistic to think that people at the Founding would commit perjury lightly, see *infra* notes 184–85 and accompanying text, and so Stuntz's argument fails to explain the Framers' vision. Second, it is morally inexcusable to condone lying when the lie merely compounds the liar's underlying crime. Third, Stuntz's argument rests on a faulty Perry Mason–like view of confessions. Lies are still useful to prosecutors in a variety of ways. *See infra* notes 170, 173, 186, and accompanying text. In fairness to Stuntz, he claims not that his theory is historically rooted or normatively appealing but only that it fits the cases.

154. *See supra* note 128.

155. In the past decade, our knowledge of the origins of the privilege has been significantly expanded and perhaps revolutionized. The earlier-received account was built on two works: Wigmore's massive treatise and Levy's heroicizing work, which built on Wigmore's version. 8 Wigmore, *supra* note 134, §2250; Levy, *supra* note 18.

156. A variant of the maxim is *nemo tenetur accusare seipsum,* "no one is obliged to accuse himself." Simeon E. Baldwin, *Preliminary Examinations in Criminal Proceedings,* 6 A.B.A. Rep. 225, 229 (1883); Edward S. Corwin, *The Supreme Court's Construction of the Self-Incrimination Clause,* 29 Mich. L. Rev. 1, 3 (1930). Two recent articles powerfully argue that the *nemo tenetur* maxim was imported from the Continent for use in inquisitorial procedure, thus casting doubt on Leonard Levy's argument that the privilege was an English invention. *See* R. H. Helmholtz, *Origins of the Privilege Against Self-Incrimination: The Role of the European* Ius Commune, 65 N.Y.U. L. Rev. 962, 967–69 (1990); Michael R. T. Macnair, *The Early Development of the Privilege Against Self-Incrimination,* 10 Oxford J. Legal Stud. 66, 67–70 (1990).

157. Langbein, *supra* note 1, at 1072; Helmholtz, *supra* note 156, at 982.

158. E. M. Morgan, *The Privilege Against Self-Incrimination,* 34 Minn. L. Rev. 1, 4 (1949).

159. Coke's early-seventeenth-century discussion of the oath *ex officio* reveals distrust of its use to uncover thoughts. The Privy Council on a motion from the House of Commons asked Coke and Chief Justice Popham when the oath could properly be administered. As part of their answer, they stated: "No Man . . . shall be examined upon secret Thoughts of his Heart, or of his secret Opinion: But something ought to be objected against him what he hath spoken or done." *An Oath before an Ecclesiastical Judge ex Officio, in* 12 Coke's Rep. 26 (3d ed., 1727). They were particularly concerned about questioning involving "heresy and errors of faith." *Id.* They also objected to the lack of any preliminary showing of suspicion via accusation or presentment or the like. *See* Corwin, *supra* note 156, at 7–8.

160. *See* Mary H. Maguire, *Attack of the Common Lawyers on the Oath* Ex Officio *as Administered in the Ecclesiastical Courts in England, in* Essays in History and Political Theory 199 (Carl Wittke ed., 1936).

161. Accordingly, in John Lilburne's first trial, in the Star Chamber, his objection was not that he had a right not to answer incriminating questions but that he had a right to a proper accusation before he did so. 8 Wigmore, *supra* note 134, §2250, at 291, 298; Corwin, *supra* note 156, at 8. He refused to answer to any matter not included in the information against him. For this he was whipped, pilloried, fined, and imprisoned. With the victory of the parliamentary forces, the Long Parliament abolished the Star Chamber and the High Commission and forbade ecclesiastical courts to use the oath *ex officio*. For a discussion, see Charles M. Gray, *Prohibitions and the Privilege Against Self-Incrimination, in* Tudor Rule and Revolution 345 (Delloyd J. Guth and John W. McKenna eds., 1982).

162. Wigmore placed the origin of the modern privilege with Lilburne's assertions in his later trials, when he was faced with questions on treason and related charges. Wigmore claimed that the privilege was well established by the late seventeenth century. 8 Wigmore, *supra* note 134, §2250, at 298–99. Now, however, the work of several historians suggests that Wigmore's evidence was flawed. *See, e.g.,* Langbein, *supra* note 1, at 1071–84.

163. Langbein, *supra* note 1, at 1065–66; Eben Moglen, *Taking the Fifth: Reconsidering the Origins of the Constitutional Privilege Against Self-Incrimination,* 92 Mich. L. Rev. 1086 (1994); *see also* J. M. Beattie, *Crime and the Courts in England 1600–1800,* at 364–66 (1986).

164. Langbein, *supra* note 1, at 1066–71.

165. *See* Moglen, *supra* note 163, at 1094–1104; Morgan, *supra* note 158, at 18–19.

166. *See* Office of Legal Policy, U.S. Dept. of Justice, "Truth in Criminal Justice" Series Report No. 1, *The Law of Pre-Trial Interrogation* (1986), *reprinted in* 22 U. Mich. J.L. Ref. 437, 482 (1989).

167. Bram v. United States, 168 U.S. 532 (1897) (holding an involuntary confession made to a police official inadmissible).

168. Professor Stuntz claims that his descriptive theory can explain the pattern of current cases. *See supra* note 153. Whether or not this is so, Stuntz's theory—that one can excusably lie to cover up earlier crimes one has committed—seems historically implausible and morally unattractive. *See supra* note 153. On both these grounds, the theory proposed below is superior, and it also better fits the Court's recent trends.

169. A government could choose a less compulsive scheme, of course, such as one that "compelled" answers by allowing a later jury or fact finder to draw adverse inferences from a suspect's pretrial silence in the face of pointed questions.

170. If a defendant can be shown to have lied at his deposition, his words—or the fact that he lied—still could not be introduced at his trial for the underlying offense. His words could be introduced, however, in a subsequent prosecution for

perjury. This caveat is necessary because otherwise defendants could effectively render the entire deposition process worthless simply by lying. The Supreme Court has adopted a similar rule in holding that immunized grand jury testimony cannot be used for impeachment purposes at the witness's trial involving the matter about which he testified, *see* New Jersey v. Portash, 440 U.S. 450 (1979); Mincey v. Arizona, 437 U.S. 385 (1978), but it can be used against the witness in a later perjury prosecution, *see* United States v. Apfelbaum, 445 U.S. 115, 127–32 (1980); Glickstein v. United States, 222 U.S. 139, 141–42 (1911). For a powerful discussion, see Lushing, *supra* note 4.

In effect, a pretrial deposition helps freeze and lock in a suspect's story, and—via the threat of perjury charges—deters post hoc concoctions. Under a testimonial immunity regime, perjury would become a much more significant weapon in the fight against crime—just as the scope of current self-incrimination doctrine creates strong incentives for wiretaps and sting operations. *See supra* text at notes 3–4. In a case where a suspect lies, a prosecutor may be able to prove perjury even if she cannot prove the predicate offense. If a murder suspect lies about his whereabouts at the time of the murder, for example, a prosecutor may be able to prove he is a liar, even if she cannot prove he is a murderer—just as a prosecutor today can sometimes nail a racketeer for tax evasion. In response to a testimonial immunity regime, legislatures might well choose to boost the penalties for perjury.

171. Defense lawyers have traditionally been excluded from the grand jury room, and I, at least, would not require their presence there. Unlike a police station interrogation, there is little risk of violence against a witness, and so a lawyer is not needed on that account. It is in fact quite useful for society to have at least one nonviolent but secret interrogation place, so that individual members of organized conspiracies can be brought in one by one, and their partners in crime will never know for sure whether they ratted or stood mute. (The secrecy of the grand jury room is in effect the wall between prisoners that creates a classic "prisoner's dilemma" to confess the truth.) Defense lawyers, if present in the grand jury room, can actually muzzle an underling who wants to tell all, for the underling's lawyer may really be the agent of the mob boss; such lawyers often help a group of conspirators to maintain a joint stonewall defense. *Cf.* Pamela S. Karlan, *Discrete and Relational Criminal Representation: The Changing Vision of the Right to Counsel,* 105 Harv. L. Rev. 670, 693–97 (1992). Even in the case of a lone criminal, a defense attorney may at times impede rather than promote the truth-seeking process. *See* Stuntz, *supra* note 52, at 1944–54. Because a lawyer-less witness in a grand jury room may be tricked or intimidated by a clever prosecutor into making misleading or inaccurate inculpatory statements, a testimonial immunity regime would not allow these statements themselves to be admitted in a criminal case, unless the defendant so authorized.

172. Preserving secrecy in the magistrate hearing would protect the witness from having to make potentially embarrassing public revelations and would prevent potential jurors in the public from being tainted by preliminary exposure to excludable testimony.

173. An additional possibility is to allow a polygraph test to be conducted on the defendant, with the proviso that the results of the test would not be admissible at trial. Polygraph tests, while less helpful in the employment context, have been shown to be of some help in the context of criminal investigations in enabling the police to decide which trails to follow. Office of Technology Assessment, U.S. Congress, *Scientific Validity of Polygraph Testing* 8, 58 (1983).

174. This last restriction obviates the Court's concern in *Fisher, Doe,* and *Bouknight* that the act of producing documents or objects itself has testimonial value. *Cf. supra* note 123; *infra* note 249.

175. The Sixth Amendment provides the accused, in all criminal prosecutions,

with the right, *inter alia,* "to be confronted with the witnesses against him" and "to have compulsory process for obtaining witnesses in his favor." U.S. Const. amend. VI. The treason provision provides that "[n]o Person shall be convicted of Treason unless on the Testimony of two Witnesses to the same overt Act." U.S. Const. art. III, §3. For more discussion of the word *witness* in these clauses, *see infra* Chapter 3, text at notes 165–97.

176. *See* Friendly, *supra* note 55.

177. Canada Evidence Act, R.S.C., ch. E-10, §5(1) (1970) (requiring that the witness answer); R.S.C., ch. E-10, §5(2) (1970) (prohibiting the prosecution from using testimonial admissions of a witness who objects that he will incriminate himself). A coparticipant must also testify, if he is charged separately from the defendant. *Re* Regan, 2 D.L.R. 135, 137–38 (N.S. 1939).

178. *See Report of the Federal/Provincial Task Force on Uniform Rules of Evidence* §33.3(b) (1982) (considering and rejecting proposals granting an indicted witness use-fruits immunity); *see also* Tague, *supra* note 5, at 3 n. 11.

179. *See, e.g.,* Friendly, *supra* note 55, at 676.

180. Current doctrine, of course, recognizes this too. A person can never be compelled, upon pain of contempt, to witness in his own criminal trial, but he can be obliged—with immunity—to witness in someone else's trial, civil or criminal. This immunity is enforced by a rule of exclusion in his own case. *See supra* notes 55–56 and accompanying text. The only question is how broad that immunity must be—exactly what must be excluded in his own criminal case.

181. *See generally* Westen, *supra* note 8, at 182–84.

182. 388 U.S. 14 (1967).

183. 388 U.S. at 19 (emphasis added).

184. *See* Barlow, *supra* note 134, at 189 (stating that oaths "might serve instead of the Rack, to the Consciences of some Men, although they have been guilty of Offenses"), *quoted in* Langbein, *supra* note 1, at 1085 n. 157.

185. For the details *see infra* Chapter 3, note 185.

186. Simon, *supra* note 49, at 198.

187. *See* Griffin v. California, 380 U.S. 609 (1965), discussed *supra* text at notes 19–21. *But see* Office of Legal Policy, U.S. Dept. of Justice, *Report to the Attorney General on Adverse Inferences from Silence,* No. 8 (1989), *reprinted in* 22 U. Mich. J.L. Ref. 1005, 1078–81 (1989).

188. This in-court inducement to testify differs arguably from much out-of-court compulsion by the police in that the prosecutor is merely trying to persuade the defendant to *testify*—simply to take the stand—while the police often encourage a suspect to testify *against himself*—to confess, to provide a certain substantive slant. The latter leads to more reliability difficulties. It is useful here to note that a defendant's testimony is *voluntary* even when it is shaped by various strategic considerations.

189. *See supra* text at note 133.

190. It could do the former by immunizing its employees, making them sing, and then taking appropriate employment action in light of their song. It could do the latter by refusing to confer sweeping immunity that might compromise later criminal prosecutions.

191. *Cf.* Friendly, *supra* note 55, at 707–8 (drawing an analogy between public and private employers).

192. The argument here is not that government employment action is not state action, nor that mimicking the market can never violate constitutional provisions, such as the First Amendment. Rather, it is that market mimicry should not be understood as the kind of compulsion that offends the letter or spirit of the self-incrimination clause. This conclusion is not the product of unreflective labels about "natural baselines" distinguishing between government as "sovereign" law enforcer

and government as "mere" employer; but instead it follows Professor Sunstein's invitation to reflect self-consciously on the "baseline" that best vindicates a particular provision's purposes. *See* Cass R. Sunstein, Lochner's *Legacy*, 87 Colum. L. Rev. 873 (1987); Cass R. Sunstein, *Why the Unconstitutional Conditions Doctrine Is an Anachronism (With Particular Reference to Religion, Speech, and Abortion)*, 70 B.U. L. Rev. 593 (1990). For an earlier exposition that makes very similar points, see Westen, *Incredible Dilemmas, supra* note 12.

193. 1 *See* Baltimore City Dept. of Social Servs. v. Bouknight, 493 U.S. 549 (1990).

194. *See* California v. Byers, 402 U.S. 424 (1971); *see also* Shapiro v. United States, 335 U.S. 1 (1948).

195. This interpretation of the Fifth Amendment arrives at Judge Friendly's solution without the need for a constitutional amendment. Friendly advocated "[r]equiring registration or reporting reasonably necessary for a proper governmental purpose, provided that no registration or report so compelled shall be admissible as evidence of any crime revealed therein." Friendly, *supra* note 55, at 722. But, he argued, "the government should not be forced to show it would have been able to prosecute quite apart from the information furnished by the registration or report or be prohibited from using leads obtained therefrom." *Id.* at 720.

196. Even with this quandary solved, however, the required records doctrine still presents thorny issues. Sometimes the government will need to introduce the records themselves to get a conviction. At least two theories are plausible here. First, if a required record is of a type a person would have kept anyway, the government could make a kind of inevitable discovery argument as follows: the defendant would have kept the record voluntarily, so the government did not really "cause" or "compel" its creation, and it should be subject to subpoena under Fisher v. United States, 425 U.S. 391 (1976), with immunity provided merely for the testimonial act of compelled production itself. *See infra* text at notes 248–49 and note 249. This theory builds on Justice Harlan's first prong in Marchetti v. United States, 390 U.S. 39 (1968), discussed *supra* text at note 40, but tries to give it more rigor. (Even if a new, noncustomary record is required as a condition of doing a certain kind of business, perhaps the government could also argue here that no real Fifth Amendment compulsion exists, because a person is free not to engage in that business. *Cf. supra* text at notes 191–92.) Second, it might be argued that certain kinds of records, required of broad classes of persons not suspected of criminal wrongdoing, and not involving face-to-face encounters with interrogators, need not be seen as akin to criminal "witnessing" even though these records are testimonial and ultimately introduced in a criminal case. This theory repackages Justice Harlan's third *Marchetti* prong as a textual argument about "witness" and reflects the Big Idea that at the Founding compelled criminal witnessing would often be unreliable because of the imbalance of power, interruptions, traps, and the like in face-to-face exchanges between citizens and prosecutors. I do not necessarily embrace either theory here (though both seem intriguing); their elaboration must await another day.

Note finally that corporate required records have long been given only minimal Fifth Amendment protection. *See* Hale v. Henkel, 201 U.S. 43, 75 (1906) ("While an individual may lawfully refuse to answer incriminating questions unless protected by an immunity statute, it does not follow that a corporation, vested with special privileges and franchises, may refuse to show its hand when charged with an abuse of such privileges.").

197. Brown v. Mississippi, 297 U.S. 278 (1936); Miranda v. Arizona, 384 U.S. 436 (1966); Escobedo v. Illinois, 378 U.S. 478 (1964).

198. In civil discovery, magistrates are not typically present during depositions but oversee the general deposition process. In my proposal, magistrates would gen-

erally be physically present for criminal depositions of suspects. *See supra* text at notes 171–74.

199. Rogue police behavior will call for special remedies, including punitive damages against the police department and strict administrative disciplinary mechanisms to punish abusive officers. (An appropriate remedial regime is sketched out *supra* Chapter 1, text at notes 196–221.) Neither the Fourth Amendment nor the Fifth, properly construed, requires exclusion of reliable fruits of unreasonable seizures of persons. Moreover, since in theory a suspect can be lawfully obliged to truthfully tell all to a magistrate under my approach, the fruits should have come to light anyway and thus would fall under the "inevitable discovery" doctrine, *see infra* text at note 244. Legislatures, of course, would nonetheless be free to require exclusion if they were determined to "teach the cops a lesson." But since abusive cops must be punished and deterred even when they expect to find no evidence, and (unsurprisingly) find no evidence, exclusion is not constitutionally sufficient. A proper punitive damage and administrative disciplinary scheme, by contrast, is both constitutionally necessary and constitutionally sufficient—it protects the innocent but avoids windfalls for the guilty. (I develop this theme in more detail in Chapter 4.)

200. Again, silence in the face of some kinds of informal accusation may be far more suspicious than silence in certain formal, legalistic, forensic judicial settings. *See supra* notes 21, 28. *But see supra* note 188. *See also* Jenkins v. Anderson, 447 U.S. 231, 243 (1980) (Stevens, J., concurring) (stating that jurors may draw a "reasonable inference from [suspicious prearrest] silence in a situation in which the ordinary citizen would normally speak out").

201. Pretrial proceedings are not best read as included within a self-incrimination clause "case." The clause is concerned with a "witness" in a "case" who in effect testifies before the jury. *Miranda* does not hold otherwise. To be sure, it holds that the self-incrimination clause applies to pretrial police compulsion, but only because the clause applies to all sorts of compulsion *outside* a criminal case. *See supra* note 55. The rule of exclusion, however, exists *within* a criminal case, *see id.,* and *Miranda* does not hold that the police station is somehow a courtroom. *Escobedo* does contain language linking police stations and courtroom rights, *see* Escobedo v. Illinois, 378 U.S. 478 (1964), but later Supreme Court cases broke with *Escobedo* here, and *Escobedo*'s language, read literally, is hard to take seriously. *See* Henry J. Friendly, *The Bill of Rights as a Code of Criminal Procedure,* 53 Cal. L. Rev. 929, 946–47 (1965). A police station is not a courtroom, and nothing is tried there. There is no judge, no jury, no public, no confrontation right, and no compulsory process right; and if a right of counsel exists in the police station, it is best understood as a due process right, not a Sixth Amendment right. *See id* at 944–46; *see also* United States v. Gouveia, 467 U.S. 180, 187–88 (1984) (holding that the Sixth Amendment right to counsel does not attach until the initiation of formal adversary criminal proceedings); Moran v. Burbine, 475 U.S. 412, 428–30 (1986) (following *Gouveia* and finding no Sixth Amendment right to counsel in a police station).   Nor does the grand jury proceeding fall within a self-incrimination clause "case." Typically, a grand jury sits before an indictment has issued and often before a clear suspect has emerged. Historically, persons were obliged to tell all in a grand jury hearing, with testimonial immunity enforced only in a later criminal trial. *See infra* text at notes 206–7. In Article III, the word *case* refers not to a factual transaction but to formal legal proceedings with parties to a lawsuit: a "case" begins when a prosecutor or plaintiff files an indictment or complaint. Indeed, the word *case* is linked to the word *cause,* as in a formal legal "cause of action." *See* Akhil Reed Amar, *Law Story,* 102 Harv. L. Rev. 688, 718 n. 154 (1988). Functionally, it does not make much sense to bar postindictment depositions while allowing preindictment hearings, because indictments could often be postponed or dismissed in order to conduct the desired

depositions. The key exclusion is thus exclusion of testimony from the trial, where the jury sits to find the facts. *Cf.* United States v. Williams, 112 S. Ct. 1735, 1743 (1992) (suggesting that evidence previously obtained "in violation of the privilege against self-incrimination" may be used in the grand jury, but not in a criminal trial, a suggestion that would be hard to sustain if the grand jury were itself a "case" within the meaning of the self-incrimination clause).

This notion of what a self-incrimination clause "case" is fits with the way we apply rules of evidence, such as hearsay. Rules of evidence, of course, apply at trial—but they do not apply in pretrial proceedings such as depositions and grand jury hearings. *See* Fleming James, Jr., et al., *Civil Procedure* §5.3, at 238 (4th ed. 1992) (stating that at a deposition the matter inquired into "need not itself be admissible evidence"); *see also* Costello v. United States, 350 U.S. 359 (1956) (refusing to quash an indictment based exclusively on hearsay testimony). Like the privilege against compelled self-incrimination, rules of evidence such as hearsay are meant to improve reliability. Reliability of individual bits of information is critical at trial, where final decisions are made, but not so critical where the goal is simply to gather as much relevant information as possible before sifting, as in pretrial proceedings. The different burdens of proof at the pretrial and trial stages—probable cause for an indictment as opposed to proof beyond a reasonable doubt for a criminal conviction—lead to differences in the need for rules emphasizing reliability.

Note finally that the question is *not* whether the word *case must* mean "at trial but not before" but whether it most sensibly *should* mean this to achieve maximum textual coherence, structural harmony, common sense, and so on. My reading of the word *case* enables the words of the self-incrimination clause to fit together and make good policy sense; it coheres with the idea of "witness" "in" a "case"; it fits with the cognate words and principle of the Sixth Amendment, which is about "witnesses" *at trial* (there is no right to confront grand jury witnesses or those who give investigators pretrial statements that are never introduced at trial); it meshes tolerably with the wording of Article III; and it draws support from American history. *See infra* text at notes 205–21. Overall, this is more than other readings of *case* can do, especially when unsupported by a clear and coherent theory of the overall meaning and purpose of the self-incrimination clause.

202. Kastigar v. United States, 406 U.S. 441 (1972).

203. New York v. Quarles, 467 U.S. 649, 660–74 (1984) (O'Connor, J., concurring in part and dissenting in part), *discussed supra* text at notes 88–94, 116–17.

204. Murphy v. Waterfront Commn., 378 U.S. 52 (1964), *discussed supra* text at notes 64–68.

205. *See* New York *ex rel.* Hackley v. Kelly, 24 N.Y. 74 (1861); *infra* note 210 (citing cases). Early manuals for justices of the peace also stressed testimonial immunity for pretrial examinations, which were routine. A Georgia manual announced: "No man shall be compelled to give evidence against himself. Hence it is that if a criminal be sworn to his examination taken before a justice, it shall not be *read* against him." Augustin S. Clayton, *The Office and Duty of a Justice of the Peace* 132 (Milledgeville, Ga., S. Grantland 1819) (emphasis added).

206. New York *ex rel.* Hackley v. Kelly, 24 N.Y. 74 (1861). Early federal cases shed little light on the scope of the privilege. The most often cited is the opinion of Chief Justice Marshall in United States v. Burr, 25 F. Cas. 38 (C.C.D. Va. 1807) (No. 14,692e). In Aaron Burr's trial for high treason, the prosecution sought to examine Burr's secretary, a Mr. Willie, about whether he understood a letter in code. Willie objected, claiming his Fifth Amendment privilege and suggesting that he feared prosecution for misprision of treason. After hearing argument on the point for two days, the Chief Justice required Willie to answer, on the somewhat flimsy basis that the question only referred to current knowledge of the code, and current knowl-

edge would not justify an inference that Willie knew the code at the time the letter was sent. 25 F. Cas. at 40. Marshall went on to state a general rule that "the court ought never to compel a witness to give an answer which discloses a fact that would form a necessary and essential part of a crime which is punishable by the laws." 25 F. Cas. at 40. United States v. Burr was quoted at length in Counselman v. Hitchcock, 142 U.S. 547, 565–66 (1892), but the case does not support the *Counselman*, or even the *Kastigar*, position. There were no immunity statutes at the time, and so Marshall's opinion does not concern the scope of immunity. Anything Willie said in Burr's trial could be repeated against him at Willie's subsequent trial. If Willie's testimony were considered self-incriminating, compelling him to testify in Burr's case would have been tantamount to compelling him to testify against himself in his own case. Thus, in Marshall's era, the key question was not the scope of immunity but the definition of *self-incriminating*. Marshall's broad language does not apply to a world where a witness can be given testimonial immunity. (Interestingly, Marshall's holding is far narrower than his language. Willie was compelled to answer after all. Marshall's definition of *self-incriminating* could be quite narrow in practice.)

The later merging of the rule against coerced confessions and the privilege against self-incrimination makes Marshall's language all the more obsolete. *See infra* note 221. When a coerced confession occurred, the *words* were excluded from the defendant's trial but the *fruits* came in.

207. 24 N.Y. at 84. The New York Constitution of 1846 tracked the federal Fifth Amendment virtually word for word. *See* N.Y. Const. art. I, §6 (1846) (amended 1938, 1949, 1959, and 1973) ("No person . . . shall . . . be compelled in any criminal case, to be a witness against himself . . . ").

208. 24 N.Y. at 83–84 (emphasis added).

209. 24 N.Y. at 83–84.

210. For federal cases upholding such statutes, see, for example, United States v. McCarthy, 18 F. 87, 89 (C.C.S.D.N.Y. 1883) (relying on *Kelly* for proper interpretation of the privilege and scope of immunity) and *In re* Counselman, 44 F. 268 (C.C.N.D. Ill. 1890), *revd sub nom.* Counselman v. Hitchcock, 142 U.S. 547 (1892). The *Counselman* court held: "If, through threats or fears of violence, a man confesses that he has committed murder, and states who was present at the time, and where the weapon and the dead body may be found, and he is afterwards put on his trial for the offense, he cannot be confronted with his confession; but the person who saw the crime committed is a competent witness, although the prosecutor might never have known there was such a witness but for the confession, and it may be shown by others that the weapon and dead body were found where the defendant said they could be found." 44 F. at 271. For state cases, see, for example, *Ex parte* Rowe, 7 Cal. 184 (1857) (upholding a testimonial immunity statute); Higdon v. Heard, 14 Ga. 255, 259 (1853) (holding that immunity satisfies the federal constitutional privilege if the answers given by witnesses "cannot be read in evidence against them, in any criminal case whatever"); Bedgood v. State, 17 N.E. 621, 623–24 (Ind. 1888) (holding that a testimonial immunity statute fully guarantees the privilege); Wilkins v. Malone, 14 Ind. 153, 156–57 (1860) (holding that facts revealed by immunized testimony may be proved against the witness in his later criminal trial, "although the confessions are wholly inadmissible," and that even if the fruit comes in, so long as the testimony is excluded, "the party cannot be said, in any just sense, 'to be compelled to testify against himself' in the criminal prosecution"); *Ex parte* Buskett, 17 S.W. 753, 754–55 (Mo. 1891) (relying on *Kelly* and holding that a witness is not protected from the introduction of the fruits of immunized testimony); Lathrop v. Clapp, 40 N.Y. 328, 332 (1864) (approving a testimonial immunity statute after *Kelly*); LaFontaine v. Southern Underwriters Assn., 83 N.C. 132, 141–43 (1880) (relying on and quoting *Lathrop*).

211. Not all federal immunity statutes were as clear as the Act of 1862, discussed *infra* text at notes 215–18. For a list of the relevant statutes, see J. A. C. Grant, *Immunity from Compulsory Self-Incrimination in a Federal System of Government*, 9 Temp. L.Q. 57, 64 n. 47 (1934).

212. Act of Jan. 21, 1857, ch. 19, §2, 11 Stat. 155, 156.

213. Cong. Globe, 34th Cong., 3d Sess. 437 (1857); *cf.* United States v. North, 920 F.2d 940 (D.C. Cir. 1990) (allowing the escape of Oliver North after his congressional testimony).

214. *See* Cong. Globe, 37th Cong., 2d Sess. 364, 428–29 (1862).

215. Act of Jan. 24, 1862, ch. 11, 12 Stat. 333.

216. Grant, *supra* note 211, at 64.

217. Cong. Globe, 37th Cong., 2d Sess. 429 (1862).

218. *See* Akhil Reed Amar, *The Bill of Rights and the Fourteenth Amendment*, 101 Yale L.J. 1193 (1992). On the "feedback effect" of the Fourteenth Amendment on a proper understanding of the original Bill of Rights and its limits on federal power, see *id.* at 1281–82.

219. *See* Langbein, *supra* note 1.

220. *See id.* at 1055.

221. Note that under this chapter's proposed regime, in which truthful answers are required under threat of punishment but (testimonial) immunity is automatically granted, immunity statutes are technically unnecessary. The privilege becomes self-executing; compelled self-incriminating statements are automatically excluded from the person's own criminal trial. The privilege thus operates exactly like the common law rule excluding coerced confessions. So why were immunity statutes thought to be necessary in the mid-nineteenth century? Because, formally, the rule against coerced confessions and the privilege against compelled self-incrimination were distinct legal doctrines. *See supra* text at note 167. Coerced confessions made outside the courtroom were automatically excluded from one's own criminal case, but testimony within courtrooms was not. Before immunity statutes, therefore, courts had no way to threaten courtroom witnesses with punishment if they did not answer and still preserve the privilege. (The trial of Aaron Burr illustrated the difficulties of trying to get self-incriminating testimony from a witness in the pre–immunity statute era. Indeed, Chief Justice Marshall strained the definition of non-self-incriminating testimony to get Willie's testimony in. *See supra* note 206.) But *Miranda* merged the two doctrines. After the merger, any compelled self-incriminating statement, whether made inside or outside a courtroom, would automatically trigger immunity, without the need to invoke immunity statutes. (A finding that the statement had been compelled—formally or informally—would of course still be necessary.) Courts have been unwilling to recognize this logic under the regimes of transactional and use-fruits immunity because those immunities are so broad, so they have clung to the requirement of immunity statutes. But with testimonial immunity, practice can be reconciled with theory.

222. 8 Wigmore, *supra* note 134, §2283, at 527 and n. 6.

223. 107 Mass. 172, 182 (1871). *Emery* explained that because the Massachusetts Constitution forbade that one "be compelled to accuse, or *furnish evidence* against himself," 107 Mass. at 180 (emphasis added), the privilege was broader in Massachusetts than in New York and protected a witness "so long as he remains liable to prosecution criminally for any matters or causes in respect of which he shall be examined or to which his testimony shall relate." 107 Mass. at 185. The case thus required transactional immunity.

224. The highest court of New Hampshire followed *Emery* in State v. Nowell, 58 N.H. 314, 314 (1878), which required transactional immunity. The court noted that the New Hampshire constitution provided that no one "shall . . . be compelled to

accuse or *furnish evidence* against himself." 58 N.H. at 314 (quoting N.H. Const. art. I, §15 (emphasis added)). In addition, the New Hampshire immunity statute was very broad; it provided that "no testimony . . . given by [the witness] shall, in any prosecution, be used as evidence, either directly or indirectly, against him, nor shall he be thereafter prosecuted for any offence so disclosed by him." 58 N.H. at 315.

225. The Virginia Supreme Court required transactional immunity in Cullen v. Commonwealth, 65 Va. 624, 633 (1873). The Virginia Bill of Rights stated that no one could "be compelled to give evidence against himself." Va. Const. art. I, §8. In any event, *Cullen* was questioned by a member of the court in Temple v. Commonwealth, 75 Va. 892, 902 (1881).

226. *See* Counselman v. Hitchcock, 142 U.S. 547, 586 (1892). The Court noted the differences in the wordings of the federal and Massachusetts constitutional provisions but stated that "there is really, in spirit and principle, no distinction arising out of such difference of language." 142 U.S. at 586.

227. Ironically, New York's highest court repudiated *Kelly* as a result of the *Counselman* decision. *See* People v. O'Brien, 176 N.Y. 253 (1903) (requiring transactional immunity and explicitly following *Counselman*).

228. Boyd v. United States, 116 U.S. 616 (1886).

229. *Id.* at 633 (emphasis added).

230. *Id.* at 637 (stating that the subpoena in this case "is surely compelling [the defendant] to *furnish evidence* against himself" (emphasis added)).

231. 468 U.S. 897, 905–6 (1984) (citing *Boyd's* Fourth-Fifth Amendment fusion progeny).

232. 425 U.S. 391, 408 (1976) ("[T]he Fifth Amendment does not independently proscribe the compelled production of every sort of incriminating evidence but applies only when the accused is compelled to make a *testimonial* communication that is incriminating").

233. *Leon*, 468 U.S. at 906 ("The Fifth Amendment theory has not withstood critical analysis or the test of time. . . ."); *Fisher*, 425 U.S. at 407 ("Several of *Boyd's* express or implicit declarations have not stood the test of time.").

234. Schmerber v. California, 384 U.S. 757 (1966).

235. 168 Eng. Rep. 234 (K.B. 1783).

236. *Id.* at 234.

237. The Crown witness system was a major force leading to the rule against coerced confessions. John H. Langbein, *Shaping the Eighteenth-Century Criminal Trial: A View from the Ryder Sources*, 50 U. Chi. L. Rev. 1, 105 (1983). Under this system, witnesses were granted immunity from prosecution if they testified against their partners in crime. If several gang members tried to become Crown witnesses, the one who could reveal the most was granted immunity. This led to contests between gang members to tell all—and more than all. Incentives to lie were great, because the crimes involved usually carried the death penalty. If a suspect tried and failed to become a Crown witness, his confession could and would be used against him. Thus the exclusionary rule for tainted confessions was born of a concern for reliability.

238. 168 Eng. Rep. at 235 (footnote omitted). The court emphasized: "The rules of evidence which respect the admission of facts, and those which prevail with respect to the rejection of parol declarations or confessions, are distinct and independent of each other." 168 Eng. Rep. at 235. In America, it was hornbook law as late as 1960 that courts would *not* exclude the fruits of coerced confessions. *See* 2 Francis Wharton, *Wharton's Criminal Evidence* §§357–58 (Ronald A. Anderson ed., 12th ed. 1955); 3 Wigmore, *supra* note 134, §§856–59; Yale Kamisar, Wolf *and* Lustig *Ten Years Later: Illegal Evidence in State and Federal Courts*, 43 Minn. L. Rev. 1083, 1115 n. 109 (1959). In fact, I am aware of no U.S. Supreme Court case—before or after 1960— that actually excludes physical fruits of a coerced confession that occurred outside

formal proceedings. *Miranda* does contain an ambiguous sentence about fruits, *see* 384 U.S. 436, 479 (1966) (speaking of "evidence obtained as a result of interrogation"), but that sentence has since been repudiated. *See supra* text at notes 85–94. *But cf.* Wong Sun v. United States, 371 U.S. 471, 484–88 (1963) (excluding, on *Fourth* Amendment grounds, physical evidence as fruit of illegal arrest).

239. 168 Eng. Rep. at 235.

240. *Id.* at 234 (emphasis added). Note the court's explicit and emphatic rejection of a broad noninstrumentalization theory.

241. 121 Eng. Rep. 589 (Q.B. 1861).

242. *Id.* at 593 (Crompton, J.). Contemporaneous American cases explicitly following the same logic in the self-incrimination/testimonial immunity context include Wilkins v. Malone, 14 Ind. 153, 156–57 (1860) and *In re* Counselman, 44 F. 268, 271 (1890), *revd sub nom.* Counselman v. Hitchcock, 142 U.S. 547 (1892).

243. 121 Eng. Rep. at 592–93 (Crompton, J.); *see also id.* at 594 (Blackburn, J.) ("[A]n enactment that nothing, the first clue to which was given by a witness under examination by the Commissioners, should be provable against him by evidence aliunde, would have been very unwise; would have encouraged rather than checked the corrupt practices which the Act seeks to put a stop to; and would have introduced excessive practical inconvenience. . . .").

For further statements of the English rule of testimonial immunity, see Commonwealth v. Knapp, 26 Mass. (9 Pick.) 495, 510–11 (1830) and 1 J. F. Archbold, *Practice, Pleading, and Evidence in Criminal Cases* 424 (Thomas W. Waterman ed., 7th ed. 1860).

244. 487 U.S. 533, 536–44 (1988). The Canadians have a well-developed inevitable discovery doctrine and draw sharp distinctions between physical evidence and testimony for purposes of exclusion. *See* R. v. Collins, [1987] 1 S.C.R. 265, 284 (Can.) (Lamer, J.) ("Real evidence that was obtained in a manner that violated the *Charter* [constitutional protections against self-incrimination, unreasonable search and seizure, and so on] will rarely operate unfairly for that reason alone. The real evidence existed irrespective of the violation of the *Charter* and its use does not render the trial unfair."); Mellenthin v. Regina, [1992] 3 S.C.R. 615 (Can.) (drawing a distinction between real evidence that the defendant has been forced to *create* by constitutional infringement and real evidence that the defendant has been forced to *locate* or *identify* by constitutional infringement, and also distinguishing between independently existing evidence that *could* have been found without compelled testimony and independently existing evidence that *would* have been found without compelled testimony); Black v. Regina [1989] 2 S.C.R. 138 (Can.) (holding that physical evidence obtained as a direct result of a statement taken in violation of a defendant's right against self-incrimination is admissible where the evidence would have been uncovered by the police in any event). The author of a leading Canadian treatise has noted the "overwhelming tendency of our courts to characterize any tangible evidence such as weapons or drugs as real evidence not going to the fairness of the trial and hence, under the *Collins* regime, generally admissible." Don Stuart, Charter Justice in Canadian Criminal Law 401 (1991). He does cite a few exceptions, however, mainly in cases where the constitutional violation was "flagrant." *Id.* at 406–7, 414.

245. Schmerber v. California, 384 U.S. 757 (1966).

246. A sensible definition is found in Justice Thomas's concurrence, joined by Justice Scalia, in White v. Illinois, 502 U.S. 346, 358 (1992). This definition includes "any witness who actually testifies at trial" and anyone who gives "extrajudicial statements . . . contained in formalized testimonial materials, such as affidavits, depositions, prior testimony, or confessions." 502 U.S. at 365 (Thomas, J., concurring). The extension to extrajudicial statements prepared for trial is analogous to the

self-incrimination clause's application to out-of-court compulsion. *See supra* note 55. Obviously, the government should not be able to evade a defendant's right to confront government witnesses by recessing a trial, walking across the street and deposing a witness without the defendant or his lawyer present, and then returning to court and introducing into evidence a transcript and videotape of the deposition. *Cf. id.* For much more discussion *see infra* Chapter 3, text at notes 165–97.

247. *Compare* U.S. Const. amend. V *with* Mass. Const. pt. I, art. XII (1780) ("furnish evidence against himself") *and* Pa. Const. art. I, §9 (1776) ("give evidence against himself"). Several other state constitutions use the phrase *give evidence. See* 8 Wigmore, *supra* note 134, §2252, at 321–24 n. 3. Wigmore thought that these differences were "immaterial" and that "[t]hese various phrasings have a common conception, in respect to the *form* of the protected disclosure." 8 *id.* §2263, at 362. However, Wigmore thought that New York's *Kelly* case should be the uniform rule. 8 *id.* §2283, at 525–28.

248. Fisher v. United States, 425 U.S. 391 (1976), *discussed supra* notes 123–24 and accompanying text.

249. Under testimonial immunity, the subpoenaed object could be used at trial but not the testimonial fact that defendant supplied the object. This clean rule contrasts dramatically with the *Kastigar* regime, under which the proper scope of "act of production" immunity is a huge unsolved—and perhaps metaphysically insoluble—puzzle. To get a sense of the *Kastigar* complexities here, see Kenneth J. Melilli, *Act-of-Production Immunity*, 52 Ohio St. L.J. 223 (1991); Reitz, *supra* note 145, at 618–27.

250. In the lineup case of United States v. Wade, 388 U.S. 218 (1967), Justice Fortas articulated a rationale that sounds like a Fourth Amendment, not a Fifth Amendment, interpretation: the lineup was "an incident of the State's power to arrest, and a reasonable and justifiable aspect of the State's custody resulting from arrest." 388 U.S. at 260 (Fortas, J., concurring).

251. *See supra* Chapter 1, text at notes 154–95.

252. If the defendant refuses to comply, there are several options available. Depending on the circumstances, the defendant could either be held in contempt or evidence of the refusal could be introduced at trial. *See* South Dakota v. Neville, 459 U.S. 553 (1983). There, the Court held that "a refusal to take a blood-alcohol test, after a police officer has lawfully requested it, is not an act coerced by the officer, and thus is not protected by the privilege against self-incrimination." 459 U.S. at 564. Moreover, the officer was not required to give warnings that evidence of refusal might be introduced at trial. 459 U.S. at 566.

253. *Compare* Rochin v. California, 342 U.S. 165 (1952) (invalidating stomach pumping) *with* Schmerber v. California, 384 U.S. 757 (1966) (upholding the taking of blood). *See also* Winston v. Lee, 470 U.S. 753 (1985) (disallowing unnecessary surgery).

254. *See supra* Chapter 1, text at notes 177–80; *see also* Taylor, *supra* note 97, at 66–68; Eric Schnapper, *Unreasonable Searches and Seizures of Papers,* 71 Va. L. Rev. 869 (1985).

255. *Cf.* Fisher v. United States, 425 U.S. 391, 401 n. 7 (1976) (noting "[s]pecial problems of privacy which might be presented by subpoena of a personal diary").

256. *See* Henry E. Smith, *Two Reliability Rationales for the Privilege Against Self-Incrimination* (Mar. 1995) (unpublished manuscript) (proposing "communicative" reliability rationale based on concern about risk of misunderstanding, and applying rationale to case of diaries).

257. *See supra* text at notes 123–24.

258. *Cf.* Friendly, *supra* note 55, at 712 n. 176 (observing that physical leads are often more important to law enforcement than getting statements for use in court). Because of huge leaps in technology, physical evidence can yield far more reliable

information today than at the Founding. This enhanced reliability only strengthens the wisdom of respecting the testimony-fruits distinction established as early as 1783. *See supra* text at notes 235–40. "Fruit" here of course also encompasses reliable third-party testimony.

259. I shall return to this theme in Chapters 3 and 4.

260. 4 Blackstone, *supra* note 8, at *357. Blackstone, always influential, is particularly important in this context because of the paucity of legislative history concerning the self-incrimination clause at the ratification of the Bill of Rights. He retained an enormous legal influence at the time the Fourteenth Amendment was ratified. Note how Blackstone's emphasis on reliability parallels the analysis in the 1783 case of The King v. Warickshall, 168 Eng. Rep. 234 (K.B. 1783), discussed *supra* text at notes 235–40. *See also* Barlow, *supra* note 134, at 189 (claiming that using "the Rack or Torture to compel Criminals to accuse themselves" is not only "cruel" but "at the same Time uncertain, as being rather Trials of the Strength and Hardiness of the Sufferer, than any Proof of the Truth"), *quoted in* Langbein, *supra* note 1, at 1085 n. 157.

261. Friendly, *supra* note 89, at 281–82.

262. Compare Blackstone's suggestion that statements from the defendant's own lips have a peculiarly devastating impact. *See supra* text at note 260.

263. Gideon v. Wainwright, 372 U.S. 335 (1963) (establishing the right of indigent defendants in noncapital cases to have the assistance of appointed counsel). *Gideon* is discussed in greater detail *infra* Chapter 3, text at notes 224–27.

264. Wilson v. United States, 149 U.S. 60, 66 (1893) (emphasis added). Note how these concerns are not present in the typical case where the government secretly wiretaps a suspect in his home and later introduces his words—his "testimony"—in open court against his will. Although noninstrumentalists might have a hard time distinguishing between using a defendant on the stand and using him in a wiretap, *see supra* note 141, a reliability approach shows why these two cases are different.

265. Nor are reliability concerns always cured by a physical corroboration test, because many confessions may concern internal mental states, where misunderstandings are quite likely. In short, physical evidence can at best partially rather than fully corroborate a statement. To the extent the physical evidence partially corroborates, it can be introduced itself. To introduce the confession in addition risks introduction of unreliable and uncorroborated aspects of the confession—say, about the defendant's mens rea. Perhaps, however, the trier of fact could be told merely that "something defendant said" led the police to the victim's body, the stolen goods, or what have you. On the other hand, this paraphrase looks rather like defendant witnessing—it is an account of defendant's own words—and, as with all paraphrases, introduces reliability concerns of its own.

266. Thus the self-incrimination clause strongly harmonizes with the doctrine of corpus delicti. Both sharply distinguish, on reliability grounds, between a suspect's self-accusatory words on the one hand, and reliable physical fruit and third-party witnesses' reliable testimony on the other.

267. Thought crimes have not been confined to the eighteenth century. Persecution of thought crimes, especially political crimes, has continued to generate praise for a right to remain silent. The anti-Communist hearings and trials of the 1950s, for instance, provoked fervent defenses of the privilege, most notably from Erwin Griswold. *See* Griswold, *supra* note 29. For a more general discussion of how the Fourth and Fifth Amendments have been pressed into the service of First Amendment values, see Stuntz, *supra* note 100.

268. To fully protect mere "thought criminals," we need to supplement the Fifth Amendment with an absolute privilege of associational privacy for purely

political and religious confederates, lest a person be compelled to divulge the identity of his thoughtmates who could then be forced to testify against him. *Cf.* Shelton v. Tucker, 364 U.S. 479 (1960) (holding that states cannot compel teachers to disclose their associational ties because to do so deprives teachers of their right to associational freedom); NAACP v. Alabama, 357 U.S. 449 (1958) (holding that a political association may assert its members' constitutional right not to be compelled to disclose their affiliation with the association). In the absence of this absolute privilege, testimonial immunity could not protect a political or religious group very well. But neither could *Counselman* or *Kastigar:* one person with immunity could be obliged to furnish a list of members, and to testify against all the members on the list, members who in turn might scramble to cut deals with the government to rat on one another.

    269. New York v. Quarles, 467 U.S. 649 (1984).

    270. Rhode Island v. Innis, 446 U.S. 291 (1980).

    271. Baltimore City Dept. of Social Servs. v. Bouknight, 493 U.S. 549 (1990).

    272. Brewer v. Williams, 430 U.S. 387 (1977).

    273. *Quarles,* 467 U.S. at 663–64 (O'Connor, J., concurring in part and dissenting in part).

    274. Eben Moglen quotes a Boston pamphlet from 1769 attacking *ex officio* oaths as inviting customs commissioners in Vice Admiralty courts to harass their political opponents with vexatious, impertinent, and groundless questions such as "Pray Sir, when did you kiss your maid Mary?—Where? and in what manner? . . . Did you lay with her in a barn? or in your house?" Moglen, *supra* note 163, at 1116. On the obviously gendered nature of this example and of privacy discourse generally, *see supra* Chapter 1, text at notes 185–86.

    275. Schmerber v. California, 384 U.S. 757 (1966).

    276. Kastigar v. United States, 406 U.S. 441 (1972).

    277. Murphy v. Waterfront Commn., 378 U.S. 52 (1964).

    278. Counselman v. Hitchcock, 142 U.S. 547 (1892).

    279. New York v. Quarles, 467 U.S. 649, 660–74 (1984) (O'Connor, J., concurring in part and dissenting in part).

    280. Boyd v. United States, 116 U.S. 616 (1886).

    281. *See supra* Chapter 1, text at notes 102–30. For a long list of cases documenting that the so-called Fourth Amendment exclusionary rule was really a joint Fourth-Fifth affair, under a theory that the Court has now rightly discredited, *see infra* Chapter 4, note 28.

3. Sixth Amendment First Principles

    1. I say "generally" because, as we shall see, the Sixth Amendment also protects other values, such as popular sovereignty and republican political participation—values that in general complement rather than contradict innocence protection and truth-seeking.

    2. Consider, for example, the *Winship* due process principle, which requires proof beyond reasonable doubt in criminal cases. *See In re* Winship, 397 U.S. 358, 362–64 (1970). Though the rule will have the incidental statistical effect of freeing some guilty defendants, the purpose of the rule is obviously to protect the *innocent* defendant from *erroneous* conviction. Although many accused persons are indeed guilty, we cannot know which ones before reliable Sixth Amendment trials have occurred. A person who is, at the time of the crime, factually and normatively guilty is legally presumed innocent until proved and found guilty; and until then, the guilty defendant incidentally benefits from Sixth Amendment rules designed to protect innocent defendants from erroneous convictions.

3. At times, guilty defendants should enjoy less freedom than do innocent ones. As we shall see, a guilty defendant should at times be less free to try to demolish a truthful witness via cross-examination, than would an innocent defendant facing a lying witness. So, too, when it comes to remedies, the guilty may at times recover less than the innocent because, as we shall see, the guilty may have suffered less constitutionally cognizable legal injury. For example, if guilty *A* endures one month of unlawful pretrial detention, but upon conviction gets a one-month sentencing discount for time served, *A* has suffered less cognizable injury than innocent *B* who endures the same unlawful pretrial detention and is then acquitted.

4. A more general discussion of the upside-down effect appears in Chapter 4.

5. At other times, however, the Supreme Court has rejected and even inverted this premise. *See infra* text at notes 95–97.

6. *See supra* Chapter 1, text at note 157.

7. *See id.* text at notes 2, 44, 158.

8. It is often argued that no exclusionary rule windfall exists because if the government had never violated the Fourth Amendment, it never would have gotten the evidence in the first place. Thus (the argument goes), the exclusionary rule creates no windfall but simply restores the status quo ante. This argument is slick, but wrong. It ignores what I have called the "causation gap"—in many situations the government would have ultimately found the evidence or some substitute even if no constitutional violation ever occurred. *See id.* text at notes 136–37. For more discussion *see generally infra* Chapter 4.

9. *See, e.g.,* Kastigar v. United States, 406 U.S. 441 (1972).

10. *See supra* Chapter 2, text at notes 5–17.

11. *See* Strunk v. United States, 412 U.S. 434, 440 (1973); Barker v. Wingo, 407 U.S. 514, 522 (1972).

12. *See* U.S. Const. amend. V ("[N]or shall any person be subject for the same offence to be twice put in jeopardy of life or limb . . . ."). *See generally* Akhil Reed Amar and Jonathan Marcus, *Double Jeopardy Law After Rodney King,* 95 Colum. L. Rev. 1 (1995). A plain-meaning reading of the double jeopardy clause, however, must be supplemented by basic due process principles prohibiting vexatious or innocence-threatening multiple prosecutions generally. *See id.* at 28–38.

13. *See, e.g.,* Maryland v. Craig, 497 U.S. 836, 849 (1990); Ohio v. Roberts, 448 U.S. 56, 63 (1980).

14. The maxim *expressio unius est exclusio alterius* means that the expression of one thing by implication excludes other things.

15. U.S. Const. art. III, §2, cl. 3.

16. If the accused pleads guilty, there is, strictly speaking, nothing to *try,* and no *trial. See* Akhil Reed Amar, *The Bill of Rights as a Constitution,* 100 Yale L.J. 1131, 1199 and n. 301 (1991).

17. *Contra* Patton v. United States, 281 U.S. 276 (1930). For discussion and criticism of *Patton,* see Amar, *supra* note 16, at 1196–99.

18. *See* U.S. Const. amend. IX ("The enumeration in the Constitution, of certain rights, shall not be construed to deny or disparage others retained by the people").

19. For a similar invocation of the Ninth Amendment to affirm the people's right to a public trial, and to rebut an *expressio unius* reading of the Sixth Amendment reference to a right of "the accused," see Richmond Newspapers, Inc. v. Virginia, 448 U.S. 555, 579 n. 15 (1980) (plurality opinion).

20. A clever textualist might note implicit textual support from the juxtaposition of the confrontation clause, which speaks of "*the* witnesses" for the prosecution, and the compulsory process clause, which speaks only of the defendant's right to subpoena "witnesses"—not "*the* witnesses"—he plans to present. This juxtaposition implicitly points to the existence of *other* witnesses—presumably nonsubpoe-

naed—that the defendant might want to put on. But even this juxtaposition does not explicitly make clear that the defendant has a constitutional, as opposed to a possible statutory or common law, right to put on witnesses who volunteer.

21. *See* U.S. Const. amend. V ("No person shall be . . . deprived of life, liberty, or property, without due process of law . . . "); *see also id.* amend. XIV, §1 ("[N]or shall any State deprive any person of life, liberty, or property, without due process of law . . . ").

22. Monaco v. Mississippi, 292 U.S. 313, 322 (1934).

23. Griswold v. Connecticut, 381 U.S. 479, 484 (1965).

24. *See* United States v. Ewell, 383 U.S. 116, 120 (1966); Smith v. Hooey, 393 U.S. 374, 378 (1969); United States v. Marion, 404 U.S. 307, 320 (1971); Barker v. Wingo, 407 U.S. 514, 532 (1972); United States v. Loud Hawk, 474 U.S. 302, 312 (1986); Doggett v. United States, 505 U.S. 647, 654 (1992).

25. *Marion,* 404 U.S. at 320.

26. *Id.* at 313–21.

27. *See* United States v. MacDonald, 456 U.S. 1, 6–9 (1982); *Loud Hawk,* 474 U.S. at 310–12.

28. *See Ewell,* 383 U.S. at 122; *Marion,* 404 U.S. at 322–25; United States v. Lovasco, 431 U.S. 783, 789 (1977).

29. *Barker,* 407 U.S. at 522.

30. Strunk v. United States, 412 U.S. 434, 439–40 (1973); *Barker,* 407 U.S. at 522.

31. Though I disagree with his analysis at key points in what follows, I have greatly profited from Anthony G. Amsterdam, *Speedy Criminal Trial: Rights and Remedies,* 27 Stan. L. Rev. 525 (1975).

32. This assumes that Andy does not, for example, knowingly and intelligently waive his speedy trial rights by asking for a postponement to better prepare his defense. The precise *cardinal* figure here—one month—is arbitrary, and used merely for illustrative simplicity. As we shall see, my point focuses on the *ordinal* relation between this number and later numbers in our hypothetical.

33. The speedy trial legal interest in avoiding unduly long pretrial detention will not have been violated because Andy will have spent only the allowable one month in jail. And the speedy trial legal interest in avoiding undue anxiety and loss of reputation because of an extended accusation will not have been violated so long as the "accusation period" is less than one year. This is the lesson of Bill's case. (This assumes, for illustrative simplicity, that pretrial jail time does not exacerbate the reputation damage caused by criminal accusation simpliciter. If we suspend this assumption, the precise math changes, but not my basic point. Assume for example that one month in jail is, in terms of *damage to reputation,* equivalent to two months of mere (undetained) accusation. If so, then when Andy is released from jail on day 30, our prosecutor would have only ten rather than eleven more months of accusation left.)

34. This last assumption is made here only for illustrative simplicity. Later I shall explore this assumption and analyze situations where it does not hold.

35. *See* United States v. MacDonald, 435 U.S. 850, 861 (1978) ("It is the delay before trial, not the trial itself, that offends against the constitutional guarantee of a speedy trial. . . . Proceeding with the trial does not cause or compound the deprivation already suffered.").

36. *See* United States v. Marion, 404 U.S. 307, 320 (1971) ("[T]he major evils protected against by the speedy trial guarantee exist quite apart from actual or possible prejudice to an accused's defense.").

37. *See* Barker v. Wingo, 407 U.S. 514, 533 (1972) ("Imposing those consequences [of pretrial detention] on anyone who has not yet been convicted is serious. It is especially unfortunate to impose them on those persons who are ultimately found to be innocent.").

38. *See infra* text at notes 74–93.

39. Again, I introduce this assumption here only for ease of exposition. Later, we shall examine this assumption more carefully.

40. *See supra* note 35.

41. *See* United States v. MacDonald, 456 U.S. 1, 6–9 (1982); United States v. Loud Hawk, 474 U.S. 302, 310–12 (1986); *see also* United States v. Marion, 404 U.S. 307, 320 (1971). As the *MacDonald* Court noted, Congress, in enacting the Speedy Trial Act of 1974, likewise believed that dropping an indictment would toll the amendment. *See MacDonald*, 456 U.S. at 7 n. 7. According to *MacDonald*, a person whose indictment has been dropped, with leave to refile, is in no different position than one who has never been indicted, but who has come under suspicion and is the subject of an ongoing (and perhaps highly publicized) "investigation." *See id.* at 8–9. Since the speedy trial clock doesn't run preaccusation, neither should it run in nonaccusation intervals, according to *MacDonald*. *See id.* at 7. (Even if this view were rejected, the speedy trial clock could be deemed to run—but more slowly—during nonaccusation intervals: preaccusation months don't count, accusation months count fully, and nonaccusation-interval months could count somewhere in between on the theory that the first indictment creates special stigma not wholly dissipated by dismissal.)

42. Suppose instead that Bill's indictment had stretched out seventeen years rather than seventeen months. In this case we should still compare Bill's suit to a comparably situated Cindy who was indicted for the first time seventeen years after the crime. If the case against Cindy would be barred by the applicable statute of limitation, so might the case against Bill. Pending indictments typically toll applicable statutes of limitation. *See, e.g.,* Klopfer v. North Carolina, 386 U.S. 213, 214 (1967); *cf.* Dickey v. Florida, 398 U.S. 30, 32 n. 3 (1969) (arrest warrant). But this tolling rule should arguably not apply to any period of *unconstitutional* indictment—any period after one year in Bill's case. Indeed, after one year, Bill should arguably have a right to treat the indictment as constitutionally lapsed, and to insist on a new indictment. This would ensure a rough contemporaneousness of judgment of the grand and petit juries—the two panels of the people who must both pass judgment against a federal defendant before any conviction can occur. This analysis may help explain both the result and some of the language of Justice Souter's opinion for the Court in Doggett v. United States, 505 U.S. 647 (1992), a drug case where more than eight years lapsed between indictment and arrest. Despite a powerful dissent from Justice Thomas distinguishing statute of limitations concerns from speedy trial clause concerns, *id.* at 667–71 (Thomas, J., dissenting), the Court's interpretation of the clause was influenced by concerns about evidentiary staleness. *Id.* at 654–56 (opinion of the Court). The relevant statute of limitations for the underlying offense was five years. *See* United States v. Doggett, 906 F.2d 573, 583 (11th Cir. 1990) (Clark, J., dissenting) (same case).

Justice Souter's opinion draws some support from *Dickey*, 398 U.S. 30, but *Dickey* was decided prior to *Marion, MacDonald,* and *Loud Hawk,* and some of its language and logic do not survive those cases. *See, e.g., Dickey*, 398 U.S. at 37–38 (apparently linking Sixth Amendment to delay between *crime* and trial); *id.* at 40 (Brennan, J., concurring) (noting that Court leaves open issue of prearrest delay).

43. *See Marion*, 404 U.S. at 320.

44. *See Klopfer*, 386 U.S. at 216 (holding that unconstitutional delay denies accused "an opportunity to exonerate himself").

45. *Cf.* 3 William Blackstone, Commentaries *125 ("[I]f the defendant be able to justify, and prove the words to be true, no action will lie, even though special damage hath ensued: for then it is no slander or false tale.").

46. *See supra* note 42. Unlike most of the Bill of Rights, the Fifth Amendment requirement that serious criminal prosecutions be preceded by a grand jury indict-

ment has not been "incorporated" against states via the Fourteenth Amendment. *See* Beck v. Washington, 369 U.S. 541, 545 (1962); Hurtado v. California, 110 U.S. 516, 538 (1884). For criticism of this, see Akhil Reed Amar, *The Bill of Rights and the Fourteenth Amendment*, 101 Yale L.J. 1193, 1218–43, 1263–64 (1992).

47. *See* United States v. Marion, 404 U.S. 307, 313–21 (1971); United States v. MacDonald, 456 U.S. 1, 6–9 (1982); United States v. Loud Hawk, 474 U.S. 302, 310–12 (1986).

48. *See* Doggett v. United States, 505 U.S. 647, 662–63 (1992) (Thomas, J., dissenting) (asserting that speedy trial clause meant only to protect defendant from oppressive incarceration or anxiety of known criminal charges caused by accusation, not prejudice to defense caused by passage of time). *But see id.* at 654–55 (opinion of the Court, per Souter, J.) (asserting that speedy trial inquiry must weigh effect of delay on accused's defense). *Cf. supra* note 42 (suggesting a better way—between Thomas and Souter—to analyze the problem posed by *Doggett*).

49. For a very similar analysis, see United States v. Ewell, 383 U.S. 116, 122 (1966).

50. *See Ewell*, 383 U.S. at 122; *Marion*, 404 U.S. at 322–25; United States v. Lovasco, 431 U.S. 783, 789 (1977).

51. *In re* Winship, 397 U.S. 358, 362–64 (1970).

52. *See* United States v. Loud Hawk, 474 U.S. 302, 315 (1986) (holding that possibility of prejudice due to delay not sufficient to support speedy trial claim; passage of time may make it "difficult or impossible" for government to prove case beyond reasonable doubt).

53. What's more, as a practical matter, the extreme nature of the dismissal remedy often leads judges to strain to deny, on the facts of the case at hand, that the Sixth Amendment was indeed violated. These strained denials undermine the values of the clause, as articulated in propositions (1)–(6). *See* Amsterdam, *supra* note 31, at 539–43. For a possible example in the case law, see *Loud Hawk*, 474 U.S. at 317. Twice calling attention to the severity of dismissal, *id.* at 314, 317, the Court glossed over troubling delay created by the Ninth Circuit's egregious and unexplained foot-dragging in processing interlocutory appeals. *See id.* at 324–25 (Marshall, J., dissenting). *But see id.* at 325 n. 8 (noting that, on the facts of the case, defendants perhaps invited delay and thus might deserve to lose).

54. If the damage is not irreversible, then other remedies may undo the damage and make a fair trial possible. Such remedies might include, for example, court-appointed special detectives to help find lost evidence, and continuances at Andy's request to put together those parts of his defense that incarceration impeded.

55. In addition to Andy's independent remedies for illegal detention simpliciter, see *supra* text at note 38.

56. This might also be the best response to government-created impediments that may not be independently unconstitutional, as when a defendant charged with crime *A* is already lawfully serving time for a separate crime *B*, perhaps even in another jurisdiction. (The latter situation also raises nice questions of dual sovereignty.) The wrinkles raised by these permutations lie beyond the scope of this chapter. In the case law, see Dickey v. Florida, 398 U.S. 30 (1970); Smith v. Hooey, 393 U.S. 374 (1969). On dual sovereignty generally, see Amar and Marcus, *supra* note 12, at 4–27.

57. Dismissal could be granted either before or after trial. In unclear cases, holding the trial will enable the judge to better gauge precisely how much the delay has impaired an adequate defense. *See* United States v. MacDonald, 435 U.S. 850, 858–59 (1978).

58. For another example of curable injury created by overlong accusation, suppose that Bill can show that during the last five months of his accusation period—the

five unconstitutional months—he lost his job because of the extra stigma caused by overlong public accusation, and now he can no longer afford his high-priced defense lawyer. Bill has indeed suffered an accusation-based injury that has created a risk of trial unfairness, but dismissal with prejudice is hardly the only possible remedy. Direct payment of Bill's high-priced lawyer by the government itself would—for *fair trial* purposes—put Bill in the same position he would have been in had the government dropped the indictment for the last five months or tried Bill five months earlier.

59. *See supra* notes 42, 46, *infra* note 71.

60. *See* United States v. Lovasco, 431 U.S. 783, 795–96 (1977) (holding that investigative delay, as opposed to bad-faith tactical delay, not due process violation even if defense somewhat prejudiced by time lapse); United States v. Marion, 404 U.S. 307, 324 (1971) (holding that due process clause might require dismissal of indictment if shown at trial that preindictment delay caused substantial prejudice to fair trial rights and delay was intentional device to gain tactical advantage).

61. It is possible to imagine an interesting variant of due process dismissal in the context of an outrageous search and seizure, a variant that might be seen as an "inverse exclusionary rule." Suppose the government is planning to introduce Exhibit A against Cindy, but knows that Cindy will counter with Item B, which will dramatically undercut or neutralize A's impact. Suppose that the cops illegally and outrageously break into Cindy's house, find B, seize it, and destroy it. Beyond Cindy's obvious compensatory and punitive Fourth Amendment tort remedies, Cindy has a great due process, fair-trial, innocence-protection argument that the government's Exhibit A should be excluded from the trial. But this *inverse* exclusionary rule differs from its standard Fourth Amendment evil twin in key ways. It excludes Exhibit A, rather than Item B—the thing actually seized. Most important, it excludes A because government conduct has rendered A presumptively unreliable (if A was really so accurate, why did the government destroy B?); the standard exclusionary rule excludes evidence of the highest reliability and probative value. Inverse exclusion is designed to protect the innocent because of their innocence; standard exclusion is designed to protect the guilty defendant as such. For a case whose logic might support inverse exclusion as a response to malicious destruction of evidence, see Arizona v. Youngblood, 488 U.S. 51, 56–59 (1988) (finding no due process violation in absence of bad-faith destruction of evidence).

62. For a statutory case reflecting many of the same intuitions and ideas, *see* United States v. Montalvo-Murillo, 495 U.S. 711 (1990) (pretrial release is a remedially inapt and disproportionate response to governmental failure to hold prompt pretrial detention hearing).

63. *Marion*, 404 U.S. at 314–15. A contrary argument would concede that of course the amendment in one sense does not apply unless and until one becomes "accused": an unaccused person has no right to demand immediate arrest or indictment. But once one becomes "accused," the argument goes, one can retroactively insist that the speedy trial clock started ticking when the crime occurred. This is textually possible, but strained. No other clause in the amendment sensibly applies "retroactively," and there is next to no historical support in the Founding era for this textual and temporal somersault.

64. *Id.* at 313–14.

65. *See* Edward Coke, *The Second Part of the Institutes of the Laws of England* 43 (Brooke, 5th ed. 1797) ("[Justices] have not suffered the prisoner to be long *detained*, but at their next comming have given the *prisoner* full and *speedy* justice, . . . without *detaining him long in prison*.") (emphasis added); Habeas Corpus Act of 1679, 31 Car. 2, ch. 2. For more on the act, *see infra* text at notes 74–76.

66. U.S. Const. amend. VIII ("Excessive bail shall not be required . . . "). The protections of the Eighth Amendment, of course, in no way eliminate the need for

the independent safeguards of the Sixth. Not all offenses are bailable—several capital crimes, for example, were historically not subject to bail. *See, e.g.,* 4 Blackstone, *supra* note 45, at *298–99. Even nonexcessive bail might be set at high levels in the event of a high objective risk of flight, and many defendants might not be able to post such high bail.

67. *See* U.S. Const. amend. V ("No person shall be held to answer for a capital, or otherwise infamous crime, unless on a presentment or indictment of a Grand Jury.").

68. U.S. Const. amend. IV (affirming Americans' right to "be secure in their persons, houses, papers, and effects, against unreasonable searches and seizures" and mandating that warrants particularly describe "the persons or things to be seized").

69. U.S. Const. amend. V ("[N]or shall any person be subject for the same offence to be twice put in jeopardy of life or limb . . . "). A critic of plain-meaning textualism in constitutional criminal procedure might try to make hay of this double jeopardy phrase. Surely, the argument goes, the clause must apply to all serious criminal charges, even if death and dismemberment are not authorized punishments. I agree that a strict *expressio unius* reading of "life or limb" would be obtuse. But I also suggest that a plain-meaning approach to the clause would read the phrase as a term of art, a grimly poetic synecdoche for all serious punishment. There is, I submit, a big difference between plain-meaning textualism and tin ear textualism. *See Ex parte* Lange, 85 U.S. (18 Wall.) 163, 170–73 (1873) (reading phrase to encompass all punishment, even misdemeanors); People v. Goodwin, 18 Johns. 187, 201 (N.Y. Sup. Ct. 1820) (reading phrase as metaphor for felonies); Joel P. Bishop, *Commentaries on the Criminal Law* 543 (1856) (similar). *But see* United States v. Gibert, 25 F. Cas. 1287 (C.C.D. Mass. 1834) (No. 15,204) (Story, Circuit J.) (offering narrow reading).

70. *See, e.g.,* 3 Blackstone, *supra* note 45, at *123.

71. Three situations suggest themselves. First, the clause must prevent extended pretrial detention that would itself materially impede the incarcerated defendant's ability to assemble his defense. *See supra* text at notes 54–57. Likewise, the clause must prevent extended accusations that may ostracize and impoverish the accused in civil society, and thus undermine his ability to pay for his defense. *See supra* note 58. Finally, the clause might plausibly be read to demand that after a certain time period a grand jury indictment necessarily lapses. *See supra* note 42. This would ensure that the two public verdicts rendered by two different panels of the people—the grand jury and the petit jury—are roughly contemporaneous. The textual proximity of the Fifth Amendment grand jury clause and the Sixth Amendment petit jury clause, with the speedy trial clause somewhere in between, is perhaps suggestive of a desired temporal proximity of the two juries' verdicts. Temporal proximity would help safeguard innocence by limiting the ability of prosecutors to forum shop over time. (Imagine a prosecutor who cajoles a single, unusually proprosecutor grand jury to issue stacks of indictments, and then stockpiles these—perhaps without even making them public, to avoid triggering any reputation interest—until unusually proprosecutor petit venires materialize from time to time.)

72. In many cases, however, long delay may be wholly justifiable. The crime may not come to light for many years; or the government, despite due diligence, may not have sufficient evidence early on to warrant prosecution; or prosecutors may hold back to avoid compromising ongoing investigations; or . . . In many of these cases, defendants may gain more from delay than they lose, given that evidentiary staleness can create reasonable doubts that must, under *Winship*, be resolved against the government. *See* United States v. Loud Hawk, 474 U.S. 302, 315 (1986). A constitutional superstatute of limitations rooted in due process should bar prosecutions only in cases where prosecutors manipulate timing solely for tactical advantage or to vex defendants, and leave the rest to *Winship*.

73. In the speedy trial clause case law, see Barker v. Wingo, 407 U.S. 514, 521 and n. 15 (1972); United States v. Ewell, 383 U.S. 116, 120 (1966). *See also* Powell v. Alabama, 287 U.S. 45, 71 (1932) (holding that "failure of the trial court to give [defendants] reasonable time and opportunity to secure counsel was a clear denial of due process"); Peter Westen, *The Compulsory Process Clause*, 73 Mich. L. Rev. 71, 109 (1974) (arguing that trying a defendant "before he can call witnesses violates the right of compulsory process").

74. Habeas Corpus Act of 1679, 31 Car. 2, ch. 2.

75. *See* Amar, *supra* note 46, at 1205.

76. U.S. Const. art. I, §9, cl. 2 ("The privilege of the Writ of Habeas Corpus shall not be suspended, unless when in Cases of Rebellion or Invasion the public Safety may require it."). On the uniqueness of this clause as an explicit statement about remedies in the Constitution, see Alfred Hill, *Constitutional Remedies*, 69 Colum. L. Rev. 1109, 1118 n. 42 (1969).

77. A complementary and more modern scheme of prevention—an administrative law "translation" of the common law habeas scheme—would feature a regulatory framework statute like the federal Speedy Trial Act, 18 U.S.C. §§3161–74 (1994), laying down parameters for reasonable case management. For a discussion of the importance of such regulatory regimes, see John C. Godbold, *Speedy Trial: Major Surgery For a National Ill*, 24 Ala. L. Rev. 265 (1972). *Cf. supra* Chapter 1, text at notes 221–23 (discussing need for similar legislative and administrative regimes in Fourth Amendment context).

Though my focus is on constitutional doctrine, this focus must not obscure the hugely important role that framework statutes, like the Speedy Trial Act, have played and must continue to play.

78. Bivens v. Six Unknown Named Agents of the Fed. Bureau of Narcotics, 403 U.S. 388, 390–97 (1971).

79. *See* United States v. Place, 462 U.S. 696, 707–10 (1983); Money v. Leach, 19 Howell's State Trials 1001, 1026 (K.B. 1765) (Mansfield, C.J.); *supra* Chapter 1, text at notes 67, 182.

80. *See* Boyd v. United States, 116 U.S. 616, 634–35 (1886).

81. *See, e.g.,* Weeks v. United States, 232 U.S. 383 (1914); Silverthorne Lumber Co. v. United States, 251 U.S. 385 (1920); Gouled v. United States, 255 U.S. 298 (1921); Amos v. United States, 255 U.S. 313 (1921); Agnello v. United States, 269 U.S. 20 (1925). *See generally* Osmond K. Fraenkel, *Recent Developments in the Law of Search and Seizure*, 13 Minn. L. Rev. 1, 4–5 and nn. 48–52 (1928) (citing cases from five states declining to apply *Weeks* rule to contraband). For a long list of Supreme Court cases, spanning almost a century, showing that exclusion rested on Fourth-Fifth fusion, *see infra* Chapter 4, note 28.

82. *See* United States v. Leon, 468 U.S. 897, 905–6 (1984); Fisher v. United States, 425 U.S. 391, 407 (1976).

83. 1 342 U.S. 519, 522 (1952). Though decided prior to the era of general "incorporation" of the Bill of Rights against the states, *Frisbie* was authored by the Court's leading proponent of total incorporation and contains no language suggesting that federal kidnapping would somehow be different from the state kidnapping at issue in *Frisbie*.

84. *See also* INS v. Lopez-Mendoza, 468 U.S. 1032, 1039 (1984) ("The 'body'. . . of a defendant . . . is never itself suppressible as a fruit of an unlawful arrest."); United States v. Crews, 445 U.S. 463, 474 (1980) (opinion of the Court, per Brennan, J.) ("An illegal arrest, without more, has never been viewed as a bar to subsequent prosecution, nor as a defense to a valid conviction. . . . Respondent is not himself a suppressible 'fruit.'"); Gerstein v. Pugh, 420 U.S. 103, 119 (1975) (reiterating "established rule that illegal arrest or detention does not void a subsequent con-

viction"). All of these cases cite *Frisbie*. *Cf.* United States v. Blue, 384 U.S. 251, 255 (1966) ("[The exclusionary rule] does not extend to barring the prosecution altogether. So drastic a step . . . would also increase to an intolerable degree interference with the public interest in having the guilty brought to book.").

85. On the unsuitability of mandamus to solve all speedy trial problems, see Note, *Dismissal of the Indictment as a Remedy for Denial of the Right to Speedy Trial,* 64 Yale L.J. 1208, 1209 n. 9 (1955).

86. Bivens v. Six Unknown Named Agents of the Fed. Bureau of Narcotics, 403 U.S. 388, 390–97 (1971).

87. *See* Akhil Reed Amar, *Of Sovereignty and Federalism,* 96 Yale L.J. 1425, 1466–92 (1987).

88. *See supra* Chapter 1, text at notes 196–211.

89. For a general discussion of this remedial vision, see Amar, *supra* note 87, at 1484–95.

90. *See* Marbury v. Madison, 5 U.S. (1 Cranch) 137, 163 (1803) (quoting 3 Blackstone, *supra* note 45, at *23, *109):

> The very essence of civil liberty certainly consists in the right of every individual to claim the protection of the laws, whenever he receives an injury. One of the first duties of government is to afford that protection. . . .
>
> . . . .
>
> "[I]t is a general and indisputable rule, that where there is a legal right, there is also a legal remedy by suit or action at law, whenever that right is invaded." . . . "[E]very right, when withheld, must have a remedy, and every injury its proper redress."
>
> The government of the United States has been emphatically termed a government of laws, and not of men. It will certainly cease to deserve this high appellation, if the laws furnish no remedy for the violation of a vested legal right.

91. This *Bivens*-like remedial regime might sensibly borrow from administrative law as well as the common law. *Cf. supra* note 77. (For a similar suggestion of administrative law remedies for Fourth Amendment violations, see Chapter 1, text at notes 221–22.) A workers' compensation–like formula for determining damages could significantly lower adjudicatory transaction costs. Note also that further transactional economies exist because: (1) defendant and the government are already parties before a court that (2) is already supposed to be attending to the effect of time on the case and (3) the defendant already has legal counsel (by court appointment in a case of indigence). Thus, instead of pursuing *Bivens*-like remedies in collateral civil proceedings, perhaps defendants should be allowed to bring their claims in a kind of contempt proceeding pendent to the criminal prosecution itself.

92. *See, e.g.,* 18 U.S.C. §3585(b) (1994) (authorizing set-offs for pretrial detention in federal cases).

93. *See* Amsterdam, *supra* note 31, at 535–36 n. 81 (arguing that trial judges may inflate sentence to offset reductions for pretrial confinement). *But see* Recent Case, 108 U. Pa. L. Rev. 414, 422 n. 59 (1960) (authored by Anthony Amsterdam) (arguing that sentence reduction may be appropriate remedy).

94. If an acquitted Billy Jo barely wins acquittal—with a trial that suggests that she is probably guilty, but not beyond reasonable doubt—she may receive lower damages than if she wins acquittal by a mile. Analytically, her damages should be measured by the *difference* in her reputation pre- and posttrial, and by the length of the unconstitutional delay. The more innocent the trial shows her to be, the more she wrongly suffered by unconstitutional trial delay.

95. United States v. Jacobsen, 466 U.S. 109 (1984); United States v. Place, 462 U.S. 696 (1983).

96. *See Jacobsen,* 466 U.S. at 122–24; *Place,* 462 U.S. at 706–7.

97. *See Jacobsen,* 466 U.S. at 122–23 and nn. 22–23 (testing to determine whether substance is cocaine "does not compromise any legitimate interest in privacy"). *See generally* Arnold H. Loewy, *The Fourth Amendment as a Device for Protecting the Innocent,* 81 Mich. L. Rev. 1229 (1983) (generalizing the insight).

98. If, pretrial, it is unclear whether a trial itself would be unduly unreliable because of pretrial detention, a judge could hold the trial. At trial, the amount of unreliability caused by delay should be much easier to measure than it was to estimate pretrial; and the judge could grant a proper motion to dismiss during or at the end of the trial itself. *See* United States v. MacDonald, 435 U.S. 850, 858–59 (1978) (recommending this approach).

99. *In re* Winship, 397 U.S. 358, 362–64 (1970) (requiring proof beyond reasonable doubt in criminal cases).

100. In one context, a defendant can be tried after conviction: If his conviction is overturned because of government-induced error, he generally may be tried again. It's tempting to claim that retrial is allowed because a defendant waives his double jeopardy claim when he takes an appeal, but this will not wash. The system *forces* the defendant to "waive" this objection as a condition of allowing his appeal in the first place—an appeal that seeks to undo a *government-induced* error. The true logic allowing retrial is that a government acting in good faith should be allowed one fair trial, with a chance to prove guilt and win a conviction that will stick. *See* Peter Westen and Richard Drubel, *Toward a General Theory of Double Jeopardy,* 1978 Sup. Ct. Rev. 81, 102–6, 125–28. To vindicate that interest we force some defendants to run the traumatic trial gauntlet twice, through no fault or real choice of their own. *A fortiori,* the government should be allowed to try Bill once, even if it has already erroneously subjected him to an overlong and traumatic accusation period.

In asserting the contrary, the Court's wooden and conclusory opinion in *Strunk* failed to ponder the implications of double jeopardy doctrine for highly analogous speedy trial issues. *See* Strunk v. United States, 412 U.S. 434, 438–39 (1973). Doctrinally, the *Strunk* Court could have applied the lesson of double jeopardy law not via "waiver" doctrine but by holding that some delays between indictment and trial are, for *fair trial* purposes, "harmless error." *See* Chapman v. California, 386 U.S. 18, 22 (1967) (discussing various constitutional errors that may not require automatic reversal); Dickey v. Florida, 398 U.S. 30, 55 (1970) (Brennan, J., concurring) (noting possible relevance of *Chapman* to speedy trial issue). For an approach directly at odds with *Strunk,* see United States v. Ewell, 383 U.S. 116, 121 (1966): "[This Double Jeopardy rule] has been thought wise because it protects the societal interest in trying people accused of crime, rather than granting them immunization because of legal error at a previous trial, and because it enhances the probability that appellate courts will be vigilant to strike down previous convictions that are tainted with reversible error. . . . These policies, so carefully preserved in this Court's interpretation of the Double Jeopardy Clause [should not be] seriously undercut by the interpretation given the Speedy Trial Clause. . . ." This *Ewell* passage was quoted in its entirety and heavily relied on in the post-*Strunk* case of United States v. Loud Hawk, 474 U.S. 302, 313 (1986). *Strunk,* by contrast, wrongly "grant[ed] immunization because of legal error at a previous [stage]." *Ewell,* 383 U.S. at 121; *cf.* Pollard v. United States, 352 U.S. 354, 362 (1957) ("Error in the course of a prosecution resulting in conviction calls for the correction of the error, not the release of the accused.").

101. Although the Court has at times denied that collateral estoppel is rooted in due process rather than the double jeopardy clause, the *logic* of the leading collat-

eral estoppel case, Ashe v. Swenson, 397 U.S. 436 (1970), belies this denial. *See* Amar and Marcus, *supra* note 12, at 30–31.

102. For more analysis, see Amar and Marcus, *supra* note 12, at 30–38.

103. *Strunk,* 412 U.S. at 440; Barker v. Wingo, 407 U.S. 514, 522 (1972).

104. *Barker,* 407 U.S. at 522 (quoted *supra* text at note 29); United States v. Blue, 384 U.S. 251, 255 (1966) (quoted *supra* note 84).

105. *See* Frisbie v. Collins, 342 U.S. 519, 522 (1952); *see also supra* note 84.

106. *See* Kastigar v. United States, 406 U.S. 441, 453–62 (1972) (excluding fruits of immunized testimony).

107. *See generally* Yale Kamisar, *On the "Fruits" of Miranda Violations, Coerced Confessions, and Compelled Testimony,* 93 Mich. L. Rev. 929 (1995) (championing these exclusionary rules).

108. Massiah v. United States, 377 U.S. 201, 207 (1964) (excluding reliable recitation of defendant's uncoerced statements). The *Massiah* Court thought the Sixth Amendment right of counsel was somehow implicated by the facts at hand, but it is hard to see how. *See id.* at 209 (White, J., dissenting) ("Massiah was not prevented from consulting with counsel as often as he wished. No meetings with counsel were disturbed or spied upon.").

109. There are, of course, important counterexamples—such as the work of Tony Amsterdam, John Jeffries, Dan Meltzer, and Mike Seidman. *See, e.g.,* Amsterdam, *supra* note 31; John C. Jeffries, Jr., *Damages for Constitutional Violations: The Relation of Risk to Injury in Constitutional Torts,* 75 Va. L. Rev. 1461 (1989); Daniel J. Meltzer, *Deterring Constitutional Violations by Law Enforcement Officials: Plaintiffs and Defendants as Private Attorneys General,* 88 Colum. L. Rev. 247 (1988); Silas J. Wasserstrom and Louis M. Seidman, *The Fourth Amendment as Constitutional Theory,* 77 Geo. L.J. 19 (1988).

110. *See generally* Philip Bobbitt, *Constitutional Fate* (1982); Richard H. Fallon, Jr., *A Constructivist Coherence Theory of Constitutional Interpretation,* 100 Harv. L. Rev. 1189 (1987).

111. *See* Bivens v. Six Unknown Named Agents of the Fed. Bureau of Narcotics, 403 U.S. 388 (1971); *Ex parte* Young, 209 U.S. 123 (1908).

112. *See* U.S. Const. amend. V ("[N]or shall private property be taken for public use, without just compensation . . . "). The phrase "liability rights," of course, comes from the classic analysis of Guido Calabresi and A. Douglas Melamed, *Property Rules, Liability Rules, and Inalienability: One View of the Cathedral,* 85 Harv. L. Rev. 1089 (1972). For important refinements, see Jules L. Coleman and Jody Kraus, *Rethinking the Theory of Legal Rights,* 95 Yale L.J. 1335 (1986).

113. This qualification, I submit, is the root idea underlying various cases and doctrines. *See, e.g.,* Lockhart v. Fretwell, 506 U.S. 364, 372 (1993) (unavailability of ineffective assistance of counsel claim when lawyer's mistake does not result in fundamentally unfair or unreliable trial); McCleskey v. Zant, 499 U.S. 467, 494 (1991) (actual innocence and miscarriage of justice exceptions to abuse of the writ doctrine in habeas); Teague v. Lane, 489 U.S. 288, 313 (1989) (exception to rule of nonretroactivity in habeas for new rules "without which the likelihood of an accurate conviction is seriously diminished"); Murray v. Carrier, 477 U.S. 478, 495–96 (1986) (actual innocence and miscarriage of justice exceptions to procedural default in habeas); United States v. Bagley, 473 U.S. 667, 678 (1985) (material omission standard for prosecutorial nondisclosure); Stone v. Powell, 428 U.S. 465, 494 (1976) (unavailability of habeas to review exclusionary rule error); Chapman v. California, 386 U.S. 18, 22 (1967) (harmless error).

114. In a case where the only criminal penalty is a fine, isn't dismissal with prejudice similar to damages: an after-the-fact financial boon (here, via a fine not charged) for a pretrial loss of liberty or reputation? The difference, of course, is that

an explicit damage scheme can be expressly tailored (via compensatory damages) to the precise legal injury caused in the past and (via punitive damages) to the precise need for future deterrence. Like the exclusionary rule, dismissal almost never achieves the right measure of compensation and deterrence, and if it does so, it is only by the wildest of coincidences—like a real-life Inspector Clousseau who always stumbles onto his man. I return to this theme in Chapter 4.

115. *See* Coleman and Kraus, *supra* note 112 (analyzing legal rights underlying liability rules).

116. *See supra* Chapter 1, text at notes 213–14.

117. Barker v. Wingo, 407 U.S. 514, 519 (1972).

118. *In re* Oliver, 333 U.S. 257, 266 (1948); Gannett Co. v. DePasquale, 443 U.S. 368, 414, 420–21 (1979) (Blackmun, J., concurring in part and dissenting in part). *See also infra* note 121 and sources cited therein.

119. 3 Joseph Story, *Commentaries on the Constitution of the United States* §1785, at 662 (1833) (emphasis added).

120. *See supra* note 16.

121. In his influential *Institutes*, Sir Edward Coke declared that the very word *court* implied public access: "[A]ll Causes ought to be heard, ordered, and determined before the judges of the kings courts openly in the kings courts, *wither all persons may resort;* and in no chambers, or other private places: for the judges are not judges of chambers, but of courts, and therefore in open court." Coke, *supra* note 65, at 103. (emphasis added); *see also* Richmond Newspapers, Inc. v. Virginia, 448 U.S. 555, 566–67 (1980) (plurality opinion) ("'[O]ne of the most conspicuous features of English justice, that all judicial trials are held in open court, to which the public have free access, . . . appears to have been the rule in England from time immemorial.'") (quoting Edward Jenks, *The Book of English Law* 73–74 (6th ed. 1967)); *id.* at 597 (Brennan, J., concurring in judgment) (noting that "public access is an indispensable element of the trial process itself"); *id.* at 599 (Stewart, J., concurring in judgment) ("With us, a trial is by very definition a proceeding open to the press and to the public."); *Oliver*, 333 U.S. at 267 n. 14 ("'By immemorial usage, wherever the common law prevails, all trials are in open court, to which spectators are admitted.'") (quoting 2 Joel P. Bishop, *New Criminal Procedure* §957 (2d ed. 1913)); Craig v. Harney, 331 U.S. 367, 374 (1947) ("A trial is a public event."); Bridges v. California, 314 U.S. 252, 271 (1941) ("The very word 'trial' connotes decisions on the evidence and arguments properly advanced in open court.").

To be sure, at some point the general innocence-protecting principles of the due process clause and the Sixth Amendment will influence the precise mode in which a trial must be public. At some extreme point, a trial that is too speedy could become a farce, and so too, a trial that is too public could become a circus. *See* Moore v. Dempsey, 261 U.S. 86, 91 (1923) (holding that verdict "produced by mob demonstration" is contrary to due process of law); *cf.* Estes v. Texas, 381 U.S. 532, 545–50 (1965) (enumerating situations in which televising trial might prejudice proceedings). For a particularly tart description of the circus problem, and the suggestion that the newspaper media can typically represent the public in the courtroom itself, see Max Radin, *The Right to a Public Trial*, 6 Temp. L.Q. 381 (1932).

122. *See* U.S. Const. amends. I, II, IV, IX, X.

123. *See generally* Akhil Reed Amar, *The Central Meaning of Republican Government: Popular Sovereignty, Majority Rule, and the Denominator Problem*, 65 U. Colo. L. Rev. 749 (1994).

124. Gannett Co. v. DePasquale, 443 U.S. 368, 428–29 (1979) (Blackmun, J., concurring in part and dissenting in part).

125. Matthew Hale, *The History of the Common Law of England* 344 (6th ed. 1820).

126. 3 Blackstone, *supra* note 45, at *372. Though this passage occurs in the context of a discussion of evidence law in civil cases, Blackstone elsewhere makes clear that the same principles apply to criminal cases. *See* 4 *id.* at *350.

127. *See In re* Oliver, 333 U.S. 257, 270 (1948) ("The knowledge that every criminal trial is subject to contemporaneous review in the forum of public opinion is an effective restraint on possible abuse of judicial power.").

128. *See* 6 John H. Wigmore, Evidence §1834 (J. Chadbourn rev. ed. 1976); *Gannett Co.,* 443 U.S. at 383; *id.* at 427 (Blackmun, J., concurring in part and dissenting in part); *Oliver,* 333 U.S. at 270 n. 24.

129. Sir John Hawles, *Remarks upon Mr. Cornish's Trial, in* 11 Howell's State Trials 455, 460 (London, Hansand 1811).

130. 3 Blackstone, *supra* note 45, at *373. For very similar language, see Hale, *supra* note 125, at 345.

131. *See* Richmond Newspapers, Inc. v. Virginia, 448 U.S. 555, 571–72 (1980) (plurality opinion) (discussing how public trial can promote "public acceptance of both the [judicial] process and its results" and "confidence in the fair administration of justice") (quoting State v. Schmit, 139 N.W.2d 800, 807 (Minn. 1966)); *id.* at 595 (Brennan, J., concurring in the judgment) ("Public access is essential, therefore, if trial adjudication is to achieve the objective of maintaining public confidence in the administration of justice."); *Gannett Co.,* 443 U.S. at 429, 448 (Blackmun, J., concurring in part and dissenting in part) (similar).

132. Charles Nesson, *The Evidence or the Event? On Judicial Proof and the Acceptability of Verdicts,* 98 Harv. L. Rev. 1357, 1367 n. 31 (1985).

133. *See* Amar, *supra* note 16, at 1183.

134. *See* U.S. Const. art. III, §2, cl. 3 ("The Trial of all Crimes, except in Cases of Impeachment, shall be by Jury . . . ").

135. *See* U.S. Const. amend. V (grand jury); *id.* amend. VI (petit jury); *id.* amend. VII (civil jury).

136. In light of my extensive discussion of juries in the Appendix, I shall devote less space in this chapter to the jury than its intrinsic importance would otherwise dictate.

137. Letter from Thomas Jefferson to David Humphreys (Mar. 18, 1789), *reprinted in The Papers of Thomas Jefferson,* 1788–89, at 676, 678 (Julian P. Boyd ed., 1958) [hereinafter *The Papers of Thomas Jefferson*].

138. U.S. Const. art. III, §2, cl. 3 (emphasis added).

139. *See* Insurance Co. v. Morse, 87 U.S. (20 Wall.) 445, 451 (1874) (stating that criminal defendant must be tried by jury); Thompson v. Utah, 170 U.S. 343, 353–54 (1898) (holding that criminal defendant must be tried by court and twelve-person jury); *cf.* Schick v. United States, 195 U.S. 65, 67 (1904) (allowing defendant to waive right to jury in case involving petty offense, which Court found was not covered by Article III mandate); *see also* Callan v. Wilson, 127 U.S. 540, 549 (1888) (noting that Sixth Amendment was not "intended to supplant" Article III mandate).

140. *See* Patton v. United States, 281 U.S. 276, 299 (1930), *criticized in* Amar, *supra* note 16, at 1196–99.

141. Of course, just as the Senate may act without the House in some areas—treaties, confirmations, expelling its own members, and so on—so a judge may act without a jury in some areas, such as accepting guilty pleas, setting bail, and sentencing.

142. *Letters from the Federal Farmer (IV), in* 2 *The Complete Anti-Federalist* 249–50 (Herbert J. Storing ed., 1981) [hereinafter *The Complete Anti-Federalist*].

143. *Essays by a Farmer (IV), in* 5 *id.* at 38.

144. Letter from Thomas Jefferson to L'Abbe Arnoux (July 19, 1789), *reprinted in* 15 *The Papers of Thomas Jefferson, supra* note 137, at 282–83.

145. *Id.*

146. *See generally The Federalist No. 84* (Alexander Hamilton).

147. *The Federalist No. 83,* at 500–501 (Alexander Hamilton) (Clinton Rossiter ed., 1961).

148. *Letters from the Federal Farmer (IV), in* 2 *The Complete Anti-Federalist, supra* note 142, at 250.

149. *See generally* Vikram D. Amar, *Jury Service as Political Participation Akin to Voting,* 80 Cornell L. Rev. 203 (1995) [hereinafter Vikram D. Amar, *Jury Service*].

150. Alexis de Tocqueville, *Democracy in America* 273, 728 (Jacob P. Mayer ed., 1969).

151. *See* U.S. Const. amend. XV (race); *id.* amend. XIX (sex); *id.* amend. XXIV (class); *id.* amend. XXVI (age). *See generally* Vikram D. Amar, *Jury Service, supra* note 149.

152. *See* Powers v. Ohio, 499 U.S. 400, 406–9 (1991) (striking down prosecutorial race-based peremptories in a criminal case); Edmonson v. Leesville Concrete Co., 500 U.S. 614, 616, 625–26 (1991) (striking down race-based peremptories in a civil case); Georgia v. McCollum, 505 U.S. 42, 59 (1992) (striking down defendant's race-based peremptories in a criminal case). Nor are such limits on peremptories any violation of an accused's right to an *impartial* jury. Surely the trial judge and appellate panel—the upper house in our bicameral judiciary—should also be impartial, yet defendants have never enjoyed a constitutional right of peremptory challenge against judges. And so the Supreme Court has repeatedly and correctly held that peremptory challenges are in no way required by the idea of impartiality. *See, e.g.,* Stilson v. United States, 250 U.S. 583, 586 (1919); Swain v. Alabama, 380 U.S. 202, 219 (1965); Batson v. Kentucky, 476 U.S. 79, 91 (1986); *McCollum,* 505 U.S. at 57.

153. *See* Westen and Drubel, *supra* note 100, at 124–34.

154. *See id.* at 124–32, 133 and n. 241; Peter Westen, *The Three Faces of Double Jeopardy: Reflections on Government Appeals of Criminal Sentences,* 78 Mich. L. Rev. 1001, 1012–25, 1033–34 and n. 99 (1980); *see also* Gregg v. Georgia, 428 U.S. 153, 199 n. 50 (1976) (plurality opinion) (linking Sixth Amendment and double jeopardy clause). For further documentation, see Amar and Marcus, *supra* note 12, at 57–58 and n. 279.

155. U.S. Const. amend. VII ("[A]nd no fact tried by a jury, shall be otherwise re-examined in any Court of the United States, than according to the rules of the common law."); *see* Ian Ayres, *Pregnant with Embarrassments: An Incomplete Theory of the Seventh Amendment,* 26 Val. U. L. Rev. 385, 401 (1991).

156. *See* Amar, *supra* note 16, at 1193.

157. *See* Georgia v. Brailsford, 3 U.S. (3 Dall.) 1, 4 (1794).

158. *See* Edith G. Henderson, *The Background of the Seventh Amendment,* 80 Harv. L. Rev. 289, 299–320 (1966); Renée B. Lettow, *New Trial For a Verdict Against Law: Judge-Jury Relations in Early Nineteenth-Century America,* 71 Notre Dame L. Rev. 505 (1996).

159. *See supra* note 155.

160. For historical support for this vision, see, e.g., *Letters from the Federal Farmer (IV), in* 2 *The Complete Anti-Federalist, supra* note 142, at 249 (linking vicinage to ease of assembling oral evidence and "cross examining witnesses" thereby leading "to the proper discovery of truth"); 2 *Debates on the Adoption of the Federal Constitution* 110 (Jonathan Elliot ed., 1888) [hereinafter Elliot's *Debates*] (remarks of Mr. Holmes in Massachusetts ratifying convention) (stating that the "local situation" of jury from the place of the crime would better enable them to "judge of the *credibility* of the witnesses"); *see also* William W. Blume, *The Place of Trial of Criminal Cases: Constitutional Vicinage and Venue,* 43 Mich. L. Rev. 59, 64–65 (1944) (quoting May 16 and 17, 1769 Virginia Resolves linking venue and vicinage ideas to concerns about "speedy Justice," pretrial detention, and fair trials; transporting an American defendant overseas

for trial in England would prolong and harshen his detention—keeping him in "Fetters amongst Strangers" in a "distant land [with] no Friend, no Relation [to] alleviate his Distresses" and "no Witness[es] . . . to testify [to] his Innocence").

161. *See* 3 Elliot's Debates, *supra* note 160, at 547 (remarks of Edmund Pendleton at Virginia ratifying convention). But Article III, Section 2—which, as we have seen, dovetails with the Sixth Amendment—does speak of venue (the place of the trial) rather than vicinage (the place from whence the jurors come): "The trial of all Crimes . . . shall be held in the State where the said Crimes shall have been committed . . . " *See generally* Drew L. Kershen, *Vicinage,* 30 Okla. L. Rev. 1 (1977).

162. Historically, crime has been considered peculiarly "local" in nature; at the Founding, a court would not enforce the criminal laws of another sovereign even though it would enforce the other sovereign's civil laws. *See* Drew L. Kershen, *Vicinage,* 29 Okla. L. Rev. 801, 811 (1976).

163. *See* Kershen, *supra* note 161, at 79–94. During the late colonial period, Americans strongly objected to the so-called Murderers' Act, passed by Parliament after the Boston Massacre. The act provided "that any government or customs officer indicted for murder [in America] could be tried in England, beyond the control of local juries." John M. Blum et al., *The National Experience* 95 (3d ed. 1973). This circumvention of the judgment of the victimized community was attacked as a "Mock Trial" system in the Declaration of Independence. *See The Declaration of Independence* para. 17 (U.S. 1776). Although English and American juries might differ in their factual findings of whodunit, they were even more likely to disagree about normative issues of excuse, provocation, justification, and self-defense—issues at the heart of the Boston Massacre trials.

Note that in condemning the Murderer's Act, Americans were siding *against* certain defendants. The Sixth Amendment, by contrast, speaks of the rights of "the accused." Thus, the defendant can arguably waive the vicinage rules of the amendment. But of course the defendant generally lacks a constitutional right to demand a different vicinage, unless due process and jury impartiality so require. *See* Amar, *supra* note 16, at 1197. (Query whether the more absolute venue mandate of Article III, quoted *supra* note 161, is also waivable.)

164. To the extent that government illegality might be relevant to the defendant's culpability or to the appropriateness of moral condemnation of his conduct, jurors could decide to take illegality into account in rendering their moral verdict. But this is a scheme of evidentiary inclusion, not exclusion—and one that (by hypothesis) is linked to the defendant's normative culpability. For other proposals to give criminal juries a greater role in monitoring illegal searches and seizures, see Ronald J. Bacigal, *A Case for Jury Determination of Search and Seizure Law,* 15 U. Rich. L. Rev. 791 (1981); George C. Thomas and Barry S. Pollack, *Saving Rights from a Remedy: A Societal View of the Fourth Amendment,* 73 B.U. L. Rev. 147 (1993).

165. *See* 3 Blackstone, *supra* note 45, at *372–73; *see also* 4 *id.* at *356. Blackstone borrowed heavily, it seems, from Hale: "[O]ftentimes witnesses will deliver [in private] that, which they will be ashamed to testify publicly. . . . [M]any times the very MANNER of delivering testimony, will give a probable indication, whether the witness speaks truly or falsely. . . . [Cross-examination] beats and boults out the truth much better, . . . and [is] the best method of searching and sifting out the truth." Hale, *supra* note 125, at 345.

166. *See* Tennessee v. Street, 471 U.S. 409, 415 (1985) (quoting Dutton v. Evans, 400 U.S. 74, 89 (1970) (plurality opinion)); *see also* United States v. Inadi, 475 U.S. 387, 396 (1986) (similar); Idaho v. Wright, 497 U.S. 805, 825 (1990) (similar).

167. California v. Green, 399 U.S. 149, 158 (1970) (quoting 5 John H. Wigmore, *Evidence* §1367); *see also* Kentucky v. Stincer, 482 U.S. 730, 736 (1987) (similar); White v. Illinois, 502 U.S. 346, 356 (1992) (similar); *cf.* Pointer v. Texas, 380

U.S. 400, 404 (1965) ("[P]robably no one . . . would deny the value of cross-examination in exposing falsehood and bringing out the truth in the trial in a criminal case.").

168. *See, e.g.,* Ohio v. Roberts, 448 U.S. 56, 63 (1980).

169. *See id.*

170. *See id.;* Maryland v. Craig, 497 U.S. 836, 849 (1990) (quoting *Roberts* and italicizing and emphasizing "preference").

171. *See, e.g.,* Coolidge v. New Hampshire, 403 U.S. 443, 454–55 (1971); Johnson v. United States, 333 U.S. 10, 13–15 (1948).

172. *See* Blockburger v. United States, 284 U.S. 299, 304 (1932).

173. *See, e.g.,* Illinois v. Vitale, 447 U.S. 410, 420 n. 8 (1980); Brown v. Ohio, 432 U.S. 161, 169 n. 7 (1977); Jeffers v. United States, 432 U.S. 137, 151–52 (1977); Diaz v. United States, 223 U.S. 442, 448–49 (1912).

174. *See, e.g.,* Kastigar v. United States, 406 U.S. 441 (1972).

175. *See, e.g.,* Baltimore City Dep't of Social Servs. v. Bouknight, 493 U.S. 549 (1990); California v. Byers, 402 U.S. 424 (1971); Shapiro v. United States, 335 U.S. 1 (1948).

176. *See generally* Amar and Marcus, *supra* note 12.

177. For a similar approach, see Coy v. Iowa, 487 U.S. 1012, 1020–21 (1988).

178. For a clear example of this error, see Ohio v. Roberts, 448 U.S. 56, 63 (1980). For a discussion of the "truth of the matter asserted" wrinkle, see Tennessee v. Street, 471 U.S. 409 (1985).

179. *See infra* note 190.

180. *See* 1 Story, *supra* note 119, §451, at 436–37.

181. For an exemplary illustration of this interpretive technique, see McCulloch v. Maryland, 17 U.S. (4 Wheat.) 316, 413–15 (1819).

182. *See The Federalist* No. 84, at 510–11 (Alexander Hamilton) (Clinton Rossiter ed., 1961).

183. U.S. Const. art. III, §3, cl. 1.

184. *See* Gannett Co. v. DePasquale, 443 U.S. 368, 437 (1979) (Blackmun, J., concurring in part and dissenting in part).

185. The Constitution itself, for example, refers to and relies on oaths in several key passages. *See* U.S. Const. art. I, §3, cl. 6 (requiring "Oath or Affirmation" when Senate sits as solemn court of impeachment); *id.* art. II, §1, cl. 8 (elaborating presidential oath); *id.* art. VI, cl. 3 (requiring various officers and legislators to take an "Oath or Affirmation" to support the Constitution); *id.* amend. IV (requiring "Oath or affirmation" for search or seizure warrants); *id.* amend. XIV, §3 (disqualifying confederate oath breakers); *see also* Marbury v. Madison, 5 U.S. (1 Cranch.) 137, 180 (1803) (stressing the judicial oath); *McCulloch,* 17 U.S. (4 Wheat.) at 416 (authorizing Congress to add new oaths). For further discussion of the greater weight placed on testimony under oath than on unsworn statements, see Westen, *supra* note 73, at 86–87, 90–91, 100 and n. 122, 111, 147.

186. In Jed Rubenfeld's terminology, our theory "captures" the "paradigm" case—in this case, trial by affidavit. *See* Jed Rubenfeld, *Reading the Constitution as Spoken,* 104 Yale L.J. 1119, 1169–71 (1995).

187. *See* 3 Blackstone, *supra* note 45, at *373 (emphasis added); *see also* Hale, *supra* note 125, at 345.

188. Mattox v. United States, 156 U.S. 237, 242 (1895). Recent quotations of this passage include: Maryland v. Craig, 497 U.S. 836, 845 (1990); Kentucky v. Stincer, 482 U.S. 730, 736–37 (1987); California v. Green, 399 U.S. 149, 157–58 (1970); Barber v. Page, 390 U.S. 719, 721 (1968); Douglas v. Alabama, 380 U.S. 415, 418–19 (1965).

189. Though I disagree with his approach in important respects, I share Professor Westen's views that (1) the key to the confrontation clause is the word *witness;* (2) the confrontation and compulsory process clauses are siblings; (3) an ideal inter-

pretive theory should be able to read *witness* the same way in both clauses; and (4) once the word *witness* is properly read, it *"can* and *should* be taken literally." Peter Westen, *The Future of Confrontation,* 77 Mich. L. Rev. 1185, 1201–2 (1979).

190. As this word implies, a person who sees an underlying out-of-court event is in one ordinary-language sense a "witness"—but surely this alone cannot be the test for the confrontation clause. If she never declares anything, in court or out, she is not a confrontation clause witness even under the Court's test. More generally, even if the government gets a statement from this eyewitness pretrial, so long as her declarations are never alluded to at trial, surely she is not a confrontation clause "witness *against* [the accused]"; the government need not somehow bring her face-to-face with the defendant. *See* McCray v. Illinois, 386 U.S. 300, 313–14 (1967) (holding that confrontation clause does not require that government produce police informant to testify in court for cross-examination by defendant); *Craig,* 497 U.S. at 864–65 (Scalia, J., dissenting) (contending that "witness" refers to one who gives testimony at trial). (Of course, the defendant may well want to subpoena her and use her testimony on the stand under the compulsory process clause, and is free to do so.)

191. *Cf.* Fed. R. Crim. P. 15(a) (providing for defendant-initiated pretrial depositions in "exceptional circumstances"); Abraham S. Goldstein, *The State and the Accused: Balance of Advantage in Criminal Procedure,* 69 Yale L.J. 1149, 1180–92 (1960) (noting various pretrial disparities between government and defendant, but not relying on compulsory process clause); Westen, *supra* note 73, at 128–29 (analyzing same issue through lens of compulsory process clause).

192. For similar reminders, see White v. Illinois, 502 U.S. 346, 355 (1992); United States v. Inadi, 475 U.S. 387, 397–99 and nn. 7, 9 (1986). Obviously, the right to compulsory process must encompass, where appropriate, the right to treat the witness as "hostile," to cross-examine him with leading questions, and even to impeach his testimony: the very notion of *compulsory* process suggests the possibility of an obvious conflict of interest between the witness and the accused. Evidentiary rules that prohibit a defendant from impeaching his "own" witness, *see, e.g.,* Chambers v. Mississippi, 410 U.S. 284, 295–98 (1973), violate the obvious spirit of the compulsory process clause, and basic innocence-protecting and truth-seeking principles to boot. For a thoughtful analysis, see Peter Westen, *Confrontation and Compulsory Process: A Unified Theory of Evidence for Criminal Cases,* 91 Harv. L. Rev. 567, 601–13 (1978).

193. The one possible exception is the 5–4 ruling in Idaho v. Wright, 497 U.S. 805 (1990) (finding a confrontation clause violation when pediatrician testified about incriminating statements concerning sex abuse that were made to him by defendant's young daughter). Even here, however, the result might well be justifiable on my approach. For the reasons, see Brief for the United States as Amicus Curiae, *White,* 502 U.S. 346 (No. 90-6113) [hereinafter Brief for the United States].

194. Two Justices, however, have properly drawn this distinction, accepting the views propounded by the United States, as amicus curiae. *See White,* 502 U.S. at 358–66 (Thomas, J., concurring, joined by Scalia, J.). *But see id.* at 352–53 (opinion of the Court, per Rehnquist, C.J.) (brushing aside this approach as coming "too late in the day" without considering how much more coherence it could offer to explain the results of past cases). Professors Friedman and Graham have also suggested that not all out-of-court declarants are confrontation clause "witnesses." Alas, both scholars sweep some friend *B*–like statements into their "witness" definitions. *See* Richard D. Friedman, *Toward a Partial Economic, Game-Theoretic Analysis of Hearsay,* 76 Minn. L. Rev. 723, 726 n. 10 (1992); Michael H. Graham, *The Confrontation Clause, the Hearsay Rule, and Child Sexual Abuse Prosecutions: The State of the Relationship,* 72 Minn. L. Rev. 523, 593–98 (1988).

195. As the solicitor general put the point in a brief outlining a theory of the confrontation clause very similar to mine: "The right to confrontation is a feature of

criminal procedure intended to benefit the defendant. By contrast, the hearsay rule is a feature of the law of evidence applicable to all litigants in both civil and criminal proceedings." Brief for the United States, *supra* note 193, at 24; *see also* Dutton v. Evans, 400 U.S. 74, 97 n. 4 (1970) (Harlan, J., concurring) (similar).

196. *See, e.g., Chambers,* 410 U.S. 284 (defendant sought admission of hearsay evidence of another man's confession to the murder charged against defendant).

197. Imagine, for example, a certain reliable subcategory of hearsay that the government seeks to introduce against a defendant. If the Court strikes down, on confrontation clause grounds, governmental efforts to introduce this type of hearsay, the government may respond by not letting defendants in other cases introduce this type of hearsay either. And this will hurt some innocent defendants in other cases. These defendants may object to the hearsay rule, arguing that it violates their right to subpoena and put on their own witnesses under the compulsory process clause. But the government can now respond by hiding behind parity—*neither* side in any case can ever introduce this kind of hearsay.

198. *See* Westen, *supra* note 73, at 182–84.

199. Washington v. Texas, 388 U.S. 14, 19 (1967) (emphasis added).

200. Similarly, the Fourth Amendment's reference to Americans' right to be secure in their "persons, houses, papers, and effects" plainly presupposes background rights of tort and property law, and their accompanying remedies—trespass law and the like.

201. *See* Nix v. Whiteside, 475 U.S. 157 (1986) (holding that Sixth Amendment right to assistance of counsel not violated when attorney refuses to cooperate with defendant in presenting perjured testimony).

202. *See* U.S. Const. amend. XIV, §1 (equal protection); *id.* art. IV, §2, cl. 1 (interstate privileges and immunities); *see also* McCulloch v. Maryland, 17 U.S. (4 Wheat.) 316, 436 (1816) (state may tax real property of federal bank on same terms as it taxes like private real property); John Hart Ely, *Democracy and Distrust* 77–87 (1980) (developing similar themes).

203. 7 Will. 3, ch. 3, §7 (1696).

204. Pa. Charter art. V (1701).

205. N.J. Const. art. XVI (1776).

206. 4 Blackstone, *supra* note 45, at *351 (emphasis deleted). On Blackstone as Madison's inspiration here, see Westen, *supra* note 73, at 97–98 and n. 114.

207. Federal Crimes Act of 1790, ch. 9, 1 Stat. 112, 118; *see also* 8 Wigmore, *supra* note 128, §2191 (stating that clause merely gives defendant "the common right . . . possessed both by parties in civil cases and by the prosecution in criminal cases").

208. *See* Webb v. Texas, 409 U.S. 95, 96, 98 (1972) (noting that trial judge intimidated sole witness for defense, but not prosecution witnesses); Washington v. Texas, 388 U.S. 14, 22 (1967) (noting that accomplices were allowed to testify for government but not for defendants); *see also id.* at 24–25 (Harlan, J., concurring in the judgment) (stressing this fact); Pennsylvania v. Ritchie, 480 U.S. 39, 57 and n. 14 (1987) (distinguishing between symmetric and asymmetric privileges in due process analysis); *cf.* Green v. Georgia, 442 U.S. 95, 97 (1979) (invalidating, on due process grounds, exclusion of hearsay statement that defendant sought to introduce, where government introduced same statement in another criminal proceeding); Cool v. United States, 409 U.S. 100, 103 n. 4 (1974) (rejecting as "fundamentally unfair" instruction telling jury it could convict solely on basis of accomplice testimony but not telling jury it could acquit solely on this basis, in case where defendant put accomplice on the stand); Chambers v. Mississippi, 410 U.S. 284, 295–98 (1973) (invalidating, under due process clause, trial in which defendant was barred from impeaching his own witness while government was free to impeach that witness).

209. Kastigar v. United States, 406 U.S. 441 (1972).

210. *See* United States v. North, 920 F.2d 940 (D.C. Cir. 1990), *cert. denied,* 500 U.S. 941 (1991) (amending United States v. North, 910 F.2d 843 (D.C. Cir. 1990)). The case is discussed *supra* Chapter 2, text at notes 79–84.

211. *See generally* Peter W. Tague, *The Fifth Amendment: If an Aid to the Guilty Defendant, an Impediment to the Innocent One,* 78 Geo. L.J. 1 (1989) (collecting and analyzing lower-court cases).

212. Government may also execute surprise searches with search warrants. Though "compulsory" in a sense—a target must honor the warrant—these searches do not involve subpoena-like "process," and thus seem to fall outside the scope of the compulsory process clause and the parity principle. Perhaps, however, if a defendant can show probable cause that a specific person has stolen goods or contraband in a specific place and would destroy the stuff if served with a subpoena, then the government must execute a defendant-initiated search warrant under the parity principle. If prosecutors may use warrants when subpoenas would predictably be defied, perhaps defendants should have similar power to assure true subpoena parity.

213. For a similar suggestion, see Westen, *supra* note 73, at 133–36, 156–57, 159.

214. *See* Alfred Hill, *Testimonial Privilege and Fair Trial,* 80 Colum. L. Rev. 1173, 1175 (1980). Consider also the case where a prosecution witness asserts a privilege in response to a defendant's vigorous cross-examination—a confrontation clause, rather than compulsory process clause, context. If the privilege passes the parity test, a court could uphold the privilege but strike the witness's other testimony on the ground that the privilege may not be invoked selectively to present possibly misleading half-truths. *See* Davis v. Alaska, 415 U.S. 308 (1974) (invalidating conviction where government witness testified and then, on cross-examination, hid behind a half-truth about his juvenile arrest record—a half-truth defendant was not allowed to expose). Note, however, that *Davis* did not involve a true privacy privilege but instead involved a prosecution witness's attempt to exclude "public" information.

215. *See* Westen, *supra* note 73, at 173–77.

216. *See* Mapp v. Ohio, 367 U.S. 643 (1961) (holding that evidence obtained by unconstitutional search is inadmissible in criminal case against searchee); Weeks v. United States, 232 U.S. 383 (1914) (similar); Boyd v. United States, 116 U.S. 616 (1886) (similar).

217. In rare situations, the evidentiary introduction of certain illegally obtained items might itself be a privacy violation—say, reading a woman's diary in open court. But typically this privacy violation does not depend on the illegality of a prior governmental search. Reading the diary in open court, civil or criminal, would be a privacy violation even if the government lawfully obtained the diary—in a proper search, or by subpoena, or if handed to the government by some third-party thief. Although the exclusionary rule is inapplicable in all these situations, a true privacy-based analysis might allow for a "diary privilege" in all proceedings, criminal or civil. *See supra* Chapter 2, text at note 255.

218. Further elaboration of this theme appears in Chapter 4.

219. So too, under First Amendment doctrine, it is one thing to prevent the press from ever gaining access to a certain bit of information, and a very different— and far more problematic—thing to prevent the press from publishing that same bit of information if the press already knows of it. *See* Gannett Co. v. DePasquale, 443 U.S. 368, 393 n. 25 (1979); *id.* at 411, 447 (Blackmun, J., concurring in part and dissenting in part).

220. *See* Kirby v. Illinois, 406 U.S. 682, 689–90 (1972) (plurality opinion) (suggesting that all Sixth Amendment guarantees are accusation-based).

221. For similar analysis tightly linking the counsel right to legal complexity, see, e.g., United States v. Gouveia, 467 U.S. 180, 188–89 (1984); Gagnon v.

Scarpelli, 411 U.S. 778, 789 (1973); *Kirby,* 406 U.S. at 689–90; Coleman v. Alabama, 399 U.S. 1, 9–10 (1970); Johnson v. Zerbst, 304 U.S. 458, 462–63 (1938); Powell v. Alabama, 287 U.S. 45, 69 (1932). Note also that the Treason Act of 1696, the font of the right of counsel, spoke of "[c]ounsel learned in the law." 7 & 8 Will. 3, ch. 3, §1.

222. *See* Moran v. Burbine, 475 U.S. 412, 428–30 (1986) (finding no Sixth Amendment right to counsel during interrogation in police station prior to accusation and rejecting contrary language of Miranda v. Arizona, 384 U.S. 436 (1966) and Escobedo v. Illinois, 378 U.S. 478 (1964)).

223. For a functional defense of this established practice, *see supra* Chapter 2, note 171.

224. *See, e.g., Johnson,* 304 U.S. at 462–63 (noting that Sixth Amendment right to be heard would often be of little avail if it did not include right to assistance of counsel); Gideon v. Wainwright, 372 U.S. 335, 344–45 (1963) (same).

225. *See* Federal Crimes Act of 1790, ch. 9, 1 Stat. 112, 118.

226. *See, e.g.,* John H. Langbein, *The Historical Origins of the Privilege Against Self-Incrimination at Common Law,* 92 Mich. L. Rev. 1047, 1050–52 (1994) (describing this theory).

227. At one time, the precise doctrinal basis for the right to appointed counsel—the counsel clause or the due process clause—mattered a great deal; today it matters not. In the late 1930s the Court located the right not in due process, but in the Sixth Amendment. *See Johnson,* 304 U.S. at 462. As a result, states were not bound by the *Johnson* rule since the Sixth Amendment was then viewed as applying only to federal trials. A Fifth Amendment due process rationale in *Johnson,* by contrast, would have applied to states by dint of the Fourteenth Amendment's parallel due process clause. In the 1960s, however, the provisions of the Sixth Amendment were held applicable against states; and so today, little turns on the due process clause/counsel clause distinction. *See generally* Henry J. Friendly, *The Bill of Rights as a Code of Criminal Procedure,* 53 Cal. L. Rev. 929, 942–46 (1965) (explaining interplay of incorporation debate and appointed counsel doctrine).

228. For an example of "unbending loyalty" ideology, see Monroe H. Freedman, *Professional Responsibility of the Criminal Defense Lawyer: The Three Hardest Questions,* 64 Mich. L. Rev. 1469 (1966).

229. 475 U.S. 157, 171 (1986).

230. *Id.* at 166.

231. *Nix* involved compulsory process clause principles, which are implicated when a defendant puts on his own witnesses; but as we have seen, these principles tightly intertwine with confrontation clause principles implicated by cross-examination of government witnesses.

232. *Cf.* Stephen A. Saltzburg, *Lawyers, Clients, and the Adversary System,* 37 Mercer L. Rev. 647, 676 (1986) ("The lawyer should not use her courtroom experience and the nervousness of the witness . . . to make an honest witness appear less than honest.").

233. *See* David Luban, *Are Criminal Defenders Different?,* 91 Mich. L. Rev. 1729, 1759–62 (1993) (discussing playacting).

234. These ethical restrictions need not take the form of rules enforced by external sanction; they could instead simply stand as norms of appropriate professional conduct internalized by members of the bar. A lawyer bent on evading the spirit of ethical standards can often do so by pretending to hear no evil from his client and, where inconvenient facts come to light, by asking cynically (along with Pontius Pilate) "what is truth?" But I write here not about a bad-man lawyer, but about a good-woman lawyer, who seeks to do the right thing. English practice is far closer to my ideal, and so were ABA standards only twenty years ago. *Compare* American Bar Association Project on Standards for Criminal Justice, Standards Relating to

the Administration of Criminal Justice 132 (1974) (The Defense Function §7.6(b)) (defense lawyer "should not misuse the power of cross-examination or impeachment by employing it to discredit or undermine a witness if he knows the witness is testifying truthfully") *with* American Bar Association Standards for Criminal Justice §4–7.6 (2d ed. 1986 Supp.) (abandoning earlier standard).

4. The Future of Constitutional Criminal Procedure

1. *See, e.g.,* Donald A. Dripps, *Akhil Amar on Criminal Procedure and Constitutional Law: "Here I Go Down That Wrong Road Again,"* 74 N.C. L. Rev. 1559 (1996); Yale Kamisar, *On the "Fruits" of Miranda Violations, Coerced Confessions, and Compelled Testimony,* 93 Mich. L. Rev. 929 (1995); Tracey Maclin, *When the Cure for the Fourth Amendment is Worse than the Disease,* 68 S. Cal. L. Rev. 1 (1994); Carol S. Steiker, *Second Thoughts About First Principles,* 107 Harv. L. Rev. 820 (1994).

2. 5 U.S. (1 Cranch) 137 (1803); *see generally* Akhil Reed Amar, *Marbury, Section 13, and the Original Jurisdiction of the Supreme Court,* 56 U. Chi. L. Rev. 443, 445–53 (1989).

3. 14 U.S. (1 Wheat.) 304 (1816); *see generally* Akhil Reed Amar, *The Two-Tiered Structure of the Judiciary Act of 1789,* 138 U. Pa. L. Rev. 1499, 1499–1505 (1990); Akhil Reed Amar, *A Neo-Federalist View of Article III: Separating the Two Tiers of Federal Jurisdiction,* 65 B.U. L. Rev. 205, 205–19 (1985) [hereinafter *Article III*].

4. 17 U.S. (4 Wheat.) 316 (1819); *see generally* Akhil Reed Amar, *Of Sovereignty and Federalism,* 96 Yale L.J. 1425, 1451–55, 1512–17 (1987).

5. 10 U.S. (6 Cranch) 87 (1810); *see generally* Akhil Reed Amar, *The Bill of Rights and the Fourteenth Amendment,* 101 Yale L.J. 1193, 1198 n. 21 (1992).

6. 17 U.S. (4 Wheat.) 518 (1819); *see generally* Akhil Reed Amar, *The Creation and Reconstruction of the Bill of Rights,* chapter 7 (forthcoming 1997).

7. 32 U.S. (7 Pet.) 243 (1833). For discussion of *Barron,* see Amar, *supra* note 5, at 1198–1203.

8. *See* Akhil Reed Amar, *Some New World Lessons for the Old World,* 58 U. Chi. L. Rev. 483, 483–91 (1991); Denis P. Duffey, Note, *The Northwest Ordinance as a Constitutional Document,* 95 Colum. L. Rev. 929, 942–44, 949–66 (1995).

9. *See* Amar, *Article III, supra* note 3, at 222 and n. 63; Lawrence Gene Sager, *The Supreme Court 1980 Term—Foreword: Constitutional Limitations on Congress' Authority to Regulate the Jurisdiction of the Federal Courts,* 95 Harv. L. Rev. 17, 53 n. 105 (1981).

10. Akhil Reed Amar, *Reports of My Death Are Greatly Exaggerated: A Reply,* 138 U. Pa. L. Rev. 1651, 1670 (1990).

11. *See, e.g.,* Harris v. New York, 401 U.S. 222 (1971) (distinguishing but not overruling Miranda v. Arizona, 384 U.S. 436 (1966)); Kirby v. Illinois, 406 U.S. 682 (1972) (distinguishing but not overruling United States v. Wade, 388 U.S. 218 (1967)); United States v. Leon, 468 U.S. 897 (1984) (distinguishing but not overruling Mapp v. Ohio, 367 U.S. 643 (1961)).

12. *E.g.,* Chimel v. California, 395 U.S. 752, 760–62 (1969); Katz v. United States, 389 U.S. 347, 357–59 (1967).

13. 392 U.S. 1, 16–20 (1968).

14. *Id.* at 8.

15. *See* Mapp v. Ohio, 367 U.S. 643 (1961).

16. 392 U.S. at 15.

17. *See, e.g.,* Malloy v. Hogan, 378 U.S. 1, 8–9 (1964); Murphy v. Waterfront Comm'n, 378 U.S. 52, 74 (1964); Ker v. California, 374 U.S. 23, 30 (1963); *Mapp,* 367 U.S. at 646–47, 646 n. 5, 656–57; *id.* at 661–66 (Black, J., concurring).

18. 384 U.S. 757, 760–65, 766–72 (1966).

19. *See also* Akhil Reed Amar and Renée B. Lettow, *Self-Incrimination and the*

Constitution: A Brief Rejoinder to Professor Kamisar, 93 Mich. L. Rev. 1011, 1012 n. 5 (1995).

20. *See* United States v. Leon, 468 U.S. 897, 905–6 (1984).

21. Los Angeles v. Lyons, 461 U.S. 95 (1983).

22. *See, e.g.,* New Jersey v. T.L.O., 469 U.S. 325, 340–41 (1985); Zurcher v. Stanford Daily News, 436 U.S. 547, 559–60 (1978).

23. 436 U.S. at 565.

24. The post-Burger members are, in order of seniority, Justices Scalia, Kennedy, Souter, Thomas, Ginsburg, and Breyer.

25. Because of the current flux on the Court, almost every one of the Justices stands as a possible swing vote on at least some current issues of constitutional criminal procedure.

26. Examples include "victims' rights" bills, various death penalty proposals, habeas restrictions, "three strikes" laws, evidence proposals concerning prior bad acts, and jury reform bills (to name just a few).

27. Here I echo the plea of the great Henry Friendly. *See* Henry J. Friendly, *The Bill of Rights as a Code of Criminal Procedure,* 53 Cal. L. Rev. 929 (1965).

28. Malloy v. Hogan, 378 U.S. 1, 8–9 (1964); Murphy v. Waterfront Comm'n, 378 U.S. 52, 74 (1964); Ker v. California, 374 U.S. 23, 30 (1963); Mapp v. Ohio, 367 U.S. 643, 646–47, 646 n. 5, 655–57 (1961); *id.* at 661–66 (Black, J., concurring); Feldman v. United States 322 U.S. 487, 489–90 (1944); United States v. Lefkowitz, 285 U.S. 452, 466–67 (1932); Olmstead v. United States, 277 U.S. 438, 462 (1928); *id.* at 477–78 (Brandeis, J., dissenting); Gambino v. United States, 275 U.S. 310, 316 (1927); Marron v. United States, 275 U.S. 192, 194 (1927); Agnello v. United States, 269 U.S. 20, 33–35 (1925); Hester v. United States, 265 U.S. 57, 57–58 (1924); Burdeau v. McDowell, 256 U.S. 465, 474–76 (1921); Amos v. United States, 255 U.S. 313, 315–16 (1921); Gouled v. United States, 255 U.S. 298, 306, 311 (1921); Perlman v. United States, 247 U.S. 7, 13 (1918); Weeks v. United States, 232 U.S. 383, 393, 395 (1914); Adams v. New York, 192 U.S. 585, 594, 597–98 (1904); Boyd v. United States, 116 U.S. 616, 630, 633–35 (1886); *see generally* Edward S. Corwin, *The Supreme Court's Construction of the Self-Incrimination Clause,* 29 Mich. L. Rev. 1, 1–2, 13–16, 203–4 (1930) (carefully reading exclusionary case law as based on a Fourth-Fifth fusion theory).

The only major Supreme Court exclusion case that does not invoke the Fifth Amendment is Silverthorne Lumber Co. v. United States, 251 U.S. 385 (1920). The government stressed the Fifth Amendment issue at length: under Hale v. Henkel, 201 U.S. 43, 75 (1906), corporations lacked self-incrimination clause rights, and thus they could not demand exclusion. *See* 251 U.S. at 385–90 (argument of the United States). Justice Holmes's three-page opinion for the Court never carefully addresses this argument but instead offers us an epigram: illegal evidence and its fruits "shall not be used at all" (251 U.S. 392). But an epigram is not analysis—even when (I would say, especially when) it comes from Holmes. Analytically, Holmes's statement is simply false. The government has always been allowed to use illegally obtained evidence in civil cases, in criminal cases against others, in keeping contraband, in returning stolen goods to their rightful owners, and so forth. Perhaps *Silverthorne's* technical disposition could be upheld nevertheless on the narrow theory that the case, in effect, did not exclude evidence in a criminal case on the basis of a constitutional mandate but simply quashed a subpoena in a collateral proceeding on supervisory power grounds.

29. *See, e.g.,* United States v. Leon, 468 U.S. 897, 905–6 (1984) (rejecting Fourth-Fifth fusion theory); Fisher v. United States, 425 U.S. 391, 405–14 (1976) (same).

30. *See* United States v. Leon, 468 U.S. 897, 905–6 (1984); United States v. Calandra, 414 U.S. 338, 354 (1974).

31. *See supra* text at note 18; note 29.

32. Mapp v. Ohio, 367 U.S. 643, 661–66 (1961) (Black, J., concurring).

33. *Id.* at 646–47, 646 n. 5, 655–57 (opinion of the Court) (quoting *Boyd* that Fourth and Fifth Amendments run "almost into each other"; noting "close connection between the concepts later embodied in these two Amendments"; stressing "conceptual nexus" between Fourth Amendment and rules against coerced confessions; suggesting that Constitution gives an "accused" a "privilege" against being "forced to give" "evidence"; suggesting that unreasonable seizures are "tantamount" to "coerced testimony"; and insisting that "the Fourth and Fifth Amendments" enjoy an "intimate relation").

34. Duncan v. Louisiana, 391 U.S. 145, 165–67 and n. 1 (1968) (Black, J., concurring).

35. *See, e.g.,* Chimel v. California, 395 U.S. 752, 760–62 (1969); Chapman v. United States, 365 U.S. 610, 613–15 (1961).

36. Gideon v. Wainwright, 372 U.S. 335, 339–40, 341 (1963).

37. Miranda v. Arizona, 384 U.S. 436, 439, 442, 457–62, 467 (1966).

38. U.S. Const. art. III, §3 (generally requiring "two witnesses to the same overt Act" for treason).

39. *See generally* Richard H. Fallon, Jr., *A Constructivist Coherence Theory of Constitutional Interpretation,* 100 Harv. L. Rev. 1189 (1987). For other powerful and illuminating accounts of interpretive methodology in constitutional law, see Phillip Bobbitt, *Constitutional Interpretation* (1991); Phillip Bobbitt, *Constitutional Fate* (1982); Jed Rubenfeld, *Reading the Constitution as Spoken,* 104 Yale L.J. 1119 (1995).

40. Counselman v. Hitchcock, 142 U.S. 547 (1892).

41. *See* United States v. Jacobsen, 466 U.S. 109, 122–23 and nn. 22–23 (1984); Arnold H. Loewy, *The Fourth Amendment as a Device for Protecting the Innocent,* 81 Mich. L. Rev. 907 (1983).

42. This is, of course, a point stressed by none other than Chief Justice Warren in *Terry v. Ohio,* 392 U.S. 1, 14–15 and n. 11 (1968).

43. My analysis here calls into question the rule of *Rochin v. California,* 342 U.S. 165 (1952), as a constitutional mandate. To forcibly pump a person's stomach against his will and without sufficient justification is horribly wrong—an obvious Fourth Amendment violation—but the violation occurs when the stomach is pumped, not at some later point. Thus, the pumping is wrong regardless of whether the forced vomit is ultimately found to contain illegal drugs, whether the drugs are ever introduced as evidence, whether the evidence is introduced in a criminal (as opposed to civil) case, or whether a case is brought against the pumpee (as opposed to, say, a third-party drug pusher). Introduction of reliable evidence—like drugs—is not *itself* an independent wrong, and exclusion of such evidence does not properly remedy the antecedent wrong of pumping: exclusion provides an upside-down aid to the guilty, and no remedy to the innocent whose vomit is drug-free. Consider also the possible "causation gap" created by exclusion: a timely and perfectly lawful *Schmerber*-like blood test might have generated comparable evidence of drug ingestion, and so exclusion may confer a kind of windfall on a guilty pumpee.

44. *See generally* Stanley S. Surrey, *Pathways to Tax Reform: The Concept of Tax Expenditures* (1973); Stanley S. Surrey, *Federal Income Tax Reform: The Varied Approaches Necessary to Replace Tax Expenditures with Direct Government Assistance,* 84 Harv. L. Rev. 352 (1970); Stanley S. Surrey, *Tax Incentives as a Device for Implementing Governmental Policy: A Comparison with Direct Government Expenditures,* 83 Harv. L. Rev. 705 (1970).

Although Professor Surrey's specific approach is controversial in tax circles, no serious tax scholar can avoid thinking about, and confronting head-on, Professor Surrey's argument about "upside-down" effects. Yet many major scholars in constitutional criminal procedure seem to have spent their entire careers without ever seriously confronting the upside-down effect of various exclusionary rules.

45. *See* Douglas Laycock, *Modern American Remedies: Cases and Materials* 143 (2d ed. 1994); Daniel J. Meltzer, *Deterring Constitutional Violations by Law Enforcement Officials: Plaintiffs and Defendants as Private Attorneys General,* 88 Colum. L. Rev. 247, 270 (1988).

46. *See, e.g.,* Yale Kamisar, *Remembering the "Old World" of Criminal Procedure: A Reply to Professor Grano,* 23 U. Mich. J.L. Ref. 537, 568–69 (1990); Yale Kamisar, *"Comparative Reprehensibility" and the Fourth Amendment Exclusionary Rule,* 86 Mich. L. Rev. 1, 36 n. 151, 47–48 (1987).

47. *See* William J. Stuntz, *Warrants and Fourth Amendment Remedies,* 77 Va. L. Rev. 881, 905 (1991).

48. *See* Bivens v. Six Unknown Federal Agents, 403 U.S. 388, 410 (1971) (Harlan, J., concurring in the judgment).

49. *See* William J. Stuntz, *Privacy's Problem and the Law of Criminal Procedure,* 93 Mich. L. Rev. 1016, 1060–77 (1995).

50. Professor Stuntz seems to recognize this problem, *see id.* at 1072, but then breezes by it in a way that would make "Leavenworth lottery" fans cheer and traditional-remedies scholars wince. His approach has also been squarely rejected in case law, *see* Frisbie v. Collins, 342 U.S. 519 (1952); Maryland v. Macon, 472 U.S. 463, 471 (1985). *Cf. id.* at 475–76 (dissenting opinion by Brennan and Marshall arguing for Stuntz-like approach while conceding that the Court's contrary approach was "following precedent"). A bit later in his discussion, *see* 93 Mich. L. Rev. at 1074 n. 210, Professor Stuntz again seems to miss the obvious ways that exclusion can overdeter because of causation gaps—gaps his approach two pages earlier would of course dramatically widen. And he continues to reveal real confusion about how damage remedies fit into his world, *compare id.* at 1072 n. 201 *with id.* at 1073 and n. 203. Some of this confusion may stem from an uncharacteristic inattention to the Coase Theorem.

51. *See* Frank I. Michelman, *Property, Utility, and Fairness: Comments on the Ethical Foundations of "Just Compensation" Law,* 80 Harv. L. Rev. 1165, 1214 (1967).

52. *See generally* Frank Easterbrook, *The Supreme Court, 1983 Term—Foreword: The Court and the Economic System,* 98 Harv. L. Rev. 4, 10–12 (1984). Among constitutional criminal proceduralists, Professor Stuntz has been a leading practitioner of ex ante incentive analysis in a wide range of intriguing and illuminating articles. *See, e.g.,* Robert E. Scott and William J. Stuntz, *Plea Bargains as Contract,* 101 Yale L.J. 1909 (1992); William J. Stuntz, *Lawyers, Deception, and Evidence Gathering,* 79 Va. L. Rev. 1903 (1993); William J. Stuntz, *Implied Bargains, Government Power, and the Fourth Amendment,* 44 Stan. L. Rev. 553 (1992).

53. *See generally* Lawrence Lessig, *Fidelity in Translation,* 71 Tex. L. Rev. 1165 (1993).

54. *See generally* William J. Stuntz, *The Substantive Origins of Criminal Procedure,* 105 Yale L.J. 393 (1995).

55. In a recent essay, Professor Schulhofer seems to tiptoe up to, but not quite admit, the many and profound ways that feminism may call into question the generally prodefendant stance of now-orthodox criminal procedure scholarship (including Schulhofer's own oeuvre). *See* Stephen J. Schulhofer, *The Feminist Challenge in Criminal Law,* 143 U. Pa. L. Rev. 2151 (1995).

Appendix. Reinventing Juries

1. For much more elaboration and documentation of my claims over the next few pages, see generally Akhil Reed Amar, *The Bill of Rights as a Constitution,* 100 Yale L.J. 1131 (1991).

2. In addition to Amar, *supra* note 1, at 1190 and n. 261, see Akhil Reed Amar and Jonathan Marcus, *Double Jeopardy Law After Rodney King*, 95 Colum. L. Rev. 1, 57–58 and nn. 279–81 (1995). This protection of the jury's role is asymmetric; a defendant can appeal a jury verdict of *conviction*, and a trial judge may overturn a jury *conviction* via a motion for judgment of acquittal. But the Constitution protects acquittals by *juries* with more finality than acquittals by *judges*. *See generally* Peter Westen and Richard Drubel, *Toward a General Theory of Double Jeopardy*, 1978 Sup. Ct. Rev. 81, 124–34.

3. In addition to Amar, *supra* note 1, at 1190 and n. 262, see Akhil Reed Amar, *The Bill of Rights and the Fourteenth Amendment*, 101 Yale L.J. 1193, 1248–50 (1992).

4. In addition to Amar, *supra* note 1, at 1199–1201, see generally Akhil Reed Amar, *The Consent of the Governed: Constitutional Amendment Outside Article V*, 94 Colum. L. Rev. 457, 489–94 (1994), and Akhil Reed Amar, *Of Sovereignty and Federalism*, 96 Yale L.J. 1425, 1429–51 (1987).

5. Letter from Thomas Jefferson to David Humphreys (Mar. 18, 1789), *quoted in* Amar, *supra* note 1, at 1195 n. 284.

6. 32 U.S. (7 Pet.) 242 (1833).

7. For much more documentation and elaboration, see generally Amar, *The Bill of Rights and the Fourteenth Amendment*, *supra* note 3.

8. Or as Professor Lessig might say, "translated." *See generally* Lawrence Lessig, *Fidelity in Translation*, 71 Tex. L. Rev. 1165 (1993).

9. This material initiative analysis will be developed at greater length in a forthcoming essay with Professor Ian Ayres.

10. *See, e.g.,* Amar, *The Bill of Rights and the Fourteenth Amendment*, *supra* note 3, at 1266 n. 309 and sources cited therein.

11. *Letters from the Federal Farmer* (IV), *reprinted in* 2 *The Complete Anti-Federalist* 249–50 (Herbert Storing ed., 1981).

12. *See* Amar, *supra* note 1, at 1188–89.

13. Alexis de Tocqueville, *Democracy in America* 273, 728 (Mayer ed., 1969).

14. *See, e.g.,* Edmonson v. Leesville Concrete Co., 500 U.S. 614, 625–26 (1991); Powers v. Ohio, 499 U.S. 400, 406–8 (1991).

15. The jury/voting analogy has been analyzed quite powerfully by Vikram D. Amar, *Jury Service as Political Participation Akin to Voting*, 80 Cornell L. Rev. 239 (1995).

16. Long trials lasting more than a week raise distinct problems—the longer the trial, the greater the difficulty in assembling a truly cross-sectional jury. Not all citizens will be able to serve without huge sacrifice, and when they drop out, the remaining pool can be skewed by self-selection. Note, however, that grand juries do typically sit over extended periods, though they do not always meet full-time.

17. Though the Twenty-Fourth Amendment by its terms applies only to voting in federal elections—and thus by analogy to federal juries—its anti–wealth discrimination principles have been deemed applicable against states. *See* Harper v. Virginia Bd. of Elections, 383 U.S. 663 (1966).

18. *See generally* John Stuart Mill, *Considerations on Representative Government* 154–58 (Currin V. Shields ed., 1958) (Chapter X: "Of the Mode of Voting").

19. Actually, in the North case, there was a seemingly strong reason to excuse jurors who had seen North testify on television, because this testimony was procured under a grant of immunity, and thus strictly inadmissible under the Fifth Amendment. (I am indebted to Betsy Cavendish for this reminder.) But this Fifth Amendment wrinkle does not exist in most other high-profile cases, where intelligent and well-informed jurors are dismissed precisely because they are intelligent and well informed. And if someone is intelligent and well informed, should we not at least consider using the scalpel of strict instructions—"you must base your verdict only on the evidence admitted in this trial"—rather than the sledgehammer of

exclusion? A judge with comparable knowledge is not disqualified here. Why do we trust judges so much and jurors so little?

For fascinating data on how a multilayered jury selection process "dumbed down" the original jury pool (as measured by percentage of college graduates and knowledge of Watergate) in a high-profile case involving political figures, see Hans Zeisel and Shari S. Diamond, *The Jury Selection in the Mitchell-Stans Conspiracy Trial,* 1976 Am. B. Found. Res. J. 151, 158–61.

20. It might be feared that a single eccentric juror today might simply sit mute and refuse to engage her peers. For my suggested corrective, see *infra* text at note 45.

21. *See generally* Amar, *supra* note 1, at 1196–99. This shift cannot be defended on the libertarian ground of giving defendants more constitutional choices, since the Court has not recognized any constitutional right of a defendant to a bench trial over the objection of a prosecutor. *See* Singer v. United States, 380 U.S. 24 (1965).

22. *See generally* Amar, *The Bill of Rights and the Fourteenth Amendment, supra* note 3, at 1260–72.

23. Consider, for example, the data discussed in Zeisel and Diamond, *supra* note 19.

24. *See, e.g.,* Stilson v. United States, 250 U.S. 538, 586 (1919); Swain v. Alabama, 380 U.S. 202, 219 (1965); Batson v. Kentucky, 476 U.S. 79, 91 (1986); Georgia v. McCollum, 112 S. Ct. 2348, 2358 (1992).

25. In conversation, Professor Stan Krauss has expressed some reservations about this point. I look forward to the eventual publication of his historical work on American juries, and may well adjust or abandon my hunch when this work comes out. As my next sentences make clear, my most important historical and structural claims here focus less on the Founding, and more on the Reconstruction and Progressive Era visions.

26. *See* John H. Langbein, *The Criminal Trial Before the Lawyers,* 45 U. Chi. L. Rev. 263, 274–75 (1978).

27. One advantage to this plan is that a jury whose members have become acquainted in one trial might be expected to deliberate better in the next, having learned a bit about what to expect from one another. At the same time, in the short span of a week, group power hierarchies won't have much chance to harden.

28. *See* Ronald F. Wright, *Why Not Administrative Grand Juries?* 44 Admin. L. Rev. 465, 516 (1992).

29. Professor Krauss has informed me that American juries were quite active in trials at least through the middle of the nineteenth century. Some juries even caused witnesses to be recalled, and asked witnesses clarifying questions after the cases had been submitted to the jury and deliberation had begun.

30. For a discussion of the empirical evidence, see Nancy J. King, *The Effects of Race-Conscious Jury Selection on Public Confidence in the Fairness of Jury Proceedings: An Empirical Puzzle,* 31 Am. Crim. L. Rev. 1177, 1185–86 (1995).

I am heartened here by a recent conversation with Justice Joyce Kennard, who now sits on the California Supreme Court. When she served as a trial judge, she always made a point of thanking jurors and soliciting their observations and suggestions about their jury experience. Indeed, she routinely administered questionnaires to jurors who had completed their service, inviting them to comment on all aspects of their jury experience. This is exactly the sort of thing I am calling for here.

31. Tocqueville, *supra* note 13, at 272, 275.

32. At the federal level, this videotaping would require a change in the law. *See* 18 U.S.C. §1508 (1988) (prohibiting recording or observing jury deliberations).

33. Bob Woodward and Scott Armstrong, *The Brethren: Inside the Supreme Court* (1979).

34. My views of juries and jury secrecy here may well differ from those of my

distinguished colleague, Abe Goldstein. *See* Abraham S. Goldstein, *Jury Secrecy and the Media: The Problem of Postverdict Interview,* 1993 U. Ill. L. Rev. 295. With due respect, I think Professor Goldstein fails to give enough stress to the jury as a political institution in an open, democratic society. For Goldstein, the "genius" of the jury lies in its "inscrutability." *Id.* at 314. For me—and, I submit, for the Framers—the genius of the jury lies in its democratic character.

For a thoughtful and more narrow argument that the public need not be given private information about individual jurors—their addresses, their questionnaire responses, even their names—see Nancy J. King, *Nameless Justice: The Case for More Routine Use of Anonymous Juries in Criminal Trials,* 49 Vand. L. Rev. 123 (1996).

35. *See* Duncan v. Louisiana, 391 U.S. 145, 158 n. 30 (1968).

36. *See* Williams v. Florida, 399 U.S. 78 (1970); Ballew v. Georgia, 435 U.S. 223 (1978).

37. *See* Colgrove v. Battin, 413 U.S. 149 (1973).

38. *Williams,* 399 U.S. at 86–100.

39. *Ballew,* 435 U.S. 223.

40. For a similar observation, see *The Federalist* No. 55, at 342 (James Madison) (Clinton Rossiter ed., 1961).

41. *See* Apodaca v. Oregon, 406 U.S. 404 (1972). *Apodaca's* current status is hardly clear-cut, since it failed to generate a majority opinion. A four-Justice plurality upheld Oregon's rule allowing nonunanimous jury verdicts on the theory that the Sixth Amendment does not require unanimity to convict. A fifth Justice concurred, but on the very different theory that the Sixth Amendment does not incorporate jot-for-jot against states. *See also* Burch v. Louisiana, 441 U.S. 130 (1979).

42. Thus, we may have an example of what Professor Lessig has termed an "*Erie* effect" calling for a changed reading. *See* Lawrence Lessig, *Understanding Changed Readings: Fidelity and Theory,* 47 Stan. L. Rev. 395, 426–38 (1995) (discussing background changes in broader culture or legal theory that trigger changed readings of old legal texts).

43. The jury in ancient Athens—the cradle of democracy—was large and randomly selected, often heard more than a single case, and operated by majority rule. (I am indebted to Shawn Chen for this reminder.) *See generally* Mogens Herman Hansen, *The Athenian Democracy in the Age of Demosthenes* (J. A. Crook trans., 1991).

44. Note, however, that a two-thirds vote in defendant's favor is not necessary for an acquittal in impeachment. Civil libertarians may well wonder whether jury unanimity should be necessary to *acquit* a criminal defendant. If so, the consequence is that the prosecutor needs only one sympathetic juror to hang a jury and inflict another trial on defendant. As the impeachment analogy reminds us, logic does not mandate symmetry (though other reasons for symmetry may exist).

45. Tocqueville, *supra* note 13, at 273.

46. In ancient Athens, juries could sometimes decide upon the constitutionality of a law under the system of *graphe paranomon.* (Here too, I am indebted to Shawn Chen.) *See generally* Mogens Herman Hansen, *The Political Power of the People's Court in Fourth Century Athens, in The Greek City from Homer to Alexander* 225 (O. Murray and S. Price eds., 1990).

47. *See* Marbury v. Madison, 5 U.S. (1 Cranch) 137 (1803).

48. To give jurors more familiarity and confidence with Fourth Amendment issues, and to create more uniformity across decisions so as to give more guidance to police officers, perhaps it might be sensible to convene a special "Fourth Amendment" jury. Such a jury would sit for several weeks and hear a string of cases alleging "unreasonable" government conduct. This may also be an especially good place to use jury clerks. *See supra* notes 28, 34 and accompanying text.

49. *See supra* note 28.

50. Once again, I borrow from Professor Lessig's ideas about "faithful translations." *See* Lessig, *supra* note 8.

51. 2 *Works of James Wilson* 537 (Robert McCloskey ed., 1967).

52. *See* Renée Lettow, Note, *Reviving Grand Jury Presentments,* 103 Yale L.J. 1333 (1994).

Cases

Index of Names and Authorities